Changing Minds with Clinical Hypnosis

AF711601

This book is a scientifically current, integrative, and practical guide for understanding clinical hypnosis and its place within a new health care paradigm.

Blending four original short stories with a treatise, it alternates narrative prose with health science discourse to create a framework for embracing systemic emotional and relational elements that lie beyond diagnosis, medication, surgery, and psychotherapy. Following the stories of four characters, the authors establish an empirically-grounded conceptualization of the mind, then demonstrate how practical applications of therapeutic hypnosis can help readers use individual and family resources in health and healing.

Clinicians will learn to improve their care by embracing emotional, relational, and narrative elements that powerfully affect health beyond diagnosis, medication, surgery, and psychotherapy. Further, health care educators and policy makers will find inspiration that enriches professional training.

Laurence Irwin Sugarman, MD, is a general pediatrician, author, and research professor at Rochester Institute of Technology. He focuses on mind-body health.

Julie Hope Linden, PhD, is a psychologist and past president of the International Society of Hypnosis. She teaches globally and specializes in the treatment of trauma.

Lee Warner Brooks, MA, JD, has written in a variety of genres, including the Shakespearean sonnet. He has recently retired from teaching writing at the University of Michigan–Dearborn/Ann Arbor.

"This book should be read by anyone working and interacting with patients. It provides an excellent background and understanding of hypnosis, not only a therapeutic intervention but a window to better medical care."

Fabrizio Benedetti, MD, University of Turin Medical School

"*Changing Minds with Clinical Hypnosis* is a mind changer! Innovative, creative, and profoundly thought-provoking. This beautifully written book delves deep, dissolving myths about hypnosis to elucidate how change happens, integrating neurobiological evidence with current knowledge of the therapeutic process. I couldn't put it down! The authors, through cogent arguments, creatively engaged conversations and story, convincingly present 21st century hypnosis as an embodied mind-changing therapy. Enjoy how it changes your mind on the critical principles of hypnosis as therapy."

Leora Kuttner, PhD, Clinical Professor, BC Children's Hospital and University of British Columbia

"This is a numinous book. *Changing Minds with Clinical Hypnosis* aligns gratifyingly with what Ernest learned at the feet of Milton H. Erickson, MD. Among the many alternate understandings of Erickson's work, this book builds solidly on the scientific foundations and furthers the practical clinical approaches within his worldview. Sugarman, Linden, and Brooks have done excellent work combining the science and storytelling that are the essence of therapeutic hypnosis. This book will change your mind."

Ernest Lawrence Rossi, PhD, and Kathryn Lane Rossi, PhD, PsychoSocial Genomics Research Institute, authors of *Creating New Consciousness in Everyday Life: The Psycho-Social Genomics of Self Creation, The Psychobiology of Gene Expression, A Discourse with Our Genes*, and many others

"This powerful book embraces the nexus of health care and freedom of mind. As a work of exquisite scholarship, it makes an impactful case for recognizing the transformative power of hypnosis in health and care. Its four compelling and beautifully written stories portray our struggle for growth and transformation. So, linking science and art, *Changing Minds with Clinical Hypnosis* places compassion at the core of healthcare. A must read."

Steven Hassan, author of *Combating Cult Mind Control, Releasing the Bonds: Empowering People to Think for Themselves*, and *The Cult of Trump: A Leading Cult Expert Explains How the President Uses Mind Control*

"This extraordinary book rests on a foundation of an exceptionally gentle and respectful humanism while advocating an active approach to caring for people's wellbeing based on the newest understandings of hypnosis and the science of human relationships. The authors have created a tight and inspiring weave of ideas and methods and a respectful and empowering use of hypnosis. Their unique style of sharing case examples lends a practicality and authenticity to their writing that readers will undoubtedly find compelling. My suggestion: read this important book—and soon!"

Michael D. Yapko, PhD, clinical psychologist and author of *Trancework: An Introduction to the Practice of Clinical Hypnosis (5th ed.)* and *The Discriminating Therapist*

"This is not your ordinary hypnosis book. It is a delightful and highly instructive compilation of the various aspects of hypnotic experience, told from different viewpoints, and through a variety of pertinent voices. It includes masterfully woven clinical stories (that make you want to read on), a thoroughly researched scientific background, and expert analysis of the evolution of the field. All of this is topped with the extensive clinical wisdom of the authors. This is an extraordinary book."

Elvira Lang, MD, PhD, Founder and CEO of Comfort Talk®, former Associate Professor, Harvard Medical School

Changing Minds with Clinical Hypnosis

Narratives and Discourse for a New Health Care Paradigm

Laurence Irwin Sugarman,
Julie Hope Linden, and
Lee Warner Brooks

Routledge
Taylor & Francis Group
NEW YORK AND LONDON

First published 2020
by Routledge
52 Vanderbilt Avenue, New York, NY 10017

and by Routledge
2 Park Square, Milton Park, Abingdon, Oxon, OX14 4RN

Routledge is an imprint of the Taylor & Francis Group, an informa business

Library of Congress Cataloging-in-Publication Data
Names: Sugarman, Laurence I., author. | Linden, Julie Hope, author. | Brooks, Lee Warner, author.
Title: Changing minds with clinical hypnosis : narratives and discourse for a new health care paradigm / Laurence Irwin Sugarman, Julie Hope Linden,
Lee Warner Brooks.
Identifiers: LCCN 2019058338 | ISBN 9780367251956 (paperback) |
ISBN 9780367256678 (hardcover) |
ISBN 9780429288975 (ebook)
Subjects: MESH: Hypnosis | Narration
Classification: LCC RC499.A8 | NLM WM 415 | DDC 615.8/5122–dc23
LC record available at https://lccn.loc.gov/2019058338

ISBN: 978-0-367-25667-8 (hbk)
ISBN: 978-0-367-25195-6 (pbk)
ISBN: 978-0-429-28897-5 (ebk)

Typeset in Baskerville
by Swales & Willis, Exeter, Devon, UK

Contents

Acknowledgments

We reach goals such as producing this book with the encouragement of others. We cannot begin to acknowledge the countless teachers and mentors who collectively compelled us to compose this volume. The most impactful among these have been those who have come to us as clients, patients, and students over our careers. Some of them are represented in this volume's stories and vignettes. All have challenged us to learn more. Our families and loved ones have taught us, supported us, cheered for us, and kept our priorities and values clear, as we have often needed them to do.

There are individuals whom we wish to acknowledge by name. Ernest and Kathryn Rossi encouraged us to dare to undertake this book, even though, or perhaps especially because, it was a strange hybrid. As it was being conceived, Peter Schafer, ever audaciously, kept cheerleading for more creativity and risk. Michael Yapko provided sound advice on the book proposal. Elgan Baker, Richard Comeau, Owen Gottlieb, Janet Isaacs, Leora Kuttner, Steve Lankton, Maren Lindheim, Michael Scharf, and John Teleska all carefully read through early chapter drafts and offered valuable and critical feedback. Sean Zion helped us consider aspects of placebo research. We went to artist James Perkins for advice about cover design. He offered to take it on himself, providing us with an inspirational metaphor. Mark Jensen and Amy Banks supported our efforts by contributing an insightful Foreword and Afterword, respectively. Marcia Weinert efficiently and skillfully worked through the detailed references and citations, while gently clarifying our dense prose, to make the book accurate, valid, and more readable. Finally, we are thankful that editor Nina Gutapalle and the folks at Routledge agreed to take this project on, made the process easy, and brought this book to you.

Foreword

In the last few decades there has been an explosion in our scientific understanding of health and well-being. We now know more than ever about the biological, psychological, and social factors that underlie illness and distress. This knowledge is gradually being translated into new treatments that have the potential to improve our health and well-being.

And yet, something is seriously wrong. Despite significant advances in our understanding about the mechanisms underlying illness and health, the rates and the severity of illness around the world are increasing rather than decreasing. We are witnessing an alarming upsurge in the rates of diabetes, obesity, insomnia, attention deficit disorder, depression, drug abuse, and their precursors. At the same time, more resources than ever are being devoted to health care and the prevention of illness.

Clearly, our methods for translating the discoveries we are making about disease into effective clinical practice are not working. And everyone knows, at least at some level, about the rule of holes: If you find yourself in one … stop digging! To help us change direction, to get out of the hole we have dug ourselves into, we need new ways of thinking. We need new paths for action that will move us toward the effective and sustainable care and the promotion of well-being.

With the publication of *Changing Our Minds,* Laurence Sugarman, Julie Linden, and Lee Brooks offer *both* clear thinking *and* practical strategies for finding and walking on new paths that will lead to healing. The unique perspectives of a physician (Sugarman), psychologist (Linden), and storyteller (Brooks) blend to communicate more effectively than any one perspective ever could. The authors understand and make the convincing argument that hypnosis and hypnotic interactions lie at the heart of all effective clinical interactions. Indeed, they understand that hypnosis is central to a truly biopsychosocial model of health and care.

The ideas presented in *Changing our Minds* are both comprehensive and accessible. The approaches are grounded in theory yet are practical. The scholarship and state-of-science knowledge presented is of the highest order. Also, the combination of scholarly non-fiction with fiction as a way to present and illustrate concepts is very effective. The clarity of the background knowledge that is presented in the first section builds a solid foundation for the very practical ideas for effective healing presented in the latter sections of the book.

After reading *Changing our Minds*, you will have new insights about the role of hypnosis in everyday life and for appropriate and effective health care. You will understand that hypnosis can be viewed as much more than simply the ritual of a hypnotic induction followed by suggestions (what the authors refer to as the "legacy model" of hypnosis). Instead, clinical hypnosis can be understood as a set of four specific clinical skills that incorporate four key principles. When exercised as an integrative discipline across the continuum of clinical care, hypnotic practice becomes the core—the essence—of health and care.

If you are healer (and every one of us is or can be a healer) or clinician familiar with hypnosis, you will discover new ways to organize and think about what you already know and what you already do. Health care providers new to hypnosis will come to recognize the hypnotic strategies that they already use when they are able to join with their patients and be most effective. These readers will be inspired to learn more, and perhaps someday in the not-to-distant future become some of the leaders in the field of hypnosis.

If you are a policy maker (and every one of us is or can be a policy maker) you will see how the traditional biomedical model needs to become something different; that policies, including polices regarding how health care is provided and paid for, need to change, if we are going to have a sustainable and effective model of health care.

Reading books and pondering their messages often help us evolve and make important discoveries about ourselves. A book is "satisfying read" when it changes us. And *Changing Our Minds* is a very satisfying read indeed. Somehow, if you are reading this Foreword, the book has ended up in your hands. Now, please feel free to enjoy how it changes your mind.

Mark P. Jensen, Ph.D.
Seattle, WA, USA

Introduction

This is a book about changing our minds. In part, its chapters are about what science and clinical experience teaches us, so far, about how we grow and develop as we alter the functioning of all those embodied systems (including our brains) that make up our minds. Clinical hypnosis can drive that change. Hypnosis is about disrupting patterns of information and energy flow in our minds. That transformation can be as strange and uncomfortable as it is enlightening. It helps to have motivating companions and role models. Throughout human history, hypnotic stories of inspirational characters with whom we can identify have served this purpose.

That is why we made this book a hybrid. It is a treatise on the power of communication and relationship in clinical care. It is also a quartet of stories. The fictions are about people at different points in their lives. The characters struggle and progress. They are subject to interactions with others, mostly outside of clinical settings. In this way, the treatise and the stories intertwine to form the book. The tales wind through the discourse like four trails in the forest. The forest is more than the sum of its trails, but how else does one get into it?

The imaginative synthesis of the stories confirm the principles that we promote in our treatise. The clinician-authors (LIS and JHL) shared myriad clinical stories to illustrate concepts and principles while the poet-author (LWB) listened and wrote them into the form of people with lives. In this process we gave primacy to our relationships with each other; attended to the narrative arcs in our story-telling; and considered our own development as children, spouses, parents, professionals, and writers.

This is how we enacted the four principles we advocate in this text: *Relational Being, Narrative Listening, Temporal Touring,* and *Systems Thinking.* As a result, the characters whom you will meet—George, Robinson, Lulu, Lyle, Stevie, and their families—have inhabited our minds, looking over our shoulders as we wrote the chapters. In this sense, the poetic prose of their minds and lives feels more real than the scholarly treatise around which their stories wind. That was our intention. Health and care are about the unique lives of individual people, not their diagnoses and treatment.

We also mean "changing our minds" as shifting our thinking, beliefs, and attitudes about something. In this case that something is health and care. We are writing, at this moment, from atop a cresting wave of a revolutionary change in the dominant western health care paradigm. We authors are in the US, arguably the epicenter of practice in the biomedical model. Among its economic competitor nations, the US holds an accelerating lead in health care spending as percentage of gross domestic product while it trails, pulling farther behind, in life expectancy (OECD, 2019). There are many reasons for these diverging trajectories. We will look at some of them, but that is not our primary purpose. Our primary purpose is to wonder about improving our health care paradigm: our beliefs, tools, and practices for how we help people preserve well-being over their lives.

We hold that the current biomedical model is cracking beneath the weight of its morbidity. A tectonic paradigmatic shift is grinding. We are experiencing an avalanche of illness born of our physical inactivity, economic disparities, increasingly processed foods, and the inadequacy of the current medical construct to prevent or address these poverties. The opioid epidemic, our declining health, and the crushing cost of medical care become manifestations of anomalies of the dominant biomedical paradigm. We speculate that a new standard must include practices and perspectives for a broader ecology of mind, one that embraces the rich and idiosyncratic experiences of each individual within the stories of their culture. This is our vantage point. Between this introduction and the epilogue—through the stories, clinical vignettes, and treatise—this book explores and narrates the principles and practices underlying that paradigm shift.

Since hypnosis, and this book, are largely about therapeutic communication, and since the shared meanings of our words factor into that, we have included a glossary at the end. Words that appear in the glossary feature in bold in the chapters containing their first use. Terms like "hypnosis," "mind," and "paradigm" are commonly used and commonly misunderstood. You may read the word "hypnosis" here, but we don't know if you are imagining swinging pocket watches, cults, or pain relief. Does "mind" conjure some vague, unscientific ephemera; a verb that means "to obey"; or a reference to an empirically grounded system? We will discuss "paradigm" as Thomas Kuhn (2012) defined it, but in common usage its implications are fuzzy. Some of our proposed definitions—for mind and hypnosis for example—vary even from usual clinical and scientific convention. Our use may seem idiosyncratic. But our intention is to place these terms carefully and precisely into a more coherent and holistic frame. Our use of "trauma," for example, not as an event or even an injury, but as a way of living, very specifically reflects how it can be impacted by each of the four principles we describe. Still other terms and concepts, such as Porges' polyvagal theory (2011), are familiar to those in specific domains of clinical care and research, but remain peripheral in the biomedical model. We define them clearly to bring them into the center of what we propose is a new paradigm.

This book is the creation of three minds: one belonging to a physician, another to a clinical psychologist, and the third to a poet/novelist. One is a woman's mind. Two are men's minds. Actually, with yours, there are now four minds. We are writing this book with all of our roles in mind: as clinicians, as people receiving health care, as family and community members related to people receiving heath care, and as people concerned about the evolution of health, care, and healthcare.[1] It will be apparent that sometimes we write from within our clinical roles and at other times we write as children, parents, spouses, and citizens. At points throughout our lives, all of us become patients. That is common ground.

We authors have changed our minds while collaborating. We intended to. We knew that reconciling our different orientations—medical, psychological, and literary—would require the learning struggles and thinking breakthroughs that emerge when vibrant, reflective, exacting minds challenge each other. We struggled, argued, and overcame obstacles together. We inspired "AHA!" moments in each other. We lived what we were writing about.

This overall process aligns with, and so affirms, the cyclic and discontinuous bursts of neuroplasticity and creative change that we reference repeatedly throughout the book. Such episodes of enlightenment are the purpose of both effective therapeutic and creative encounters.

So, in composing this book, we have modeled what we envision for the place of hypnosis skills in the delivery of health and care. Our goal was to enact our goals by writing this book hypnotically. In our writer's trances, you, dear reader, were with us with each sentence, thought, and image. We hope your minds will change as have ours.

Note

1 Throughout this book we refer to health and care as separate words, meaning well-being and the act of support for well-being, respectively. We reserve the term "healthcare" to refer to the combined industries that are involved with production and delivery of products, running hospitals, providing insurance, their representatives to government regulation agencies, and those governmental agencies themselves.

References

Kuhn, T. S. (2012). *The structure of scientific revolutions* (4th ed.). Chicago, IL: University of Chicago Press.

Organisation for Economic Co-operation and Development (OECD). (2019). *Life expectancy at birth*. doi: 10.1787/27e0fc9d-en

Porges, S. W. (2011). *The polyvagal theory: Neurophysiological foundations of emotions, attachment, communication, and self-regulation*. New York, NY: W. W. Norton.

Robinson's Story

George with Carol

Here is the scene: an older couple, in the fading light of a chilled autumn evening, hurrying through the wind-driven leaves, up the stone steps to the glowing, brass-framed, glass doors of the public library. Actually, that's not quite it. He is all wiry and angular, moving in lurches and tugs, hurrying *her*. She is shorter, round, slow, patient, but yielding as they proceed up the steps.

"Please, George, I am moving as fast as these legs can carry me."

"I just hope we can find it. You sure you have the card?"

"For the tenth time, yes, dear. What has gotten into you? I don't know the last time you wanted to go *with* me to the library, of all places!"

"I'll show you. We just need to find it."

"Okay. Okay," she says, shaking her head in wonder, pulling forward on his outstretched arm.

An aging but fit security guard holds the door open for the couple. "Good evening, Carol. This must be your husband."

"Yes, this is my George. George, Franklin started working here just as I retired."

George pauses and shakes Franklin's hand as if it is a turnstile, mumbling "Good to see you," in passing.

Franklin calls after them, "Closing in 45 minutes, folks."

Inside, George stops, confused. He is looking for the wooden drawers that used to house the card catalog. Carol, takes his arm and leads him to the bank of touchscreen monitors that have replaced the worn oak cabinets. Her fingers deftly sort through the windows on the monitor display to select "In-Library Collection." She turns and asks her husband, "Now what is it that you are so hot to find?"

"Orwell. *Nineteen Eighty-four.*" George answers, deliberately.

She shakes her head, sighs, and repeats. "Well, I just don't know *what* has gotten into you … But here it is. Fiction. 823.913 ORW. Follow me, George."

George is following Carol's slow, competent pace. They are on her turf, now. But he is so eager to get wherever it is she is leading him that he follows right at her heels, like a determined dog. Along the ends of the stacks, she leads. Right at "753–879," then along the shelves, eyes scanning up and down as she walks, he fervently watches her find it. She stops, turns left, leans down, and carefully slides out the hardcover gray and black binding. She holds the book, then looks at him. He is looking at her, face tense, suddenly fighting back tears. She hands the book to him, an offering. He receives it in both hands as if it is both fragile and powerful. As if it could detonate.

She has known him far too long to say anything more, now. She leads him back to the circulation desk, reaches into her purse pocket, fishes out the library card that she hands to the young librarian, and a tissue that she hands to George. George hands over the book, wipes his eyes and blows his nose. The librarian says, "Three weeks. Good night."

Now, later, home at the kitchen table with a pot of tea, they sit facing each other. Jimmy is in the other room watching TV.

"It is hard to explain, Carol," says George, haltingly.

"It happened when I went to see that doctor today. You know about my sleeping … or not sleeping … and everything. You know. That second visit with the new doctor. He told me where he was from … uh, … yeah, Haiti. He's from Haiti. That's why he has that accent."

She nods. She knows to wait.

"I told him about the dreams, and my retiring, and my worrying about you and about Jimmy. And I told him about this book. Of all things! I was telling him about this book, I don't know why … and poor old Winston and the rats. And then, … I don't quite know how it happened. I remember asking him what he thought. I asked him … I wanted to know what he was thinking …"

George pauses. He lets go of his teacup, his hands on the table. His eyes close. His right fist clenches … then relaxes as he exhales, slowly, deeply. And the tears return … pouring this time. Through them he says,

"I have been so worried about taking care of everything for so long that I haven't told you that I care, … how much I care … about you and Jimmy. How much I love you. I am afraid that I haven't been very … uh … very lovable."

She reaches over and holds his right hand.

"I don't know what that doctor said. But he did something. No. He helped me do something … inside … here." George lays his left palm on his chest.

"I got angry … not at him … I told him that. Not *at* him. Kind of a *righteous* anger, I told him. I don't know. But it was really good … No … It is *going to be* really good. We're going to take better care of each other, starting now. Do you know I used to read? I used to read *a lot.* I never told you. I wanted to be a writer."

George moves his right hand from Carol's, reaches the book and places it between their hands. "You and I, we're going to read this book, together."

1 Prologue

> **Main Ideas**
>
> 1. Kuhn's thesis on scientific revolutions and Engel's advance of a biopsychosocial model can be viewed together as predicting a paradigm shift for health care.
> 2. The current biomedical health care paradigm is moving toward change due to increasing morbidity, mortality, and cost.
> 3. Clinical hypnosis, as a discipline for driving multisystem change—or psychobiological plasticity—lies at the heart of a new health care paradigm.
> 4. Four principles are introduced as clinical stances within a new health care model.

To know something is to transcend it.

Anonymous

This book is about how clinical **hypnosis** fits into our shifting health care **paradigm**. Why **clinical hypnosis**? Because it is the practice, within clinical settings, of communication and relationship to drive beneficial change in the **embodied** mind. We dare to refer to hypnosis as the heart of the healer's art. We will explore this in our first four chapters, starting with relevant aspects of the history of hypnosis. But the foundational concepts of this book do not lie in hypnosis's history. They start with a confluence of the work of physician George Engel and philosopher-physicist Thomas S. Kuhn.

More than 50 years ago, George Engel (1977)[1] tilted at the trajectory of **biomedicine**—the dominant **paradigm** of healing practice—by conceiving a "**biopsychosocial model**." In a reaction to what he viewed as the increasingly technical, reductionist, and dispassionate practice of medicine, he sought to bring personal experiences, relationships, and culture into the therapeutic mix. In so doing, Engel acknowledged and welcomed a broader range of inputs into an open and evolving system of mind and healing. Essentially, he raised two questions. First, how does the reductionist biomedical model expand to include psychological, relational, and cultural factors? Second, how do those factors interact to affect health outcomes? These queries spawned the development of new integrative health research endeavors including, but not limited to, psychoneuroimmunology (Ader, 2006)[2], placebo effect research (Benedetti, 2014), and psychosocial **genomics** (Rossi, 2003). Findings generated from these new fields reveal that both our social relationships and the stories we tell ourselves can modify and sometimes even override the effects of medicine and surgery. These discoveries unveil interactive intricacies that challenge the **monistic**—singular and linear—core of biomedicine. They hint at an ecology of health and care with complexity, unexpected possibilities, and wonder: what we could call "psychobiological care."

While Engel was still formulating his model, Thomas Kuhn (2012) produced his classic thesis on the making of scientific revolutions. Kuhn "single handedly changed the currency of the word *paradigm* so that a new reader attaches very different connotations to the word than were available to [Kuhn] …" (Hacking, 2012, p. xvii; italics original). He adopted the word paradigm to mean a system of scientific explanations, tools, and practices. A "dominant paradigm" was that system of explanations, tools, and practices that became so authoritative that it governed our perception of reality. For example (ours, not Kuhn's), until the 1700s the dominant paradigm of the universe was geocentric: the earth was central and heavenly bodies moved around it. Kuhn proposed that as-yet unexplained phenomena, or **anomalies**, acted as disruptive quakes in a formerly coherent and dominant paradigm. In our example, anomalies arose as early astronomers applied the practice of mathematics and the tools of optics to the heavens to discover that heavenly objects behaved in ways (e.g., retrograde motion) that challenged geo-centrism. Kuhn observed that as anomalies increasingly threaten the coherence, and so the dominance, of the current model, they compel a revolutionary shift; e.g., in our case, to a heliocentric system and a new cosmological paradigm. Kuhn likened paradigm shifts to a "gestalt switch" (2012, p. 118). The new paradigm re-framed the previous facts, changed our perspective, and thus our reality. The heavenly bodies were still there and moving, but through a new frame of reference, shaped by a new paradigm.

Kuhn's thesis furthered our pursuit of explanatory paradigms to fit our evolving understanding of the world within a rational system called science (see also Kant, 1781/1998). But there is a critical piece beneath that epistemology: the *how* of it. Kuhn's thesis, after all, was entitled "The Structure of Scientific Revolutions," not "The Existence of Scientific Revolutions." Kuhn defined anomalies not only in relationship to the paradigm, but also to the scientist. An anomaly, he wrote, was a phenomenon "… for which his paradigm has not readied the investigator" (p. 57). The "structure" of the revolution was embedded *within* the investigators' minds. Kuhn was not a psychologist, so he did not discuss the self-affirming and **liminal** nature of our minds and our behaviors. Despite this exclusion, Kuhn's thesis was fundamentally about *how we changed our minds*: how we require a system of explanation to fit together with a rationality (in this case, science) and within a social structure. In essence, Kuhn revealed how science provides us stories with which to understand and form our world, stories that we prefer to stick with, despite evidence of their fallacy, until the burden of those errors drives us to change our minds.

Kuhn's work was necessarily historical, focusing on previous paradigmatic revolutions in physics and chemistry; for example, the discoveries of oxygen and x-rays. But he was also prophetic. He acknowledged dispute—nearly 60 years before this writing—about whether social sciences and psychology were really scientific:

> Nowhere does this show more clearly than in the recurrent debates about whether one or another of the contemporary social sciences is really a science. These debates have parallels in the pre-paradigm periods of fields that are now unhesitatingly labeled science.
>
> (p. 159)

Kuhn mentioned neither medical science, nor health care, nor the healing arts. No one was suffering or dying as a direct result of the inadequacy of the dominant paradigmatic revolutions he described.

As we noted in our introduction, we are writing at a critical time in the evolution of the dominant western health care[3] paradigm. Currently in the US, at least 60% of adults and 40% of children have body mass indices greater than the upper limit of the "average risk" range of 25, thereby increasing their likelihood of developing cardiovascular and metabolic diseases (NIDDKD, 2018), and half of these at-risk children are obese (BMI > 29). US children also lead the world by five-fold in the consumption of prescribed psychoactive medications, especially in their use of the psychostimulants methylphenidate and amphetamines (Insel, 2014). Opioid addiction affects an increasing proportion of the US population, with estimates that as many as 40% of those suffering from addiction take the drug as prescribed. Overdose deaths have risen nearly three-fold nationally in the last decade (NIDA, 2018). In the US, and increasingly in westernized countries, children who eat average diets, participate in normal (sedentary) activities, and are exposed the dominant culture, are more and more likely to be less healthy than their parents, requiring increasing health care resources to treat metabolic, cardiovascular, and stress-related diseases. It can be argued that the current cohort of US youth is the first generation since the industrial revolution who may die at a younger age than will their parents (SSA,

2018). As such, they represent the last generation of those we may describe as the "accidentally well," who incur a rising tide of healthcare bills coming due. We consider these factors and more as representing cracks in a shifting paradigm. We imagine that we are ripe for something new.

Putting Hypnosis into Practice

The two clinician-authors (LIS and JHL) of this book explicitly use clinical hypnosis to provide **person-centered**, mind-integrative, and systems-informed care. We are not alone. We are informed by the work of Daniel Siegel (2012), Bruce Perry (Perry & Szalavitz, 2017), Urie Bronfenbrenner (2005), Yvonne Agazarian (Agazarian & Janoff, 1993), Ernest Rossi (2002, 2003), and many others who have brought concepts together that underscore the benefits of hypnotically-informed communication across the range of the healing arts. Because it utilizes the power of communication and relationship, we consider clinical hypnosis a skill set for ethically influencing "**psychobiological plasticity**" toward healing and optimizing health. We are going to use the word "**plasticity**" a lot. It is in the glossary for that reason. But since this is the first time we have used it, we owe you a ready explanation. By plasticity we mean, generally malleability and agility, both physical or imaginative. This can mean, susceptibility to external influence, but it can also be intentionally self-determined, as in being flexible and "open-minded." This agility can refer to both cognitive and emotional domains. Since we are mostly referring to our embodied minds, with both psychological and biological workings, by "psychobiological plasticity" we mean how able and willing we are to change our minds, whether or not we are aware of it. This has strongly informed our theory and practice of care. We have found that hypnosis and the phenomena it evokes are increasingly congruent with research findings in psychoneuroimmunology, placebo effects research, psychosocial genomics, and other areas that are consistent with the tenets of Engel's biopsychosocial model. Hence, we regard hypnotic skills as the heart, not the fringe, of health and the healing arts.

In this book, we intend to reorient the principles and practice of clinical hypnosis to align with evolving findings in psychobiology and "mind-body" health, or psychobiological care. We are paying particular attention to the psychobiology of human **development**, attachment, and **trauma** in relation to genomics, **epigenetics**, and the social environment. We believe that an expansive range of evocative, open-ended, and conversational hypnotic interactions must augment the traditional directive and premeditated methods of health care. We hold that hypnosis, as we conceive it, allows for individualistic—even idiosyncratic—person-centered approaches, to produce deeper and more lasting effects than problem-, technique-, or diagnosis-centered strategies. In this way, we expect that hypnosis allows a translation of psychobiological research findings into clinical care. In short, we believe these skills form the heart of a new health care paradigm. This book orients clinical hypnosis to align with the evolving science of mind and inform evolution in the healing arts.

First Principles of Hypnosis-Oriented Communication

1. ***Systems Thinking***—The client/patient always functions as part of, and is influenced by, a nested set of systems.
2. ***Temporal Touring***—Problems and their treatment travel in time with people.
3. ***Relational Being***—We are designed to influence each other. The intensity of our relationships correlates with the intensity of the influence.
4. ***Narrative Listening***—We have a need for coherent and congruent stories, the oldest form of healing art.

In the daily work of clinical care, we can lose sight of the principles and conceptual framework that influence our professional behavior; for example, that each patient is a unique individual within a social system (Engel, 1977). When we take these principles for granted and they are neither freshly delineated nor defined, their influence and meaning can recede, as when simply prescribing takes less time and engagement than listening some more. Our beliefs also need to be challenged regularly. This book endeavors to bring into the foreground concepts and perspectives that deserve clarification and naming so that we may more consciously, even mindfully, welcome their influence.

We consider four principles in the paradigm of psychobiological care to supersede, but not replace, the prevalence of biomedical cause-and-effect reductionism. They are listed at the beginning of this section. These principles are not really new. We are merely aligning and configuring them. We bring them into the core of the new paradigm from their previous place on the anomalous periphery of the biomedical model. Similarly, we believe that these principles interact and, like our integrative narratives, cut across all aspects of professional clinical behavior. They serve as cardinal directions to orient oneself in relationship to a person in care. These orientations are simply introduced here. Their significance unfolds in discussion, clinical application, and the narrative stories of this book.

1. *Systems Thinking*. Borrell-Carrió, Suchman, and Epstein (2004) note that in formulating his model, Engel rejected the (false) dichotomy contrasting the purely materialist-reductionist perspective (e.g., pills and procedures) on one hand with the ephemeral holistic-energy views (e.g., healing spiritual energy) of clinical care on the other. Instead,

> He endorsed what would now be considered a complexity view, in which different levels of the biopsychosocial hierarchy could interact, but the rules of interaction might not be directly derived from the rules of the

> higher and lower rungs of the biopsychosocial ladder. Rather, they would be considered **emergent properties** that would be highly dependent on the persons involved and the initial conditions with which they were presented, much as large weather patterns can depend on initial conditions and small influences.
>
> (p. 577)

Among the many implications and decades of clinical research that derived from this principle, three are particularly relevant to this book. First, at whatever level of the system one starts, from intracellular processes to family interactions, "the system" is open and evolving, and therefore unpredictable. Thinking (while being) in systems requires developing comfort with uncertainty. Second, so-called involuntary phenomena, like Kuhn's anomalies, originate outside of the practical or operational boundaries one has chosen. For example, if one believes that their immune system operates independently from other embodied mechanisms, then any conditioned effects of perceived psychological stress and emotional response on inflammation are anomalous and circumstantial. But if our boundaries broaden to a model in which immunity is a manifestation of a larger integrative system (i.e., an embodied mind), then thoughts, emotions, and inflammation are all collaborative processes amenable to intentional control. Put simply, we change by transcending system boundaries. Finally, within mind-as-a-system, as within collections of minds as social structures, changes are liminal. Activation energy, a build-up of potential dynamism, is required for change. We need to struggle for a while before we have moments of enlightenment and epiphanies. In short, we grow in spurts.

2. *Temporal Touring.* Similar to the progression of systems thinking from linear to complex/chaotic, this orientation holds that our approach must evolve from static clinical snapshots, frozen in time, to a chronobiologic/developmental perspective. Temporal Touring is not time travel. It simply involves appreciating the ever-shifting oscillations in the system. From short-duration epochs—breathing and heart rate variability changes over minutes—to **ultradian rhythms** (90–120-minute cycles) that pertain to shifting genomic expression, diurnal rhythms, monthly menstrual cycling, seasonal emotional changes, multi-year developmental periods and, of course, transgenerational life-times. This fourth-dimensional or temporal view recognizes that we are all traveling together in currents of time, at different rates. This means that clinicians need to help those in their care while thinking about interventions and changes progressively. Future and past orientation create plasticity in the fluid present.

3. *Relational Being.* We are biologically designed to be influenced by others. Biology is a model for co-existence. For us mammals, perhaps the most potent factors influencing our complex, open, evolving, dynamic,

roller-coastering minds are the other people in our lives. Autonomy is universally valued because it is vanishingly rare. The exploration, curiosity, and defiance of early childhood can be framed as a search for congruence, patterns and, most importantly, limits and structure on autonomy. This principle evolves from attachment research that suggests much of our mental health derives from these early relational models (Brown & Elliott, 2016; Siegel, 2012; Wallin, 2007). The bottom line is that the intensity of human relationships (and relationships with our pets, and even with interactive media; see also Spike Jonze's *Her*, 2014) can moderate or override our responses to medical and surgical interventions. Placebo research suggests that relationships may be equipotent with the effects of narrative, conditioning, and expectation in changing our response to health interventions. *Relational Being* means that the clinician is conscious of and skilled in developing and enriching therapeutic **rapport** by cultivating a relational **mindset** or "**clinician's trance**."

4. *Narrative Listening.*[4] I (LIS) was listening to an interview with a novelist in which the interviewer asked, "There are so many elements of your life in this book. Is it autobiographical?" The writer laughed, then responded, "Well, we write what we know, but it couldn't be an autobiography. Lives have no narrative arc." In the same way that we are motivated by illusions of autonomy, we are also driven by a need for coherent and congruent narratives and stories. As children, we often read the same books repeatedly. We search for security and predictability in the notion that life "makes sense." Further, we learn by association. That is what metaphors, narratives, and stories are for. Because we cannot change the system from inside of it, we are often myopic within dominant narratives and paradigms. What is outside the paradigm's boundaries does not seem real. Biomedicine is the dominant western health care paradigm. But placebo effect research demonstrates that suggestion, couched in a coherent, culturally aligned narrative, can drive physiologic effects in the mind of the listener. Common clinical usage is to "take a history." In reality, we are co-constructing a narrative. How we tune, or co-author, our therapeutic narratives to align with the internal health resources of the person seeking care may have as "direct" a biologic effect as the prescription. Storytelling is perhaps the oldest form of the healer's art.

These are our guiding principles. As we travel through the layers of this book, we will continue to draw from these four ways of being in relationship with those who seek care.

How the Book Goes on from Here

With the aforementioned principles as guideposts, this book builds a concentric model of hypnosis and the factors that influence it. We use the word concentric because we are building our thesis from the inside out, like nesting dolls. The chapters of Part I describe and illustrate a conceptualization of hypnosis and its role in therapy, scaling up from cell to mind. In Part II we add the consideration of developmental drives that act as imperative forces to direct psychobiological plasticity, ideally within an agile, open mind. The brittle, traumatized mind is discussed in Chapter 8. For Part III we broaden our understanding of changing minds to consider the influence of attachment, relationships, and the narratives they can originate to build resilience. Finally, in the last chapter, we enlarge these ideas to consider the changing health care paradigm and the evolution of health and care beyond the biopsychosocial model. The book ends with an epilogue that brings the stories flowing through the chapters to their ends, or at least to the thresholds of their futures.

About the Stories

Integrating fiction into a clinical text challenges the dominant clinical standard. In clinical writing it is common, and arguably necessary, to illustrate principles and practice with encounters drawn from experiences with people in the context of their care. We do that, too. Historically, biomedicine and evidence-based psychological care have promoted an objective and detached stance when reporting such interactions and findings (Engel, 1977). Of course, this detachment is idealized and illusory. Even when these clinical narratives are verbatim transcripts, or written by persons receiving care, they still only represent the clinicians' or clients' subjective perspectives (see also Axline, 1964; Erickson & Rossi, 1989). This subjectivity is a valid representation of experience from within the system, as long as it does not pretend to be more.

Objectivity cannot arise from *within* the system. The clinical encounters we cite in professional texts do not report on the lives of those seeking care that occur *outside* of the examination, consultation, or operating room, in the vast open worlds of people's lives. Artists—in their painting, sculpture, music, dance, and here, with poetic prose—more completely represent the fullness and potential of lived phenomena. Artists know what to leave out. Art allows uncertainty. It explicitly includes the implicit and knowingly plays with the unknowable. Art evokes. Science tries to explain. In this sense, art is more valid than science. Besides, we repeat that storytelling has always been part of the healer's art.

As we have claimed, thinking systemically, relationally, and narratively in clinical care was, at least in retrospect, fundamental to Engel's revolutionary biopsychosocial model and part of what this book is about. So, within this book, and without apology, we include fictional stories to more richly illustrate our clinical principles in lives that move through and exist beyond clinical agencies.

The first story started before this chapter. The stories will continue on, passing between successive chapters, like the aforementioned trails in the woods, illustrating and animating principles and practices as they go.

Questions and Assignments for Further Discussion

1. In this chapter, psychoneuroimmunology, placebo research, and psychosocial genomics are cited as evidence of scientific pursuits that threaten and transcend the current biomedical paradigm. What additional areas of science, or potential areas, may also emerge as paradigm-changers?
2. Within this book's stories find one example of each of the four principles listed in the chapter: *Systems Thinking, Temporal Touring, Relational Being,* and *Narrative Listening.*
3. Discuss some examples of health narratives, often precautionary (such as, "You will catch a cold if your feet get wet in the rain") that formed your own views of health and sickness. Do you still hold them? Why or why not?

Notes

1 George Engel was neither a psychiatrist nor primarily an academic. He was an internal medicine clinician who studied and was a proponent of psychoanalysis, but never trained or worked as a psychiatrist. Nevertheless, he gained significant influence with the leadership in the Psychiatry Department at the University of Rochester School of Medicine, and in particular with John Romano, chief of the Department of Psychiatry. This speaks to the phenomenon and theme that impactful change often originates from outside of a system.

2 Robert Ader was Engel's first post-doctoral trainee, first within the Department of Psychology, then in the Department of Psychiatry, both at the University of Rochester.

3 Throughout this book we refer to health and care with separate words, meaning well-being and the act of support for well-being, respectively. We reserve the term "health-care" to reference the combined trades that are involved with production and delivery of products, the processes of running hospitals, providing insurance, their representation to government regulatory and oversight agencies, including those governmental agencies themselves, all of which comprise, *in toto*, the healthcare industry.

4 We distinguish this principle from the practice of "Narrative Therapy" as introduced by Michael White and David Epston (1990). Narrative therapy is a clinical strategy involving intentional collaborative "re-authoring" as a means to confront problems. This approach, as a clinical strategy, certainly aligns with and is congruent within our meaning of narrative. But we are more broadly using the term to refer to the generic need for the "narrative arc" and for "making sense" to drive change, rather than a specific story or narrative for therapeutic intent.

References

Ader, R. (2006). *Psychoneuroimmunology* (4th ed.). Amsterdam, Holland: Academic Press/ Elsevier.

Agazarian, Y. M., & Janoff, S. (1993). Systems theory and small groups. In I. Kaplan & B. Sadock (Eds.), *Comprehensive textbook of group psychotherapy* (3rd ed., pp. 33–44). Baltimore, MD: Williams & Wilkins.

Axline, V. M. (1964). *Dibs: In search of self.* New York, NY: Houghton-Mifflin.

Benedetti, F. (2014). *Placebo effects: Understanding the mechanisms in health and disease.* New York, NY: Oxford University Press.

Borrell-Carrió, F., Suchman, A. L., & Epstein, R. L. (2004). The biopsychosocial model 25 years later: Principles, practice, and scientific inquiry. *Annals of Family Medicine, 2*(6), 576–582. doi:10.1370/afm.245

Bronfenbrenner, U. (2005). *Making human beings human: Bioecological perspectives on human development.* Los Angeles, CA: Sage.

Brown, D., & Elliott, D. (2016). *Attachment disturbances in adults: Treatment for comprehensive repair.* New York, NY: W.W. Norton.

Engel, G. L. (1977). The need for a new medical model: A challenge for biomedicine. *Science, 196*(4286), 129–136.

Erickson, M. H., & Rossi, E. L. (1989). *The February man: Evolving consciousness and identity in hypnotherapy.* New York, NY: Routledge.

Hacking, I. (2012). Introductory essay. In T. S. Kuhn, *The structure of scientific revolutions* (4th ed., pp. vii–xxxviii). Chicago, IL: University of Chicago.

Insel, T. (2014). Post by former NIMH Director Thomas Insel: Are children over-medicated? Retrieved from: www.nimh.nih.gov/about/directors/thomas-insel/blog/2014/are-children-overmedicated.shtml

Jonze, S. (2014). *Her [Motion picture].* United States: Annapurna Pictures.

Kant, I. 1998. *The critique of pure reason.* (P. Guyer & A. W. Wood Eds., Trans.) Cambridge, UK: Cambridge University Press. (Original work published 1781).

Kuhn, T. S. (2012). *The structure of scientific revolutions* (4th ed.). Chicago, IL: University of Chicago.

National Institute of Diabetes and Digestive and Kidney Diseases (NIDDKD). (2018). Overweight and obesity statistics. Retrieved from www.niddk.nih.gov/health-information/health-statistics/overweight-obesity

National Institute on Drug Abuse (NIDA). (2018). Overdose death rates. Retrieved from www.drugabuse.gov/related-topics/trends-statistics/overdose-death-rates

Perry, B., & Szalavitz, M. (2017). *The boy who was raised as a dog: And other stories from a child psychiatrist's notebook—What traumatized children can teach us about love, loss and healing.* New York, NY: Basic Books.

Rossi, E. L. (2002). *The psychobiology of gene expression: Neuroscience and neurogenesis in hypnosis and the healing arts.* New York, NY: W. W. Norton.

Rossi, E. L. (2003). Gene expression, neurogenesis, and healing: Psychosocial genomics of therapeutic hypnosis. *American Journal of Clinical Hypnosis, 45*(3), 197–216.

Siegel, D. (2012). *The developing mind.* New York, NY: Guilford.

Social Security Administration (SSA). (2018). Actuarial life tables. Retrieved from www.ssa.gov/oact/STATS/table4c6.html

Wallin, D. (2007). *Attachment in psychotherapy.* New York, NY: Guilford.

White, M., & Epston, D. (1990). *Narrative means to therapeutic ends.* New York, NY: W. W. Norton.

Lulu's Story

Introduction

How come I came to be so all alone? When I have two sisters and a brother and a Mom and Dad. And friends at school.

I'm not alone, but I seem to be alone. Some people cry because "No one likes me!" I don't cry, but I'm sad because "No one is like me."

My family—my American family—my Mom, mostly—tells me I had a different language when I first came here, but she never knew that language and I don't remember it. Or I know that there are words that float up out of the back of my mind once in a while, words that aren't English, and I assume they come from my old language, the one I used to know, but they're not connected to anything, so there is no meaning, no usefulness to it. They are more like broken parts of feelings and memories. They are like shards of pottery

Or—maybe there are a few words. Maybe just a few. I know them, but I don't know them. I hear the sounds of singing and talking in my mind, I hear words like faraway music, but I don't know what the sounds mean. Although—I know this. I know there's a word that means "water". I can't quite catch hold of it, I can't write it, I can't even say it, but it means "water". I remember that. *Water.*

Lulu Tries to Write

It is 3,500 miles from Europe to North America by airplane. And the deepest place in the Atlantic Ocean is 27,498 feet. I know it's there, but I can't imagine that much water.

In elementary school, we learned that human blood is mostly sea water; that's where life began. A guy at school, Roger Furlong, told me I don't have the same blood as my family has. He said I'll never really be part of my family because I don't have the same blood. But I know Roger just said that to be mean; my Dad told me that's wrong. All of us—all humans, all mammals—have the same blood. I have memory pieces where blood is spilled.

They tell me my America Mom is my mother now, but—Isn't someone else my mother, too? Isn't there some far-off person in Africa who is also my real mother, who looks dark, like me? But, if there is, why would she give me away? I'm afraid to ask that question. I guess I fear that I will not like the answer I get. I fear that no one else has questions like that. I'm so confused. I don't even know what questions to ask.

I have learned that family is more than looking alike. I look different from the rest of my family because I was adopted. But my America family is my family.

My America Mom tells me that when I don't understand something I should write down my thoughts, and then maybe I can write my way to an answer. I don't know if that will work for me. Do I even know the questions to ask? I think I have a lot of questions. I'm going to write down what I know.

Sometimes when I was a kid people would ask me where did I come from. My brother and sisters are pale all over and I'm dark all over. And back then, I didn't talk like everyone else. My brother and sisters would tell those people that they're being really rude. The fact is that they *were* being rude, but still, I want to know, too. I want to know where I came from. And I want to know who my birth family is. I want to know why I live in America instead of Africa.

And I want to know why I don't feel happy lately.

I can't tell my America Mom and Dad that I'm not happy. That would be ungrateful. They helped me when I was in trouble. They brought me here, they gave me water to drink and food to eat. They gave me clothes to wear and a soft bed to sleep on. And it's safe here where I'm living now. I think maybe we were in trouble back in Africa. I don't know what the trouble was. But it's been a long time. Shouldn't it be over by now? But there are those shards … and dried blood.

My America family even gave me a new name. Lulu. It isn't my real name, but they told me it's an America name, and I needed to have an America name. So it's good, I guess. It seems like everyone here doesn't care about Africa because of course I'll stay in America my whole life because America is the best place in the world. No one asks me what I think about that. But at least for now I guess I need to live here. I wouldn't know where else to go. But I don't think that's why I'm not happy.

I asked my Mom those questions and she said we need to sit down together and find answers, the best answers we can. We need to have a family meeting. So that's what we decided to do. But then we decided not to have the meeting yet, because my Dad has an idea that could help us find answers.

Lulu Does Gymnastics

Here's one idea of why I'm not happy: I've been doing gymnastics since I was six years old. I'm very good at gymnastics. My coach says I'm "fearless." She says that when I approach the vault I let go of my fears and fly. And I always ask myself—*Truly, what do I have to fear?* I ask that ... and feel that there are answers, hiding. Answers lurk in the puzzle-piece-memories. There is in me something worth fearing. When I do gymnastics—when I run and twist and fly—I feel fear*ful. As if* I am getting away from something. Someone told me courage isn't fearless. They don't see what's in me.

But a month ago I touched that deep-inside fear: I lost focus on the balance beam. I was worried my tampon might overflow and blood would run down my leg. So I flubbed a landing. I fell. I have fallen before. Everyone does. But this time it was different. The moment I hit the mat I felt ... terror. I don't remember this but coach said that when she went to help me I pulled back into a ball, my eyes went wide. "Like a deer in the headlights," she said. Then she helped me up and I was shaking. I did not know why. And the others stared. I ended up with this cracked ankle. The broken pieces are close together and will heal.

I had never heard that expression, "Like a deer in the headlights." Why would a deer be in the headlights? It must be a thing. My memory-puzzle-pieces felt the headlights. The headlights flashed "Fear" in those back-of-my-mind non-English words, shaking me.

So—I used to fly, and now I'm crawling, limping along on a crutch. And it hurts, obviously. But I'm not afraid of pain. I've been lucky so far, not to have an injury like this. But I've seen a lot of girls get injured and heal up 100%. And anyway, people say a healed bone is stronger than a bone that's never been broken.

And bodies change after puberty. It's true. My center of gravity has shifted. But, for now, not by much. My periods have never been regular. Learning about our bodies and paying close attention to them is part of being an athlete. So that's not it. That's not why I'm not happy.

Sometimes I think that maybe I don't really care about gymnastics anymore. Maybe it's just a phase I went through. Maybe my body is already outgrowing it. I keep assuming that when my ankle is healed and the bone is in one piece I'll lose the weight I've put on and go back to the gym and pick up right where I left off. But what if that's just a fantasy?

Well, what if it is? If I want to do it, I'll do it. If I realize I don't really care anymore, then I won't do it, and I won't cry over it. Courageous is not fearless.

But I still don't know why I'm unhappy. Although maybe it isn't actual unhappiness I'm feeling. What about this? What if what I'm feeling is my body waking up? When we're kids, we just hurl our bodies into whatever movements the coach calls for. But eventually even gymnasts become self-conscious; we become aware of who's watching—could be college coaches, even Olympic coaches—and what those people are thinking. We feel the power of all those eyes. I went to the gym yesterday (in my sweats, leaning pathetically on my crutch!) and watched the little girls practice for a while. I thought—they're terrific—spinning and flipping and landing—I was like that. They are determined, and making it easy. Having fun. I was *not* exactly like that. Something in me was running, jumping, and hiding to save my life. Something they don't know about. I don't know if *I* know. Eventually these little girls are going to stop performing like little machines. Eventually they'll have to deal with the enormous pressure of all that awareness, all those expectations, even fear in the headlights.

Maybe sometimes kids have just had enough. They don't want it anymore. They need to turn off all the pressure. Maybe I messed up that landing on purpose because there was no other way out. Maybe because I wanted to learn something about myself. Wow. What a thought. Where did I come up with that?

Part I

Hypnosis and Changing Minds

2 What Was Hypnosis? What Is It Now? What Is It Becoming?

Main Ideas

1. Our understanding and application of hypnosis has evolved in parallel with our evolving understanding of mind, health, and care.
2. Hypnosis is most functionally defined as communication skill set, not a ritual or procedure.
3. When applied as a research probe, hypnosis can yield new insight into understanding relational aspects of mind.
4. Given its far-reaching effects, hypnosis lies at the heart of clinical interactions, whether we recognize it or not.

When I (LIS) was in medical school, one of my mentors, a respected professor of internal medicine, was hospitalized with lymphoma. I went to visit him. I arrived in the hospital ward to search for his room, feeling ambivalent. I hadn't been exposed yet to life-altering illness in people I knew. I was both attracted to and repelled by the gravity of his illness. I was used to chatting in his office, surrounded by books and across his paper-strewn desk, not seeing him in a hospital bed, tethered with wires and tubes. I was confused, curious, uncertain, and therefore vulnerable. I know now that this emotional mix drove my psychobiological plasticity, the novel **trance** of this encounter, and that was why it would prove to be so formative.

As I entered, he weakly smiled his welcome and invited me to come around his bed to sit by him on the only chair. Just as I did, a doctor entered. I stood up to leave. My teacher told me to stay, introduced me, and motioned for me to sit. So I did, tenuously. The confident, white-coated clinician asked his questions, skillfully examined and considered, then discussed plans, while I hunched in my chair, feeling intrusive. He finished, shook our hands, and left.

When the silence cleared, my teacher started to ask me how I was. A woman entered the room and introduced herself as a social worker. Again, I popped up to leave, was introduced, then motioned back down by my teacher. I sat and attempted invisibility as they discussed practical options and preparations for home care; then she left.

As the door closed, my teacher turned to me and smiled, again…when the door reopened abruptly to frame a bearded, gregarious man who warmly announced my teacher's first name. I leapt to my feet. My teacher introduced me to his rabbi and motioned me down. I sat, trained. I remember the earnest, lilting bass melody of the rabbi's voice more than the English and Hebrew lyrics from the two friends' conversation. I stared at my hands in my lap. Eventually, he left.

Once more, the doors closed. My teacher lay back in bed, sighed, then nodded thoughtfully to himself. He turned and, index finger pointing at me, declared, "You know, there was a time when all of these roles were played by the same person."

What is hypnosis? "Hypnosis" is a word that evokes curiosity, mystery, confusion, suspicion, quackery, anxiety, and also promise. Coined in the mid-19th century, hypnosis started as a label for psychophysiological phenomena in medical contexts (e.g., Braid, 1843). It evolved into the monster embodied in the rogue character "Svengali," in George Du Maurier's novel, *Trilby* (1894); the nefarious focus of dozens of popular movies such as *The Cabinet of Caligari* (Kay, 1962), *The Manchurian Candidate* (Demme, 2004), and *Get Out* (Blum & Peele, 2017); the medium for undue influence and cult indoctrination (Hassan, 2018); as a stage entertainment phenomenon; a health care panacea; and, recently again, the subject of clinical investigation of mind-body interactions. Perhaps the most succinct response to "What is hypnosis?" is "Misunderstood."

The origins of this misunderstanding are significant. Disputed terminologies are often symptoms of deeper dissent. We contend that, in large part, the controversy surrounding hypnosis stems from it being a *system for interpersonal influence*, and thus a threat to our autonomy. Human beings cherish autonomy. We value our individuality. We are also designed biologically to influence each other profoundly. Christakis (2019) has pointed out the "paradox that individuality is actually essential for community" (p. 66). Our individual characteristics, and reciprocal recognition of these characteristics (e.g., our faces), form a basis for unique connections. We are evolutionarily engineered, Christakis writes, to connect, relate, love, and cooperate, as we develop our identities, and to be part of nested systems. Our health and care are related to our survival as a species of exceptional individuals. Banks and Hirschman (2015) take this further, to propose that clinicians ought to thoroughly evaluate and teach those in their care the significance of our unique constellations of relational networks in the creation of well-being.

Hypnosis more generally, then, is the relational equivalent of a two-edged sword. Without question, focused interpersonal influence can do harm and be traumatizing. But, when ethically applied in therapeutic settings, **clinical hypnosis** can cultivate profound and enduring benefit. We will excavate the developmental and biological roots of this influence in the remaining chapters of this first section of our book. In this chapter, we will discuss the historical origins of hypnotic phenomena, and then its evolution into a clinical skill set.

What Was Hypnosis?

We do not intend to be exhaustive in the following historical review. Readers and students of the health care and hypnosis histories may be interested in texts dedicated to those subjects (see Pintar & Lynn, 2008; Tinterow, 1970). In this opening chapter, we consider the evolution of hypnosis as a phenomenon and a clinical practice through a paradigmatic lens—in other words, by examining how the components of what we now call "hypnosis" have served progressive frameworks for understanding the mind in health and disease.

What we call hypnosis was originally rooted in a system of beliefs and rituals in early civilizations, when science and religion were the same and constituted one cultural dominion; back when, as the medical school professor at the beginning of this chapter said, "all of these roles were played by the same person." Within medieval Europe and into the Enlightenment, those spiritual rituals were extracted as the effects of insensible forces or magnetic fluids and subjected to early scientific study. With the emergence of the biomedical model over the last two centuries, hypnosis has been dissected in an attempt to reduce it to one element or another, concordant with our reductionist and categorical approach to health and care. Hypnotic communication and its benefits have always been lurking within the practice of health care—often peripherally, and sometimes as anomalies (in Kuhn's sense). Our thesis is that hypnosis has been awaiting its place at the heart of a new health care paradigm. So we will begin, in this opening chapter, to move hypnosis from the fringe to the core.

Creating Hypnosis

A Scottish surgeon, James Braid (1795–1860), is often credited with coining the term *hypnosis*, first as *Neuro-Hypnosis* or "nervous sleep."[1] In his monograph,

Neurypnology; or, the Rationale of Nervous Sleep, Considered with Animal Magnetism, Illustrated by Numerous Cases of its Successful Applications in the Relief and Cure of Disease (1843), he described first attending a demonstration of mesmerism—or animal magnetism—by famed French Mesmerist Charles LaFontaine as "a complete skeptic" (p. 2). He felt compelled to return to the demonstration for two consecutive performances, intrigued and speculative. While he discounted animal magnetism as the medium of the phenomena—catalepsy, amnesia, suggestibility—he came to believe that he was engaging with the poorly understood juncture of psychological and physiological domains.

Braid viewed hypnotic phenomena (more accurately termed *trance* phenomena, as we will explain) as innate and biological. He began his ardent and alliteratively-titled final monograph, *The Physiology of Fascination: And the Critics Criticised* (1855), by speculating how it is that the snake who is "destined to wander pronely upon the earth" (p. 3) can fix with its gaze a bird that is otherwise free to fly away and, doing so, ultimately consume it. He described numerous similar reflexes, such as gaze fixation and catalepsy, as occurring when people encountered novel or traumatic events. He noted that sometimes this resulted in residual and ongoing behavioral and physiological symptoms. In this, he foretold post-traumatic disorder. Braid endeavored to replicate, then study these phenomena and their enduring effects.

From his precise observations of the mesmerist's subjects, and subsequently his own, Braid determined that producing fatigue by way of a prolonged upward gaze was one way to achieve the mesmerists' trance. He would hold a candle or his reflective lancet case at a distance of "eight to fifteen inches from the eyes" (Braid, 1843, p. 27), while directing his subjects to stare at it, noting their tremulous eyelids, pupillary responses and, eventually, swooning into a repose during which they were more responsive to his successive instructions.

Initially, Braid's focus was on the physiological and behavioral aspects achievable with hypnosis. His direction later shifted toward the subject of concentration and the nature of interpersonal influence. He even attempted to rename the methods of the field of study he had established "monoideism" (Braid, 1855, p. 5). But the word "hypnotism" rapidly gained popularity and, perhaps fortunately, his new term never caught on.

Through his clinical exploration, Braid attempted to replicate and parse these natural phenomena by studying **induction** of eye-fixation, catalepsy, and amnesia. He emphasized that these clinical findings were only the surface of a deeper understanding of health and disease. He coined the term *psychophysiology* and noted that "… the attempt made to study these two branches of science so much apart from each other, has been a great hindrance to the successful study of either" (Braid, 1855, p. 7). Of his discoveries about hypnosis, Braid (1843) wrote:

> I feel quite confident that we have acquired in this process a valuable addition to our curative means; but I repudiate the idea of holding it up as a universal remedy; nor do I even pretend to understand the *whole range of diseases* in which it may be useful ... Whether these extraordinary physical effects are produced through the imagination chiefly, or by other means, it appears to me quite certain, that the imagination has never been so much under our control, or capable of being made to act in the same beneficial and uniform manner, by any other mode of management hitherto known.
>
> (p. 5, italics original)

Oddly, current major American texts in the field that he christened—psychophysiology—neither credit nor mention Braid (Cacioppo, Tassinary, & Berntson, 2019; Carlson, 2004; Schwartz & Andrasik, 2016). The most famous aspect of his legacy seems to be his methodology of eye-fixation with an upward gaze in the practice of hypnotic induction. This distillation from broadly person-centered, innate, and naturalistic phenomenology to clinical procedure—from what we can do *for* ourselves (autogenic) to what we can do *to* others (allopathic)—seems, in retrospect, to be typical of the subsequent practice of hypnosis particularly, and biomedicine more generally, over the ensuing history of health and care. We doubt Braid would be pleased with this outcome. We will return to the subsequent evolution of hypnosis into the current biomedical paradigm later in this chapter (and further in Chapter 12). Before that, let's look back at hypnosis before it became "Hypnosis."

What Was Hypnosis Before It Was Hypnosis

What we now call hypnosis has a long history of benefitting the sick and unwell. Prehistoric mystics, shamans, and medicine women utilized the orienting response—the inherent fight/flight/freeze reflex generated by way of our protective amygdalae—that opens avenues to survival, adaptability, and change, long before Pavlov. Those primordial healers used their knowledge of the traditions, beliefs, and imaginations of their community to produce benefit. Like the lesson from the author's memory retold above, there was a time when healing in physical, social, and metaphysical realms was not disassembled into distinct professional roles.

Over 4,000 years ago, in the Egyptian Sleep or Dream Temples, the Priest Imhotep used chanting, fasting, baths, sacrifices, and dream interpretation. The earliest known physicians successfully used dream interpretation, often of induced dreams, to help the sick heal. The Delphic Oracles of Greece were involved with the Aesculepian rituals. Aesclepius was the Greek god of healing, whose cult of followers encouraged pilgrimages to temples for priests' blessings, then promoted dreams for healing and counsel. The legendary doctor Hippocrates may have begun his career as an Aesclepion.

It is perhaps historically presumptuous, if not chauvinistic, to retroactively refer to these early practices as hypnosis. Doing so is akin to reducing Buddhism to the practice of mindfulness meditation, relegating prayer in Abrahamic religions to "self-hypnosis," or giving modern interpretation to ancient works of art. Such secular reductions deny the deeper meaning of these religious and cultural practices in their connections and attributions to systems of belief and symbols. Again, we argue that it is more authentic to view these practices from within their contemporaneous paradigmatic context, not retrospectively. We cannot fully understand the cultural mindset of those in the first millennium toward health and healing, any more than they could conceive of our current biomedical paradigm. We can surmise from historical records that the paradigms—again: beliefs, practices, and tools—of these cultures were wholistic and communal. There were neither mind-body, science-spirit, nor individual-social dualities. All of these dichotomies, arguably false, are relatively modern creations of the last seven centuries of human invention.

The connection between beliefs and practices, with the evocation of naturally-occurring trance for healing primarily in religious contexts, began to dissolve early in the next millennium. This was typified by the work of Paracelsus (c.493–1541), who was a keen observer and investigator of both treatment and toxicology, and who conceptualized the role of the imagination in illness (Ehrenwald, 1976, p. 200). The schism widened with the impact of René Descartes (1596–1650). Called the "father of 'rationalism,'" he was famously, and perhaps unfairly, accused of proposing a separation, if not a divorce, of spirit from science by questioning the divinity of the soul. In his *Passions of the Soul* (1649/1989), Descartes championed theories of body mechanics linking perception, emotion, and physiology that would become foundational to the modern era and heralded the Enlightenment, or Age of Reason (c.1600–1800). This period of reorganization of science, religion, and philosophy could be considered a period of parsing or dis-integration. Psychiatrist-Philosopher Iain McGilchrist (2009) speculates that this period foreshadowed a growing divide between left- and right-brain function that is emblematic of a larger health care crisis. We imagine that this birthing of scientific reason as the centerpiece of healing was the start of the shift to what became the biomedical paradigm.

In 1643, Athanasius Kircher (1601–1680), a German Jesuit Priest and polymath, described animal magnetism as a force in nature responsible for health and disease (Kircher, 1643). His work is rumored to have inspired Franz Anton Mesmer (1734–1815), the person from whom the term *Mesmerism* derives. Mesmer was a Viennese physician who, like many of his forbearers and contemporaries, studied astronomy and the theories of Isaac Newton on gravity. It is likely that Mesmer was influenced by Kircher's ideas and the contemporaneous influence of "insensible forces." Distressed by the bloodletting and purges that were pervasive and standard in medicine at that time, Mesmer was looking for gentler and more enlightened methods to bring about cures (Mesmer, 1779/2016). Hypothesizing a natural transference of energy between all things, animate and inanimate, he advocated the theory that disease was caused by imbalances of a force subject to magnetic influence, and that cures could be achieved by manipulating the body's magnetic fluids.

Arranging his clients around a large wooden tub fixed with projecting metal rods—a baquet—and filled with water containing iron filings, the afflicted would fall into "crises," perhaps psychogenic seizures, and then awaken, cured. Similar effects were obtained by movements of magnetic rods, and later, "magnetized" hands over the surface of, but not touching, the body. Mesmer was reportedly charismatic, enthusiastic, and successful with many of his cures, including those of ladies of the royal court in France. But he also established a private hospital in his own home for treating the indigent. The popularity of his cures and the mounting contempt of the medical establishment developed into fulminant controversy. Unfortunately, Mesmer compounded this by establishing a secret society, La Société de L'Harmonie (The Society of Harmony), through which he charged disciples to learn magnetic techniques (Tinterow, 1970, p. 74).

Ultimately, this notoriety attracted the attention of the royal court (Kihlstrom, 2002). King Louis XVI commissioned an investigation, chaired by Benjamin Franklin and including the chemist Antoine Lavoisier, the doctor Joseph-Ignace Guillotin, and the astronomer Jean Sylvain Bailly, to investigate Mesmer's claims by examining the practices of one of his disciples, Charles D'Eslon. Their careful examination, including wooden rods painted to mimic iron rods, constituted one of the first published, prospective, peer-reviewed, placebo-controlled trials. The commissioners concluded, within the limits of contemporary science, that magnetic influence did not directly cause the beneficial effects attributed to it.

The commissioners did not, however, dispute the reality of those favorable effects. In this way, as Kihlstrom (2002) pointed out, the Franklin Commission left Mesmer's claims of benefit "both unchallenged and unexplained." Their report presumed that the cures were due to imagination, imitation, and touch, rather than magnetic influence. Further, they claimed that the crises or convulsions that occurred around the baquet were harmful and "pernicious" (Tinterow, p. 127). But this was a century before William James, the Father of American psychology, gave credence to the power of the imagination. Within the mechanistic model of the time, disproving magnetism sufficed to protect the medical establishment. Any salutary effect was—to recall Kuhn's thesis—anomalous.

Mesmer's passionate work ignited interest throughout Europe. He brought interpersonal influence—by whatever means—into scientific study and into the world of medicine, which itself was only beginning to find its professional footing. A contemporary of Mesmer, an Indo-Portuguese priest, Abbé Faria (1746–1819), introduced an oriental practice of influence to Paris (Perry, 1978). Unlike Mesmer, Faria claimed that this influence "generated from within the mind," presumably by the power of expectancy and cooperation. His theoretical position and the subsequent experiences of the Nancy School of Medicine were contributors to "autosuggestion" techniques of another French physician, Émile Coué, and later to autogenic training techniques of German psychiatrist, Johannes Heinrich Schultz.

Interest in animal magnetism spread across the channel and into the United Kingdom. A London surgeon, John Elliotson (1791–1868), the first British doctor to use the stethoscope and practice acupuncture, was intrigued with the potential of mesmerism to provide anesthetic experiences for his patients. He founded and published the 13 volumes of the journal *Zoist*, the first professional publication to focus on mesmeric study. He eventually resigned in protest from the London University Hospital, when mesmerism was banned there.

James Esdaile (1808–1859), a Scottish surgeon practicing in India as Civil Assistant Surgeon to the East India Company, is credited with inducing anesthesia by mesmeric passes. He reportedly first used mesmerism in 1845. He documented over 400 major surgical procedures, as well as many minor ones, while claiming to have successfully transferred magnetic energy for anesthesia and analgesia (Tinterow, 1970, pp. 252–254). In addition to the decreased suffering attributed to Esdaile's application of mesmerism, there were two unanticipated correlates. Postoperative infection rates decreased from 50% to 5%, and there was a notable decrease in perioperative bleeding. However, there is doubt about the efficacy of Esdaile's work. James Braid's retrospective review revealed that only 30% of Esdaile's patients actually experienced analgesia (Braid, 1847), nor did he actually "mesmerize" the patients. Instead he hired native boys to spend hours per day in darkened rooms, employing a technique that involved breathing on the patient's body. When his practices were rejected by the British Royal Academy of Medicine, Esdaile lost interest. Concurrently, ether was introduced for surgical anesthesia and interest in perioperative use of hypnosis and magnetism waned.

While we include Esdaile's work in this hypnosis pre-history, it is important to recognize that Esdaile was a student of neither Mesmer nor Braid. He introduced his interpretation of mesmerism out of desperation, to relieve suffering, based on written description, and having never seen it demonstrated. His technique was reportedly to have his patient recline in a darkened room while Esdaile silently moved his hands in claw-like positions over, but not touching, the patient's body, as if to direct magnetic fluid. Nothing was spoken. If not magnetism or perhaps electromagnetic influence, only mystery, expectancy, suggestion, and motivation for change could have brought about the insensibility and other benefits that sometimes occurred in Esdaile's subjects. His practice was nothing like procedures of Braid or the "hypnotists" that followed, leaving one to attribute these results to intention and expectancy. Nonetheless, Esdaile's work figures prominently in the lore of hypnosis history and the early evolution of the science of psychobiology, as another early fragmentary attempt to reduce the phenomena to a single component.

Hypnosis and the Revolution in Scientific Medicine

This returns us to the period during which James Braid began his study of psychophysiology, after skeptically viewing and re-viewing LaFontaine's mesmerism demonstration. He stripped the technique of its magnetic trappings and developed a ritualized and physiologically based method of replication with which to study the phenomena that he termed hypnosis. With his strategy of fixed gaze and focus on a single idea, borrowed from its mesmeric origins, the analytic study of hypnosis, within the increasingly respected and powerful field of scientific medicine, was born.

The parsing began back across the channel with the founding of the "Suggestion School" in Nancy, France. There, Ambroise-August Liébeault (1823–1904) focused on the cooperation and rapport that seemed requisite between the hypnotist and the participant, emphasizing the primacy of the subject's suggestibility. Liébeault was opposed to the theories of his peer, Jean-Martin Charcot (1825–1893), Chief of Neurology at the Salpêtrière hospital in Paris. Charcot, working with traumatized patients, thought hypnosis was pathological. He hypothesized that it induced hysteria, since its catatonic and other behavioral effects appeared similar to psychogenic seizures observed in patients diagnosed with hysterical conditions. From our current perspective on the biology of hypnosis and trauma, both men were correct: rapport, suggestibility, and the evocation of unusual behaviors were associated with hypnosis. But they were describing aspects of a broader range of responses than they suspected.

The dissection of hypnotic phenomena deepened. Liébeault mentored Hippolyte Bernheim (1837–1919), professor of internal medicine at the School of Nancy. Bernheim furthered the study of suggestion and the malleability of memory under its influence as "suggestive therapeutics," by demonstrating and documenting the creation of false memory. It was Bernheim's demonstration of the power of suggestion and the evocation of nonconscious processes beyond the subject's awareness that later turned Sigmund Freud toward his practice of psychoanalysis. Exploring similar phenomena from a more pathological perspective, Parisian psychiatrist Pierre Janet (1859–1947) was the first to use hypnotic regression to uncover the presumed traumatic origin of symptoms (affirming Braid's earlier prediction of traumatic residua). He had studied at Salpêtrière and produced cathartic cures prior to Freud's psychoanalytic techniques.

The exploration of hypnotic phenomena in clinical settings spread. The first International Congress for Experimental and Therapeutic Hypnotism was held in Paris in 1889, with Janet, Bernheim, and Freud in attendance. Professional societies were formed. The first professional society was formed in the Netherlands in the late 1800s. Then, in the aftermath of the First World War, physicians faced an upsurge in medical and psychological causalities, traumas that responded well to hypnotic approaches and compelled experimentation with it. The medical community kept returning to hypnosis because of its apparent benefits, while they studied it to understand what its mechanisms revealed about our own inner workings.

Sigmund Freud (1856–1939) initially studied and practiced these hypnotic techniques in the manner demonstrated by the French schools, but he found them too rigid and impractical for summoning the **depth** of response he desired from his patients. At this time the practice of hypnosis involved authoritative and prescriptive direction and influence, almost completely by male physicians upon relatively passive, often infirm and, more often than not, female subjects, according to rigidly structured, and thus reproducible, protocols derived from the best scientific practices. This aligned with the prevailing and emerging medical culture. Writing about the evolution of professional education in clinical hypnosis, Alter and Sugarman (2017) described the prevailing scientific medical climate in this way:

> The prescriptive pole of the hypnotic continuum aligns with the medical model that developed during the mid-19th century in Vienna and Paris, then was championed by Osler and others into the 20th century in the United States (Rosenberg, 2002). The reductionist, clinico-pathologically-correlated, disease-based, allopathic approach was founded on three principles: (1) measurable and predictable biological factors led to pathological states that could be modeled as diagnoses; (2) different individuals with common diagnoses therefore manifested common pathophysiology and so could and should be treated similarly; and (3) to optimize reproducibility and results, prescriptive therapies ought to be delivered in a formalized and structured manner. This is the basis of the disease-defined, diagnosis-driven revolution in medicine and in medical education in the United States (Flexner, 1910) that set the standard of accurate diagnosis and refined treatment based upon measurable, evidence-based outcomes. There is no doubt this revolution markedly improved modern health and care globally from where it started in the mid-19th century.
>
> (p. 240, see also Ludmerer, 1999)

This, then, was the birthing of the monistic paradigm of biomedicine that would come to govern the direction of global health care and to which the broader and mysterious range of hypnotic phenomena were forced to conform. Western societies were in the thrall of the industrial and medical revolution that urged a materialistic approach to therapy. There was enthusiasm for what we could produce to cure a host of maladies. Hypnosis was wielded as a medical procedural mechanism for investigation and treatment of diseases of the mind. In retrospect, this medical coming-of-age was an inflection point in the history of clinical hypnosis.

In this time period, the social phenomenon and stigma of hypnosis was iconically represented in Du Maurier's novel *Trilby,* published in 1894 and set in Bohemian Paris of the 1850s. In this story, the Semitic rogue hypnotist, Svengali, subjected the young and suggestible Trilby to his will, forcing her to perform for money that he pocketed. *Trilby* presented what was to become the archetype of hypnosis used for undue influence: the attraction of exposing our vulnerability and questioning our sense of autonomy. It was also the first published book to outsell the Bible (Pintar & Lynn, 2008).

In this Western cultural climate, Freud abandoned the hypnotic techniques he had employed for subconscious exploration in favor of free-association techniques that he developed. He rejected the ritual and authoritarian directives of hypnosis in favor of more free-form and what we would now consider person-centered approaches. The revolutionary influence of his theoretical constructs moved psychotherapy and medicine away from hypnotic practice for a few decades.

Twentieth-Century American Hypnosis

In the same period in which medical hypnosis was the focus in Europe, American philosopher William James (1841–1910) was establishing the first Department of Psychology at Harvard. The area of study was initially an extension of the Department of Philosophy, and James, as did Kuhn, 70 years hence, claimed, "This is no science; it is only the hope of a science" (James, 1892/1985, p. 335). Meanwhile, during his recovery from polio, 24-year-old Clark Leonard Hull (1884–1952) became such a rapt student of James' writing that he decided on a career in psychology with a focus on learning and motivation. He was introduced to hypnosis while teaching in the graduate program at the University of Wisconsin, where he was asked to teach hypnosis as part of a premedical course. Dissatisfied with the unscientific basis of the phenomena he was being asked to demonstrate, he sought to develop academic and scientific rigor in the field. This culminated in his work, *Hypnosis and Suggestibility: An Experimental Approach* (1933). Like Bernheim, Hull insisted that the essence of hypnosis was that it fostered a condition of increased responsiveness to influence and suggestibility.

One of Hull's medical students was Milton H. Erickson (1901–1980), another polio survivor. He was so taken by Professor Hull's demonstration of hypnosis that he convinced one of the subjects to come back to his room for further hypnosis and discussion (Haley, 1967). It is an interesting coincidence that Erickson's initial behavior upon encountering hypnosis mirrored Braid's reaction to LaFontaine nearly a century prior, though absent Braid's skepticism. For each, witnessing hypnotic phenomena was life-changing. Erickson completed his medical education to study and practice psychiatry with a profound and creative focus on hypnosis as a foundational skill.

Over his 50 years of practice, investigation, writing, and teaching, Erickson became the single most transformative person in the modern history of clinical hypnosis. While his clinical approaches were initially quite authoritarian and directive, over the course of his career he demonstrated an uncanny ability to focus on the deeply personal, unique, and individual manifestations of each person. Erickson's practice of hypnosis turned it from a prescriptive ritual to an astoundingly creative and person-centered evocation for self-actualization. Central to his custom and teaching was what he termed the "utilization approach," which he claimed was essentially a means of evoking an individual's ability to access and utilize their own, often nonconscious, experiences as beneficial resources in their own, unique ways (further discussed in Chapter 5). Erickson often claimed that hypnosis was not a "cure" as much as method to cultivate a climate for therapeutic change (Rossi, 1993). This naturalistic and responsive methodology contrasted dramatically with the directive and prescriptive style of his predecessors, and opened a broader range of possibilities for the application of hypnosis.

Erickson was a tremendously influential clinician and behavioral phenomenologist. His insight and experience were sought by Margaret Mead and Aldous Huxley, to mention two notables of thousands internationally. Study of his efficient and strategic therapeutic methods spawned a wide range of study in interpersonal influence, therapeutic linguistics, memory, and altered states: all efforts to parse something both integral and complex (see also Lankton & Lankton, 1983; Rossi, 2002; Zeig, 1994). In 1958, Erickson established the American Society of Clinical Hypnosis and its publication, the *American Journal of Clinical Hypnosis,* with himself serving as its first Editor-in -Chief. Despite this leadership and recognition, his strategic approaches, often labeled "Ericksonian," were considered by many to be too enigmatic, even idiosyncratic, and not easily subjected to the type of reductionist scrutiny required by biomedical hegemony. In the previously considered perspective of Kuhn's thesis, Erickson's contributions were anomalies. In this way, Erickson brought hypnosis to the beginning of a new inflection point and one that, we contend, is still evolving.

While Erickson was cultivating creative clinical approaches and documenting their phenomenology, rigorous laboratory research was initiated to continue dissecting psychobiological mechanisms of hypnosis. At the University of Pennsylvania, the Viennese-born psychiatrist Martin Orne (1927–2000) established a hypnosis research laboratory and became the editor of the highly respected *International Journal of Clinical and Experimental Hypnosis* for three decades. Orne questioned the validity of hypnosis research by noting the implicit "**demand characteristics**," the desire to please the examiner (1962). Orne's wife of 40 years, Emily Carota Orne, was instrumental in developing the Harvard Group Scale of Hypnotic Susceptibility with Ronald Schor and made significant contributions to the forensic use of hypnosis and the debates about "false memory." Psychologist and learning theorist Ernest Ropiequet "Jack" Hilgard (1904–2001), together with his wife, child psychiatrist and developmental psychologist Josephine Hilgard (1906–1989), and André Weitzenhoffer (1921–2004), founded a laboratory for Human Development at Stanford University to focus primarily on the study of hypnosis. In their laboratory-controlled settings, they studied effects of reproducible hypnotic protocols on induced pain, demonstrated induced dissociated ("neodissociation") states, and established the Stanford Susceptibility Scales, the first standardized scales for measuring hypnotic phenomena.

Others produced alternative scales of hypnotic susceptibility or "**hypnotizability**." Based upon various responses and tasks that were labeled hypnotic or non-hypnotic, even non-hypnotic behaviors (upward gaze or "eye-roll") correlated with responses to demands within a hypnotic frame (Council, 2002). But there was reason to question whether the scales for determining potential "hypnotic susceptibility" that were derived from research with volunteers remained relevant in the clinical context, where motivated people engaged with their doctor or therapist to alleviate their suffering. Overall, there was little evidence that hypnotic susceptibility scale results predicted response to hypnosis in clinical settings in which the demand characteristics differed from the laboratory, and clients and patients were differently motivated.

This pursuit of hypnotizability scales was emblematic of what would become a growing irrelevance between the prevailing scientific methodology applied to hypnosis and its clinical practice. Hypnotizability scales used a circular—so, flawed—logic. All of these scales defined hypnosis in terms of responses to tasks which had been defined as "hypnotic." When a subject did not adequately respond, they were considered to be "low hypnotizable." The flaw lay in limiting hypnosis to the tasks tested. This can be illustrated with an admittedly simplistic, ludicrous, and hypothetical example. If we define hypnotizability as correlating with the degree to which a person involuntarily raises their right arm while imagining that it is tethered to a helium balloon, then it stands to reason that right-arm-amputees are not hypnotizable. Of course, a much broader range of abilities is tested in the standardized hypnotizability scales; but there will always be abilities that are unique to the subject and therefore not tested by the scale, yet quite relevant to their health. This may be even more true amongst the neurodiverse (e.g., people with autism spectrum disorder) and differently-abled.

Despite originating the Stanford Hypnotic Susceptibility Scales (Weitzenhoffer & Hilgard, 1959), Weitzenhoffer (2002) questioned their clinical utility as follows:

> This is not a well-recognized fact, but it has never been independently, empirically, or theoretically shown that (a) hypnosis has or should have depth or degrees, and (b) that suggestibility is or should be a measure of this depth or degree.
>
> (p. 212)

Regarding his own clinical practice, he added,

> How useful is it to know, for instance, that a patient can do an age regression when all one needs to do is to produce an analgesia? Generally, not greatly. For this reason, in my own practice … I do essentially no pretesting of suggestibility. My advice is not to spend the time on testing, which can be better spent doing something more productive.
>
> (p. 217)

Considering the assessment of "hypnotic abilities," Teleska and Sugarman (2013) put it this way:

> Assigning a specific set of behaviors/responses as The-Hypnotic-Phenomenon-To-Use-As-Metrics-Of-Hypnotic-Ability serves primarily to measure the extent of the intersection of the measurer's preconceived (and perhaps rigid) notions of what constitutes hypnotic ability with the patient's naturally evolved subconscious talents and competencies. Working on a problem that matters to them, clinical patients are differently motivated.
>
> (p. 85)

They conclude:

> We suggest the clinician is better served by studying the unique coordination of abilities, subconscious and otherwise, that each young person already *has* in order to help him or her do what he or she *can*, rather than what he or she *cannot.*
>
> (Teleska & Sugarman, 2013, p. 85, italics original)

The notion of hypnotizability, however useful as a (contrived) metric in research, essentially acted to objectify and constrain a person's resourcefulness, while ignoring the complex systemic and relational aspects of hypnosis. This would need to be resolved, in order for research to benefit clinical practice.

While not directly related to hypnosis and hypnosis research, the work of Abraham Maslow (1908–1970) was contemporary with Erickson, the Ornes, the Hilgards, Weitzenhoffer, Engel, and others, and also relevant to the shift toward person-centered approaches toward health and care. Maslow's framing of the construction of human well-being with a "hierarchy of needs" included an individualized aspiration toward "self-actualization" that included "peak experiences" (Maslow, 1943, 1964, 1968). This "humanistic psychology," as it was called, was innovative in that it focused on health as more than absence of disease. As Maslow put it, "It is as if Freud supplied us the sick half of psychology and we must now fill it out with the healthy half" (Maslow, 1968, p. 274). Maslow's conceptualization became widely integrated into both psychological and medical training.

There was another shift occurring. The principle of *Relational Being* in our reconceptualization frames hypnosis as an interpersonal phenomenon (Baker, personal communication, July 29, 2019). Baker and Spiegel (2019) noted a shift in the use of hypnosis from the first half of the 20th century to the second half. From a focus on abreactions and regression designed to promote insight, it moved to an emphasis on more relationally oriented approaches, in which the interactive moments between caregiver and the person in care were used to repair developmental disruptions and promote growth. The psychoanalytic lens of Baker (1981), Brown and Fromm (1986), and Diamond (1984, 1987) reflected the cultural swing from a self and internalized focus to a community and external focus which foreshadowed our principles of people functioning in nested systems and growing (healthy or otherwise) as a result of relating.

Hypnosis with Children

Concurrent with the blossoming of clinical hypnosis study in the latter 20th century arose a separate and distinct focus on hypnosis with children and adolescents. Perry London and Leslie Cooper (1978) and, separately, developmental psychiatrist Josephine Hilgard and psychologist Arlene Morgan (1978), took an interest in measuring correlates of hypnotic ability with young people. Not surprisingly, they found greater problems with demand characteristics and the limitations on validity. There was evidence, for example, that younger children scored higher on the Stanford Hypnotizability Clinical Scale for Children when they were asked to imagine rather than asked to relax and that, when assessed by the Children's Hypnotic Susceptibility Scale, children found eye-closure a much more difficult task than did adults on the Stanford Hypnosis Susceptibility Scale (Kohen & Olness, 2011). There was general consensus that children were especially gifted hypnotically, since they were in the business of learning how to work their embodied minds. This further questioned the clinical relevance of assessment scales used with children.

On the clinical practice side, German-born pediatrician Franz Baumann (1912–2001), who learned hypnosis from Erickson, began to integrate it into his care of children in San Francisco, publishing papers on therapy for the adolescent drug abuser and for children with enuresis. Increasing numbers of pediatricians, child and adolescent psychiatrists, and child psychologists began to gather to teach about hypnosis with children, and the first workshop on child hypnosis took place in the early 1970s at meetings of the American Society of Clinical Hypnosis and the Society for Clinical and Experimental Hypnosis, giving rise to a pediatric hypnosis faculty. This faculty, in 1986, inaugurated an annual child and adolescent hypnosis skills training workshop associated with the annual meeting of the Society for Developmental and Behavioral Pediatrics and, in 2010, the National Pediatric Hypnosis Training Institute. Psychologist Gail Gardner and pediatrician Karen Olness authored the first child-focused hypnosis text in 1981, as the field grew into a movement (1981).

Daniel Kohen, Karen Olness, and their colleagues in a behavioral pediatrics group at the University of Minneapolis, published a prominent and auspicious research paper during this ferment. Their report of 505 pediatric encounters using hypnosis for a wide range of childhood conditions demonstrated that (1) most children developed usable skills and benefit after the second visit, (2) there was a "spillover effect of therapeutic efficacy" beyond the presenting problem, and (3) parental reminders to use the hypnosis skills negated benefit (Kohen, Colwell, Heimel, & Olness, 1984, p. 24). As a result of these types of findings, in this and many more clinical studies, child-centered hypnosis came to focus beyond the initial problem of diagnosis and toward teaching self-regulation that invested in the young person's **self-efficacy**, resilience, and psychobiological health (Sugarman, 1996). This shift in the purpose of hypnosis with young people was part of a broader change that, aligned with the contributions of Erickson, contributed to the movement of hypnosis from beneath the biomedical frame and toward a new health care paradigm.

Four themes that emerged from the use of hypnosis with children heralded this change and will play out in our book. First, hypnosis with children was found to be most successful when clinicians followed the child's lead, evoking their interests and motivations. This aligned with the hypnotic methods professed by Erickson in his later work and, though not explicitly hypnotic, the work of Carl Rogers (1951), the play therapy of Virginia Axline, so compellingly portrayed in her case report, *Dibs: In Search of Self* (Axline, 1964), and, more recently the practice of motivational interviewing by William Miller and Stephen Rollnick (2013). Next, hypnosis with children and adolescents prioritized teaching self-hypnosis, helping children help themselves, in accord with their developing autonomy imperatives. This in turn modified the relationship with the clinician, who became no longer an authoritarian director of care but a coach, a teacher, and "sorcerer's apprentice." Third, hypnosis with children and adolescents necessarily became hypnosis within the family system. The ecology of the family and primary attachments therein required that clinicians using hypnosis to help children change would reverberate immediately beyond the child (Roffman, 2013). Finally, given the impact of life's first two decades on the remainder, it was clear that these core aspects of hypnosis with children were also true for adults, especially when they regressed in treatment. Techniques and strategies of child hypnosis could be used with adults. The reverse was not true. Developmental awareness became critical for the effective practice of clinical hypnosis across the lifespan.

Modern Hypnosis

Well into the 21st century, the evolution of clinical hypnosis continued along two divergent trajectories: one in clinical practice and the other in research. An integrative, translational, and promising third rail began to emerge between them with the advent of new research methods.

Along the clinical trajectory, there are more reports of clinical hypnosis documenting efficacy as adjunctive and primary therapy for defined problems than ever before in its history. Professional conferences and continuing professional development courses on hypnosis clinical skills are now prevalent globally and increasing in frequency and number of offerings. Evidence supports a primary role for hypnosis in the treatment of migraine headaches (Hammond, 2007), especially juvenile migraines (Olness, MacDonald, & Uden, 1987), and irritable bowel syndrome (Palsson, Turner, Johnson, Burnett, & Whitehead, 2002). There is compelling evidence that including hypnosis and especially the teaching of self-hypnosis to young people early in the course of chronic disease has long-term and increasing benefit, perhaps due to that "spillover effect" cited above. To allow scientific scrutiny, the clinical trials employ reproducible protocols. Some, such as the program used by Vlieger, Menko-Frankenhuis, Wolfkamp, Tromp, and Benninga (2007) for children with irritable bowel syndrome, provide a wide range of choices for imagery and self-direction. But it is likely that even better outcomes could be achieved by tailoring such diagnosis-based protocols to the abilities of the individual. Similar to the issue of hypnotizability scale, this raises the difficult problem of **ecological** and **construct validity** in clinical research: when we subject our clinical approaches to the most stringent methodological requirements of reproducibility and consistency, we study models of interventions that are impractical, abstract, and unresponsive to unique and complex individuals in their real worlds.

The problems of ecological and construct validity are more pronounced and compelling when it comes to laboratory-based research into components of hypnosis. The revolutionary tools in both anatomical and functional neuroimaging have permitted astonishing views into brain correlates of both behavior and internal experiences within and after rituals and procedures identified as hypnotic. At McGill University, for example, Canadian neuroscientist Amir Raz and his colleagues combined functional magnetic resonance imaging with electroencephalography to demonstrate the changes in information and energy flow through the brain that correlate to scripted hypnotic **inductions** and suggestions (Landry & Raz, 2015). With similar research methods, Kosslyn and colleagues have shown that when subjects are asked to see colored images as gray-scale, they suppress signals in the visual cortex of their brains triggered by color perception (Kosslyn, Thompson, Costantini-Ferrando, Alpert, & Spiegel, 2000). At the time of this writing, we could fill another volume with fascinating findings from neuroimaging research that correlate changes in brain function with reproducible and scripted instructions that have been labelled "hypnotic," based upon the nature of the procedure conducted with subjects who scored high on the aforementioned measures of hypnotizability. These findings purport to demonstrate some of the mechanisms that underlie responses to hypnosis and its influence. They may well do that. And, if nothing else, they demonstrate the feasibility of this exciting research methodology. But this line of research purposefully excludes relationship factors, effects of illness and disease, and the nuances of language that are tuned and adapting to the needs of a specific and unique individual. Would these same correlates hold? What new factors and responses would come to light? What does this have to do with the medical professor with lymphoma in the hospital bed at the opening of this chapter?

A Complex and Integrative Understanding of Mind as a Domain for Hypnosis

It is the aforementioned emerging third rail of research and care that holds promise to provide both a more wholistic understanding of how hypnosis helps us change our minds, as well as methods for psychobiological care. To better understand this perspective, it is helpful to back up and look at the history of health care science again, this time including some integrative perspectives.

William James—who was 13 years old when Braid's *Physiology of Fascination* was published—went on to presage, by a century, Engel's (1977) biopsychosocial model. James (1950) described the human capacity for attention, habit formation, memory, and imagination as innate features fundamental to our interpersonal neurobiology. But even before James, French physiologist Claude Bernard (1813–1878), like his contemporary Braid, was determined to bring scientific scrutiny to the then-archaic practice of medicine. Unlike Mesmer's more inductive approaches, Bernard (1974) was much more "hands-on": he used vivisection. He conceived of autonomous regulation of the *milieu interieur* as a vital function of the organism. This would later be translated and codified by William Bradford Cannon (1872–1945) under the rubric *homeostasis*, and launch Cannon's exploration of the autonomic nervous system (1939).

From these beginnings, the subsequent evolution of a more integrated and complex study of human systems paralleled the more dominant reductionist biomedical therapeutics revolution. It included Selye's (1982) elucidation of the General Adaptation Syndrome and the role of hypothalamic-pituitary-adrenal axis as a pathway into the embodied mind; the exploration of bidirectional co-influence of perception, conditioning, and immune response in Ader, Felten, and Cohen's *Psychoneuroimmunology* (1994); Pert's (1997) *Molecules of Emotion*, which revealed how emotions are a coordinated, intercellular symphony of cell receptor responses throughout the body; Bennedetti's (2014) ground breaking and meticulous research on placebo effects; Porges' (Harris, Porges, Clemenson, & Vincenz, 1993; Porges, 2011) furthering of autonomic homeostasis into the emotional and social realms with his ***Polyvagal Theory***; Siegel's (2012) interpersonal neurobiology; and on to Rossi's (1993) grand synthesis—from genomics to behavior—of a complex yet accessible psychobiology of therapeutic hypnosis. In short, there has long been emerging a more cybernetic and holistic study of our thought, feelings, perception, brain, and physiology as integral facets of our embodied minds. If he knew of it, we believe that Braid would have been more satisfied with this inclusive trajectory of study as his legacy than the biomedical one.

The contributions of Ernest L. Rossi, a student, collaborator, and primary co-author with Milton H. Erickson, has culminated a near-inclusive study of hypnosis by combining the interpersonal, chronobiological, physiological, genomic, and even quantum aspects of consciousness. His work is at once accessible, through clinical teaching of techniques such as *Mirroring Hands* (2017), and feasibly studied at a genomic level by measurement of early gene transcription products that signal activation of neural plasticity. These hypnotic formulations and strategies are neither diagnosis-based nor formally scripted. These approaches regard psychophysiological plasticity/adaptability as a vital and innate resource for health and healing. They allow for the heterogeneity of individual mind-systems and the primacy of unique and innate risks and resources in driving therapeutics over the externally-applied diagnostic narrative. There are as many different experiential paths into anxiety disorders, irritable bowels, or asthmatic pulmonary hyper-reactivity as there are individuals who experience them. There are even more paths out.

As Rossi (1993) summarizes:

> These approaches are all explorations of how we can best actualize human potential rather than manipulate and control behavior. Our work does not involve overt or covert conditioning, "influence communication," or programming. We do not even use "suggestion" in the conventional sense of putting an idea into another person's mind. Rather we simply access state-dependent learning, memory, behavior (SDLMB) systems and make their encoded information available for problem

> solving. The locus of control of the process remains within the patient at all times. The therapist is a facilitator, guide, and consultant.
>
> (p. 90, emphasis original)

This brings us to the growing edge of hypnosis as mind-changing. It was coined in reference to "nervous sleep," has been studied as sets of research protocols, investigated as some kind of innate ability or susceptibility, fractured into component experiences and behaviors, and subjected to forces during magnetic resonance imaging that would have mesmerized Mesmer. But what do we mean by hypnosis now?

Reorienting Hypnosis

We used the metaphor of the "third rail" earlier as another path in the evolution of hypnosis. But it would also be apt to use the term in its more colloquial sense, when referencing an electrically ungrounded train track: the thing to avoid. Although Braid tried and failed to rename his discovery, he would likely be disheartened by the taboos that have grown around it. The second title of Braid's (1855/1970) *Physiology of Fascination* was … *And the Critics Criticised*, since this, his last monograph, was also a lengthy rebuttal to the condemnations he took from both the medical and religious establishments. Still now, we, your authors, sigh and ready our defenses when asked, by bemused people in casual social settings, "So, how do you do hypnosis?"

Hypnosis suffers from a lack of consensual definition, clear boundaries of what it is and isn't, a defined set of practices and sloppy language usage. As Hope and Sugarman (2015) put it in their argument for a simple and cohesive definition,

> In both research and practice, clinical hypnosis is not yet mainstream nor gaining significant momentum towards integration. There is ignorance of the abundant evidence for efficacy in medical and psychological contexts.… Misrepresentation also contributes. But we hold that the primary problem is the lack of a consensual, evidence-based delineation of the hypnotic domain, distinct from the non-hypnotic, as well as its relationship to trance. Without a clear distinction and context, the word hypnosis gets so overused that it becomes nearly meaningless. Being bored while driving on the thruway becomes *highway hypnosis*. Focused attention in conversation or at work becomes *naturalistic hypnosis* and part of the *hypnotic trance of everyday life*. Research on hypnosis and cognition becomes research on *hypnotic states* when the only basis for the adjective is a procedure labeled hypnosis. Further, there is the tendency, even chauvinism, to disregard other explanations of phenomena in favor of hypnotic processes. A person sits quietly, eyes closed, breathing slowly with a paucity of spontaneous movement, while someone else talks. Competing proponents of hypnosis,

> meditation, prayer, and other contemplative practices vie for their orientation and training to have hegemony over this condition. Can there be both teleological commonality among, and clear boundaries between these practices? The quiet person with closed eyes could be sleeping.
>
> (p. 12, italics original)

To resolve this confusion, and before we finally clarify our terms, we want to return to what we believe is a fundamental reason for the alienation of hypnosis in western culture, and in biomedical practice. We mentioned it in the opening paragraphs of this chapter. We think it gets to the essence. Since hypnosis is a practice of influence, it is a threat to autonomy. We human beings value our autonomy, our self-determination, and our liberty. We take great care to protect it. We are capable of doing great harm to each other. This is why, in hypnotic contexts, we often use "suggestion" euphemistically when we really intend to direct, however indirectly. It is why our suggestibility attracts us to watch stage hypnotists and "mentalists" perform, why we are drawn to stories of cults and why Du Maurier's *Trilby* outsold the Bible. We wonder if we are so gullible. We are. We are designed to be. We have evolved to change our minds in concert with others.

Theories of hypnosis have glowed, then burnt out like shooting stars. For an analysis, the reader is referred to Lynn's and Rhue's (1991) comprehensive review. We argue that a comprehensive theory must await a consensual definition. But we favor a biological and evolutionary approach, since it can be grounded in evidence. Hope and Sugarman (2015) began a biological explanation by separating the notion of "trance"—which they define as a process of psychobiological plasticity or change—from hypnosis. They build on the work of Pavlov (1927) and others (Green, Barabasz, Barrett, & Montgomery, 2005) to make the case that novel stimuli trigger orienting responses that have autonomic nervous system, attentional, and cognitive effects. They summarize their basis for trance this way:

> Grouped together, we interpret this research as autonomic, neural, and physiological features of the OR [orienting response] as a framework for understanding "trance-opening." We are "hard-wired" to respond to the intensity and significance of perceived stimuli by shifting autonomic states, considering the emotional valence of the perception, and shifting attentional awareness and cognitive processing to various degrees in response to a significant and novel stimulus. In this way, the OR can be considered a model for simultaneous and efficient triggering of the systems that subsume mind, preparing them for changing degrees of connectivity. What happens next most likely depends on the persistence and intensity of the novel stimulus.
>
> (Hope & Sugarman, 2015, p. 221)

Hence, we are offering a frame in which clinicians may find a richer, more effective set of options on behalf of navigating therapeutic transactions with their patients and clients. We consider hypnosis an intentional interpersonal skill set for influencing that process of psychobiological change that we call trance, as defined above. With this framing we do not intend to contest other models or theories of hypnosis, though these all tend to conflate trance and hypnosis. We simply explain clinical hypnosis as an interpersonal communication discipline. It cultivates trance and, in clinical contexts, affects therapeutic change.

Where We've Been: The Legacy Model

The practice of hypnosis, both in clinical settings and at seminars for "lay hypnotists," has traditionally mirrored the original techniques of Braid and the early French schools. The practice starts with some type of "induction," during which a passive subject is instructed to become more relaxed, close their eyes, and become more or less aware of their body. Often the hypnotist counts down from some number to pace this change, softening their voice with each successive number. Some behavioral change such as arm levitation is "suggested" with an end point (the arm touching the face or falling back to the lap) to indicate that the induction is now complete and the subject is ready. Inductions are followed by "intensification" or "deepening" (itself a metaphor and "suggestion" without psychobiological correlation, like hypnotizability; see also Heap, 2006). The next step is a series of instructions, suggestions, and metaphors designed to produce the behavioral change (for therapeutic benefit or, in the case of the stage hypnotist, for entertainment). Often instructions, called "post-hypnotic suggestions," to return to this experience in response to some cue are introduced at this point in the process. The experience ends with instructions, often with the hypnotist counting them "alert" or "awake" as a reverse of the induction. The research participant or therapy client or stage subject resumes their previous apparent awareness, sometimes with amnesia (as "suggested" or spontaneously). Sometimes the post-hypnotic suggestion is activated and the stage subject, at the clap of the hypnotist's hands quacks like a duck or jumps off the chair as if it is charged with electricity (there is that "third rail" again).

Where We're Going

This linear, directive Induction-Deepening-Suggestion-Awake model, often referred to as "formal hypnosis," has been the basis for professional clinical hypnosis education for decades (Hammond & Elkins, 1994). In their argument for a more progressive approach, Alter and Sugarman (2017) term it the "legacy model" and, while acknowledging that learners have to start somewhere, place it at the "prescriptive" pole of a continuum of hypnotic interaction. They and many others (see also Teleska & Roffman, 2004) note that this practice "aligns purposefully with the predominant Diagnose-and-Treat Western allopathic model of therapeutics" (Alter & Sugarman, 2017, p. 239). At the other end of the continuum contrasts a conversational, non-linear model that Alter and Sugarman describe this way:

> The naturalistic end of the hypnosis continuum focuses on the uniquely individual, intrapersonal, and often remote phenomenology of trance wholly owned by the subject. The formulation of hypnotic skills in this case concerns how we may creatively interact with those unique personal **experiential resources** to disrupt them beneficially. This type of practice, notable for indirect and evocative strategies, is especially ascribed to Milton H. Erickson in his later years as "intuitive" and "idiosyncratic," and has been formalized by many, notably, Lankton and Lankton (1983). In professional settings, this type of skill development is primarily reserved for the advanced level workshops, consultations, and supervision. It is generally not offered to beginners. They are being trained prescriptively.
>
> (Alter & Sugarman, 2017, p. 239)

Given the range of the continuum, Teleska and Roffman (2004) write:

> Our primary concern is the emergence of new experiential domains more viable than those from which we and our clients start. Ultimately our bias is that the realm of hypnotic conversation offers a more capacious framework for us to enact a wider range of therapeutic interactions with our clients, including more formal and ritualized hypnotic work.
>
> (p. 113)

The more "capacious framework" gives room for the relational aspects of trance to play out as one's mind copies and mirrors others, and watches itself do so (see also Hilgard, 1977 on "neodissociation"). Observing and experiencing trance is dissociative. It is a reasonable hypothesis that trance affords increased ability to tune our networks of "mirror neurons": those systems that learn from the behaviors of others (Rizzolatti & Fabbri-Destro, 2010). In their promotion of the teaching of conversational hypnosis, Sugarman, Schafer, Alter, and Reid (2018) point out that it is different from the prescriptive pole in three ways, ultimately likening it to a form of performance art:

> First, there are no **formal induction**s, because the client is presumed to be engaged in trance prior to and in anticipation of the encounter (Hope & Sugarman, 2015; Alter & Sugarman, 2017; see also Reid, 2016). Second, because the format is a dialogue, clinicians do not deliver monologues of

> scripted suggestions to influence receptive clients. Conversational hypnosis is reciprocal, spontaneous, and creative. Its direction and structure are determined by the expressions of abilities, resources, and strengths that unfold in a unique and, in clinical settings, therapeutic encounter. Third, because the client engaged in conversation is neither passively reposed nor focused on some other behavioral context, the full range of communicative performance art is in play.
>
> (p. 141)

A Few Words about Hypnotic Language

We will delve into the specifics of the hypnosis skill set in Chapter 5. But we ought not leave this discussion of what hypnosis has come to mean without commenting on the emergence of the central role of therapeutic language in hypnosis.

Nuances of interpersonal communication have become fundamental to the practice of hypnosis. Early on, when hypnosis was directive, commands were given to a passive and obedient subject. Again, the legacy model of formal hypnosis was a stepwise, linear, prescriptive procedure to treat a defined problem, regardless of the person who had it. In this context, the confidence and forcefulness of the hypnotist was likely the dominant factor, not the idiosyncrasies of the subject's mind. So, timing and reciprocity was contingent simply upon the subject indicating that they had completed the assigned task. The subject focused on the shiny object. The eyes closed. The arm slowly raised. The head nodded. These were directives, not suggestions.

With the emergence of more conversational, multidimensional, and person-centered therapeutic and hypnotic strategies, a broader consideration of interpersonal communication came into consideration. We have noted Erickson's pivotal place in the history of hypnosis. His lifetime of learning, practice, teaching, and writing on the rich art and science of therapeutic language is perhaps the most significant of his many contributions. More than any other individual, Erickson shifted the focus of hypnosis to working with the spontaneous, natural, "common everyday trance" of the individual and, by extension, to the innate resources of the individual, tuning his language to their experiences (Erickson, Rossi, & Rossi, 1976). Erickson modeled and taught an uncanny ability to both read and interpret the range of verbal and non-verbal cues that acted as clues to his patients' internal organization and proclivities for change. He discerned and spoke the patient's language. Then he utilized it to catalyze therapeutic change.

We can gather insight into multiple dimensions of language that pertain to hypnosis from Mehrabian's (1971) analysis of feeling and attitude in communication. He posited that only 7% of interpersonal communication was verbal semantics. Of the remainder, 38% was prosody and rhythm and 55% was composed of posture, gestures, and facial expression. In terms of performance art: 7% lyrics, 38% music, and 55% dance. When used in an informal, conversational, and naturalistic context, the hypnosis skill set enlarges to include both attention and response to the subtle, presumably nonconsciously-derived dance, music, and lyrics on the part of both the clinician and the person(s) in care. This includes "pacing" these behaviors and semantics with emphasis or encouragement, then often "leading" with additional meaning. For example, the patient may spontaneously sigh in response to a question. Whatever the reason for the sigh, the clinician knows that it is an effort (often nonconscious) to self-regulate autonomically and emotionally. So, the clinician may sigh more obviously in response, and say, "Yes," or even comment, "You certainly know how to care for yourself, do you not?" In so doing, the clinician is driving awareness and change. Simultaneously, the clinician is tuning their volume, rhythm, pitch and gesture to evoke and provoke. They wonder.

> Shall I lean back and give this person space to consider or lean in with curiosity? Shall I slow my pace or speed it up? Will I respond to that sad joke with laughter, sadness, or a mix? Is this a good time to be quiet… and for how long? I wonder what I will do next that evokes within this person what is most useful for them at this moment.

The semantics of hypnosis have developed into a rich science and art. The word-choice, order, and innate metaphorical representations that volley between the patient and clinician have great potential for driving change. If one purpose of a hypnotically-informed therapeutic conversation is to build self-efficacy beneath the treatment of the person's problem, then person-centered language carries meaning and coherence. So, in hypnosis training clinicians are taught to say, "You may discover, to your surprise, that you are feeling more and more confident …" instead of, "I have every confidence in you." And instead of focusing on *not* getting a headache or *not* wetting the bed, the clinician expresses interest in "How you already know to how to keep your head comfortable most of the time," and "How you let your bladder wake you so effectively so you can keep the bed dry."

Beneath the semantics of intent and self-determination, powerful associative learning goes on in our minds. We learn and understand by making one thing like another, by using metaphors. This conceptualization is illuminated by Lakoff and Johnson's (2003) rich discourse on metaphors that are embedded in and underlie our common use of language. David Gordon (2017) developed an understanding of metaphor as a reflection of sensory representational systems for encoding experiences. For example, "I couldn't *see* my way through it" refers to visual representation. While, "There's just no way *around* it," refers to a more tactile, physical representation. If we imagine that these language forms are manifestations of deeper components and connections of state-dependent learning memory and experiences, then we can drive change with hypnosis by both matching, disrupting, or altering these language forms. "I *see* what you mean. What does a solution *look* like to you?" and "That's *hard.* I know it *feels* like an obstacle. That's a lot to *go through.*"

When we return to discuss the language of hypnosis in Chapter 5, we will lay out a more comprehensive map of its domain. So far, let it suffice that the emergence of clinical hypnosis as a skill set for multilevel and therapeutic communication now focuses more on *how* we can help the person in care bring unique and personal internal experiences—or, better, experiential resources—to bear, to heal, and grow. With this comes an increased self-awareness about how the person in our care is affecting us and how we tune our perceptions and responses to them: what we may call the "clinician's trance." Within this mutual trance interplay (Banyai, 1998), while using our therapeutic communication to facilitate plasticity and benefit for the person in our care, we grow much more interested in what our questions *do* than what the answers are.

Gender in the History of Hypnosis

The roles of women in the history of hypnosis reveals both gender bias as well as the importance of women's life experiences and perspectives in this field. Women made up the majority of subjects in early hypnosis research, demonstrations, and reports by Mesmer, Bernheim, and Janet in the French schools; to a lesser extent Freud; and for demonstrations by Milton Erickson. Most of those in the audiences and reading the reports were men. While credit is due to the female subjects, from a social constructionist view this phenomenon displays the stereotypical role of women: attractive, subservient, weak, uneducated, and so, susceptible. This clinical subjugation cannot be separated from the roles of Trilby and countless women on the stage as hypnotists' assistants. At the same time, most of hypnotic practice, by men, as we have pointed out, was directive, authoritarian, and aimed at recipients who were expected to passively receive it, if not swoon into histrionic crises. As we have shown, most of the male-driven history of hypnosis research is reductionist and categorical, attempting to reduce hypnosis to this or that element.

Since the mid-20th century, as they entered academia and professional life in record numbers, women brought new orientations with them, and to the fields of medicine, psychology, and hypnosis. Josephine Hilgard's recognition of the importance of child development and relationships in hypnosis coincided with the balancing of the previously compartmental, categorical, and authoritarian male model. Similarly, Gail Gardner and Karen Olness, in promoting the power of hypnosis with children, shifted the foundations of clinical hypnosis toward a more person-centered investment beyond the presenting problem and diagnosis for all persons in care. Kay Thompson, the first woman board member of the American Dental Association and the first woman president of the American Society of Clinical Hypnosis, was a dominating figure who encouraged the creative and organic use of language and a belief in the possible in clinical hypnosis. We would argue that it took a woman—Candice Pert, the first woman to head a laboratory at the US National Institute of Mental Health—to bring us the holistic realization that our neurotransmitters, hormones, immunoglobulins, etc., were all "**messenger molecules**" that transcended our categorical body systems and were actually embodied "molecules of emotion" (see Chapter 3).

The list of women who have changed the course of hypnosis to make it more accessible and beneficial is long and worth exploring beyond the scope of this book. It includes such additional notables as Emily Orne, Helen Crawford, Marlene Hunter, Erika Fromm, Helen Watkins, Joan Jobsis, Lillian Fredericks, Eva Banyai, Leora Kuttner, Maggie Phillips, Claire Fredericks, Lynne Hornyak, Consuelo Casula, Marie-Elisabeth Faymonville, Elvira Lang, and Katalin Varga. The list goes on. They have provided a holistic perspective that is captured in the "5 E's Model of Feminist Hypnotherapy" that I (JHL) proposed over 20 years ago (Linden, 1999). Each E—Empathic, Empowering, Egalitarian, Ego-strengthening, and Embodying—is both a principle and a strategy for how to enact hypnosis naturally. It is no coincidence that these same concepts are woven throughout this volume.

Women have long been the healers of the species. Franz Baumann (1996) quipped that "Pediatric hypnosis started when the first mother kissed it and made it better." As in so many endeavors, hypnosis has neither adequately recognized nor given due credit to the women who have made major contributions that shifted its course for the better. But beyond an effort to rectify that, we mean to value inclusion of all kinds of minds to the mix of changing minds. All of the women noted above, and countless more, had to overcome a bias that their perspectives and contributions were not rigorous or "hard" enough. This is how they pushed boundaries and moved the foundational bases of the field. As both our cultural and biological understanding of gender, as well as ethnicity and race, become more fluid, we will be required to expand our practice of how to care enough to help people change their minds.

Conclusion

Hypnosis was born in the Egyptian Dream Temples of Aesculapius, conducted through the *baquets* in Mesmer's salon, inspired Braid's fascination, became the subject of the French schools, drove Erickson's enlightened utilization, and cultivated the imaginations of children. Throughout its controversial history, hypnosis has emerged as both a clinical practice and a research probe into the intricacies and idiosyncrasies of embodied minds and how we change them. Hypnosis has defied containment by and restriction to biomedical models or psychological theories. It transcends reductionist, categorical, and monistic representation by affecting minds systemically and individually. We think that this places hypnosis at the heart of an emerging, more systemic, and more effective paradigm of health and care.

Before we let that thesis unfold, we will take a step back and consider how we build, then change our minds, in Chapters 3 and 4, respectively. Then we will return to putting hypnotic skills and principles into contemporary practice in Chapter 5.

Questions and Assignments for Further Discussion

1. This chapter describes two parallel histories of hypnosis. The "legacy" model developed in line with the biomedical paradigm as generally prescriptive and problem-based. The roots of the more person-centered and evocative approach are just as old. Speculate on why the former became dominant.
2. There is continuing controversy within related fields of medicine, psychology, neuroscience, and psychophysiology about whether the terms "hypnosis," "mind," and "trance" ought to be used given their vague definitions and cultural implications. Discuss both sides of this debate.
3. Distinguish clinical hypnosis from both other forms of contemplative practice (e.g., meditation, prayer, and daydreaming) and influence (e.g., advertising, organized religion, and team membership).
4. Discuss how the inclusion of child development and women researchers and clinicians affected the evolution of the field of hypnosis.

Note

1 There is controversy as to whether Braid deserves credit for originating the term "hypnosis" and its other forms (e.g., "neurohypnology"). Gravitz (1993) notes that Etienne Félix d'Hénin de Cuvillers, a student of Mesmer, started prefixing terms with "Hypn-" in reference to the effects of magnetic influence prior to Braid.

References

Ader, R., Felten, D., & Cohen, N. (1994). Psychoneuroimmunology: Interactions between the nervous system and the immune system. *Lancet, 345*(8942), 99–103. doi:10.1016/S0140-6736(95)90066-7. Retrieved from: www.sciencedirect.com/sdfe/pdf/download/eid/1-s2.0-S0140673695900667/first-page-pdf

Alter, D. S., & Sugarman, L. I. (2017). Reorienting hypnosis education. *American Journal of Clinical Hypnosis, 59*(3), 235–259. doi:10.1080/00029157.2016.1231657

Axline, V. M. (1964). *Dibs: In search of self.* New York, NY: Houghton-Mifflin.

Baker, E. L. (1981). A hypnotherapeutic approach to enhance object relatedness in psychotic patients. *International Journal of Clinical & Experimental Hypnosis, 29*, 136–147. doi:10.1080/00207148108409154

Baker, E. L., & Spiegel, E. B. (2019). Dancing in the in-between: Hypnosis, transitional space and therapeutic action. *American Journal of Clinical Hypnosis, 62*(1–2), 31–59. doi:10.1080/00029157.2019.1585328

Banks, A., & Hirschman, L. (2015). *Wired to connect: The surprising link between brain science and strong, healthy relationships.* New York, NY: Jeremy Tarcher/Penguin.

Banyai, É. I. (1998). The interactive nature of hypnosis: Research evidence for a social-psychobiological model. *Contemporary Hypnosis, 15*(1), 52–63. doi:10.1002/ch.116

Baumann, F. (1996). Personal communication at annual meeting, Society of Developmental and Behaviorial Pediatrics, San Francisco, CA.

Benedetti, F. (2014). *Placebo effects* (2nd ed.). London, UK: Oxford University Press.

Bernard, C. (1974). *Lectures on the phenomena of life common to animals and plants* (H. E. Hoff, R. Guillemin, & L. Guillemin, Trans). Springfield, IL: Charles C. Thomas (Original work published 1872/1873).

McKittrick, S., Blum, J., Hamm, E. H. (Producer), & Peele, J. (Director). (2017). *Get out* [Motion Picture]. United States: Universal Pictures.

Braid, J. (1843). *Neurypnology; or, the rationale of nervous sleep, considered in relation to animal magnetism* [pdf]. Retrieved from https://books.google.com/books?id=rLMnuwEACAAJ&dq=neurypnology&hl=en&sa=X&ved=2ahUKEwjApZTEz7zkAhVFUt8KHbTgAtYQ6AEwBHoECAUQAQ

Braid, J. (1847). Facts and observations as to the relative value of mesmeric and hypnotic coma, and ethereal narcotism, for the mitigation or entire prevention of pain during surgical operations. *Medical Times, 15*(385), 381–382. *16*(387), 10–11. Retrieved from: https://books.google.com/books?id=vRkCAAAAYAAJ&pg=PA10#v=onepage&q&f=false

Braid, J. (1855). *Physiology of fascination: And the critics criticised* [pdf]. Manchester, UK: Grant & Co. Retrieved from https://wellcomecollection.org/works/vu9sncqd

Brown, D. P., & Fromm, E. (1986). *Hypnotherapy & hypnoanalysis.* Hillsdale, NJ: Lawrence Erlbaum Associates.

Cacioppo, J. T., Tassinary, L. G., & Berntson, G. G. (Eds). (2019). *Handbook of psychophysiology* (4th ed.). Cambridge, UK: Cambridge University Press.

Cannon, W. (1939). *The wisdom of the body.* New York, NY: W. W. Norton.

Carlson, N. R. (2004). *Foundations of physiological psychology* (6th ed.). Boston, MA: Allyn & Bacon.

Christakis, N. A. (2019). *Blueprint: The evolutionary origins of a good society.* New York: Little, Brown Spark.

Cooper, L. M., & London, P. (1978). The children's hypnotic susceptibility scale. *American Journal of Clinical Hypnosis, 21*(2–3), 170–185. doi:10.1080/00029157.1978.10403970

Council, J. R. (2002). A historical overview of hypnotizability assessment. *American Journal of Clinical Hypnosis, 44*(3), 199–208. doi:10.1080/00029157.2002.10403480

Demme, J. (2004). *The manchurian candidate.* Hollywood, California, USA: Paramount Pictures.

Descartes, R. (1989). *Passions of the soul* (S. H. Voss, Trans.). Indianapolis, IN: Hackett (Original work published 1649).

Diamond, M. J. (1984). It takes two to tango: Some thoughts on the neglected importance of the hypnotist in an interactive hypnotherapeutic relationship. *American Journal of Clinical Hypnosis, 27*(1), 3–13. doi:10.1080/00029157.1984.10402582

Diamond, M. J. (1987). The interactional basis of hypnotic experience: On the relational dimensions of hypnosis. *International Journal of Clinical & Experimental Hypnosis, 35*, 95–115. doi:10.1080/00207148708416046

Du Maurier, G. (1894). *Trilby*. Paris: C. Reinwald. Retrieved from https://books.google.com/books?id=3A0OAAAAYAAJ&printsec=frontcover&dq=editions:ISBN1775416143#v=onepage&q&f=false

Ehrenwald, J. (1976). *The history of psychotherapy: From healing magic to encounter*. Lanham, MD: Jason Aronson.

Engel, G. L. (1977). The need for a new medical model: A challenge for biomedicine. *Science, 196*(4286), 192–136.

Erickson, M. H., Rossi, E. L., & Rossi, S. I. (1976). *Hypnotic realities: The induction of clinical hypnosis and forms of indirect suggestion*. New York, NY: Irvington.

Fletcher, J. E. (2011). *A study of the life and works of Athanasius Kircher, 'germanus incredibilis.'*. Leiden, The Netherlands: Brill.

Flexner, A. (1910). *Medical education in the United States and Canada*. New York, NY: The Carnegie Foundation for the Advancement of Teaching.

Olness, K., & Gardner, G. G. (1981). *Hypnosis and hypnotherapy with children*. New York, NY: Grune & Stratton.

Gravitz, M. A. (1993). Etienne Félix d'Hénin de Cuvillers: A founder of hypnosis. *American Journal of Clinical Hypnosis, 36*(1), 7–11. doi:10.1080/00029157.1993. 10403033

Green, J. P., Barabasz, A. F., Barrett, D., & Montgomery, G. H. (2005). Forging ahead: The 2003 APA Division 30 definition of hypnosis. *International Journal of Clinical and Experimental Hypnosis, 53*(3), 259–264. doi:10.1080/00207140590 961321

Haley, J. (Ed.). (1967). *Advanced techniques of hypnosis and therapy: Selected papers of Milton H. Erickson, M.D.* New York, NY: Grune & Stratton.

Hammond, D. C. (2007). Review of the efficacy of clinical hypnosis with headaches and migraines. *International Journal of Clinical and Experimental Hypnosis, 55*(2), 207–219. doi:10.1080/00207140601177921

Hammond, D. C., & Elkins, G. (1994). *Standards of training in clinical hypnosis*. Chicago, IL: ASCH Press.

Harris, R. M., Porges, S. W., Clemenson, M. E., & Vincenz, L. M. (1993). Hypnotic susceptibility, mood state, and cardiovascular reactivity. *American Journal of Clinical Hypnosis, 36*, 15–25. doi:10.1080/00029157.1993.10403035

Hassan, S. (2018). *Combating cult mind control*. Newton, MA: Freedom of Mind Press.

Heap, M. (2006). Defining hypnosis: The UK experience. *American Journal of Clinical Hypnosis, 48*(2–3), 119. doi:10.1080/00029157.2005.10401505

Hilgard, E. R. (1977). *Divided consciousness: Multiple controls in human thought and action*. New York, NY: Wiley.

Hill, R., & Rossi, E. L. (2017). *The practitioners' guide to mirroring hands: A client-responsive therapy that facilitates natural problem-solving and mind-body healing* (pp. 22). Carmarthen, UK: Crown House.

Hope, A. E., & Sugarman, L. I. (2015). Orienting hypnosis. *American Journal of Clinical Hypnosis, 57*(3), 212–229. doi:10.1080/00029157.2014.976787

Hull, C. L. (1933). *Hypnosis and suggestibility: An experimental approach*. New York, NY: Appleton-Century.

James, W. (1950). *The principles of psychology*. New York, NY: Dover (Original work published 1890).

James, W. (1985). *Psychology: A briefer course*. Notre Dame, IN: University of Notre Dame Press. (Original work published 1892).

Kay, R. (1962). *The Cabinet of Caligari.* Motion picture. United States: 20th Century Fox.

Kihlstrom, J. F. (2002). Mesmer, the Franklin commission, and hypnosis: A counterfactual essay. *International Journal of Clinical and Experimental Hypnosis, 50*(4), 407–419. doi:10.1080/00207140208410114

Kircher, A. (1643). *Magnes sive de arte magnetica.* Coloniae Agrippina apud iodocum Kalcoven. Retrieved from http://diglib.hab.de/drucke/218-25-quod-1/start.htm

Kohen, D. P., & Olness, K. N. (2011). *Hypnosis and hypnotherapy with children.* New York, NY: Routledge.

Kohen, D. P., Olness, K. N., Colwell, S. O., & Heimel, A. (1984). The use of relaxation-mental imagery (self-hypnosis) in the management of 505 pediatric behavioral encounters. *Journal of Developmental and Behavioral Pediatrics, 5*(1), 21–25. doi:10.1097/00004703-198402000-00005

Kosslyn, S. M., Thompson, W. L., Costantini-Ferrando, M. F., Alpert, N. M., & Spiegel, D. (2000). Hypnotic visual illusion alters color processing in the brain. *American Journal of Psychiatry, 157*(8), 1279–1284. doi:10.1176/appi.ajp.157.8.1279

Lakoff, G., & Johnson, M. (2003). *Metaphors we live by.* Chicago, IL: University of Chicago Press.

Landry, M., & Raz, A. (2015). Hypnosis and imaging of the living human brain. *American Journal of Clinical Hypnosis, 57*(3), 285–313. doi:10.1080/00029157.2014.978496

Lankton, S. R., & Lankton, C. H. (1983). *The answer within: A clinical framework of Ericksonian hypnotherapy.* New York, NY: Routledge.

Linden, J. H. (1999). Discussion of symposium. Enhancing healing: The contributions of hypnosis to women's health care. *American Journal of Clinical Hypnosis, 42*(2), 140–144. doi:10.1080/00029157.1999.10701731

Ludmerer, K. M. (1999). *Time to heal: American medical education from the turn of the century to the era of managed care.* New York, NY: Oxford University Press.

Lynn, S. J., & Rhue, J. W. (Eds.). (1991). *Theories of hypnosis: Current models and perspectives.* New York, NY: Guilford.

Maslow, A. H. (1943). A Theory of human motivation. *Psychological Review, 50*, 370–396.

Maslow, A. H. (1964). *Religions, values, and peak experiences.* Columbus, Ohio: Ohio State University Press.

Maslow, A. H. (1968). *Towards a psychology of being.* New York, NY: John C. Wiley.

McGilchrist, I. (2009). *The master and his emissary: The divided brain and the making of the western world.* New Haven, CT: Yale University Press.

Mehrabian, A. (1971). *Silent messages.* Belmont, CA: Wadsworth.

Mesmer, F. A. (2016). *Mesmerism: The discovery of animal magnetism.* V. R. Myers, Trans. Vancouver, BC: Soul Care Publishing. (Original published 1779).

Miller, W. R., & Rollnick, S. (2013). *Motivational interviewing: Helping people change* (3rd ed.). New York, NY: Guilford.

Morgan, A. H., & Hilgard, J. R. (1978). The Stanford hypnotic clinical scale for children. *American Journal of Clinical Hypnosis, 21*(2–3), 148–169. doi:10.1080/00029157.1978.10403969

Olness, K., MacDonald, J. T., & Uden, D. L. (1987). Comparison of self-hypnosis and propranolol in the treatment of juvenile classic migraine. *Pediatrics, 79*(4), 593–597. Retrieved from: https://pediatrics.aappublications.org/content/79/4/593.long?sso=1&sso_redirect_count=1&nfstatus=401&nftoken=00000000-0000-0000-0000-000000000000&nfstatusdescription=ERROR%3a+No+local+token

Orne, M. T. (1962). On the social psychology of the psychological experiment: With particular reference to demand characteristics and their implications. *American Psychologist, 17*(11), 776–783. doi:10.1037/h0043424

Palsson, O. S., Turner, M. J., Johnson, D. A., Burnett, C. K., & Whitehead, W. E. (2002). Hypnosis treatment for severe irritable bowel syndrome: Investigation of mechanism and effects on symptoms. *Digestive Diseases and Sciences, 47*(11), 2605–2614. doi:10.1023/A:1020545017390

Pavlov, I. P. (1927). *Conditioned reflexes*. Oxford, UK: Oxford University Press.

Perry, C. (1978). The Abbé Faria: A neglected figure in the history of hypnosis. In F. H. Frankel & H. S. Zamansky (Eds.), *Hypnosis at its bicentennial* (pp. 217–249). Boston, MA: Springer.

Pert, C. (1997). *Molecules of emotion: Why you feel the way you feel*. New York, NY: Scribner.

Pintar, J., & Lynn, S. J. (2008). *Hypnosis: A brief history*. Chichester, UK: Wiley-Blackwell.

Porges, S. W. (2011). *The polyvagal theory: Neurophysiological foundations of emotions, attachment, communication, and self-regulation*. New York: W. W. Norton.

Reid, D. B. (2016). Hypnotic induction: Enhancing trance or mostly myth? *American Journal of Clinical Hypnosis, 59*(2), 128–137. doi:10.1080/00029157.2016.1190310

Rizzolatti, G., & Fabbri-Destro, M. (2010). Mirror neurons: From discovery to autism. *Experimental Brain Research, 200*(3–4), 223–237. doi:10.1007/s00221-009-2002-3

Roffman, A. E. (2013). Family therapy as hypnotic conversation. In L. I. Sugarman, W. Wester, III, & W. C. Wester (Eds.), *Therapeutic hypnosis with children and adolescents* (2nd ed., pp. 325–350). Bethel, CT: Crown House.

Rogers, C. R. (1951). *Client-centered therapy: Its current practice, implications and theory*. London, UK: Constable.

Rosenberg, C. E. (2002). The tyranny of diagnosis: Specific entities and individual experience. *Milbank Quarterly, 80*(2), 237–260. doi:10.1111/1468-0009.t01-1-00003

Rossi, E. L. (1993). *The psychobiology of mind-body healing: New concepts of therapeutic hypnosis* (2nd ed.). New York, NY: W.W. Norton.

Rossi, E. L. (2002). *The psychobiology of gene expression: Neuroscience and neurogenesis in hypnosis and the healing arts*. New York, NY: W. W. Norton.

Schwartz, M. S., & Andrasik, F. (Eds.). (2016). *Biofeedback: A practitioner's guide* (4th ed.). New York, NY: Guilford.

Selye, H. (1982). History and present status of the stress concept. In L. Goldberger & S. Breznitz (Eds.), *Handbook of stress* (pp. 7–20). New York, NY: Free Press.

Siegel, D. J. (2012). *Pocket guide to interpersonal neurobiology*. New York, NY: W. W. Norton.

Sugarman, L. I. (1996). Hypnosis: Teaching children self-regulation. *Pediatrics in Review, 17*, 5–10. doi:10.1542/pir.17-1-5

Sugarman, L. I., Schafer, P. M., Alter, D. S., & Reid, D. B. (2018). Learning clinical hypnosis wide awake: Can we teach hypnosis hypnotically? *The American Journal of Clinical Hypnosis, 61*(2), 140–158. doi:10.1080/00029157.2018.1437710

Teleska, J., & Roffman, A. (2004). A continuum of hypnotherapeutic interactions: From formal hypnosis to hypnotic conversation. *American Journal of Clinical Hypnosis, 47*(2), 103–115. doi:10.1080/00029157.2004.10403629

Teleska, J., & Sugarman, L. I. (2013). Hypnotic abilities. In L. I. Sugarman & W. Wester (Eds.), *Therapeutic hypnosis with children and adolescents* (2nd ed., pp. 63–88). Bethel, CT: Crown House.

Tinterow, M. (1970). *Foundations of hypnosis, from Mesmer to Freud*. Springfield, IL: Charles C. Thomas.

Vlieger, A. M., Menko-Frankenhuis, C., Wolfkamp, S. C., Tromp, E., & Benninga, M. A. (2007). Hypnotherapy for children with functional abdominal pain or irritable bowel syndrome: A randomized controlled trial. *Gastroenterology*, *133*(5), 1430. doi:10.1053/j.gastro.2007.08.072

Weitzenhoffer, A. M. (2002). Scales, scales and more scales. *American Journal of Clinical Hypnosis*, *44*(3/4), 209–219. doi:10.1080/00029157.2002.10403481

Zeig, J. K. (1994). *Ericksonian methods: The essence of the story*. Levittown, PA: Brunner/Mazel.

Robinson's Story

George and Robinson

(The afternoon before the previous episode)

In his first visit, George had time to get comfortable with Doctor Robinson's dark complexion and unusual accent. Africa, maybe? George was too polite to ask. But it occurred to George that he was supplying all the information in this encounter. Maybe it wouldn't hurt if—George glanced toward the doctor, who seemed to read George's mind. "I'm from Haiti," Doctor Robinson said, "I grew up speaking a form of French."

This second visit was less formal. It took place in Robinson's office, not the examination room. Soft chairs faced across from each other in front of the desk. Robinson entered, removed his stethoscope and white coat and laid them on the desk, next to the framed photo portrait of his beaming wife, toddler son, and infant daughter. George partially rose from his chair as Robinson motioned him to sit. Robinson lowered himself in the chair opposite, and leaned back with an expression of interest and curiosity. Here is the conversation they had:

R: So, George. What did you want to tell me?
G: What do you mean?
R: You came here for a reason.
G: Because Carol said to.
R: Of course. And you naturally want to help Carol.
G: And the kids.
R: Because you've always taken care of your family.
G: [Tears suddenly well in George's eyes.]
R: Tell me about it.
G: [George wipes his eyes on the elbow of his shirt.]
R: [Waits. Points to the box of tissues.]
G: [Clears his throat.] I haven't cried since I was ten years old … When my dog Nicky died.
R: And now you've cried again … probably for good reason.

G: I don't know … yeah, I guess so.

R: Right. So …

G: I worry. I worry about Carol. And Jimmy, I told you about him last time. Carol's always been the one to look after Jimmy. Nobody else understands. She takes Jimmy everywhere. And now—

R: [Waits.]

G: I don't think I told you. Carol has diabetes. She—and her heart.

R: And now?

G: And I've always handled everything. Now more than ever.

R: You've always been the breadwinner.

G: And paid the bills. And fixed the house … and pretty much whatever else was broken … And—I'm not complaining … I mean, it's what I do.

R: You care for your family.

G: I didn't smoke. I didn't drink. I wasn't perfect. I—[Tears well up again.]

R: [Waits.]

G: I wasn't perfect. I admit that. I talked to God about that. I talked to Jesus. There was forgiveness there. You understand?

R: [Nods.]

G: I'm about set to retire. We won't have much to live on. The County was steady work for 22 years. But didn't leave us with much.

R: And now?

G: Here's my—[Stops talking abruptly. Waves a hand in the air as if to brush these things away.]

R: [Leans forward in the chair—brow furrowed, head tilted to the side—and waits.]

G: Was going to say I don't have enough money to get my roof fixed. And I need to get my roof fixed. And I can't be going up on my roof anymore. But that's not the point. The point is—I'm getting old. Most of the time I don't feel old. I get on OK. I can still get down under the car to change the oil. But lately—that's not the point either. Listen.

R: [Robinson nods, attentive.] I am.

G: Back in high school we read a book called *Nineteen Eighty-Four*, you know, Orwell. I don't read books much … anymore, but I read this book all the way through, maybe because it was by someone named George, like me. At the end of the story, Winston, like the cigarettes, is being tortured, and what they do to him is—see, the torturers know what everyone's biggest fear is, and Winston's biggest fear is … rats.

I always remember that because I have a terrible feeling about rats, too. It's like disgust, but stronger. Rats just seem so dirty and nasty to me. I don't want to see them or even hear about them. And in the book, the torturers put a cage of hungry rats on Winston's head. So repulsive. I don't know how George Orwell was able to think of a person doing such a disgusting thing to someone—to another human being.

And here's what's been happening. Well, for a long time I've had this thing—my doctor, before you, told me it sounded like what he called "REM Sleep Disorder." It means that sometimes I move around in the bed when I'm asleep and dreaming. It even seems like I'm maybe acting out my dreams. Sometimes I yell, a few times I've even jumped out of bed. So there's a name for it—great—but the doctor, he couldn't do anything about it. Except for saying my wife and me should sleep in different beds. So I won't hurt her when I'm sleeping.

I'd never hurt her. [Tears.] Never on purpose, but—you know.

So I was talking to a buddy of mine about mice and rats getting into the compost or the garbage or the birdseed. This got me thinking about rats. And that made me start dreaming about rats. And the rats I dreamed of were vicious, hungry ones. And the dream I had about them was one of those super realistic dreams. And so in my dream I was dreaming I was in my bed, and it was all real except that there were rats on the floor next to my bed, and there was rat filth on the floor by the bed, and the rats were making jibbery rat noises.

So I woke up. I didn't wake Carol because like I say we can't sleep in the same bed now, but I woke up and I had this strong feeling that the rats were under the covers at the foot of my bed, so if I reached out with my feet toward the foot of the bed I'd feel a rat there, and the rat would feel me and start scratching and biting. So I got out of bed and turned on the lights and didn't see any rats, so I lay down on my belly and looked under the bed and there weren't any rats there either.

So there's no rats in my bedroom, it's just a dream, but I keep having the same dream, and in one dream I even thought I was awake, and my mind was telling me—*Now don't be fooled; there really is a rat at the foot of the bed, and if you put your feet down there it will bite you!* And I keep having dreams so strong that I wake up and jump out of bed and yank back the covers to make sure there's no rats there.

So why am I talking about rat dreams?

Well. I feel like—I don't know. It's like—like my brain is coming apart. Like my brain got rewired overnight so it stopped working right.

You know that fairy tale about the shoemaker and the elves? And how overnight the elves show up and sew the shoes together so they're all finished and perfect in the morning? That's how it is for me, except in reverse: instead of the elves sewing shoes together overnight, the elves take the finished shoes apart every night.

No one knows about this. I feel like I can't even talk to Carol about it. It will just frighten her, and she wouldn't be able to fix it anyway. She can't help because she's too busy helping Jimmy. And Jimmy can't help because he's *never* been able to look after himself. And now it's worse. Now I have this problem that really bothers me, that I can't understand, that I can't fix myself. I mean—I've tried to wait it out. And it just got worse. [Falls silent …]

R: [Nods slowly and watches what George does as he finishes talking.]

G: [Realizes Robinson is being silent so he sits back in the chair. Sighs audibly and his shoulders drop. After a full minute of silence, he asks …] So, what do you think, Doc?

R: [Slowly, gently.] I'm *thinking* about a lot of things. I'm *thinking* that Carol didn't really need to ask you to come see me, but it is *loving* of you to be here for her … And I'm *thinking* of how much you care and how much you've given of your self …

G: [Begins to weep, softly.]

R: [Moves the tissue box to George's chairside table. Points to it and George's eyes. He speaks again, a little more firmly.] Good. *One* of us ought to cry … Can I go on now?

G: [Gestures with his hand to continue while taking tissue to his eyes and nose.]

R: [Standing, then pacing.] And I'm thinking that you are struggling mightily … certainly courageously … I mean [with a wry smile, shaking his head.] Voracious rats … And in your bed! My God … [pauses, stops pacing.] You sure know how to gnaw at yourself.

G: [Looks up at Robinson, startled.] You think I'm doing this to myself? On purpose?!

R: [Smiling, softly.] I think you are here, right now, to start making some sense of all of this. I think that you've felt pulled apart in a lot of directions. I think you deserve to feel a lot better about yourself, … and to have better dreams … even good dreams.

G: [Wiping his tears, straightening his posture.] You know, Doc, I'm getting kind of pissed off … not at you … just … I don't know how to say it …

R: [Smiling and sitting back down, leaning forward toward George with interest.] Yes. Every right to be.

G: [Sits more erect and clenches both fists while he inhales deeply.]

R: Great. George, please, the way you feel right now? Hang onto that feeling … It's even in those hands of yours, those fists. Got it?

G: [Nods slowly, looking straight ahead into space, breathing deeply.]

R: As you stay with that, George, allow being "pissed off," that feeling, to move, to concentrate, into just one of those hands … whichever one is *right* for it … you don't have to know which one it is going to be … you can just surprise yourself.

G: [Again, nods slowly, staring ahead, breathing. His eyes close as his left hand begins to fall open and rotate outward on his left thigh and his right fist slowly closes.]

R: [Enthusiastic whisper.] Yes. Wow. Really. Feel that! Even more of that now.

G: [Face slowly reddens, slowly, subtly shakes his head once as his left hand continues to unfold, opening and stretching.]

R: Yes. [Looking at G's hands.] *Opening*. Even more happening over there. *Wondering* what it is *learning* to do as it does that.

G: [Subtle, tenuous smile and a tear forming in the corner of his right eye.]

R: Isn't that a good thing to know? … To discover? … and will you continue to do that until you come to a good place, a good time to pause? This learning, this new understanding can go on inside … even surprising you.

R & G: Sit together in silence for a full eight minutes. George's facial muscles relax and the color softens. His one tear dries. Robinson observes him, watches the clock and audibly scratches some notes on a pad of paper with his fountain pen.

G: [Opens his eyes. Looks at and opens his right hand. Leans back and stretches both arms, then folds his hands in his lap, smiling and nodding at Robinson.]

R: You look like you did something interesting. I am wondering what you would *like* to tell me about what that was … while you keep the rest private.

G: [Chuckles.] Well, doc, I am not sure I can explain it … or really want to right now. I mean I still feel this anger, but it's like I have it kind of with me. And it's … uh … yeah … it's righteous. And I spent time with my boy … my other boy, not Jimmy … but he was part of it … I mean myself as a boy, reading Orwell and thinking about poor Winston. I really don't want to explain it right now …

R: [Smiles and nods.] I think that's really meaningful, George. Do you think you have started something good and important?

G: [A bit distracted.] Yeah. I do. Wait. What time is it? [Sees the clock.] Huh! It's been that long? [Gets up.] I'm sorry, Doc, I need to go … home and talk with Carol.

R: [Stands. Gives George his coat, helps him put it on.]

G: [Putting his arms in his sleeves.] Thanks. [Puts out his right hand.] I mean thanks, Doctor. I appreciate you giving me this time. I know you want to talk more, but I think I need to talk more with Carol. [To himself.] Maybe we should go out for dinner at the Big Boy … I will make another appointment … for uh … next week, Okay? I think Carol has a library card … [Pauses again, shaking Robinson's hand.] I mean it. Thank you.

R: That's quite a firm handshake. You are very welcome, George. I will walk you out.

3 How We Make Up Our Minds

Main Ideas

1. Mind is an oscillating, complex, open, and evolving system of information flow.
2. Mind is embodied and integral; there is no empiric mind-body duality. It exists in and limits our thinking, language, and cultures.
3. From gene to consciousness, information and energy transfer is a discontinuous, threshold-limited (liminal) process that requires an impetus for change. It ebbs and flows.
4. Mind evolves along developmental paths that are determined by the interplay between autogenic algorithms (self) and influences perceived as "other."
5. Minds are all different, and require creative, flexible approaches for change. Lessons from the quantum world may apply.

In Chapter 2, we described hypnosis as a skill set for influencing the mind's plasticity. We discussed how our understanding of hypnosis has evolved with our progressive merging of psychology and physiology. In the following chapter we will begin to discuss how minds change, defining "trance" as a process of plasticity or flexibility. Here, we explain what we mean by "mind" in the first place.

In this chapter we assemble various areas of research to build an empirically grounded model of mind as a complex system that is embodied, liminal (discontinuous, with thresholds), evolving, dynamic, and both idiosyncratic and familiar. Emergent properties of this complexity include consciousness, our sense of self, and our ability to form meaningful relationships with others. This latter quality allows minds to merge and form social systems. This holistic conception of mind is fundamental to the central role hypnosis plays in clinical settings and the health care paradigm. By the end of the chapter we anticipate that you will be eager to learn about trance: how minds change.

What We Mean by "Mind"

Mind is a word. It's a label, a placeholder—like all words—for something irreducible to words. In English, it is used both as verb and noun. As a verb it refers to directing attention with care—"minding one's work," "mind that you don't slip and fall"—and a degree of resentment—"If you don't mind … But I *do* mind." As a noun, it refers to the processes of thought, intellect, belief, ("I am of a mind to …"), and to those who raise those processes to a higher level, "she has [or, interestingly, 'is'] a great mind." We also refer to it as a surface, like a desk; or a container, like a frame, for what current thoughts and feelings may be forming or filtering our perceptions. "What's on your mind?," or "I'm of a frame of mind" are examples of these vessel metaphors. Some use the term "mindset" as if mind is a collection of playing pieces that will be brought to bear for what may come next. And, of course, when we feel most disoriented from that mind-as-containing-framework, when we have lost the marbles that fit comfortably into that mindset, we say that we are "out of my mind" or have "lost my mind."

Those who study the mind seem to be of two camps. More medicalized researchers and clinicians who tend to focus on identifiable brain functions and locations consider "mind" ephemeral and inexact. Mind is something to be parsed and processed into something "real" and located, mostly, in the brain. Mind is a research placeholder for what we have yet to refine and define. Once parsed, that part is no longer in "mind." It is something more distinct. Some go so far as to reduce the mind to the thalamus and surrounding limbic system of the brain, since those structures serve as the gateways to memory, consciousness, and transduction of brain signals into body function through the hypothalamus and pituitary. Clinical psychologists and other therapists are more likely to use "mind" more freely, but still as some brain-function-equivalent or an emergent neurologic manifestation.

When asked to locate their mind, most people point to their heads. That's where we tend to put our minds, these days. We have raised the central nervous system in status with the relatively recent and rapid growth of neuroscience. In past civilizations, before we placed such value on our brains, we likely gestured toward other body areas to represent ourselves, our consciousness, and our mind. After all, the ancient Egyptians "excerebrated" the brain in preparation for mummification by removing it through the nostrils and then disposed of it, preserving most of the other viscera in canopic jars for use in the afterlife. Brains used to be expendable.

Our current neuro-centrism, when it comes to mind, has reflected our ongoing categorical, classified, and reductionist habit. The brain, as integrator of subservient body systems, has been viewed as the seat of consciousness, perception, volition, knowledge, and so, self. Modern treatises on the scientific origins of these phenomena primarily have focused on the brain, populated by about 100 billion neurons

(Chalmers, 2010; Damasio, 2010). Hence, the proliferation of "neuro-" as prefix, as in neuropeptides, **neuroplasticity**, neuropharmacology, neurolinguistics, etc., even though these terms refer to things and processes that are not limited to the brain, neither in effect nor origin. Further, we have coined new terms from other researched systems, like stepping stones across a stream, to link parts of mind: psycho-neuro-immunology, psycho-neuro-endocrinology, etc. These linkages and the studied phenomena that demonstrate them have been held up as intriguing anomalies—Emotions might be related to inflammation? Food labelling can affect metabolism?—rather than surface manifestations of a much more densely integrated and interpersonal ecology of mind. It is said that George Engel warned against hyphenating the word "biopsychosocial," since punctuation inferred partition (Kreipe, 2019).

Similar to the history of hypnosis in Chapter 2, there seems to be a tendency to understand mind as only and no more than the sum of its parts and, further, to believe that the parts we carve out for study—and build into medical school departments and specialties of practice—actually exist autonomously. This may simply represent the careful conservativism of evidence-based science. But it limits our care and engagement. Our resultant specialization in health care often pulls people apart, or causes them to feel that they are being dissected. Our effort here is to shift our perspective to a more systemic model of mind. As Yapko (2009) put it, in his discussion of the tendency to dissect the psyche of people with depression, we tend to examine clients "even more closely under the microscope, analyzing ever smaller pieces of their psyche, as if depression is just their individual problem, [while] the solution lies in a broader view. We need a *macro*scope" (p. xvi). Like our understanding of health and care, our minds are essentially something we are continually making up to explain ourselves.

Mind as System

A "murmuration" is the term given to flocking starlings. You can find many videos of them online, often characterized as "mesmerizing." Grainger Hunt (2013) writes that they are "a dazzling cloud, swirling, pulsating, drawing together to the thinnest of waists, then wildly twisting in pulses of enlargement and diminution." As these starlings fly together, they look and behave like a single, marvelously agile organism. This "Darwinian Dance" (Hunt, 2013) apparently evolved in defense to the threat of predator peregrine falcons flying near the flock's periphery. The fascination of murmuration has been the subject of considerable study. Flocking starlings have been found to enact "scale-free correlation" by which, as one researcher explained, "The group respond[s] as one" and "cannot be divided into independent subparts" (Cavagna et al., 2010, p. 2). Observers of this collective behavior often claim to feel entranced and inspired by some kinship in its synchrony. Murmuration is a manifestation of a complex system (Alfano, 2013). Its form is more than the sum of its parts: an emergent property. So are our minds.

A bit of systems science—cybernetics—is necessary at this point, in order to build a concept of mind as emergent. At its simplest, a system is a group of elements that are linked by their coordinated response to a "load," which is usually a force that perturbs them. My electric kettle is a simple system. I put in cold tap water and depress the lever that turns it on. Electrical current flows through its wires, attached to the socket in the wall. The current's energy moves through the element that changes that energy into heat which is subsequently transferred to the water. Another element in the lining of the kettle, a temperature-sensing thermistor of annealed metal, turns that heat back into current, shutting off the flow of electricity at a predetermined temperature with a second, internal switch. This is a negative feedback loop. The elements are the wires, the water, the thermistor and two switches. The loads are the electricity and thermal energy in the water.

As described, the kettle is a simple, closed system. It turns on, heats up, then turns off. I make my tea. It could be diagrammed as a line. We could make it more complex by adding a second internal switch that turns it back on when the temperature goes down—a thermostat—to keep my tea water hot all the time. That would make a circle. Or we could make it the heart of a steam engine, adding a rotor with vanes to make a turbine near the spout then adding plumbing elements that keep filling the kettle with water. Then we could attach gears to the turbine to drive a knitting machine with rotors, levers, shuttles and a feeder of fiber. Or perhaps we could scale it up to run a whole textile factory, carding bales of cotton into sheets of fabric, along with a whole host of workers in various roles—and thereby part of the system—to keep it all going. It would be challenging to diagram that flow of energy.

At some point in this evolving complexity, our textile factory becomes more than the sum of its parts, more than the elements of its systems. Its collective sounds and smells, the material flow of fiber and dust affecting the machinery and the workers, the relationships and synchrony between the workers and machinery, and countless other factors all multiply (rather than sum) to emergent properties.

As you likely noticed, back when I connected my kettle to the electric socket: it isn't really a "closed" system. The current to the socket comes from somewhere outside of the kettle: a power plant, solar panels, windmills, or some dynamic combination of these. The ambient temperature in the kitchen is a factor that is controlled by another thermostatic system in my house, in addition to whether I am baking something in the oven, and what the weather is today, which is determined by the planetary climate system. Imagine diagramming that! And where would you stop? Consider the economic and social impacts of the steam engine, which propelled the cotton processing industry in Manchester, England in the 1840s, where young Friedrich Engels was composing *The Condition of the Working Class in England* (Engels, 1892). The boundaries that we place around any given system serve to focus our understanding of it, and those limits are both opportunistic and artificial.

Ultimately, our individual mind systems expand collectively to family, neighborhoods, and also to systems of beliefs, religions, rules, and paradigms. We need not look further than the internet—formerly and aptly, the "world-wide web"—to find a fitting metaphor for and manifestation of the collective mind as an open, complex, and evolving system. Scientific paradigms, as we discussed in Chapter 1, are beliefs, tools, and practices that combine to create a version of reality, an atmosphere of understanding and making sense … until it doesn't. Then, according to Thomas Kuhn, a revolution occurs and a new, usually more inclusive paradigm makes more sense, and we don't go back to the old one. This happens because our mind systems are open and learning collectively all of the time. We can think of our mindsets—our life experiences and practices, our habits, how we have come to believe life works—as our own personal paradigms. Instead of scientific methods, tools, and theories, we have our mind-systems that also evolve, then shift. As we will discuss, hypnosis is a way to help minds shift.

Minds Are Embodied

So how do the elements of our mind-systems talk with each other? If we are willing to accept the irreducible holism of our integrated mind, what holds it together? Here we need to introduce three current and salient bodies of research: **Hebb's axiom** (2009), Pert's *Molecules of Emotion* (1997), and Porges's **polyvagal theory** (2011).

Hebb's Axiom

In 1949, Canadian neuropsychologist Donald O. Hebb wrote, "The general idea is an old one, that any two cells or systems of cells that are repeatedly active at the same time will tend to become 'associated' so that activity in one facilitates activity in the other" (Hebb, 2009, p. 70). Later oversimplified to "Cells that fire together wire together," this idea became an organizing principle in neuroscience and, we would argue, the science of the embodied mind. It has been used to explain how neural cells, linked by some activating input, some novel learning experience or practice, form an engram. Allport explained,

> If the inputs to a system cause the same pattern of activity to occur repeatedly, the set of active elements constituting that pattern will become increasingly strongly inter-associated. That is, each element will tend to turn on every other element and (with negative weights) to turn

> off the elements that do not form part of the pattern. To put it another way, the pattern as a whole will become "auto-associated." We may call a learned (auto-associated) pattern an engram.
>
> (Allport, 1985, p. 44)

Thus form elements of memory. Memory, then, is not a photograph or a recording, a fly in the amber. It is the likelihood that a system of associated cells will collectively activate again. Engrams, as patterns of perception, are far more ephemeral than physical recordings, and they are subject to hypnotic influence.

While Hebbian Theory is founded on and most often applied to neural networks, it is not limited to these associations. It has much wider applicability. The engram extends from memory to somatosensory and motor nerves, muscles, tendons, and joint position. Any seasoned musical instrumentalist feels the comfort and competence of adopting their performance posture. A guitarist friend (of LIS) explained that when he needs to feel more confident in any situation (especially a non-musical one), he simply lays his right palm down and his left palm up, replicating the guitar-playing hand position. A nurse colleague (of JHL) shared that, whenever she stood next to a patient's bed, she felt an emotional surge of commitment and protection that superseded anything else that was going on elsewhere in the busy hospital ward. It was like a warm fire in her heart. These are embodied engrams forming memories.

As a basic tenet, all of our learning that has become conditioned—meaning our talents, skills, automatisms, and traumas—are embodied: stored and expressed as body memory (Levine, 2010; Ogden & Fisher, 2015; Van der Kolk, 2014). This embodiment is also discernable as we observe each other. As we will see, many non-conscious behaviors—e.g., facial expressions, breathing and gestures—in therapeutic encounters are clues to embodied memory and resources for change.

I (LIS) had an experience with Hebb's Axiom that added new dimensions of understanding. I was driving to clinic on the usual busy meshwork of highways one morning. In front of me was an old model Toyota with a unique collection of bumper stickers … a unique connection of bumper stickers that was familiar. I realized that had been behind this car on this road at this time, perhaps many times, before. It dawned on me that within the collected congestion of cars surrounding me there were probably many folks just like me, all heading to work at the same time. We were passively cooperating with each other. No one decided it was a good time to play bumper cars. We were following rules of engagement. We were all being dutiful cogs in a bigger machine—society, economy—and allowing each other to do the same. But—and here is the new dimension—we were mostly and willingly ignorant of our auto-association (pun unintended).

Moving cars on a busy road flow like starlings. We imagined ourselves autonomous elements within our individual systems: minds, cars, radio, hands-free phones, thermal mugs. At an individual level we did not know, or much care, that we were elements of a larger and dynamic system. I had always thought of my coordinated cells as somehow knowing and caring for each other, being friends, of there being an emotional element to their cooperation. After all, most of the time, unless I was sick or injured, all of my parts got along and worked as a team. I guess I always imagined a certain *esprit de corps*. As we will see shortly, there is an emotional element, just not in the anthropomorphic way I imagined.

There were two insights produced by this revelation that pertain to our understanding of mind and our book's thesis. The first is the lack of intentionality and determinism in our auto-association. Randomness plays a part. Our connections are what they are, but they could just as easily go another way. This is relevant to some quantum interpretations of mind and hypnosis that we will touch on near the end of this chapter. The second idea was the scalability or concentric nesting of systems: drivers to cars to economy to society is similar to cells to organ systems to mind. They are nesting systems that contribute irreducibly to the whole murmuration.

So, one way that our minds are orchestrated is by our auto-associated cells creating engrams that tend to persist. Before we consider Candace Pert's contribution, we must consider one more aspect of the engrams of memory. Since our minds are open and evolving systems, our memories change. Memory and life experience not fixed recordings and photographs; we constantly edit them. Each time we reroute an engram through consciousness and reconstruct it through the hippocampus—one brain structure that takes part in memory and learning—we alter it. Memory is infinitely malleable and influenced by our unique life experiences and growth.[1] That home you grew up in doesn't look the same. As artists often do, American writer and editor William Maxwell may have described the plasticity of memory better than most scientists when he wrote:

> What we, or at any rate I, refer to confidently as memory—meaning a moment, a scene, a fact that has been subjected to a fixative and thereby rescued from oblivion—is really a form of storytelling that goes on continually in the mind and often changes in the telling. Too many conflicting emotional interests are involved for life ever to be wholly acceptable, and possibly it is the work of the storyteller to rearrange things so that they conform to this end. In any case, in talking about the past, we lie with every breath we draw."
>
> (Maxwell, 1980, p. 27)

Pert's "Molecules of Emotion"

Much of Hebbian Theory has been applied to the central nervous system and the brain primarily. After all, the brain is currently held as the central integrator of the mind, and we understand much of how it transfers and regulates information across synapses. But Candace Pert's contributions from the study of cell receptors and the molecules that bind to them revealed a stunningly new level of complexity in cellular integration that threatens, or at least competes with, our "neurocentrism." It leads to a deeper understanding of how mind is both embodied and distributed. Much of Pert's work is elegantly laid out in her book, *The Molecules of Emotion* (1997).

Before explaining Pert's contribution, we need to explain some basic cell "*receptor-ology*." The outer membranes of each of the 3.72×10^{13} cells that compose our physical self are encrusted with 10,000 to 20,000 receptors, like little satellite dishes, waiting to bind a molecule. In the act of binding, we call that molecule a **ligand**. Most ligands are peptides, short strings of amino acids that twist together like a tangled rubber band to form asymmetric shapes—with embedded receptor binding sites—that hold potential energy. That potential energy is released when the ligand binds its particular receptor. The receptor, thus transformed by this energy, in turn affects change within the cell through internal "second-messenger systems." This cascade changes intracellular function: making more or less of that substance, growing faster or slower, even making more or less receptors. Of course, the ligand peptides are made and dispensed by other cells as their way of conveying information between vast systems of cells. They orchestrate disparate functions by creating a humoral climate in the blood and lymph and extracellular fluids that bathe our internal milieu.

This much was generally understood as Pert entered the field. But we had studied receptors and ligands from *within* various and, we thought, segregated systems. We studied immunoglobulins and cytokines—the ligands that mobilize the immune system—as exclusive members of that system. We studied serotonin, dopamine, glutamate, and other so-called "neuropeptides" belonging to and serving the nervous system. Insulin and glucagon were functionaries of the endocrine system, and so forth. Pert's critical discovery was that our 3.72×10^{13} cells with their 10,000 to 20,000 receptors per cell *did not know* that they belonged exclusively to these systems. Most had receptors for all sorts of ligands. Bone cells and immune cells had serotonin receptors. Nerve cells not only had insulin receptors but receptors for gastrointestinal messengers as well. Different types of cells responded differently to the same messengers in keeping with their roles. But they were all playing along with the same complex musical score in their own harmonious way. The intercellular coordination was much more widespread and cross-disciplinary than previously known. Even though the heads of the departments of endocrinology, immunology, gastroenterology, and psychiatry may not be coordinating their work, and sometimes they refused to talk to each other, the cells of their individual embodied minds were getting along just fine.

Pert stripped these peptides of their departmental affiliations, dubbing these ligands "messenger molecules." But as the emergent properties of their far-ranging effects on the internal climate became clear, she dared to call them the "molecules of emotion." Pert recognized that these dynamic intercellular influences represented the embodiment of mind, and so, collectively, as she called it, "the wisdom of the body" (Pert, 1997).

That view gained credence when, in coordination with colleagues, Pert published data supporting the hypothesis that, of the information/energy transfer within the central nervous system, less than two per cent was being transferred synaptically (Pert, Ruff, Weber, & Herkenham, 1985). The other 98% was transmitted by the receptors on the nerve cell somata, the "heads" of the nerve cells that contain the nucleus and from which the axon, the long transmitting "wire" of the nerve, originates. This receptor activity contributes to the likelihood that the nerve will fire, sending an electrical impulse down its axon. So even the central nervous system was subject to the body's climatic wisdom.

Porges' Polyvagal Theory

The third body of research that contributes to the embodied mind is Stephen Porges' Polyvagal Theory. Again, the interested reader is referred to two excellent books on the subject in addition to primary source material (Dana & Porges, 2018; Porges, 2011). Here we will summarize the essence for its relevance. Porges developed the Polyvagal Theory to resolve an apparent paradox in the function of the mammalian vagus nerve.

The vagus nerve is the main conduit of the parasympathetic portion (PNS) of the autonomic nervous system. Through much of the last century, the study of the autonomic nervous system has been focused on the sympathetic part (SNS). The SNS is the main mediator of the so-called "fight-or-flight" response. As a result of Selye's (1955) research, the SNS became the focus of brain-to-body stress communication, and the role of stress in coronary artery disease, gastrointestinal conditions, and a range of medical conditions. The PNS and the vagus nerve were relegated to the role of SNS counterbalance, a modulating force. However there was a problem with this role assignment. In infants, especially premature infants, increased vagal nerve activity (tone), instead of beneficial modulating, was associated with life-threatening slowing of the heart rate, or bradycardia. This was the "vagal paradox." The vagus seemed to have two opposing roles: life-sustaining and defeating (Porges, 2011).

Porges resolved this apparent contradiction by determining that there were *multiple* layered and evolved vagal nuclei in the back of the brain. Hence the *poly*vagal theory. The evolutionary older, earlier vagal nuclei mediated the reptilian freeze response: slowing heart rate and body metabolism to simulate, and sometimes result in, death. These portions of the vagus nerve were slower, uninsulated by the myelin sheath. That insulation produced efficiency of conduction in evolutionarily newer nerve systems. A newer mammalian myelinated system functioned to mediate between the energizing SNS and the reptilian system, what Porges termed a "vagal brake." Unfortunately, this newer system is not fully myelinated in some premature infants and so is not "up and running" at their birth. Hence, the reptilian system can cause unopposed bradycardia. The vagal brake operates reflexively, and can be evoked intentionally, with slow, deep breaths. These exaggerated breaths change barometric pressure in the chest cavity that, in turn, affect the speeding up and slowing down of the heart (called sinus arrhythmia). This keeps the heart from slowing down or speeding up too much, as well as feeding back to the vagal nerve nuclei in the brainstem. In short, this feedback from the lungs and heart through the afferent vagus nerves tells the brain that the body is safe.

But it is the forward projections of this mammalian vagal system into the higher functions of the brain that is most relevant for us here. Porges noted that the evolutionarily newest (dorsal motor) nucleus of the vagus contributed to and influenced a variety of prosocial functions, including facial expression, vocal motor control, and tuning the ear to human voice frequencies, to name a few. He posited that increased vagal tone projected forward to widely distributed, higher centers within the brain and activated a "social engagement system." Moreover, the vagal system is primarily (c. 80%) **afferent**, meaning that it mainly carries signals from the body *to* the central nervous system. These afferent vagal fibers come from the viscera, with a majority coming from the gastrointestinal tract, lungs, and heart. The regular oscillations of heart rate—slowing, then quickening, then slowing again, in concert with the barometric changes associated with breathing—seem to maximize vagal tone at the rate of about six cycles per minute, or 0.1 Hertz, about ten-second breaths. Together, Porges referred to these summed, embodied signals arriving at the brain via the vagus nerve as "neuroception," giving substance to the long-held belief in "gut feelings." Neuroception, or more inclusively, "**interoception**" informs us about the degree of stability in our internal milieu that, when activated and optimized, gives us a measure of safety and comfort, allowing us to engage socially and effectively.

These three lines of research—Hebbian Theory, widely distributed messenger Molecules of Emotion, and the Polyvagal Theory—all transcend any mind-body duality attributed to Descartes. Together, they demonstrate how the mind is necessarily embodied. To use an oversimplified computer metaphor, our brains are the mind's central processor. The computer's memory is stored and widely distributed in the entire body, like books located in various sections of a library, and indexed, for its part, in the brain's catalog system.

Why Does the Embodied Mind Matter?

Why should it matter that mind is embodied in this complex and holistic way? First of all, as we will continue to note, helping change minds involves physical and emotional change. Hypnosis skills always involve noticing and utilizing gestures, facial expressions, posture, facial blood flow, and breathing changes: non-consciously derived behavioral manifestations of the embodied mind. Much of that information flows afferently through the vagal fibers.

Next, it is the humoral/emotional climate of the embodied mind that both shapes and determines the accessibility of memory: from amnesia to vivid, eidetic imagery.[1] So attending to that climate, making some sense of its patterns, and encouraging "internal climate change," is necessary if one is therapeutically helping to change those patterns.

Third, our concentrically nested minds, from inside the cell to society, do not change form at the level of the problem. We have to move to a higher level to effect change. Returning to my driving-to-work metaphor: if we have an accident, we will need to get out of our cars, call the police, perhaps even get tow trucks and maybe even an ambulance. We won't change the situation by sitting in our cars and wondering why they don't move. Similarly, it is the job of the clinician, and, in Maxwell's world, the story-teller, to help the other move out of the problematic system in which they may find themselves stuck. Hypnosis is really good for that.

Finally, this notion of holism was—and still is—the essence of Engel's biopsychosocial model. It is *not* a rejection of reductionism or our grasp of mind processes at an inter-cellular, intracellular, and genomic levels. It *is* acknowledging the multiple interconnections between previously segregated organ systems, as well as the effects of learning and conditioning, life experiences, social relationships, and environmental exposures on the intricacies of inter-cellular, intracellular, and genomic functioning. Holism explains the intergenerational effects of trauma, for example, since we now understand that traumatizing experiences change gene expression, and how the encoding of that altered gene expression can be transmitted to the next generation. Our response to trauma is itself a hypnotic process: something that directs mind-plasticity in intense and enduring, albeit restrictive and damaging, ways. So hopeful, positive, and resilience-enhancing therapeutic experiences such as clinical hypnosis can also produce adaptive effects at a genomic level (Rossi, 1993, 2002).

Mind is Liminal

From the Latin word *limen* meaning threshold (Merriam-Webster online, n.d.), the adjective "liminal" has different meanings in different contexts. In anthropology, it refers to the ambiguity and disorientation that occurs before a rite of passage (Turner, 1974): when one "stands at the threshold" of a new state, identity or role. This can apply to our larger thesis about heath care paradigms. We have claimed that we are writing this book at the threshold of a heath care paradigm shift. When considering the (always embodied) mind, we also use liminal to mean that the mind is constructed of integrated but discontinuous systems. From inside the cell to up to our adolescent growth spurts and "AHA!" realizations, pressure-energy-information builds to a peak, then crosses a threshold, and things shift.

Here is an imagined example of liminality at a cellular level. Imagine you are an intra-cellular spectator, floating within the cytoplasm (the material inside the cell membrane, excluding and surrounding the nucleus) of one of your 3.72 x 10^{13} cells. You are aware that there has been some commotion outside the cell, evidenced by the increasing frequency of pulsations of the membrane receptors (Lodish et al., 2000). To review, like satellite dishes, these are the outward-facing binding-sites (10K–20K per cell) that receive intercellular messenger molecules, called ligands (from the Latin, *ligare*, to bind). Ligands hold information packets as potential energy that, once bound to a receptor, are transferred for use in the cell. The type of receptor on the type of cell and the activity that the cell is momentarily engaged in collectively determine the use, or meaning, of that information.

For whatever reason, those receptors are buzzing. As a result, more and more energy is being brought into the cytoplasm in the form of charged molecules and ions. These in turn bind to other proteins, changing their shape and level of excitement. There are multitudes gathering out there. Memories of crowds with torches and pitchforks in old monster movies, or zombie apocalypses in more recent ones, come to mind. Less dire, it is like the cumulative roaring of happy fans for their winning team at a sporting event. Some come from next door, in the neighborhood. Others have travelled long distances from other organ systems. In all cases, elements of inspiration are building towards some kind of response.

Suddenly, a threshold is reached. The commotion has peaked. A boundary has been breached at this higher power expenditure. That summed energy needs to be channeled, directed, to do something different. It is decision time. Internal messenger molecules travel through the nuclear membrane, towards the inner sanctum, as emissaries. You go with them.

Packed inside the nucleus is genetic material: chromosomes and the necessary machinery to decrypt and index it. Large molecules move along the winding double-stranded surface of the huge DNA behemoths, each encrusted with other large proteins and smaller molecules. The code for designing and building all of the elements that ultimately make up our embodied minds is written in the simple pairings of four nucleotide bases along the twisted core of this massive genetic structure. The genetic sequence is the history of life. These base-pairs are constantly being sequentially separated and closed, like some giant opening and closing zipper, by a complementary macromolecule. Riding along the DNA surface and attached to its own assembling machinery, RNA replicates the base-pair sequence, to allow it to be transcribed into new protein building blocks, regulating enzymes and other functionaries of the mind. The mounting pressures of the potential energy entering the nucleus turns on this magnificent apparatus. These workings used to be the central dogma of genetics.

But genetics—the inherited encoding of our potential selves, slowly evolving over multiple generations from the birth of life itself, a sacred text—is not the whole or even the most germane part of this story. There are finer thresholds within the barriers to and facilitation of genetic transcription. We have evolved a way to flag this translation, to make it more or less accessible to decryption and expression. Genomics—literally naming or expressing one's genetic potential, one's blueprint—is our tendency, our affinity to express a gene or group of genes for a given purpose. It is how *likely* we are to do what we have done before. It requires a higher threshold: more power, more novelty, to change our genomic tendency. That higher bar is the first threshold crossed when we change our minds.

In response to novelty—to things knocking loudly on the cell wall receptors, then ascending to open the doors to the hallowed nuclear mechanisms—we first express "Immediate Early Genes" (Rossi, 2002). These messenger RNAs prepare a cascade of expression, a cellular alerting, to prepare to channel energy toward making something very different ("**epithetic**") or to do much more of the same ("**conservative**").[2] Hence, there is an even finer succession of thresholds on the way to change. And there are even more intricate levels of complexity meshing away beneath this surface and out of your view, there in the nucleus.

We might consider each of these thresholds of change the edge of enlightenments, part of Maxwell's "storytelling that goes on continuously in the mind." It scales all the way up through our organ systems to mind, to beliefs, to our sense of self, and beyond that to belonging, family, society, and to life itself. These mind shifts matter because they are postured both as moments of possibility and progress. As the energy builds towards the threshold of change, the only certainty is that change is about to happen. Everything else is uncertain. All outcomes are possible. Once the threshold is crossed and the genomic realization is made, the paradigm is shifted, there is no going back. All possible outcomes collapse to one. Imagine that this what is happening beneath our mind's surface when we understand something in a new way, experiencing a new insight, when the tears begin to flow, and everything looks different. This is the kind of breakthrough that we intend to facilitate at all levels of care. It is a radically different take on health and care than the monistic, reductionist determinism of diagnosis and treatment (i.e., traditional healthcare). This is *Systems Thinking*.

Mind Engages in an Ongoing, Discontinuous, Chronobiological Dance

Our minds are ruled by time cycles as much as chemical interactions and gene expression. Ernest Rossi has studied the literature from the rapidly unfolding field of chronobiology (Groopman, 2017) in an effort to understand the contribution of the **Basic Rest Activity Cycle** (BRAC, 90-120-minute "ultradian" period) and its relationship to how minds change with therapeutic hypnosis. These tidal, ultradian periods are the summed results of shorter, humoral oscillations of messenger molecules, influenced by clock genes. Rossi notes that Milton H. Erickson preferred to see clients for 90 to120 minutes because he claimed, presciently, "That's how long it takes" (Rossi, 2019a). Rossi observes that this period correlates with the zenith of the BRAC, a peak in energy expenditure that enhances gene expression (van der Veen & Gerkema, 2017) that he (Rossi, 2002) has termed the **Novelty-Numinosum-Neurogenesis Effect**. In short, Rossi presents a chronobiological, oscillating frame that gives a rhythm for our liminal, "AHA!" events.

Rossi has divided the ultradian BRAC into four stages, derived from the work of German philosopher, Hermann von Helmholtz, and the French mathematician, Henri Pointcaré (Hill & Rossi, 2017).

1. Baseline. The beginning of questioning, discomfort, information gathering. What is this all about? What's going on? Perhaps it's triggered by someone asking, "How are you?"
2. Incubation. Wondering, struggling, and working out what might be happening. What does this mean to me? What am I to do about it? This drives toward a degree of activation and even agitation.
3. Breakthrough and Illumination—a flash of insight, resolution, or revelation (an "AHA!" moment) followed by an expansive and creative response to change. Things make sense now and I can create something better in my life.
4. Verification—the whole experience is quietly reviewed and considered, and the benefits integrated into everyday life. I understand, appreciate, and accept what I have learned.

In our relatively mindless daily lives, most of us tend to resist this inevitable disruptive roller-coaster push for growth and change. In the Baseline phase, we typically multitask and self-distract, resisting and avoiding the deeper questions that rise up. As our struggle and uncomfortable questioning builds tension during Incubation, we feel we are bored or stuck and need to do something else. So, we try to relax. We use depressants (alcohol, cannabis) or other substances to get us "out of our heads." If we can successfully bypass a Breakthrough moment of insight, we feel tired and sapped of energy. So we drink coffee or take other stimulants to cope with the Verification stage. In most economically developed countries, the schedules of work and childhood education neglect or ignore these chronobiologic waves, to our detriment.

Clinicians will sometimes join these maladaptive efforts in their care. As we will discuss in Chapter 5, the traditional teaching of hypnosis and the use of practices such as progressive muscle relaxation and guided imagery are designed to direct the client to relax, influencing them to become passive in the face of the challenge of the second stage, Incubation. Since most people come to care in, or in anticipation of, an Incubation (stage two) experience, the opposite—encouragement toward struggle—is often needed. Equally important, we tend to over-think and over-analyze the Breakthrough (stage three) and Verification (stage four) experiences, rather than letting new learning integrate and become embodied, conditioned, and verified. Contemplative practices such as mindfulness meditation—both stepping out of and appreciating the flow of the mind's currents without hindrance—are most aligned with Breakthrough and Verification. For the clinician, it is powerfully therapeutic to express faith through trust, tolerance, and silence, while being present with a person in the process of absorbing their own new realizations.

Tuning therapeutic work (of all kinds) to the actual timing of this ebb and flow—engaging in provocative evocation to a creative peak, then absorption and reflection—aligns it to the model of the ultradian BRAC. While there is an established chronobiological basis for this cycling that may affect therapeutic response (Jensen, 2016), it is impractical, if not impossible, to see all of our patients in the late morning and early evening. The therapeutic value of the Four-Stage cycle is most practically archetypal. It is in our sleep cycles. It is the form and flow of a sonata, storytelling, and a gourmet multicourse meal. It is a form that our minds know. We resonate with it. So it becomes a powerful prototype for collaboration in understanding and treatment.

This pattern—increasing tension and struggle toward a breakthrough of new understanding and enlightenment, followed by a (hopefully satisfying) verification and integration—cycles away at the heart of *Systems Thinking.* One might consider it a psychobiological engine that resonates expansively from gene expression to behavioral expression and impels us toward change. Indeed, it is built into each of our characters' stories in this book. We will affix examples of each of the other three principles—*Temporal Touring, Relational Being, and Narrative Listening*—to this shape as we move along.

Developmental Algorithms Direct Mind Plasticity

In the midst of all of this complex ferment of cells wiring and firing together—orchestrating molecules of emotion, attending autonomic balance between friend and foe, and the rising and falling of the liminal dance—common developmental programs are unfolding and switching on to govern the entire system toward life achievements. The list is long and familiar and variously categorized: rolling over, sitting up, self versus non-self, object permanence, walking, talking, imaginative play, autonomy, testing social rules, sexual exploration, adult identity, love, partnership, parenting, aging, mortality, and dying. In Chapter 6 we will discuss the effects of human development on mind and in therapy to change our minds. We will note and expand upon many who have studied and written about development. Here we simply want to include **developmental imperatives** as we explore *how* we make up our minds. There are three aspects of the developing mind to note at this point.

First, since our programmed development plays a governing role, it must be embraced, accepted, and utilized in therapeutic relationships. It is the prime directive. Ignoring—or worse, resisting—it severs the therapeutic alliance.

Second, as we will discuss in Chapter 8, the impact of both traumatizing and empowering events—the ways they affect our internal climate and shape our minds—depends upon the developmental context in which they occur. Timing is everything.

The third aspect is that our developmental trajectories are diverse and unique. Not only do we learn to talk, walk, and individuate at different rates, but we unfold those particular programs in different ways. Consider learning to speak: hearing the sounds of language, linking them with a variety of non-verbal concomitants, figuring out the nuances of meaning, deciding to risk speech, internally translating mind-state into words and prosody (the lyrics and music of language), controlling the breath to do so, controlling the apparatus of vocal chords-mouth-tongue (part of the vagal system), making verbal noise, hearing one's own voice, self-correcting speech in real time, and so on. All of these modalities must develop in precise coordination … and often don't.

Hence, we have developmental differences, or as we have proposed elsewhere, "diffabilities" (Taylor & Sugarman, 2013). Our developmental currents and how we run them are ultimately idiosyncratic. Even when we meet criteria for a described developmental condition, say autism spectrum disorder, it is *how we don't fit* that diagnostic template that is the key to how we can move beyond the condition's limitations. This is evident to different degrees and in various ways in each of our characters' stories. George and Lulu—who you have already met—and Lyle and Stevie—who you will meet soon—all struggle with the categorical and their lack of fit. As clinicians, we gain much more by focusing our therapeutic leverage on what people in care are good at—their strengths—than how well they meet criteria for a diagnosis. Ultimately, it is by learning and accepting how an individual manages their ongoing development that allows us to meet their minds where they are and at their best.

There are Ghosts in the Machine

The systemic, embodied, liminal, and developing mind is infinitely more complex than current healthcare's monistic and reductionist vision. It is both ridiculously and sublimely more than the sum of its parts. It is ineffable. Many Western philosophers and scientists, including Jaynes (2000), Damasio (2010), Edelman (2005), Chalmers (2010), and Kandel (2007), have struggled with the factoring of this complexity into these emergent properties of mind, self, and consciousness. This pondering has led many to Buddhist teaching, which is ultimately transcendent. Parsing these difficult problems is beyond the scope of this book and, frankly, the mere clinical minds of its authors. The main reason we are emphasizing our minds' impenetrable complexity is that, like the murmurating shapes of starling flocks, our minds, consciousness, and sense of self are never reducible to any single element or group of elements. Treating any one element of a biopsychosocial entity in an attempt to heal the whole is rarely, if ever, sufficient. We are far more than our diagnoses.

The systemic, embodied, liminal, and developing mind also does things in ways we cannot yet deduce from our previous models. We use the term "ghosts" not to imply some spiritual, ephemeral, or indefinable elements—though we are not excluding them—but simply to mean anomalous influences we have yet to identify and integrate. Human history, and especially our study of ourselves, has been a process of moving our understanding from the ethereal realm to the empirical one. This is happening in the relatively new field of placebo effect research. Also, in terms of finding and parsing ghosts in the mind, we find relevance in the methods of quantum science. So, in closing our chapter about how we make our minds, we will use these two fields to peer over the edge into what we don't know yet.

Placebo Effect Research

Placebo effect research studies the indirect (non-monistic) but still biological effects of the *meaning* of therapeutic rituals. Moerman (2002) argues that "placebo response" ought to be replaced with "meaning response." Again, the breadth and depth of the field of placebo effect research is well beyond our scope, and readers are referred to the works of Benedetti (2014), Kirsch (2014), Crum (Crum, Corbin, Brownell, & Salovey, 2011; Crum & Langer, 2007; Crum, Phillips, Goyer, Akinola, & Higgins, 2016), Kaptchuk (2018, Kaptchuk & Miller, 2018, Ongaro & Kaptchuk, 2018), and others who have founded the field.

The size and color of pills; the delivery system (e.g., injection versus oral); the warmth, competence, and status of the clinician; the physical office environment; the narrative or story of the mechanism of action of the intervention—all of these have measurable biological effects in a person and therefore on the condition being studied. These effects are determined by factors within our unique conditioning, expectation, attitudes, and life experience, all building to what Crum calls "mindset" (Crum, Corbin, Brownell & Salovey, 2011; Crum & Langer, 2007). In that way, placebo effects are an expression of our abilities to change our minds at biological levels. Because these factor into all health interventions (in conscious people), all health interventions are *at least* placebos, even when there is also a direct and specific biological effect. Critically, placebo effects hinge on our conviction that the intervention—the pill or device or procedure—*is doing something to us that we cannot do for ourselves.* So we can, and do, use clinical interventions without known direct specific biological effects (sugar pills and sham surgery) to evoke innate, but disowned, abilities for self-regulation.

The "ghosts" appear when we study what is happening at a cellular level in people responding to placebos, for example. Much placebo effect research focuses on Parkinson Disease (PD), in which those affected begin to fail to deliver adequate amounts of dopamine into brain pathways that govern the "want" system, as the dopaminergic system can be called. The dopaminergic system branches out from deep within the center of our brains to propel our desires. It allows us to initiate and smooth our movements (nigrostriatal pathway), to hone our thinking and attention toward motivation for reward, including delaying our gratification (mesocorticolimbic pathways), and to regulate hypothalamic and pituitary function toward social relationships, including maternal-infant bonding (tuberoindundibular pathways), among other functions. In essence, the dopaminergic system drives our plasticity. To various extents, people with PD have losses in these operations.

People with PD are treated with attempts to provide more dopamine to the brain with medication, and by electrical pacemaker stimulation of nerves deep in the brain to replace the effects of dopamine. Both interventions also work as placebos, when patients are given fake pills or told people that the nerve stimulator is on when it is not. Benedetti (2014, pp. 157–169) has studied single-neuron responses when people with PD are given placebos. To oversimplify his research and get to our point, people with PD who have been treated with nerve stimulators (conditioned) and deceived to believe that the devices are turned on when they are not, will *activate their cell receptors, in the absence of dopamine.* In short, it appears that their cell receptors are activated without ligands … as if there is "ghost dopamine." Similar findings have been made in the opiate-pain-reward system and immune systems (Benedetti, 2014).

Again, we are not proposing that there are really ghosts—meaning unknowables. We are arguing that even our transcendently embodied messenger-molecule system cannot wholly explain how our beliefs, experiences, and conditioning—our mindsets—work. There are more complex and holistic, nonpharmacological, factors at play.

Quantum Science of Mind

Quantum science and quantum field theory developed, in part, as methodology to explain the behaviors of large systems of complex and contradictory elements. We are quite aware that these concepts have been misrepresented, misapplied, and abused outside of the physics community. They only and rigorously apply to the behaviors of elementary, subatomic particles, not to multicellular organ systems, and certainly not to our minds. Most readers familiar with quantum field theory (developed to combine classical field theory, special relativity, and quantum mechanics) can argue that it is irrelevant to human behavior and relationships. So such a stretch admittedly reduces our credibility. But, with respect for the value of theory and paradigm as metaphor, and using "quantum science" in its popular, colloquial sense, we suggest that is valuable to consider it as a way of studying mind.

We have already laid the groundwork for this perspective. Minds are supremely complex and evolving systems. They are embodied with multiple, nested, and overlapping levels of energy/information. They are discontinuous and oscillating, allowing for the mounting tension of growing possibilities that suddenly collapse into resolution. Because of the absolutely unique developmental histories of each mind, the number of possibilities for various outcomes is exponential. And minds join together in social groups that, because of their reciprocal influences—for example, with placebo effects—minds' boundaries tend to dissolve.

Most intriguing is that our own insight and presence, our awareness, our practice of being mindful and open to creative exploration of the possible—in short, our consciousness—becomes part of the system. The Heisenberg uncertainty principle (1927)—that measurement itself changes what is being measured—applies to our minds. While we can measure a dizzying array of physiological and functional markers for many health conditions, and determine whether a given person meets criteria for a specific disorder, how that individual directs their own physiology and how they don't fit the diagnosis may be as critical to their healing and health. As a 12-year-old boy who used his guitar practice—both actual and in his mind's imagination—to open his airways and relieve his asthma once told me (LIS), "Maybe how I imagine it works is really how it works." He changed my mind.

We are admittedly scratching the theoretical surface of the role of quantum field theory in the mind and in therapy. We refer the intrigued reader to Rossi and Rossi (2019). Here let it suffice, risking oversimplification, that, as Kathryn Rossi says, "Quantum means that all outcomes are possible" (2019).

Minding Our Hypnotic Abilities

What does this convoluted and rich understanding of mind have to do with healing, health, and hypnosis? Well, that is what the rest of the book is about.

But so far, we hope this allows you to consider that individual minds are uniquely resourced in both content and abilities. Our engrammed life experiences that are constantly changing in the context of their use—both bad and good habits—present as diagnoses and talents for change, respectively. Hypnosis, as a skill for facilitating changing minds, involves cultivating plasticity within the system to allow utilization of those talents for change, whatever they may be. Before we discuss *how* we use hypnosis, we will next explore *what* changes our wonderful mind systems.

Questions and Assignments for Further Discussion

1. Given the categorical conditioning of mind-body duality in Western culture as compared to the systemic conceptualization of mind discussed in this chapter, how might a clinician most therapeutically respond to a person in care who has been told or has come to believe their symptoms are "all in their mind"?
2. Consider the phrase "… *how* we don't fit that diagnostic template … is the key to how we can move beyond the condition's limitations …" and provide examples of how it is illustrated in each of the characters' stories.
3. In the clinical encounter with George, how does Robinson make use of Rossi's Four-Stage process? At what stage does he join George? At what stage is George most likely to be when he leaves the office. What is the clinical evidence for this in the story?

Notes

1 Some may argue that eidetic memory, so-called "photographic memory" is an exception or a rebuttal to this contention of memory's fallibility. Some people do have better abilities than others to fix sensory (visual, auditory, olfactory, tactile, kinetic) aspects of a scene, or simply memorize a page of numbers and reproduce them on an examination: memorization. We would counter that, even in these cases, the context will continue to change with life experience and learning, even if some content does not.

2 These terms, "epithetic" and "conservative," from a mind-plasticity view, are further defined in Chapter 4.

References

Alfano, A. (2013). How do starling flocks create those mesmerizing murmurations? Cornell Laboratory of Ornithology. Retrieved September 30, 2019 from www.allaboutbirds.org/how-do-starling-flocks-create-those-mesmerizing-murmurations/

Allport, D. A. (1985). Distributed memory, modular systems and dysphasia. In S. K. Newman & R. Epstein (Eds.), *Current perspectives in dysphasia* (pp. 32–60). Edinburgh: Churchill Livingstone.

Benedetti, F. (2014). *Placebo effects* (2nd ed.). London, UK: Oxford University Press.

Cavagna, A., Cimarelli, A., Giardina, I., Parisi, G., Santagati, R., Stefanini, F., & Viale, M. (2010). Scale-free correlations in starling flocks. *Proceedings of the National Academy of Sciences*. doi:10.1073/pnas.1005766107

Chalmers, D. J. (2010). *The character of consciousness*. New York, NY: Oxford University Press.

Crum, A. J., Corbin, W. R., Brownell, K. D., & Salovey, P. (2011). Mind over milkshakes: Mindsets, not just nutrients, determine ghrelin response. *Health Psychology*, *30*(4), 424–429. doi:10.1037/a0023467

Crum, A. J., & Langer, E. J. (2007). Mind-set matters: Exercise and the placebo effect. *Psychological Science*, *18*(2), 165–171. doi:10.1111/j.1467-9280.2007.01867.x

Crum, A. J., Phillips, D. J., Goyer, J. P., Akinola, M., & Higgins, E. T. (2016). Transforming water: Social influence moderates psychological, physiological, and functional response to a placebo product. *PLoSONE*, *11*(11): e0167121. doi:10.1371/journal.pone.0167121

Damasio, A. (2010). *Self comes to mind*. New York, NY: Vintage Books.

Dana, D. A., & Porges, S. W. (2018). *Polyvagal theory in therapy: Clinical applications of the polyvagal theory*. New York, NY: W. W. Norton.

Edelman, G. M. (2005). *Wider than the sky: The phenomenal gift of consciousness*. New Haven, CT: Yale University Press.

Engels, F. (1892). *The condition of the working class in England in 1844*. F. Kelley, Trans.). London, UK: Swan Sonnenschein. Retrieved from. https://books.google.com/books?id=B4YpAAAAYAAJ&printsec=frontcover&dq=engels+condition+working+class+in+england+1844&hl=en&sa=X&ved=2ahUKEwiK-dT6usnkAhVlnVwKHbbWARkQ6AEwBHoECAEQAg#v=onepage&q&f=false

Groopman, J. (2017, October 2). The real message of the 2017 Nobel Prize in physiology or medicine. *The New Yorker*. Retrieved from www.newyorker.com/tech/elements/the-real-message-of-the-2017-nobel-prize-in-physiology-medicine

Hebb, D. O. (2009). *The organization of behavior: A neuropsychological theory* [e-book]. Retrieved from https://books.google.com/books?id=ddB4AgAAQBAJ&printsec=frontcover&dq=organization+of+behavior+hebb&hl=en&sa=X&ved=2ahUKEwjL_pSvv8nkAhV8VRUIHRZaD4UQ6AEwAHoECAMQAg#v=onepage&q=organization%20of%20behavior%20hebb&f=false

Heisenberg, W. Z. (1927). Über den anschaulichen Inhalt der quantentheoretischen Kinematik und Mechanik. *Zeitung für Physik*, *43*, 172–198. doi:10.1007/BF01397280

Hill, R., & Rossi, E. L. (2017). *The practitioner's guide to mirroring hands: A client-responsive therapy that facilitates natural problem-solving and mind–body healing*. Carmarthen, UK: Crown House.

Hunt, G. (2013). In murmurations, starlings have a Darwinian dance partner. Cornell Laboratory of Ornithology. Retrieved from www.allaboutbirds.org/in-murmurations-starlings-have-a-darwinian-dance-partner/

Jaynes, J. (2000). *The origin of consciousness in the breakdown of the bicameral mind*. New York, NY: Houghton Mifflin Harcourt.

Jensen, M. P. (2016). Brain oscillations and diurnal variations in hypnotic responsiveness: Is there an optimal time to be hypnotized? *International Journal of Clinical and Experimental Hypnosis*, *64*(1), 137–145. doi:10.1080/00207144.2015.1099408

Kandel, E. R. (2007). *In search of memory: The emergence of a new science of mind.* New York, NY: W. W. Norton.

Kaptchuk, T. J. (2018). Open-label placebo: Reflections on a research agenda. *Perspectives in Biology and Medicine, 61*(3), 311–334. doi:10.1353/pbm.2018.0045

Kaptchuk, T. J., & Miller, F. G. (2018). Open label placebo: Can honestly prescribed placebos evoke meaningful therapeutic benefits? *BMJ, 363*: k3889. doi: 10.1136/bmj.k3889.

Kirsch, I. (2014). Antidepressants and the placebo effect. *Zeitschrift für Psychologie, 222*(3), 128–134. doi:10.1027/2151-2604/a000176

Kreipe, R. (2019, April). Personal communication with the author.

Levine, P. A. (2010). *In an unspoken voice: How the body releases trauma and restores goodness.* Berkeley, CA: North Atlantic Books.

Liminal. (n.d.). In *Merriam-Webster online.* Retrieved from www.merriam-webster.com/dictionary/liminal

Lodish, H. F., Berk, A., Darnell, J. E., Zipursky, S. L., Baltimore, D., & Matsudaira, P. (2000). *Molecular cell biology.* New York, NY: W. H. Freeman.

Maxwell, W. (1980). *So long, see you tomorrow.* New York, NY: Alfred A. Knopf.

Moerman, D. E. (2002). *Meaning, medicine and the placebo effect.* Cambridge, MA: Cambridge University Press.

Ogden, P., & Fisher, J. (2015). *Sensorimotor psychotherapy: Interventions for trauma and attachment.* New York, NY: W. W. Norton.

Ongaro, G., & Kaptchuk, T. J. (2018). Symptom perception, placebo effects, and the Bayesian brain. *Pain, 160*(1), 1–4. doi:10.1097/j.pain.0000000000001367

Pert, C. B. (1997). *Molecules of emotion.* New York, NY: Scribner.

Pert, C. B., Ruff, M. R., Weber, R. J., & Herkenham, M. (1985). Neuropeptides and their receptors. *Journal of Immunology, 135*(2), 820s–826s. Retrieved from: http://candacepert.com/articles/neuropeptides-and-their-receptors-a-psychosomatic-network/

Porges, S. W. (2011). *The polyvagal theory: Neurophysiological foundations of emotions, attachment, communication, and self-regulation.* New York, NY: W. W. Norton.

Rossi, E. L. (1993). *The psychobiology of mind-body healing: New concepts of therapeutic hypnosis* (2nd ed.). New York, NY: W.W. Norton.

Rossi, E. L. (2002). *The psychobiology of gene expression: Neuroscience and neurogenesis in hypnosis and the healing arts.* New York, NY: W. W. Norton.

Rossi, E. L. (2019a, May). Personal communication with the author (LIS).

Rossi, E. L., & Rossi, K. L. (2019). A quantum field theory (QFT): Integrating Feynman's path integral of physics with Milton Erickson's pathways of effective consciousness and cognition in neuropsychotherapy. *The Neuropsychotherapist, 7*(4), 30–38. Retrieved from: www.thescienceofpsychotherapy.com/a-quantum-field-theory/

Rossi, K. L. (2019b, May). Personal communication with the author (LIS).

Selye, H. (1955). Stress and disease. *Science, 122*(3171), 625–631. doi:10.1126/science.122.3171.625

Taylor, P. G., & Sugarman, L. I. (2013). Hypnosis and young people with developmental diffabilities. In L. I. Sugarman, W. Wester, III, & W. C. Wester (Eds.), *Therapeutic hypnosis with children and adolescents* (pp. 297–324). New York, NY: Crown House.

Turner, V. (1974). Liminal to liminoid in play, flow, and ritual: An essay in comparative symbology [pdf]. *Rice University Studies, 60*(3), 53–92. Retrieved from: https://scholarship.rice.edu/bitstream/handle/1911/63159/article_RIP603_part4.pdf

Van der Kolk, B. A. (2014). *The body keeps the score.* New York, NY: Viking.

van der Veen, D. R., & Gerkema, M. P. (2017). Unmaking ultradian rhythms in gene expression. *Journal of the American Societies for Experimental Biology*, *32*(2), 743–750. doi:10.1096/fj.201600872R

Yapko, M. D. (2009). *Depression is contagious: How the most common mood disorder is spreading around the world and how to stop it*. New York: Free Press.

Lyle's Story

Lyle's Mother

This was long ago. Long before the days when elementary school kids all played with cell phones and computer games instead of actual toys. But Lyle —of course he had to be different.

I've kept this photograph. That's Mrrow Housecat. And Doggie Droopsag. And Teddy Bear. And all of the Big Cats in a line, guarding his bed: Tygee Tiger, his best friend, followed by Leo Lion, Leaper Leopard, Cheaper Cheetah, Jaggar Jaguar, Bobbie Bobcat, and Ozzie Ocelot. He never got a panther, though. Or a saber-toothed tiger. He always really wanted a saber-toothed tiger. Of course, they're extinct, so it stands to reason they're hard to locate. And he was disappointed that he never got a snow leopard, which was on his wish list for a long time. They're rare, in real life, as well as in the stuffed version, assuming it exists. And there you can see all of his army men, lined up in front of the stuffed animals, as his first line of defense.

This was, I suppose, his command center. When I asked what it was all about, he just said "games." I admit, I didn't get it. To me, it was all "bad habits."

Lyle and the Bad Habits

Lyle was in dreamville as long as he could stay inside the perimeter of his defenses.

Back then, he still wet the bed. He didn't like waking up in cold wet sheets, but he said it wasn't his fault. He couldn't help it. That was one bad habit, I suppose. Like sucking his thumb, which he also did.

And another one: he was constipated all the time. Because of what he ate, I presume, and what he didn't eat.

And sometimes back then he would go and sit down someplace and empty his bowels. I guess it was like an infantile portable dreamville. But then he'd wake up from the dream and be in trouble. That is—in trouble with me. Right. But another bad habit. To go to school, he had to stop doing that. And he did very much want to go to school, where he could find books about Big Cats. And so long as he was in school, his sisters were out of sight.

Of course, it was impossible for him to sit still at a desk all day long at school, but it was better than being at home. His favorite teacher was Mrs. Porter. She was nice. Sometimes she let Lyle write stories in class after he finished the math problems.

Food was another big problem. The only things he ate were totally not healthy: white flour, white rice, white pasta, added sugar. He ate no fruits or vegetables. No meat, not even hot dogs. Tomato sauce, but only if the tomatoes came from a can and were completely smoothed out, so there were no seeds—nothing in it that looked remotely like a tomato. And almost nothing with fiber or protein. He ate creamy peanut butter and grape jelly for lunch every school day of his life. He never bought the school lunches. I believe he would have starved if not for Peter Pan peanut butter.

But he was incredibly stubborn about it. We tried to get him to eat, but he wouldn't have it. Once at the dinner table I tried to get him to eat a hard-boiled egg. He took a small bite, but then he thought he detected a tiny fragment of egg shell and threw up all over the table. You can imagine how that went over with his sisters. So that was another bad habit.

At one point he realized he was very very hungry. The chicken I was cooking smelled delicious. But of course he couldn't eat it. If he tried, the whole family would make a huge fuss about it, especially his sisters. *Look at Lyle! Lyle's eating chicken! He's eating food he never eats! Mom, why doesn't Lyle eat like a normal person?*

Lyle Makes a Friend

Before Kenneth, his stuffed animals were his only friends. He could hold them. They were soft and fuzzy. They never hurt him. For a long time, Lyle had no friends, but then somehow he became friends with Kenneth.

He didn't know how to be with people, but with Kenneth, it didn't matter.

Which brings up another bad habit. If Kenneth called after school to invite Lyle over to play, Lyle always said "Naah." It was just a reflex. It wasn't that he had something else to do or somewhere else to go or didn't want to play with Kenneth. He would just automatically say "Naah." One afternoon, I got so tired of this that I interfered. I heard the phone ring, so I picked up the receiver and answered. Sure enough, it was Kenneth. But when I tried to hand the phone to Lyle, he wouldn't take it. So I ended up inviting Kenneth to come over and play at our house. Which worked out fine—for me. But what did Lyle learn from this?

So what was it about Kenneth? He was amazingly tactful for a nine-year-old boy. Most kids would pester Lyle, asking why there were so many things he wouldn't eat. But as soon as Kenneth learned what Lyle wouldn't eat, Kenneth didn't bring it up again. He made it easy. He even told his mother what kind of sandwich to make so Lyle wouldn't have to turn down the food Kenneth's mother offered.

Kenneth was a good athlete; Lyle was not, but somehow Kenneth found ways they could play outside together. Maybe it could be that Kenneth and Lyle made friends because they were both new to the same school, and were in the same class. There was no one left to be best friends with.

But however it began, they were friends. Lyle still would never call or invite Kenneth to come over. But once they got together, Lyle stoppped routinely saying "Naah" and started saying "Yes" to everything. Suddenly, it was, "Do you want to play frisbee?" "OK." "Do you want to play catch?" "All right."

So maybe that was Lyle's first bad habit that turned into good. Partly good, at least.

Then, in fifth grade, Kenneth's family moved away to Texas.

4 Trance-Formation

How We Change Our Minds

Main Ideas

1. Trance is a dynamic process of mind-change that alters function, occurring both intentionally and unintentionally. Trance is how we "go plastic."
2. Novelty, especially in the context of social relationships, is a common initiating/liminal element.
3. There are measurable characteristics of trance, from intercellular to behavioral.
4. Trance is not owned by its intention. As far as the mind is concerned, prayer, daydreaming, hypnosis, and yoga are all the same trance.

If you have been reading this book, you have been changing your mind. Of course, that may also be true of any other book you read. But this is the one you are reading in this passing time right now. If you stop reading for a moment, sit back, sigh, look away, or close your eyes and simply process, in your own way, what these words, "changing your mind" mean to you, then you will change your mind some more. Considering the depths of mind-building that we probed in Chapter 3, you might wonder, while you do this, whether you are simply changing it superficially by making a bit more of a certain class of messenger molecules, strengthening some synaptic connection, tweaking autonomic states, and editing some engrams. Or maybe, given the time of day, your motivating energy, and your accelerating struggle to figure things out, you are now bursting into a realization, with heightened levels of immediate early gene expression, an intense sense of enlightenment, and an "AHA!" moment. Or, perhaps, given your state of mind and the time of day, you have just read this paragraph three times and are bewildered, muttering, "Huh?"

What forces drive the wondrous, elaborate, and evolving system of mind to shift profoundly, to change course? Why and how does it sometimes do that more readily than at others? What are the internal and external influences that are most likely to drive that transformation? What does research tell us about the neurobiological correlates of these internal paradigm shifts? What has research not yet unveiled? How do we intentionally and autonomously change our own minds? And what's this word "trance" got to do with it? These are the questions for discussion in this chapter.

Actually, in the previous chapter, it was difficult to describe mind as a static system. It was like describing a bud opening into a flower or a caterpillar metamorphosing into a butterfly, using only a photograph or diagram. The changing mind, like an integrative and collaborative kind of modern dance, is more than the sum of the behaviors of the dancers. That process—the "how" of it—is an emergent property. So, our focus now turns to *how* you considered that phrase, "changing your mind," at the beginning of this chapter a couple of paragraphs back. That is your trance.

In this chapter, we continue laying the foundation for a new health care paradigm by discussing trance. As we will explain more fully, we use "trance" to mean the *process* of developing plasticity, malleability, agility, and further, resilience of mind. This is quite a different definition of trance than is commonly used. So we will start by discussing the derivation of that traditional meaning and its (limiting) associations, especially when it is linked with formal hypnotic procedures. Then we will discuss how we may redefine trance to align with a wider range of phenomena and abilities that have to do with changing our minds. Next, we will attempt to trace trance from the outside in—from our trance behavior to the biological mechanisms beneath it. We will consider relevant research that provides clues about some of the psychobiological processes that may participate in trance, even though our understanding is wonderfully incomplete. We will introduce the roles that human development—our programmed, unfolding abilities—and social relationships play in trance, in preparation for deeper and empirical discussions in parts II (Chapters 6 through 8) and III (Chapters 9 through 11) of our book. Finally, we will consider how we use trance intentionally, thereby setting the stage for the next chapter in this opening part of our book, "Hypnosis: The Healer's Art."

Defining and Redefining Trance

Merriam Webster (2019) defines trance as "a sleeplike state … characterized by partly suspended animation with diminished or absent sensory and motor activity … a state of profound abstraction or absorption." It originates from the Latin verb *transire:* to pass through, to cross. In Middle English and Anglo-French it became associated with crossing into rapture, coma, and death. Of course, it persists as a prefix in words like transition, transport, transpire, transform, and contemporarily, in reference to persons who traverse binary gender identity and expression as "trans." Trance, related to an aspect of mind we identified in the previous chapter, is liminal.

In its common usage, trance is often linked to hypnosis, as defining what hypnosis, first and foremost, *does*. Even when no intentional hypnosis procedure is taking place, we often add the descriptor "hypnotic" when one is engaged in quiet reflection, reverie, prayer, or absorbed in observation. Trance also tends to carry the implication of receptivity, possession, dissociation, or some other dissolution of boundaries of self, including being subject to undue influence (Wickramasekera, 2015; see also Hassan, 2018).

This last inference, and the imprecision of the term (like mind and hypnosis) has caused many in the field to shun it. We are keeping it, along with mind and hypnosis. It has historical roots, and can be usefully purposed. Unlike psychoneuroimmunology, for example, trance is both concise and more than the sum of its parts.

As hypnosis has traditionally been taught and practiced, trance induction (e.g., James Braid's previously described eye-fixation technique, instructions and scripts for relaxation, or suggestions for being focused, comfortable, and receptive) is a prerequisite. It is the first step in preparing the participant for hypnotic influence. From a relational point of view trance evokes demand characteristics, compliance, and expectations for suggestibility. As we will discuss in the next chapter on hypnotic skills, the necessity and value of induction is controversial. In sum, trance has come to mean a state of mind in which one has a degree of dissociation, absorption, and receptivity to influence, either naturally occurring, intentionally, or as a result of a hypnotic influence.

Aligned with our more holistic thesis, we are revising that definition of trance. First, we are divorcing it from hypnosis, prayer, meditation, yoga, indigenous healing dances, or any other means for obtaining it. While there are different kinds of trances, the differences are best attributed to the person who creates or "owns" it; in other words, the resources and talents within the mind of the person who is engaged in their trance, not the ritual or practice intended to achieve it. So there is limited, if any, validity in referring to a "hypnotic trance" to distinguish it from a prayer or reading trance. There may be validity in distinguishing *how* the person engaged in trance is *using* it, because there are likely distinct neurobiological functions activated with an individual's different intentions. But for our redefinition, different means of entering trance represent different doors into the same room.

Next, we are going to call trance a *process*, not a state. States are static, fixed: a photograph or a frame of a movie film. We define trance as dynamic, flowing, and temporal: the dance produced by the dancers, the musical waves produced by the orchestra, Heraclitus's river. It is the percolating process of producing possibilities. If trance is a state, it is a *state of change*. There is real, though limited, value in referring to trance as a state. For example, sympathetic nervous system arousal, coupled with elevated circulating levels of epinephrine and cortisol, affects sensory, motor, cognitive encoding, and memory formation in what is termed a "state-dependent" fashion. We can retrieve from memory and re-enact—i.e., "bring to mind"—state-dependent learning, memory and behavior (Rossi, 2002) in preparation for musical, athletic, or teaching performance. We can use this framework to address the residue of trauma and heal through it. The point we are making here is that the boundaries we place on that experience—when we imagine it started and ended and what we have chosen (non-consciously) to include and exclude in the state—are contrived in order to make the experience acceptable and accessible. We refer to a trance state as memory. Those boundaries are imagined. Trances always and only happen in the present.

Finally, the product of that process, what trance *creates*, is plasticity. As we discussed when considering mind in Chapter 3, we do not mean only *neuro*plasticity. There cannot be neuroplasticity without resonance throughout the integrated and embodied mind. So, what is it that is becoming more plastic or malleable in the process of trance? The big answer is mind. The specific answer is "connections." Imagine that our minds are composed of complex, redundant, and embodied information transportation systems, as they are. There are major rail lines, highways, light rail, two-lane roads, dirt roads, bike paths, and trails in the woods, complete with bridges, tunnels, and traffic signals. You might give each different course a color. Imagine the incredibly complex and wonderful map they would make, in the shape of your body. Of course, the pathways meet in various ways: hubs, stations, and even simple, at-grade crossings. The entire network is subject to weather and climate change (mediated at least by the mix of messenger molecules and the sway of the autonomic nervous system). The more established and enduring the route—the "harder" it is "wired"—the more resilient it is in this flow of accumulating experiences.

Once you have all that in mind, imagine the paths softening and melting. Like objects in a painting by Salvador Dali, they morph. They can flow into one another, changing direction, connections, and even form. A trail can become a road, and the reverse. New roads and rails can be laid down, old ones can be become grown-over through lack of use, some can slide over to make parallel connections. What happens next, and how we rearrange this network of experience, depends on what we *do* with the process of plasticity that we are calling trance. That is what hypnosis is about. Trance is simply the process of melting or softening the connections, disrupting what we believe we know and have organized. We can imagine trance as the preamble to life events. Trance is the preparation for the liminal.

Considering Trance from the Outside In

What does it look like when we "go plastic"? How does our behavior change? A look of wonder. A wrinkled brow. Eyes wide-open, mouth agape. Closed eyes. Lost in thought. A look of consternation. Being still, even momentarily catatonic, as we get our minds around an emerging understanding. Struggling, pacing back and forth, wrestling with internal demons. A wide variety of facial expressions, postures, and behaviors come to mind. All are embodied aspects of those engrams that we introduced in the previous chapter. We recognize them as signaling introspection and questioning that, in turn, lead to interoception. These behaviors can be mapped onto the Incubation and Breakthrough stages of Rossi's four-stage ultradian model, which we introduced in Chapter 3. There is a reckoning with uncertainty and novelty, in preparation for something imminent.

Because this type of experience is common, even archetypal, it has been subjected to broad scrutiny across artistic and scientific disciplines. Consider Rodin's *Thinker* (1904), Mihaly Csikszentmihalyi's *Flow* (2008), and the aforementioned work of Ernest Rossi (2002) on the "Novelty-Numinosum-Neurogenesis" effect. There is something that draws us in when we encounter these representations of trance behavior. Carl Jung (1959/2014) recognized that such archetypes

> … cannot be integrated simply by rational means, but require a dialectical procedure, a real coming to terms with them, often conducted by the patient in dialogue form, so that, without knowing it, he puts into effect the alchemical definition of the *meditatio*: 'an inner colloquy with one's good angel.'
>
> (p. 40)

In short, trance is contagious.

In order to animate this point, let's re-enact one of the more epic, iconic, and popular cinematic examples, the opening "Dawn of Man" scene from Kubrick's (1968) *2001: A Space Odyssey*. Set in the early Paleolithic Era, early hominids begin to use bones as tools, elevating their status from prey to predator, from victim to autonomous agent. The soundtrack builds from the sound of wind and the barks and howls of the ape-like, crouching pre-Neanderthals, to the swelling disharmony of the choral composition, *In Hoc Signo Vinces* (conventionally translated into English as "In this sign thou shalt conquer"; Burning Rome, 1968), as the increasingly upright Neanderthals encounter the mysterious black monolith that symbolizes truth, intelligence, and transcendence. Then, as the scene rises to a peak and the even-more-erect pre-Homo-Sapiens pick up bones, using them as weapons to attack and subdue a less-evolved, stooped clan, the score introduces Richard Strauss' (1896) *Also Sprach Zarathustra*. With the final, fading organ chord of the Strauss work, the scene closes as the triumphant early human aggressor tosses his weapon toward the sky in slow-motion, and the action cuts from the gently twirling, suspended bone to a rotating space station. Thus, Kubrick ripples the experience of plasticity through about 400,000 years of space-time, from one early man to humankind. We resonate with the ongoing theme of discovery, of "AHA!" moments.

What do we know about the psychobiology subsumed by this phenomenology we are calling trance? Like the reputed blind men describing the elephant, the methods for getting at this question are varied, overlapping, and incomplete. We divide them into three groups: (1) brain imaging that renders visual representations of *where* an activity is occurring; (2) monitoring electrical activity (electroencephalography) that can discern with less spatial accuracy *what type* of activity is occurring; and, (3) measures of gene expression (RNA microarrays) in response to provocative stimuli that tell us *when* our trance evocation crosses an evocative threshold. None of these methods have yet yielded anything resembling a thorough understanding of the psychobiology of trance phenomena. There are just too many disparate experimental approaches and conditions being applied to too many different characterizations of trance to produce coherence. But there are compelling clues in this confusion.

Brain Imaging Studies

Brain imaging in real time captures our imaginations and promises real answers to the vexing question, "What were you thinking?" Given the anatomic, localizing nature of this technology, perhaps it better answers the question, "Where were you thinking?" Much of the anatomical and functional study of trance has been done in research laboratory protocols in which standard "inductions" are delivered to those participants who meet criteria for being "high or low hypnotizables" (using assessments described in Chapter 2). Functional magnetic resonance imaging (fMRI), positron emission tomography (PET) and, to a lesser extent, magnetoecephalography (MEG) and near-infrared spectroscopy (NIR) have been employed to study the induction process, usually compared to a control condition labeled "normal waking" or "wakefulness" (Landry & Raz, 2015; Villringer, Planck, Hock, Schleinkofer, & Dirnagl, 1993). Each of these methods monitor localized changes in energy flow in the brain to develop pixels that can be summed by computers to produce multi-dimensional images. Such images represent the geography of brain activity at various points in time under controlled conditions; for example, before and after receiving instructions for trance induction.

Across various experimental contexts, images derived from trance induction without any task-specific suggestions mainly depict the engagement of the frontal and thalamic areas (Deeley et al., 2012; Demertzi et al., 2011; Egner, Jamieson, & Gruzelier, 2005; Faymonville et al., 2000, 2003; McGeown, Mazzoni, Venneri, & Kirsch, 2009; Müller, Bacht, Schramm, & Seitz, 2012; 2013; Rainville, Hobauer, Bushnell, Duncan, & Price, 2002; Vanhaudenhuyse et al., 2009). When participants report feelings of relaxation and absorption, neuroimaging shows regulation of alertness and attentional processing involving the fronto-parietal attention network areas (Rainville et al., 2002). The brain's "resting state," attributed to activity in brain regions termed the "default mode network," refers to the condition of spontaneous cerebral interactions in the absence of task-directed activities (Fox & Raichle, 2007).

Imaging resting state activity with and without hypnotic induction reveals decreased activity in the brain's default mode network and spontaneous generation of cognitions (Buckner, Andrews-Hanna, & Schacter, 2008). Simultaneously, there is increased activity in the frontoparietal attention network (Deeley et al., 2012; McGeown et al., 2009). This decrease in spontaneous background thinking co-occurring with intensified attention may fit with the notion of trance being a process of increased absorption and susceptibility to external influence.

There is also evidence of dissociation of control, and monitoring of perception and cognitive-processing after induction, such that the dorsolateral prefrontal cortex, a brain region associated with attention and cognitive control (Corbetta, Patel, & Shulman, 2008; Nee et al., 2013), and the anterior cingulate cortex, that chiefly participates in monitoring cognitive conflict (Botvinick, 2007; Botvinick, Cohen, & Carter, 2004; Shenhav, Botvinick, & Cohen, 2013), decouple with hypnotic induction (Egner & Raz, 2007). The anterior cingulate cortex also plays a role in processing noxious stimuli and negative affect, such as in pain (Faymonville et al., 2000; Maquet et al., 1999; Schulz-Stübner et al., 2004). Using fMRI, researchers have shown reduced activity in the anterior cingulate in the face of pain and after induction without specific suggestion to alter pain sensation. This has led to speculation that induction correlates with altered connectivity between the frontal (processing) and somatosensory (receiving) areas of the brain, further supporting dissociative aspects of trance (Vanhaudenhuyse et al., 2009).

As compelling as it is, this type of research has limited applicability to our model of trance as the process of plasticity. It is less an image-generating exploration of episodes of plasticity as it is imaging the effects of series of "suggestions" (or "hypnotic inductions") on the activity in different brain areas. In other words, these studies don't necessarily reveal what happens when we spontaneously or naturally "go plastic." They show what our brains do when we are invited to relax, stop thinking, and become absorbed in experimental settings. Not surprisingly, the data shows that we quiet our thoughts and increase our attention when asked to do so. They are centered around a conceptualization of trance as preparation for suggestive influence. Like all refined, highly controlled, and thus reproducible research, this body of work lacks **ecological validity**, applicable to the real world. We are not claiming that these imaging findings are irrelevant to trance as plasticity—the dissociative aspects may be particularly germane—but only that they grant a narrow view of an expansive phenomenon.

Electroencephalographic Studies

Studies of our brain's electromagnetic oscillations—as representations of our dynamic, internal conversations—may yield more ecologically valid information. We need to provide you with a cursory explanation of how these are used and interpreted before continuing. For more depth consider Buzsáki's (2006) *Rhythms of the Brain* and a review by Jensen, Adachi, and Hakimian (2015a).

Neurons "firing" and "wiring" together—the collective and coordinated pulsations of current along the axons of the 100 billion neurons that collaborate within our brains—comprise our "brain waves." Just as we may attempt to listen in through the wall while outside of a convention hall on the flow of conversation among one billion conventioneers within, an array of scalp electrodes can attempt to "listen in" on our brain's electrical activity. It may seem that little sense could be made of the cacophony of conversation in the convention hall, the flow of information contained within the various discussions, debates, and tête-à-têtes. But the exchanges are not random. While we can only monitor the "sounds," whether auditory or electrical, on the periphery, near our surface sensors, those signals are coordinated with, perhaps in response to, and so reflective of, deeper activities. Now imagine that you have happened upon a convention of musicians—100 billion of them inside the walls of that convention hall—who have brought their instruments and choral voices to perform a symphony. If we monitor their music through the wall, we can get its gist—rhythms, harmonies, and the overall flow of it. More, we can deduce what the conductor, deep in the center of hall, might be doing. This musical metaphor is more apt because functional meaning of neuronal conversations can be correlated with their frequencies, the firing rhythms of groups of neurons "wiring together."

Since the first electroencephalograms (EEGs) were reported by Berger (1929), the oscillatory nature of brain waves has been scrutinized as proxies for the activities of neuronal networks. The frequency (cycles per second, Hertz, Hz, 1 Hz = 1 cycle/second) have been conventionally grouped as bandwidths, from slower to faster: delta (0.5–4.0 Hz), theta (4.0–8.0 Hz), alpha (8.0–13.0 Hz), beta (13.0–30.0 Hz), gamma (30.0–60.0 Hz), and high gamma (60.0–200.0 Hz). The amplitude (wave height) provides an indicator of the number of neurons that are firing in each frequency band. And EEG signal power in specific frequency bands may be used as a way of gaining insight into brain states. EEG measures not only likely reflect cortical function at a network level but also (with limits) focal brain activities. The correlates of brain oscillations at different bandwidths (e.g., sleep states: Ferrara & De Gennaro, 2011; Poe, Walsh, & Bjorness, 2010; memory function: Ferrara & De Gennaro, 2011; Klimesch, 1999, 2012; mood: Davidson, 1992; Fumoto et al., 2010; Yu et al., 2011) are easier to demonstrate for lower frequency (theta and alpha) oscillations, because slower waves are easier to detect through the bone and skin between the brain and the electrode (just like the bass of a neighbor's stereo is easier than the treble to hear through the wall between apartments). But the influence of hypnosis on brain oscillations has been reported for a variety of frequency bands.

Supported by a number of lines of evidence, theta power in particular is linked to the formation and retrieval of declarative (narrative) memory in the temporal lobes and in particular the hippocampus and amygdala (which "flavors" the emotional content of memory). In addition, these structures have dense connectivity with virtually all higher brain functions, allowing theta broad spatial and, it is hypothesized, coordinating, influence. Gamma frequencies seem to be associated with specific tasks performed by groups of neurons throughout the brain, especially in sensory modes, and simultaneously across congruent and related areas. This has led to the hypothesis that theta plays a "binding" role in coordinating spatially distant functions performed by the neurons firing in faster (i.e., gamma) frequencies. Theta is hypothesized to have this effect on gamma by "phase-locking" gamma frequencies, in a sense regulating gamma's functions. As Jensen et al (2015a) put it:

> Based on these ideas, it has been speculated that the hippocampus and amygdala, via theta oscillations, communicate with neuron assemblies throughout the brain via their influence on phase-locked fast oscillations, which themselves represent specific components of memory. However, we should emphasize that this latter "binding" effect of theta via theta-gamma phase linking remains a hypothesis that has yet to be adequately tested and established as fact, although preliminary evidence from a number of laboratories—mostly using data from animal memory studies—has provided preliminary support for this model (Buzsáki, 2006) for declarative memory. If evidence is found that supports this theta-gamma mechanism as playing a role in declarative memory formation and retrieval in humans, it may also help explain the findings regarding the links between theta and gamma power and hypnotic responding.
>
> (p. 239)

This serves as background to what Jensen et al. (2015a) initially called a "Preliminary Theta/Gamma Oscillation Model of Hypnosis." They hypothesize that trance functions in part through the development and influence of increased theta power which facilitates

> … access to information needed to be able to respond to suggestions for changes in one's experience, that is, the *recall* functions necessary for hypnotic responding. In addition, theta activity may also reflect new connections and new learning, for example, an increased ability to respond to post-hypnotic suggestions or to suggestions for new ideas and perspectives on a problem, that is, suggestions that use the *record* function of the brain.
>
> (p. 242, italics original)

Because of evidence that alpha frequencies also play a role in increasing responsivity to hypnotic influence, Jensen and his colleagues have revised this theory, renaming it the "slow wave" hypothesis. Jensen's most current summary of the evidence is that:

> … faster oscillations (beta and gamma) reflect the *work* of the brain (to create our experience and our response to that experience) and that slower oscillations (theta and alpha) are used by the brain to *control* the work of the brain. Hypnosis is about, in part, getting control over the brain's response to sensory and other cues. Slower oscillations are an important part of that, and having more of these can provide the brain with greater ability to exert this control. This is the "slow wave" hypothesis. Preliminary evidence is consistent with this. More research is needed to confirm this preliminary support, flesh out how slower and faster waves work together, and then apply this understanding to enhance response to hypnosis.
>
> (Jensen, personal communication, 2019, italics original)

The preliminary evidence to which Jensen referred is proof-of-principle study in which participants with multiple sclerosis and chronic pain who were randomized to hypnosis sessions (both face-to-face and recorded) preceded by neurofeedback (EEG biofeedback) training to increase theta power reported less pain than control group participants who did not receive neurofeedback training (Jensen et al., 2016). In short, for our purposes, this research suggests that theta and alpha, slow waves, may be an important clue to the brain's role in producing plasticity.

EEG studies of hypnosis often follow the same type of protocol as imaging studies in which participants are stratified into high and low hypnotizable groups based upon their responses to standardized assessments. As such these studies may suffer from the aforementioned issues of ecological validity. But this particular EEG-based approach can access brain functions that occur outside of hypnotic frames, with and without inductions. So it provides a window into more naturalistic and uncontrived environments, including our daily lives. It is intriguing to imagine a study that aligns the development of theta (using neurofeedback) along the ultradian time course of Rossi's four-stage model, for example. Can we encourage more adaptability and mind-agility just using theta-enhancement over that (BRAC) period? Or do other processes contribute to the plasticity for which theta is a just a part or a signal? Is the theta the dog's tail or the dog's emotions? One cannot make a dog happy by forcibly wagging its tail. But, conceivably, if the mind is embodied, a dog who starts wagging its tail might, as a result, start to experience happiness.

Psychophysiological Approaches to Plasticity

Outside of a hypnotic and purely neurological frame, Hope and Sugarman (2015) have posited trance as a naturalistic and systemic (embodied mind) response to novelty. They "suggest that [since] all animals are 'hard-wired' to consider and adapt to novelty, and that adaptation necessarily requires a shift to render the mind more malleable or plastic," that the well-described orienting response (OR) ought to be considered a basis for understanding trance as a process of psychobiological plasticity (p. 218). They turn back to Pavlov's (1927) recognition that animals exhibit an investigatory reflex, a "What is it?" response as "the class of negative or inhibitory reflexes (instincts) which are often evoked by any strong stimulus or even by weak stimuli, if *unusual* ..." adding "Animal hypnotism, so-called, belongs to this category" (p. 12, emphasis added). Hope and Sugarman then review a broad range of research linking imaging studies of the hippocampus, electroencephalographic data in the face of novel stimuli, and the influence of (embodied) autonomic inputs to conclude:

> Grouped together, we interpret this research as autonomic, neural, and physiological features of the OR as a framework for understanding "trance-opening." We are "hard-wired" to respond to the intensity and significance of perceived stimuli by shifting autonomic states, considering the emotional valence of the perception, and shifting attentional awareness and cognitive processing to various degrees in response to a significant and novel stimulus. In this way, the OR can be considered a model for simultaneous and efficient triggering of the systems that subsume mind, preparing them for changing degrees of connectivity. What happens next most likely depends on the persistence and intensity of the novel stimulus.
>
> (p. 221)

Rather than trance being simply and uniformly a set of behaviors that center on relaxation and attentional absorption, it can be a spectrum of behaviors and emotions—from alienating/traumatizing to falling in love—that pivot around the disruptive and dissociative force of encountering the new or unknown. This places the propensity for "trance openings" wholly within the individual and based upon their life experience (memories and engrams: i.e., what they already know). Consider new life experiences as occurring in the numerator of a "novelty ratio." When the denominator of life experience is small, such as when we are infants, or when Lulu is in a refugee camp in Sudan, the potential for novelty and trance openings are high. We have "beginners' minds." And as we accumulate a large denominator of life experiences and melding memories, the impact of anything new on our entrenched minds shrinks.

Another powerful implication of trance-as-plasticity-stimulated-by-novelty is that every sentient person is capable of trance, in their own unique way. Taylor and Sugarman (2014) and Sugarman, Garrison, and Williford (2013) have discussed hypnosis with people with developmental "diffabilities," and specifically those meeting criteria for autism spectrum disorder, to promote a personalized and strength-based approach to finding, utilizing, and celebrating individual and unique trance openings. "Hypnotizability," the ability for a given subject to accomplish a series of tasks labeled "hypnosis"—jumping through hypnotic hoops—becomes a measure of compliance with instructions and, perhaps primarily, of relationship with the assessor. In short, hypnotizability reduces to rapport.

Novelty and the OR as "en-trancing" align with Rossi's four-stage, ultradian process that leads to the "Novelty-Numinosum-Neurogenesis" effect, and fit into the model of trance as an interpersonal process that drives gene expression, or "psychosocial genomics" (Rossi, 2002). We struggle along Stage 2 in an incubating process toward creative synthesis—novelty—at Stage 3. This frame has generated an exciting and progressive research effort, in which early sentinels of altered gene expression—transcribed RNA microarrays for immediate early genes—are monitored, as study participants move through a "Creative Psychosocial Genomic Healing Experience" (CPGHE) protocol (Rossi, 2004, 2005; Rossi et al., 2008). In contrast to the relaxation/focusing inductions, as part of previously cited imaging and EEG research, the CPGHE protocol basically invites participants to internally explore a given symptom or problem by engaging a heuristic process toward some inevitable change, if not resolution, over about 20–30 minutes. Data from an initial pilot show up-regulation of 15 early response genes and down-regulation of none (Rossi et al., 2008, 2010).

What can we conclude from this review of research into trance? First, like the mind, it is not reducible to one bio-marker. In part this is due to the lack of consensual definition by those studying it: the blind men sticking with their part of the elephant. The problem is also that trance is an emergent property of changing minds: a complex and evolving system. It cannot be reduced. Next is that exciting research is being conducted, and the findings from this research are on the horizon. Imagine combining modalities—brain imaging, measures of autonomic balance, EEG, chronobiological measures, and RNA micro-arrays—while engaging participants in various types of internal numinous internal searches (derived from the CPHGE) at different times of day? This would be fantastically difficult, not to mention (currently) prohibitively expensive, but not impossible. For now, it is enough that the challenge, opportunity, and promise of such methods can inspire our own clinical creativity.

Now that we have explored the research that attempts to describe the inner workings of the process we are calling trance, we will turn our attention to some specific aspects of trance that are pertinent to therapeutic hypnosis: how it is influenced by development and relationships, and how it gets us stuck in ruts. This will lay the groundwork for more in-depth discussion of hypnosis skills in the next chapter.

Developmental Trances

In Chapter 3 we posited developmental programs and processes as currents within the system of mind. So here we ask that you imagine developmental programs as "trance-governing." Trance-as-plasticity means these unfolding algorithms preferentially drive gene expression, ultradian cycles, messenger molecules, and what is perceived as novel. As we will detail in the next section (Chapters 6 through 8), the therapeutic use of trance (what clinical hypnosis is about) requires clinicians to recognize and utilize the power of developmental dominance.

In this light, cultivating a beginner's mind—both for the clinician and the person in care—takes on new significance. Seeing problems in a new way can be a regressive act, as in, "Let's look at this [problem] as if we have never seen it before." This promotes trance by lowering the burdening weight of the denominator of experience. It also involves stepping out of the overriding developmental current and diving into another one. We commonly encounter a manifestation of this when working with adolescents. A young person becomes so caught up in their drive (imagine it as a type of gene expression) to have their first intimate relationship and be attractive to another that they lose sight of their drive to forge their own identity and self-expression (imagine it as a different type of gene expression), to "just be myself." We can address this by helping them remember what kind of person they imagine themselves becoming. This is the essence of our principle of *Temporal Touring*: encouraging and evoking the plasticity—in the hippocampus and amygdala, by shifting autonomic balance, by increasing slow wave (theta + alpha) activity and the transcription of immediate early genes—that was (in the instance of regression) or will be (in the instance of an imagined future).

Relational Trances

And what of the trance of the clinician? How does the clinician balance the use of practiced, disciplined skills with the agility to attend to the uniqueness of each individual person's abilities? The Pulitzer prize-winning poet and physician, William Carlos Williams, while never referencing clinical hypnosis, depicted the clinician's trance when he wrote:

> It's the humdrum, day-in, day-out, everyday work that is the real satisfaction of the practice of medicine; the million and a half patients a man has seen on his daily visits over a forty-year period of weekdays and Sundays that make up his life. I have never had a money practice; it would have been impossible for me. But the actual calling on people, at all times and under all conditions, the coming to grips with the intimate conditions of their lives, when they were being born, when they were dying, watching them die, watching them get well when they were ill, has always absorbed me.
>
> I lost myself in the very properties of their minds: for the moment at least I actually became *them*, whoever they should be, so that when I detached myself from them at the end of a half-hour of intense concentration over some illness which was affecting them, it was though I were reawakening

> from a sleep. For the moment I myself did not exist, nothing of myself affected me. As a consequence I came back to myself, as from any other sleep, rested.
>
> (Williams, 1932/1984, p. 119, italics original)

This dissolution of self, becoming absorbed in the "very properties of their minds," invites plasticity. The trance behavior of the clinician, the timing of their non-verbal communication, is evocative. In essence, this dyadic trance can mutually propagate plasticity. Wickramasekera (2015) has proposed and developed an empathic involvement theory of hypnosis in which he proposes that

> … the experience of hypnosis is embodied in a system of neural networks in the brain that utilizes empathy-related processes, adaptive resonance between perceptual input and top-down expectancies, and connectionist learning algorithms to (a) empathically enact the affect, cognition, body language, response expectancies, social roles, sensations, etc. that are presented to them during hypnosis in accordance with socio-cognitive theories of hypnosis; (b) engage in a convergent psychophysiological relationship with another person in accordance with psychoanalytic, Ericksonian, and polyvagal/social engagement system theories; (c) alter the empathic self/other (theory of mind) coding of phenomenological experiences during hypnosis in accordance with aspects of the neo-dissociative and socio-cognitive traditions; and (d) develop an experiential understanding of the illusion of self that may lead, in some people, to its transcendence in accordance with Bon-Buddhist, Dzogchen, and transpersonal scholars.
>
> (p. 330)

We will detail and apply these factors further in the next chapter and the third section of this book. Here we raise them to emphasize their relevance to our principle of *Relational Being*: the intensity of our empathic presence, not to mention how our nonverbal and verbal communications can and do drive trance. The clinician's balancing act is one of holding, with one hand, the denominator of their clinical experience and training, while in the other, open palm, welcoming uncertainty and creativity about the person in their care. All the while, the clinician needs to maintain their own ability to care for their own emotional needs and mental energy. Clinician self-care, often diminished in medical practice, is a requisite. One of my (LIS) teachers often said that, of all the behaviors that clinicians promote but don't necessarily practice themselves—healthy eating, regular exercise, improved sleep, avoiding tobacco—understanding and working with our own trances is required if we are going to truly care for others and ask them to engage in their own trance-work.

The Plastic Paradox

There is one more intriguing facet of plasticity that is central to this conceptualization of trance. Doidge (2015) refers to an analogy created by Alvaro Pascal-Leone that he calls the "Plastic Paradox." He writes:

> [P]lasticity is like snow on a hill in winter. If we wish to go down that hill a first time [e.g. on sled or skis], because the hill is a virgin hill, and because the snow is plastic and pliable, we can take many different paths down that hill. However, being human, if we have a good run the next time we go down that hill, we will be inclined to take a path very similar to the first if we found it very rewarding. And if we keep repeating that, we will develop tracks in the snow, and eventually ruts—precisely because the snow is plastic and pliable and easily molded—and find ourselves unable to stray from the initial path. This is a metaphor for the fact that brain plasticity is competitive, and once we build up circuits in the brain, they get very good at doing what they do and out-compete other potential circuits and ways of doing things. Thus, plasticity can give rise initially to flexible behaviors, and over time, if repeated, to rigid behaviors as well. In other words, the brain is always plastic even if our behaviors are rigid. And if they are, we then tend —to use the psychoanalytic term—to project this rigidity back onto the brain itself and assume it too is rigid.
>
> (p. 350)

So, trance allows us to both deepen our ruts (e.g., by practicing a musical instrument, or practicing anxiety responses, and re-traumatization in the face of novelty) or to creatively synthesize new ones with numinous, "AHA!" moments. We can use this dichotomy intentionally as a method for directing trance, creating a trance dichotomy. We can deepen our ruts with practice. We can call this "conservative" trance. Alternatively, we can create new engrams of experience with creativity. We can term this "epithetic" ("epi-" meaning new, upon, over, as compared to "syn-" meaning next to or like) trance. We find this a useful frame because, as a method for directing trance, hypnosis may be used therapeutically for either of these purposes. It also raises interesting questions. Can we crave uncertainty and learning new things? Can we learn to desire new learning? Can we facilitate, within ourselves and others, the habit of creating the rut of being able to change our minds? We posit that health requires psychobiological agility in both conservative and epithetic directions.

Before leaving this chapter, and by way of conclusion, we invite you to re-read this chapter's first paragraph. In particular, consider what "changing your mind" means to you now as compared to then? At what points in this chapter did you find yourself most and least absorbed? When do you find yourself getting out of your "ruts?" Why, and more importantly, how did you do that? Isn't that interesting?

Questions and Assignments for Further Discussion

1. Cite examples from each of the stories in which characters shift to increased psychobiological plasticity, or trance. What is the evidence that is happening? What is/are the novel or reinforcing factors?
2. Discuss examples of developmental priorities influencing trance (psychobiological plasticity) in each of the stories and in your own life.
3. Given the moral neutrality of trance—from undue influence to altruism—speculate on those factors that increase our likelihood of an individual being hurt or helped by trance. Consider the roles of development and relationships.
4. The plastic paradox claims we can believe that we become psychobiologically inflexible over time, through practice and repetition. What are some ways to foster awareness of this paradox, and keep the mind flexible?
5. Discuss your answers to the questions posed in the last paragraph of this chapter.

References

Berger, H. (1929). Über das Elektroenkephalogramm des Menschen [About human electroencephalograms]. *Archiv Für Psychiatrie und Nervenkrankheiten*, *87*(1), 527–570. doi:10.1007/BF01797193.

Botvinick, M. M. (2007). Conflict monitoring and decision making: Reconciling two perspectives on anterior cingulate function. *Cognitive, Affective, & Behavioral Neuroscience*, *7*, 356–366. doi:10.3758/CABN.7.4.356

Botvinick, M. M., Cohen, J. D., & Carter, C. S. (2004). Conflict monitoring and anterior cingulate cortex: An update. *Trends in Cognitive Sciences*, *8*, 539–546. doi:10.1016/j.tics.2004.10.003

Buckner, R. L., Andrews-Hanna, J. R., & Schacter, D. L. (2008). The brain's default network: Anatomy, function, and relevance to disease. *Annals of the New York Academy of Sciences*, *1124*, 1–38. doi:10.1196/annals.1440.011

Burning Rome. (1968). In Hoc Signo Vinces [Music]. In S. Kubrick, *2001: A space odyssey*. Retrieved from www.youtube.com/watch?v=3MUV88a7RKQ

Buzsáki, G. (2006). *Rhythms of the brain*. New York, NY: Oxford University Press.

Corbetta, M., Patel, G., & Shulman, G. L. (2008). The reorienting system of the human brain: From environment to theory of mind. *Neuron*, *58*(3), 306–324. doi:10.1016/j.neuron.2008.04.017

Csikszentmihalyi, M. (2008). *Flow: The psychology of optimal experience*. New York, NY: Harper Collins.

Davidson, R. J. (1992). Anterior cerebral asymmetry and the nature of emotion. *Brain and Cognition*, *20*(1), 125–151. doi:10.1016/0278-2626(92)90065-T

Deeley, Q., Oakley, D. A., Toone, B., Giampietro, V., Brammer, M. J., Williams, S. C. R., & Halligan, P. W. (2012). Modulating the default mode network using hypnosis. *International Journal of Clinical and Experimental Hypnosis*, *60*(2), 206–228. doi:10.1080/00207144.2012.648070

Demertzi, A., Soddu, A., Faymonville, M. E., Bahri, M. A., Gosseries, O., Vanhaudenjuyse, A., & Laureys, S. (2011). Hypnotic modulation of resting state fMRI default mode and extrinsic network connectivity. *Progress in Brain Research*, *193*, 309–322. doi:10.1016/B978-0-444-53839-0.00020-X

Doidge, N. (2015). Hypnosis, neuroplasticity, and the plastic parodox. *American Journal of Clinical Hypnosis*, *57*(3), 349–354. doi:10.1080/00029157.2015.985572

Egner, T., Jamieson, J., & Gruzelier, J. (2005). Hypnosis decouples cognitive control from conflict monitoring processes of the frontal lobe. *NeuroImage*, *27*(4), 969–978. doi:10.1016/j.neuroimage.2005.05.002

Egner, T., & Raz, A. (2007). Cognitive control processes and hypnosis. In G. A. Jamieson (Ed.), *Hypnosis and conscious states: The cognitive neuroscience perspective* (pp. 29–50). New York, NY: Oxford University Press.

Faymonville, M. E., Laureys, S., Degueldre, C., DelFiore, G., Luxen, A., Franck, G., & Maquet, P. (2000). Neural mechanisms of antinociceptive effects of hypnosis. *Anesthesiology*, *92*, 1257–1267. doi:10.1097/00000542-200005000-00013

Faymonville, M. E., Roediger, L., Del Fiore, G., Delgueldre, C., Phillips, C., Lamy, M., & Laureys, S. (2003). Increased cerebral functional connectivity underlying the antinociceptive effects of hypnosis. *Cognitive Brain Research*, *17*, 255–262. doi:10.1016/S0926-6410(03)00113-7

Ferrara, M., & De Gennaro, L. (2011). Going local: Insights from EEG and stereo-EEG studies of the human sleep-wake cycle. *Current Topics in Medicinal Chemistry*, *11*, 2423–2437. doi:10.2174/156802611797470268

Fox, M. D., & Raichle, M. E. (2007). Spontaneous fluctuations in brain activity observed with functional magnetic resonance imaging. *Nature Reviews Neuroscience*, *8*, 700–711. doi:10.1038/nrn2201

Fumoto, M., Oshima, T., Kamiya, K., Kikuchi, H., Seki, Y., Nakatani, Y., … Arita, H. (2010). Ventral prefrontal cortex and serotonergic system activation during pedaling exercise induces negative mood improvement and increased alpha band in EEG. *Behavioural Brain Research*, *213*, 1–9. doi:10.1016/j.bbr.2010.04.017

Hassan, S. (2018). *Combating cult mind control* (4th ed.). Newton, MA: Freedom of Mind Press.

Jensen, M. P., Adachi, T., & Hakimian, S. (2015a). Brain oscillations, hypnosis, and hypnotizability. *American Journal of Clinical Hypnosis*, *57*, 230–253. doi:10.1080/00029157.2014.976786

Jensen, M. P., Adachi, T., Tomé-Pires, C., Lee, J., Osman, Z. J., & Miró, J. (2015b). Mechanisms of hypnosis: Towards the development of a biopsychosocial model. *International Journal of Clinical and Experimental Hypnosis*, *63*, 34–75. doi:10.1080/00207144.2014.961875

Jensen, M. P., Gianas, A., George, H. R., Sherlin, L. H., Kraft, G. H., & Ehde, D. M. (2016). Use of neurofeedback to enhance response to hypnotic analgesia in individuals with multiple sclerosis. *International Journal of Clinical and Experimental Hypnosis*, *64*, 1–23. doi:10.1080/00207144.2015.1099400

Jung, C. (2014). The archetypes and the collective unconscious. In R. F. C. Hull (Trans.). *Collected works of C. G. Jung* (2nd ed. Vol. 9). London, UK: Routledge (Original work published 1959).

Klimesch, W. (1999). EEG alpha and theta oscillations reflect cognitive and memory performance: A review and analysis. *Brain Research Reviews*, *29*, 169–195. doi:10.1016/S0165-0173(98)00056-3

Klimesch, W. (2012). Alpha-band oscillations, attention, and controlled access to stored information. *Trends in Cognitive Sciences*, *16*, 606–617. doi:10.1016/j.tics.2012.10.007

Kubrick, S. (Director, Producer). (1968). *2001: A space odyssey* [Motion picture]. United States: MGM. "Dawn of Man" scene retrieved from www.youtube.com/watch?v=ypEaGQb6dJk.

Landry, M., & Raz, A. (2015). Hypnosis and imaging of the living human brain. *American Journal of Clinical Hypnosis*, *57*, 285–313. doi:10.1080/00029157.2014.978496

Maquet, P., Faymonville, M. E., Degueldre, C., Delfiore, G., Franck, G., Luxen, A., & Lamy, M. (1999). Functional neuroanatomy of hypnotic state. *Biological Psychiatry*, *45* (3), 327–333. doi:10.1016/S0006-3223(97)00546-5

McGeown, W. J., Mazzoni, G., Venneri, A., & Kirsch, I. (2009). Hypnotic induction decreases anterior default mode activity. *Consciousness and Cognition*, *18*(4), 848–855. doi:10.1016/j.concog.2009.09.001

Müller, K., Bacht, K., Schramm, S., & Seitz, R. J. (2012). The facilitating effect of clinical hypnosis on motor imagery: An fMRI study. *Behavioral Brain Research*, *231*(1), 164–169. doi:10.1016/j.bbr.2012.03.013

Nee, D. E., Brown, J. W., Askren, M. K., Berman, M. G., Demiralp, E., Krawitz, A., & Jonides, J. (2013). A meta-analysis of executive components of working memory. *Cerebral Cortex*, *23*(2), 264–282. doi:10.1093/cercor/bhs007

Pavlov, I. P. (1927). *Conditioned reflexes*. Oxford, UK: Oxford University Press.

Poe, G. R., Walsh, C. M., & Bjorness, T. E. (2010). Cognitive neuroscience of sleep. *Progress in Brain Research*, *185*, 1–19. doi:10.1016/B978-0-444-53702-7.00001-4

Rainville, P., Hobauer, R. K., Bushnell, M. C., Duncan, G. H., & Price, D. D. (2002). Hypnosis modulates activity in brain structures involved in the regulation of consciousness. *Journal of Cognitive Neuroscience*, *14*(6), 8887–8901. doi:10.1162/089892902760191117

Rodin, A. (1904). *Penseur* [Thinker]. Paris, France: Musée Rodin.

Rossi, E., Atkinson, D., Blake-Mortimer, J., Iannotti, S., Cozzolino, M., Castiglione, S., … Krippner, S. (2010). The creative psychosocial genomic healing experience ©: Administration, rationale, & research—An open invitation to mind-body psychotherapy clinical & experimental research. Retrieved from www.ernestrossi.com/ernestrossi/Research%20Group%20Papers/Protocol%20CPGHE%20v1.3.pdf.

Rossi, E., Iannotti, S., Cozzolino, M., Castiglione, S., Cicatelli, A., & Rossi, K. (2008). A pilot study of positive expectations and focused attention via a new protocol for therapeutic hypnosis assessed with DNA microarrays: The creative psychosocial genomic healing experience. *Sleep and Hypnosis: an International Journal of Sleep, Dream, and Hypnosis*, *10*(2), 39–44. Retrieved from www.ernestrossi.com/ernestrossi/PILOT%20MIND%20GENE%20ITALIAN%20RESEARCH.pdf

Rossi, E. L. (2002). *The psychobiology of gene expression: Neuroscience and neurogenesis in therapeutic hypnosis and the healing arts*. New York, NY: W. W. Norton.

Rossi, E. L. (2004). *A discourse with our genes: The psychosocial and cultural genomics of therapeutic hypnosis and psychotherapy* (S. Iannotti, Trans. & Ed.). New York, NY: Zeig, Tucker, Theisen.

Rossi, E. L. (2005). Prospects for exploring the molecular-genomic foundations of therapeutic hypnosis with DNA microarrays. *American Journal of Clinical Hypnosis*, *48*, 165–182. doi:10.1080/00029157.2005.10401514

Schulz-Stübner, S., Krings, T., Meister, I. G., Rex, S., Thron, A., & Rossaint, R. (2004). Clinical hypnosis modulates functional magnetic resonance imaging signal intensities and pain perception in a thermal stimulation paradigm. *Regional Anesthesia and Pain Medicine, 29*(6), 549–556. doi:10.1016/j.rapm.2004.09.002

Shenhav, A., Botvinick, M. M., & Cohen, J. D. (2013). The expected value of control: An integrative theory of anterior cingulate cortex function. *Neuron, 79*, 217–240. doi:10.1016/j.neuron.2013.07.007

Strauss, R. (1896). *Also sprach Zarathustra* [Music]. Munich, Germany: Joseph Aibl.

Sugarman, L. I., Garrison, B. L., & Williford, K. L. (2013). Symptoms as solutions: Hypnosis and biofeedback for autonomic regulation in autism spectrum disorders. *American Journal of Clinical Hypnosis, 56*(2), 152–173.

Taylor, P. G., & Sugarman, L. I. (2014). Hypnosis and young people with developmental diffabilities. In L. I. Sugarman & W. C. Wester, II (Eds.), *Therapeutic hypnosis with children and adolescents* (2nd ed., pp. 297–324). Bethel, CT: Crown House.

Trance. (2019). *In Merriam-Webster online dictionary*. Retrieved from www.merriam-webster.com/dictionary/trance

Vanhaudenhuyse, A., Boly, M., Balteau, E., Schnakers, C., Moonen, G., Luxen, A., … Faymonville, M. E. (2009). Pain and non-pain processing during hypnosis: A thulium-YAG event-related fMRI study. *Neuroimage, 47*(3), 1047–1054. doi:10.1016/j.neuroimage.2009.05.031

Villringer, A., Planck, J., Hock, C., Schleinkofer, L., & Dirnagl, U. (1993). Near infrared spectroscopy (NIRS): A new tool to study hemodynamic changes during activation of brain function in human adults. *Neuroscience Letters, 154*(1–2), 101–104. doi:10.1016/0304-3940(93)90181-j

Wickramasekera, I. E., II. (2015). Mysteries of hypnosis and the self are revealed by the psychology and neuroscience of empathy. *American Journal of Clinical Hypnosis, 57*(3), 330–348. doi:10.1080/00029157.2014.978495

Williams, W. C. (1984). *The Doctor Stories*. New York, NY: New Directions (Original work published 1932).

Yu, X., Fumoto, M., Nakatani, Y., Sekiyama, T., Kikuchi, H., Seki, Y., … Arita, H. (2011). Activation of the anterior prefrontal cortex and serotonergic system is associated with improvements in mood and EEG changes induced by Zen meditation practice in novices. *International Journal of Psychophysiology, 80*(2), 103–111. doi:10.1016/j.ijpsycho.2011.02.004

Stevie's Story

Stevie Goes to Yoga Class

You can call me Stevie. I mean—*call me Stevie, dammit!* It's my name … I think. It *feels* like it's becoming my name.

So there's 14 dwarves—right?—seven on the right and seven on the left. That's *Snow White* times two—all placed at the street corners of my brain, and they've all got white bristly beards so they're easy to recognize. They're sitting on long benches, where they can conveniently take notes about all the ways my life is messed up.

One thing is, I can't stop talking. Yeah. I mean even when I've stopped talking, my brain keeps right on talking, you know? Like, obviously, now. Sometimes people tell me my lips are moving even though I'm sitting alone. Talking. Because, well, I do that. Guilty as charged.

Micky says he has a cousin who's a shaman. Micky also says this shaman is male *and* female. So, like, maybe I don't have to decide. But that therapist Dad took me to was the opposite of that. It was all about "Let's squeeze Stevie into some kind of template so we can all go to bed at night, knowing we've successfully diagnosed Stevie's little problem."

I think most of what Micky says is about half right. Which may be worse than not saying anything at all.

Oh yeah. I should have said that Micky is this person who thinks he and me are friends. His name is actually Micky, not Mick or Mack or Mike or Michael. Unlike me, who was told I was Stephanie. But part of me kind of hated it. Stephanie. The name, not the person. It's not the name of that person … who is me. And that raises the question: Who is this "me." What is this vapor they try to squeeze into some therapist's template, to liquify into some caterpillar's chrysalis soup.

Anyway, so: I'm in this yoga class. Where we're supposed to stay quiet and still and just think about our breathing. Which, actually? Makes my skin crawl. I can't just sit still. And the more I think about it, the more jittery I get.

But right now the issue is that I showed up for this 6 a.m. yoga class—that's six *are-you-kidding me?* a.m.—only a little bit late, all to stay cozy-up with the Missus.

Which refers to the person who left our family to join another family a few years ago. Which I'm only doing the yoga now because Dad insisted.

And I wouldn't stay for the class except—where would I go instead? It's effing 6 a.m. And Dad tells us "be nice to the Missus". That's a big issue. But the hit or Missus mostly misses, in her pretty new life as the pretty new wife and her pretty big tropical houseplants that she throws away as soon as they stop bleeding—I mean blooming. Stop blooming.

Missus says, she and me should do yoga together. *Hnh.* Is this going to be on the test? Does the Missus really miss us? If she does, then why is she absent today? All these questions! Doesn't matter. It's like meditation: When an unwelcome thought shows up, we just toss that thought away. So let's toss it now—nice and easy, *shwisht!* I can picture that unwelcome thought floating away to a mountaintop, catching an up-draft, landing in the courtyard of a Buddhist monastery in Nepal, where it will soon instill peacefulness and clarity upon a novice as a consequence of the shimmering perfection that unanticipated thought has conveyed.

Meditation says breathe in, pause, breathe out. In, pause, out. Same as yoga. Except that like I say no matter what you call it, I still can't sit still. And there's no way I can empty my mind. It's just another game I can't play. Same game, different name.

Worse: Something about Peter—today's yoga instructor—makes me queasy. Icky—reminds me of—Micky. That Micky—but—I'll stop there. I should have known better than to listen to Micky. In fact, I do know better. If we assume that "I" is one formed thing, entity, person. Not a vapor liquifying into soup. But I—anyway. Toss those thoughts away.

It's like the two of them think they know more about me than I do. Shaping the "I" that is "me" into another template that fits their form.

But I can't toss those thoughts away. Can't believe I'm here on my yoga mat displaying all the shapes and parts of my not-really-my-girl-body-anyway to Peter and bending and twisting so close to him. But he's in charge. And here he comes now. Grrl. Git your eyes off my flesh, cowboy. Just because you're a yoga instructor? *Ha.*

But he bends my body however he wants. Peter says he's correcting my posture. He tells me when to breathe and when to stop breathing. Peter must have a God complex. Shaping me into just the image he wants.

But what does this person want from me? Sex, everyone says. Obviously. But what is sex? I'm serious. What is it? Why are people so crazy for it?

Stop! Pause the brain please. But Micky—he *is* mean. He tries to hurt me. He makes lumps of concrete harden in my innards. But I will toss that meanness away. Toss it into the cosmos. They're all mean, but Micky's the worst. Inhale, hold, exhale, cold.

I need to get out of where I am, even if I have to step naked into outer space to do it.

In physics, we learned that if we jump into space without a space suit we'll puff up, asphyxiate, and die—all in approximately 90 seconds. Not enough time for serious pain to rev up. But then, we'd be dead, wouldn't we, and we'd orbit the earth forever at a speed of 18,000 miles per hour like a life-sized astronaut statue, frozen for all eternity to a temperature of minus 454.8 degrees Fahrenheit. That would be a good thing, I think. To be freeze-dried instantly. Like coffee in little packets for the coffee machine. Whirly-girl-body and all.

I need to not think about all this. Mr. Dougal wouldn't have told us about it if they would really let that happen. Just trying to liven up the old physics class. But I think he shouldn't have said it, anyway. It waits in me, another template, another choice for the vapor-soup to form into.

But if I have to stay where Peter is, I will explode. And at school, Micky keeps "accidentally" touching my girl-body parts, and I want to know—who put his locker next to mine? I'd gladly trade in my girl-body, but what do I get in return?

And where was the Missus today? No one's reliable. No one shows up. They tell me to show up, and then they don't show up. No one answers my questions. No one even *hears* my questions.

I could go to school today. But I could only stand it if I take one of these Micky pills. And—should I do that? Everyone except Micky says no.

But Micky writes things. He showed me this thing he wrote. He calls it a poem. I remember it. I can recite it silently in my mind while we all lie here on our yoga mats, eyes on the ceiling. It goes like this:

I can't move
I can't move

I can't breathe
I can't see

I can't smell
I can't taste

I am suffocating

I have to get through it
I have to get over it

I am in brain-pain.

Fun stuff, eh? I like it because I've felt exactly like that. Like trapped in my skin. Brain in flames. Bubbling chrysalis cauldron. Nothing works. Nothing makes sense. All bridges are out. Nothing will ever make it better. I will never get fixed.

Stevie Goes to School

The Missus arrives, just as yoga class breaks up. Totally late, way too late to participate, chattering something to me about going out for breakfast together at the new Bagel & Egg place, though I don't know why I'd want to do that. She knows I'm vegan anyway. Probably nothing I could eat.

So I make up a story. Something about an English essay I have to turn in in Ms. Abood's first period AP English Literature class. Which reminds me that—oh shit—I actually *do* have an essay due first period. And I actually read the short story we're supposed to write about—it's called "The Lady or the Tyger." Actually, I kind of skimmed it. But the point is obviously the ending. The man in the story has to go through a bizarre punishment where he has to choose from two identical doors; behind one is a hungry tiger, behind the other, a beautiful lady. And at the end, the man makes a decision—but the story ends without telling which door he opens—the Lady? Or the Tyger.

Hnnh. I always liked tigers.

So I take up the Missus on her offer of a ride to school and a Bagel & Egg—that is, in my case, something that looks like a bagel and that they claim is 100% plant-based genuine food. How can this genuine food be so fake? Tastes like dust. At this point, though, I'm dizzy from lack of nourishment, so I just eat it. Dust to dust.

So the Missus drops me off at school, and I while away the rest of the time before first period in the computer lab writing a partly true essay about the choices I need to make in my actual life. And it's easy because I just have to write down what I'm thinking about what I'm drinking.

Not that I'm drinking anything. I end up imagining that I told the Missus and my Dad to get together in a room and said "Don't come out until you've graduated from kindergarten, or until you've learned to listen instead of just yammering at each other." I'd make them write essays and exchange them and keep revising them until both essays are identical. In my made-up story, the Missus comes back to the family she left behind and realizes too late what a clown her new husband is.

And then I start to get anxious, maybe because I realize that my humpity-dumpity family will never come together again and I don't have any magical powers to fix it. And then I'm just sitting there at the computer and I realize that I'm not going to show this story to Ms Abood. Here I am pouring my miserable life out, and she's going to start correcting my punctuation and pronouns? No thanks.

But then I realize that the halls are empty except for me and for some reason I'm not in Ms Abood's first period English Lit class. I'm wandering back to my locker where I check to see if maybe Micky slipped something through the slots on my locker door. Not that I'd take the pills. But if I put the little glassy bag in my backpack, I'll have it, you know? It's calming to see they're there. Just in case.

I have learned that the key to high school is showing up to raise a hand and speak a syllable when the roll is called. But today I'm already late. The name that they think belongs to whatever I am has been called and responded to with silence and stillness. Looks like I'm absent. I am not here. And yet, where am I if I'm not "here"? And so, obviously, if I go home to my room, I'll still be "here."

Conveniently, Hayden High School, the high school I go to, or usually go to, when I am really there—or here—or—I'm getting confused—The point is, my high school is only six blocks from my house. And the parental worthies are both working today, so I will incur no wrath if I make my "here" here at home instead of in the aforesaid high school. Where, to be sure, I no longer am, as I have already departed through the south doors and commenced the hardly strenuous River Street stroll which will end with my arrival on Raven Lane where what's left of my family dwells.

So. Do I take the pill and let it chill—do what it will?

5 Hypnosis

The Healer's Art

Main Ideas

1. Trance usually starts before the induction ... on the way to the clinical appointment, for example.
2. Effectiveness of hypnosis is founded on *authentic* rapport and facilitation of novelty: the clinician's trance.
3. Hypnosis can be understood as the application of basic principles and skills.
4. Hypnosis can be viewed as performance art, encompassing gesture (dance), prosody and cadence (music), and verbalization (lyrics), in order of decreasing influence.
5. Hypnosis is most effectively applied in person-centered ways, attending to the stage of change (e.g., Rossi's Four-Stage Model, transtheoretical model), developmental imperatives, and immediate needs.

This is the last of our four foundational chapters. We started with a history, depicting hypnosis as a wandering nomad, moving from theory to theory as if from house to house, in search of a home that can embrace and understand it as a whole and without limits or prejudice. Then, in Chapter 3, as if to assemble that home, we defined the mind as a richly complex, dynamically evolving, and open system of self that encodes experiences as engrams and abilities. In Chapter 4, as if to install the utilities for hypnosis' home, we defined trance as the process of psychobiological plasticity that can be cultivated and utilized by hypnosis for adaptability and change. In this chapter, we are prepared to explore how hypnosis does its work, or more aptly, how we work hypnosis. We will detail the range of skills and strategies that comprise hypnosis as a discipline for directing our changing and embodied minds. We claim that these skills are at the center of health care's common ground, in the wild garden joining the domains of medical and psychological care, where both are at their most therapeutic. In this communion, the discipline of hypnosis merges theory and practice in psychotherapy and medicine. Ultimately, we portray hypnosis as the healer's art, since art is the highest enactment of any discipline.

We will start with a critical overview of standard methods and ethics of professional training in clinical hypnosis. We will emphasize what we see as the limitations of that linear and stepwise legacy. Next, we will categorize some basic introductory skills, then more advanced strategies that (1) cultivate rapport, (2) disrupt patterns of experience, and (3) encourage new, more beneficial and healthy engrams to re-assemble. This is the discipline of clinical hypnosis. Then we will discuss these skills through the lenses of the four principles we introduced in the introduction: *Systems Thinking, Temporal Touring, Relational Being,* and *Narrative Listening*. We will compare and contrast this hypnotic discipline with related skill sets: meditation, guided imagery, neurolinguistics programming, and eye-movement desensitization and reprocessing (EMDR). In all, we hold hypnosis is most effective when it is evocative, dynamic, and person-centered, in contrast with prescriptive, formulaic, and problem/diagnosis-based approaches. Using hypnosis skills with agility and empathy is the art. We close by reexamining, with new light, why these skills lie at the heart of health and care and, in due course, a new paradigm.

Before diving in, we must provide a caveat. There are probably hundreds of books currently in print—and hundreds more no longer in print—that claim to teach how to "do hypnosis." Ours is not one of them. This is because, as a discipline of interpersonal communication, hypnosis cannot be taught one-dimensionally, from a book. Hypnosis is as much, if not more than, the *how* of communication: as much form as content. The core of the discipline of hypnosis is the pacing, prosody, posture, facial expression, and ability to adapt all of these—in addition to the subject of communication—to the needs and behaviors of the other. These must be studied, but then also refined and practiced "live" at professional, experiential workshops and under clinical supervision. Books can provide a framework. But none of them, including this one, can be an effective "how-to-do-it" guide. This chapter describes and catalogues the principled essentials of the hypnosis skill set that follow from our conceptualization of mind and trance. It is not intended nor does it aspire to compile a comprehensive list of strategies. It cannot, because hypnotic strategies are invented and refined with each new person in care. This book is intended to change your mind about hypnosis and its central place in health and healing. In subsequent chapters we will apply those skills to developmental imperatives, social relationships, and ultimately to health and care. These chapters, then, will provide a basis for practice.

The World of Hypnosis

Of course, we all know how to do hypnosis in our own way, without knowing that we know. We learn with the wisdom of our infancy how to use influential communication to manipulate our parents in order to get our needs met—just as parents strive to manage children, and siblings contend for position in the mix. As a matter of fact, the more complex and interdependent the relationship is, the more multilayered the communication becomes. As one family therapist wryly claimed, "There is no such thing as an honest expression of emotion in families." In our relationships, all of us innately refine our language of influence: in the telling of our jokes, our stories, our excuses, and even our secrets and lies. Consider examples of this in the lives of our fictional characters. Notice how George's story unfolds to Robinson and how difficult it is for Stevie to find the courage to share what s/he feels.

In larger, nonclinical settings, this language of influence is most pervasive in politics, advertising, sales, and the nefarious use of undue influence that occurs in cults, abuse, imprisonment, and enslavement. These skills are taught, practiced, and honed via mentorship, group indoctrination, and interactive media. Acts purporting to display the "mysteries of the mind" at the hands of "mentalists" and "hypnotists" have a long, lucrative history and remain popular, both in resorts and casinos, and on the college entertainment circuit. Recall that it was the travelling mesmerist Lafontaine who inspired Braid, and Du Maurier's *Trilby* that captured the imagination of the masses. These exhibitions—when they actually select willing volunteers from the audience, rather than use paid covert collaborators—primarily reveal the power of influence in an atmosphere of obedience, if not exploitation. In that sense, they compel our morbid curiosity. As Olness (2006) has discussed, perhaps this reflects a cultural wish that some external power or person can take away our problems for us. We note that abuse, undue influence, and harm can also take place in clinical settings.

One could propose, as do Hope and Sugarman (2015), that if we simply define hypnosis as influence communication, then worldwide, most hypnosis is practiced at least to manipulate others to do things that are clearly not in their own best interests, if not to harm them. Indeed, our lives have enough ways of providing us with challenges and "trance-formative" traumas. As we have noted previously, it is these naturally occurring hardships—painful, life-changing trance experiences—that provide clinicians with patients. As Milton H. Erickson is quoted as saying, "Life will bring you pain all by itself. Your responsibility is to create joy" (Rossi & Rossi 2019, personal communication).

But we are not simply defining hypnosis as influence communication. We can call such influence communication "hypnotic" since it uses language in ways similar to hypnosis. But this communication does not necessarily consider, adapt to, nor benefit its intended audience. Instead, we are defining hypnosis as a skill set and discipline for influencing, steering, and directing trance. As we explored in Chapter 4, we define trance as a process during which we are particularly plastic, susceptible, and engaged with novelty, uncertainty, and the unknown. Trance is owned by and created within each person—and often shared between clinician and client—since, like mind, it is embodied. We acknowledge a boundary problem with this definition: separating trance from "everyday plasticity." But for our clinical, non-research purposes, trance is what trance does. We use hypnosis skills to facilitate and respond to those signs of trance—autonomic changes, disrupted flow of thoughts, wonder, and disorientation—and cultivate them with both verbal and non-verbal communication including, especially, our silences.

In clinical settings, hypnosis is bound by ethical canons in exclusive service to the person in care: non-maleficence (do no harm), beneficence (do good), respect for autonomy (truth-telling, no deception, informed consent), and respect for justice (equal access). Contrast this with stage hypnosis, in which the primary beneficiary is the entertainer. The secondary beneficiary is the audience. The last, questionably, is the "volunteer."[1] We take these principles to mean that clinicians ought to use their interpersonal skills to the best of their abilities and within the limits of their broader professional competence to evoke the best abilities for self-regulation within those in their care.

This brings us to the matter of so-called "lay hypnotists." In the US, individuals with no professional licensure in health care can practice hypnosis as the sole treatment for a variety of complaints, and are rarely cited for practicing health care without a license. They can obtain training and certification from organizations that claim to be "professional" (by asserting that being a hypnotist is a profession). The majority of these individuals are likely well meaning and believe in the value of what they are doing. They may also be filling a gap in access to care. After all, there is a dearth of licensed professionals who are competent to use hypnosis therapeutically in clinical settings.

Our concern with lay hypnotists is twofold. First, as we have defined it, hypnosis is not therapy. It is a discipline for cultivating change. Lay hypnotists primarily use a prescribed system of problem-focused statements (benignly termed "suggestions"), after some standard assessment and ritualized "induction," to influence their customers. So indeed, they are doing more than hypnosis, they are purporting to treat problems. But problems are not people. Treating problems at the expense of our individuality is one of our criticisms of the dominant biomedical paradigm (further addressed in Chapter 12). Our second concern is that, since hypnosis is not therapy, a prescriptive system of influence for given problems is neither person-centered nor holistic. Hypnosis is a discipline at the heart of effective psychobiological therapy. We expect that licensed health care professionals carefully evaluate the range of appropriate treatments—whether primarily surgical, pharmacological, physically manipulative, or psychological—for an individual's unique constellation of problems. They then use hypnosis to put those treatments into place: perioperatively, to augment the beneficial effects of medicines, or to facilitate positive behavioral change. In short, the problem with lay hypnotists is that they are "hypnotists." A professional clinician is no more a "hypnotist" than a "penicillinist" or "stethoscopist" or any other "procedurist." We are concerned that lay hypnotists treat a wide range of different kind of people with a narrow range of problem-focused rituals and suggestions. At best, they limit care.

Professionals Learning Clinical Hypnosis Linearly: The Legacy Model

For decades, training in clinical hypnosis for licensed clinicians has been offered by professional, national, and international organizations (see list in the Appendix). In most, if not all cases, hypnosis skills are introduced and taught in a linear and stepwise manner. Participants are basically trained to (1) inform and educate the client/patient about hypnosis; (2) perform an induction to initiate trance; (3) provide suggestions in a variety of ways that are geared at addressing the person's presenting problem; (4) make post-hypnotic suggestions for ongoing change; (5) bring the trance experience to a close; and (6) elicit reflection and feedback.

As Alter and Sugarman (2017) have noted, this linear training model is purposefully congruent with the allopathic approach that has evolved over the past 150 years. As noted in Chapter 2, this is a reductionist, clinicopathologically-correlated, disease-based paradigm, informed by principles that assert:

> (1) measurable and predictable biological factors [lead] to pathological states that [can] be modeled as diagnoses; (2) different individuals with common diagnoses therefore manifest common pathophysiology and so [can] and should be treated similarly; and (3) to optimize reproducibility and results, prescriptive therapies ought to be delivered in a formalized and structured manner.
>
> (Alter & Sugarman, 2017; p. 240)

Research protocols and hypnosis scripts apply to specific diagnoses, with efforts made to decrease the effects of individual differences. Structured hypnosis protocols, in which clinicians are instructed to get their clients to relax, focus on their breathing, and become receptive to an intoned monologue of suggestions, have become standard. Teaching hypnosis to professionals also adheres to this model of treatment: like learning the steps through a surgical procedure.

This teaching and training is often and best done through a course of reading, study, small group experiential learning with feedback, and supervision, either live or by reviewing video-recorded sessions. Such training is often sponsored and credentialed by professional organizations (again, such as those in the Appendix), as well as by colleges, universities, and teaching hospitals, as part of professional development programs. During this training, emphasis is often placed on tailoring language to the individual to facilitate trance. The nuances of therapeutic language, and the rationale for various metaphors and strategies, are significant parts of ongoing education in hypnosis. We will discuss those aspects in more depth later in this chapter. Our focus here is that these skills are usually taught within a linear framework that restricts their usefulness.

Even though most clinical interactions (including surgical procedures) often refuse to follow the script, this stepwise approach is nevertheless defended as a good place to start. But there are both functional and principled objections to this legacy training model. The most practical is that, as noted by Alter and Sugarman (2017), most medical and psychologically-oriented professional hypnosis workshop participants return to practice with a set of tools that they struggle fit into their practice schedule and routine.

> While they know how to perform some inductions and construct some suggestions and metaphors, they are unsure of what to do next, how to get started with individual clients, and with which clients they should get started … Simultaneously, the faculty often assert the participants were clearly instructed in just how to get started with hypnosis in practice. We suggest that this discrepancy stems in part from the uncertainty of launching into new territory with limited tools, expertise, and confidence. At a deeper level, we suspect introductory-level participants realize that integrating inductions into their practices, then engineering trance while inventing suggestions and metaphors, requires more self-awareness, sensitivity to, and knowledge about the client than they have experienced in training thus far. They first need skills that reveal and cultivate how their client and people generally "work."
>
> (pp. 254–255)

In short, the procedure of hypnosis (as taught) does not mesh with the realities of clinical practice.

Beyond this issue of fit, there is the problem of hypnosis-as-procedure: hypnosis taught, then practiced, as a separate allopathic process, similar to other therapeutic interventions under the clinician's direction, like a tooth extraction or colonoscopy. This is particularly exemplified by the notion of inductions. Iconically represented by Braid's directing his subjects to fix their gaze before swooning into trance, induction is how the clinician starts a hypnotic ritual, reasoning that it is a requisite preparation for immersion into the hypnotic marinade of suggestions. We argue, as will be clear, that it is also how the clinician interrupts, coopts and replaces the client's trance of expectation upon coming to the clinical encounter.

Clinicians go to their offices, make hospital rounds, or enter the surgical suite for yet another day at work. This is not so for those of us in their care. We come to our therapists, doctors, dentists, surgeons, and especially the emergency department, with a heightened sense of expectancy, risking vulnerability, a building readiness for or resistance against change. Seeking care requires courage. Simply coming into care evokes trance: the process of plasticity. The induction occurs on the way to the office. In their paper proposing a new model of professional hypnosis education, Alter and Sugarman (2017) exemplify this naturalistic and autonomous trance of coming-to-care in an opening clinical vignette:

> J's phone alarm reminds her that it is time to leave work for her second appointment with the new doctor. As she reaches to quiet it, she wonders if she should cancel. The last two doctors did not help. This one seemed different somehow, but it is hard to tell.
>
> The phone lies on her desk next to the framed photo of her husband and son: close, smiling, and squinting at the camera, at her. That was from before. She sighs, stands, grabs her coat, and leaves her cubicle with a quick, "I have a meeting," to her office mates. They are all too busy anyway.
>
> As the gate lifts, allowing her to exit the parking garage, she realizes that she has been on autopilot since she pushed the elevator button. Of course there is the hourly preoccupation about her son, then the heavier drag of her husband and what mood will he be in if he comes home tonight.
>
> But there is some other internal conversation going on that has to do with this new doctor. She realizes that she is autopiloting again, driving to his office. He asked her a lot of questions about her headaches and the medical history and, of course, the accident, just like the others. But there were pauses, as if there was room for her to say more. That worried her. What if he asks about more than headaches? What if he does help? What if this is her own fault? All of it.
>
> She finds herself in the waiting room and checks in with the receptionist. There is a young mother with a baby and an elderly couple there. What would she tell herself if she could travel back to that age? What will she know when she is theirs?
>
> From his tone of voice, she becomes aware that she didn't hear the doctor's first greeting at the waiting room door. She grimaces, rolls her eyes, and shakes her head slightly as if to say, "I'm sorry. I was elsewhere." He smiles and nods deliberately. He follows her to his office in silence. She chooses a chair. He closes the door, sits, studies her for a moment, then says, slowly, "I have been wondering about what has been going through your mind as you prepared yourself for this visit."
>
> (pp. 237–8)

The vignette continues with the clinician responding to the behavioral manifestations of J's "internal conversation" that she brings to the office, such that J's mindset moves toward healing.

What if, instead, the clinician in this common circumstance derails this woman's very relevant reverie to teach some sort of structured induction in order to "go deeper into trance"? Or, worse, he directs her attention away from this reverie in order to educate her about hypnotherapy and how he plans to use it to help her, then test her hypnotizability? Our primary point is that hypnosis-as-procedure—starting with a stepwise assessment, education, and then induction—is about what the clinician imposes, authoritatively, upon the person in care. It is procedure-centered. It is not about how that individual "does" trance. It is as if a toddler who had learned to pester her mother in order to get something, instead said, "Mother, I would like for you to decide to buy me a toy." It is not about utilizing those innate talents and proclivities to evoke change and develop a richer sense of self in the process. It is not person-centered. At the very least, attempting to replace and engineer her trance process is inefficient.

From a similar allopathic and prescriptive outlook, the legacy, linear model of clinical hypnosis teaches that the next steps after induction are to "deepen" or intensify the trance then embed a variety of suggestions that somehow relate to the person's problems or symptoms. We suspect that a large portion of current books on hypnosis and "guided imagery" are about prescribing metaphors, crafting inductions and suggestions, and composing teaching stories for specific contexts, such as preparing for surgery or chemotherapy, or problems like chronic pain, depression, and anxiety. Certainly, the majority of clinical hypnosis Listserv discussions involve requesting and receiving advice about how to use hypnosis for a given diagnosis or set of symptoms. Less frequently, but a close second, are queries about helping certain types of people (of a given age, development, or circumstance). It is as if hypnotic procedures can be matched to categories of people, problems, and diagnoses in the same way that medications (e.g., matching antibiotics to the vulnerabilities of the infecting germ) or surgical procedures are used to treat a diagnosis. Again, hypnosis training evolved and strove for legitimacy by intentionally aligning with this allopathic model of care.

The problem with this model is that people are not problems, diagnoses, or types. Problems, diagnoses, and types of people are categories that we have devised for specific reasons; in this case, to serve the delivery of health care methods. Through our current health care paradigm, we have made these categories seem real, and often more real than the people we treat, as we discuss in our closing chapters (Rosenberg, 2002). We are about to consider clinical hypnosis from a different perspective than this procedural one: a perspective that aligns with a new paradigm focused on *how* people *have* problems, diagnoses, and types. But since we are critically viewing hypnosis *training*—not hypnosis *per se*—before leaving this subject we must address defenders of this training status quo.

The most common defense of this assess-induce-deepen-influence-awaken procedural method for teaching hypnosis is that it is a good place to start. Clinicians are used to learning skills in a stepwise manner. Keep it simple. Clinicians who want to learn more will. Eventually we develop our own style and flexibility. Perhaps the most common defense is, "That's how I learned and it worked for me." One colleague argued that, "We all learn clinical skills that we have to unlearn later. That's just the way it is." Finally, for most clinicians using hypnosis in this way, it works. They achieve results, just as hypnosis "works" when used in uniform protocols within research protocols to treat pain, irritable bowel syndrome, and a whole host of other problems.

The rebuttals are that (1) clinicians tend to practice as they are taught; (2) the aforementioned limitations of fit likely deter clinicians from practicing much of what they are taught; (3) there are potential harms in this model; and (4) hypnosis can be used far more effectively. Our informal survey of US professional hypnosis organizations indicates that fewer than 40% of introductory workshop participants continue with more refined training. While they may also read or obtain other training about more flexible, collaborative, and person-centered practice of hypnosis, they do not tend to engage in ongoing training through those organizations. They just do what they were initially taught. Further, the hypnosis-as-procedure model is perpetuated both because it aligns with clinical practice and, more broadly, with its portrayal in books, movies, television, and stage hypnosis. So why would a clinician see the need to change their application of hypnosis? Along with Alter and Sugarman (2017), we add a deeper level of concern:

> Though the Legacy Model, as currently structured, may be easiest and most culturally syntonic to teach with a linear, prescriptive pedagogy it is not a basis for ethical practice. It certainly risks misunderstanding, at least, for introductory-level clinicians. … [W]e conceive the only types of clinical situations in which formalized induction followed by prescribed, scripted suggestions and metaphors are indicated are either within a research setting that requires a rigid and standard protocol or in a clinical context in which there is (1) little rapport, (2) significant alexithymia [difficulty knowing one's feelings], (3) little capacity for insight, and (4) tendency toward pathological dissociation. The latter would be a risky scenario for any but the most experienced and skilled clinician. Simply put, teaching formal prescriptive induction and problem-based metaphor should be reserved for advanced-level training and practice, if taught at all.
>
> (pp. 256–7)

If we view clinical hypnosis as a procedure, and use it as one, it will likely work as one. It may even work more effectively and efficiently than, or increase the efficacy and efficiency of, many non-hypnotic interventions, such as surgical procedures. But, as psychologist and author Michael Yapko (2012, p. 71) teaches, there is a difference between "doing hypnosis" and "being hypnotic." As we will discuss, recognizing and responding to the trance of the encounter, and facilitating the flow of clinical interactions with hypnosis skills, allows clinicians to better collaborate with the person beneath the problem.

There is an impressive example of effectively teaching specific aspects of hypnotic interaction. Elvira Lang, who started her career as an interventional radiologist, has successfully developed a training program to teach radiology technicians how to use language—both verbal and non-verbal—to decrease patients' anxiety, pain, and the duration of procedures, thereby improving the cost-effectiveness of the radiological procedures (Lang & Laser, 2011). Here is an example of teaching care-givers to "be hypnotic." We should add that these care-givers are not therapists, and these are not ongoing therapeutic relationships, however beneficial these procedurally related interactions may be. All of this is to support the idea that hypnosis can and ought to be taught differently from the outset.

Rick Kluft (personal communication, August, 2019) has proposed a developmental perspective to resolve the apparent polarity of teaching hypnosis starting with a problem-based, linear perspective, versus a more systemic and person-centered one. He describes five steps of professional development in the disciplined practice of clinical hypnosis as follows:

1. There are exceptions, but most of us start with the stereotypic repetition of what we have learned/read/etc. We don't have either sufficient memory or experience to draw upon, but we do have handouts and/or copies of something.
2. After repetitive use, we tend to regard the protocols we have been using as "training wheels" to prevent our losing our balance, but our actual need for them decreases. We begin to find our own way, but may keep them at hand for reminders or for security. Here I refer primarily to inductions and more general techniques. I am not referring to complex crafted approaches that have sufficient intricacy that we may need not to trust our memories or our inspiration of the moment.
3. Further along, we metabolize elements of the ways we first used, imbricating elements or portions of them into our more personal styles with added elements of our own derivation and more complex crafted interventions, usually borrowed from others with greater experience.
4. Along with metabolizing, or subsequent to it, we may engage in improvisations and recombinations [sic] in which we combine elements from several preexisting sources with our own ideas and new highly crafted interventions. We are synthesizing what we have learned into approaches, which we are increasingly comfortable in applying flexibly, and working with a greater sense of confidence and competence in deriving useful interventions and new variations. The focus of such growth is clinician-centered.
5. Superficially similar but quite different below the surface is Individualization, which may have a time line all its own. More secure in ourselves, we combine known components with novel creations to tailor and to select among approaches empathically and dynamically attuned to the individual patient. Our concern here is focused primarily not upon how we do

and use hypnosis per se, but upon how our understanding of our patients guides us in our practice. Such growth is patient-centered and relational.

We agree with this developmental view, but are concerned that most clinicians do not progress much beyond the second level due to the pressures and boundaries of allopathic care. We would hope that clinicians learning hypnosis would be exposed to modelling at the fifth level from the outset and that this model be set as the standard of care.

Imagining Domains of Clinical Hypnosis

Instead of imagining clinical hypnosis as a procedure that is done to people, or a process to which a patient or client is subjected, consider clinical hypnosis as a collection of skills that structure our communication during a therapeutic encounter. In other words, put hypnosis at the heart of the entire range of clinical interventions, from conversation to procedure to palliative care. Certainly, overhearing inadvertent comments such as, "I don't think he's going to make it," in the emergency department hallway beyond the curtain of your treatment bay is a negative influence. *Clinical* hypnosis, as therapeutic influence, ought to be salutary.

Such naturalistic, conversational, integrative applications of hypnosis, as compared to the procedural, are often considered special and exceptional uses in the legacy hypnosis realm. Designations such as "Awake," "Alert," and "Eyes-open" hypnosis are often defined as higher level practice. They deviate from the linear, legacy model in that a subject remains active; in other words, a client's eyes remain open and a client can be physically engaged in energetic behaviors while in trance. Wark asserted that the value of these alert variations on the legacy model was that "there are ways to induce hypnosis beyond the traditional eye fixation and relaxation" (2006, p. 298)

Conversational integration of clinical hypnosis differs. As Sugarman, Schafer, Alter, and Reid (2018) put it and we repeat from Chapter 2:

> Conversational hypnosis relates to alert models in that hypnosis is used with a specific active behavior: a conversation. But it departs from both the alert and legacy models in three significant ways. First, there are no formal inductions, because the client is presumed to be engaged in trance prior to and in anticipation of the encounter … . Second, because the format is a dialogue, clinicians do not deliver monologues of scripted suggestions to influence receptive clients. Conversational hypnosis is reciprocal, spontaneous, and creative. Its direction and structure are determined by the expressions of abilities, resources, and strengths that unfold in a unique and, in clinical settings, therapeutic encounter. Third, because the client engaged in conversation is neither passively reposed nor focused on some other behavioral context, the full range of communicative performance art is in play. … In active conversation, not only

> are the client's words (akin to lyrics), prosody, and rhythm (akin to music) available for expression but so are the client's postures and gestures (akin to dance). So, inviting "dance" into the hypnotic mix multiplies the resources available for appreciation, evocation, and response.
>
> (p. 141)

The lyrics, music (including silences), and dance of the interaction become the collaborative, two-way media of hypnosis in conversation. The coordination of these elements provides a meta-message: *how* we mean what we are saying. What binds these elements together, what makes them hypnotic, is that they are all employed intentionally to influence, direct, or shape the psychobiological malleability that we are calling trance. This is even more evident in the use of hypnosis with children in play, as Linden (2003) has described. This, then, is the general context in which we will consider the practice of hypnosis. It does not preclude a more structured and formal ritual of induction-deepening-suggestion-realerting. That remains an optional component within the broader encounter.

Basic Skills

When we teach other professionals about hypnosis-as-conversational, we begin with four basic skills (as distinct from our principles). Our goal is to help clinicians learn how to cultivate trance and disrupt patterns within the course of "normal" encounters. This contrasts with the "hypnosis-as-intervention" model that is less feasibly transferred from the training workshop to the office. As will be evident, these simple conversational tools make use of much of what we know about provoking plasticity. They introduce novelty, uncertainty, disorientation, and developmental time-travelling, which we have termed "*Temporal Touring.*" When clinicians, as participants in professional development workshops, first practice these skills, they report that the hardest part is adopting a "beginner's mind." By this, they do not only mean the difficulty of seasoned practitioners learning new skills. They mean that the skills themselves are best enacted from an attitude of not-knowing, of naivete, of awe and intense curiosity about the person in care. This stance of non-authority can be uncomfortable, even anxiety-provoking, for those clinicians who identify with their knowledge and confidence. It is the act of moving from diagnostic predetermination to phenomenology. And it is part of the paradigm shift toward which we are building.

Alter and Sugarman (2017) introduced these four "Basic Skills" as **kneading**, **wondering**, **wandering** and pro/regression. The last term was later changed to "con-gression." The syllable these words share, "-gress," comes from Latin and old French, and refers to stepwise movement, often through time and events. "Con," from the Latin, means "with"; thus, it refers to developmental time-travel in *both* directions, not just backwards (re-gression) or forward (pro-gression). Here is an edited excerpt from Alter and Sugarman's (2017) original definitions:

> *Kneading*[2] involves recognizing and reinforcing non-conscious manifestations (gestures, postures, verbal expression) in order to intensify trance. The term refers to kneading bread dough since that process involves repetitive folding the outside of the dough inward. … kneading always originates with the patient's behavior—not the clinician's interpretation … . Kneading drives trance by attending primarily to the non-conscious.
>
> Both *wondering* and *wandering* are intentional practices of uncertainty. Both involve loosening preconceptions of both causation and treatment as well as prioritizing the encounter's agenda with anything other than the client's cues. Both require an open posture and open-ended questions and "I wonder" statements and "How" questions (e.g., "How do you do that?") that, again, are client-centered. By presuming no foreknowledge of a pathophysiological mechanism for the client's problems or challenges—having a "beginner's mind"—the clinician implicitly places primary responsibility for creativity with the client. … Wondering is at the heart of evocation. It is the opposite of prescribing a metaphor or following a script.
>
> *Wandering* is only different from wondering in that it moves, contingent on the client's last response. Wandering is the exploration of the client's experiential domain … Wandering is not aimless. Rather, it is a curiosity-driven, non-predetermined expedition in which the client's behavior is the tour guide … .
>
> *[Con-]gression* refers to noting and facilitating access to formative and early experiences in service of plasticity. We contend that, since we often identify with being psychophysiologically plastic when we are young, trance … is often, if not always, a regressive experience.
>
> (pp. 244–5. Italics added)

We add to the authors' descriptions that, with children and adults equally, projected and imagined time travel into the future, with learned and improved competencies and contexts, i.e., "progression," can also be beneficial. So progression and regression are simplified (however awkwardly) into "**congression**."

Let's Demonstrate Each of These Skills

- "Kneading" is often an opening line: "That was a deep breath!" Or an observation like, "You closed your eyes for a moment before you answered that question." But without analysis. Just folding back in, as one would gently knead a soft bread dough.

- As in the excerpt, "wondering" often starts with "How" as in "How do you [know/do/figure] that?" It can be emphasized with a preface of "I wonder …"
- "Wandering" continues with some contingency such as "Then what do you imagine would happen?" and "If you did that, then what?"
- "Congression" is mainly expressed non-verbally—by adopting a prosody and posture as if one is interacting with a younger (regression) or more mature (progression) person—and secondarily in word choice befitting that developmental target. So, with an adult who is tearfully recalling a childhood trauma, one might say softly, slowly, and with more variation in pitch, "Oh! That hurts," as one might address a child. And, with a child who feels unfairly treated, one might adopt a tone and posture of addressing an adult when asking, "So, what exactly do you think needs to be done?"

Functional Groups of Skills: Relational, Disruptive, Renewal

The basic skills we have just described are useful for introducing trance cultivation to clinicians learning hypnosis. They are as fundamental to ongoing practice as scales are to musicians. In that sense, they replace teaching inductions. They are initial methods to engage with and enrich the aforementioned trance of expectancy that the person in care brings to the visit. Beyond trance cultivation, clinical hypnosis steers that plasticity toward health and self-efficacy. Hypnosis intensifies rapport, breaks problems into useful parts, then wonders them together toward healing. More simply, we use hypnosis to engage, disrupt, then renew. This sequence rides along the rails of Rossi's four-stage Novelty-Numinosum-Neurogenesis Effect (2002). Let's assemble these next-level hypnotic skills in terms of their functions in driving therapeutic change.

Relational skills strengthen our interpersonal attachment, and encourage those in our care. The rapport facilitated by relational skills is needed to contain the uncertainty and discomfort of the ensuing change. Next, since change is about disruption of what is, there are *disruptive strategies* that dissociate and disorient, confuse and collapse the beliefs, engrams, and ruts that keep things in place. Then comes the creative, often numinous process of *renewal*: how we get our act together, and how the clinician facilitates the ongoing and progressive processes of healing and health.

Relational Skills

Relational skills start with the clinician's trance: focused attention on the person in care. The objects of this focus include, but also go beyond, their speech and its content, breathing patterns, facial expression, eye contact, posture, and gestures. The clinician grows curious about the mindset and "habitus" of the client. By mindset, we mean the workings of their minds and, particularly, evidence of trance or momentary trance "openings." By habitus, we use Bourdieu's (1977) sense of how an individual's relationship with society affects their responses and behavior. While one part of the clinician's mind is collecting data and recording notes, another is taking in this collective impression and letting it affect, intrigue, and drive intuition and hypothesis-generation. A third part of the clinician's mind is monitoring, cautioning to avoid judgment or limiting diagnostic predetermination, reminding not to become too attached to their own clinical hypotheses about that person. Most importantly, the clinician's trance is one of appreciation for the chance to be with and learn about another human being who has the courage to seek care. It is fundamental because it informs everything that we project to the person in care. As Daniel Siegel (2012, p. 94) puts it, the clinician's trance creates the milieu in which the person in care "feels felt." A colleague called this experience one of "rapt presence," an intentional English homophone for "wrapped presents."

There are a variety of nonverbal abilities that reinforce rapport. Making eye contact, matching one's breathing with the client's, keeping an empathic facial expression, maintaining an open posture, and keeping one's head at the level of the patient's (e.g., sitting down at the bedside or examination table in medical settings, instead of towering over the other). When we are troubled and seeking care, we tend to see through these efforts if they are forced or inauthentic. Beneath these behavioral manifestations, as a foundation of the clinician's trance, there is the expression of sincere interest, appreciation, and wonder at what the person in care is communicating. Consider William Carlos Williams' (see Chapter 4) attitude when he "… lost myself in the very properties of their minds: for the moment at least, I actually became *them* …" (Williams, 1984, p.119, italics original).

Conventionally, in professional clinical hypnosis training, rapport-building with positive regard and encouragement is termed "ego-strengthening." It is typically enacted as statements of praise. "You are very good at that." "That's right." "You have done that very well." While such statements may have their place, praise risks a posture of authority and judgement. Given the clinician-patient/client relationship, such statements tend to imbue the clinician with higher authority. So the implicit (and therefore determinant) message becomes, "From my position of higher expertise about your life, I endorse what you have done." Contrast that with statements of wonder and appreciation such as, "How do you do that?" "I find that amazing," "I can imagine that was very hard to do," and even "Wow!" In these, the clinician uses a beginner's mind to value the struggle of the other. The implicit message is appreciation. In that modelling of esteem, there is the potential to evoke it. Whatever an "ego" might be, it is less likely to be sustainably strengthened by externally derived grading than from evocation.

Another aspect of relational skills is the use of "person-centered language." As outlined by Teleska and Sugarman (1997), person-centered language uses the person's own words, once elicited, to describe their condition. It emphasizes the other's agency by replacing directives such as, "I want you to …" with invitation: "You can choose to …" More implicitly, it evokes self-actualization by not simply letting symptoms or problems "just go away," but instead wonders, "What do you imagine that you did that made that better?" and (again), "How did you do that?" When improvement or worsening of symptoms, for example, are experienced as non-conscious and involuntary, we tend to attribute that change to something outside of us. So it can be challenging to be asked how we did something of which we are unaware. The common response is, "I don't know." To which we often respond, "Well, part of you does."

This interaction exposes an apparently oppositional facet of relational skills in hypnosis. Relationships develop resilience with tension and elasticity. The implicit evocation of self-worth is tested with provocation. Creating the container of the relationship requires enlarging it in preparation for the challenges of change. That provocation can be teasing, humor, and probing questions. When a patient says, "I don't think that's going to work," rather than inquiring about that belief, we often respond provocatively, "If you say so." Just like "… part of you does," the terse but kindly intoned answer challenges the other to consider that the clinician is expressing more faith and ability than patients may have in themselves. The internal search that such a question evokes is another matter that we will get to shortly. That, and the novelty of the question, expose the overlap in the domains of these hypnotic skills. Relational skills can be disruptive and provoke change leading to renewal. As introduced in Chapter 2, Linden (1999) has encoded these relational skills in the "Five E's of Feminist Hypnotherapy": being Empathic, Empowering, Egalitarian, Ego-Strengthening, and Embodying. Here we introduce this provocative aspect of relational skills to highlight that our faith in the person who comes to care is more powerfully enacted by carefully challenging them, implicitly saying, "I believe you have more resources than you are aware of in service to yourself." This is a basis for hope.

An additional dimension of relational skills has to do with exploring and utilizing the other's "representational modes" and metaphors. Gordon (2017), and Lakoff and Johnson (1980), have brought to light the implicit ways by which we encode or represent our feelings, thoughts, and concepts. For example, when we say, "I see what you mean," we are referencing the visual system. If, upon reading a message, one concludes, "It sounds to me like he doesn't want to do it," the speaker is calling upon their auditory system as a metaphor for processing an opinion. A person worries, "I just don't know how I can get through it," by representing the problem as a physical, tactile thing, an obstacle that one must somehow go through (or get "around," "over," or "past"). Similarly, and more kinetically, we say that a situation is weighing us down. Less commonly, we reference gustatory and olfactory systems: "That leaves a bad taste in my mouth," "gut feelings," "something that you can really sink your teeth into," and "that stinks." The reader is encouraged to enjoy Lakoff and Johnson's (1980) hundreds of insightful examples. Like everything else we do, these perceptual means tend to become habitual and so part of our conditioning: the paradoxical ruts we create with our plasticity.

These representational modes are significant because they provide insight into how we embody our minds. As we have previously noted, conditioned learning is embodied. These habituated methods become elements in the engrams that we call experience. When clinicians are "tuning into" a person's mindset—how they feel, think, and conceptualize something—then mirroring that person's representational mode can help the client "feel felt." This is evidenced in responsive regard: nodding, smiling, or relaxing facial muscles and saying something like, "Yeah. Like that!" and "You got it." And, as we will explain, changing representational modes can disrupt conditioned engrams of experience, further cultivating trance.

Finally, consider metaphor construction as part of relational being. How does the person in care imagine the workings of their problem? To what do they attribute it? In medical settings, patients often expect the doctor to explain the etiology and pathophysiology of their condition. We routinely turn the tables on our patients in the course of establishing a relationship by asking two types of questions that evoke metaphors. Regarding a symptom, we ask, "What is it like?" Literally we are asking for, and thus evoking, parallels and associations with previous experiences. Second, we ask, "How do you imagine this is happening?" We are requesting an invented description, a synthesis of their condition's processes within their embodied mind. The previously introduced basic skills of wondering and wandering are used in this exploration. While this line of questioning is ostensibly data gathering, it values and validates the patient's perception. Recall the boy in Chapter 4 who proclaimed, "Maybe how I imagine it works is *really* how it works!"

To assign relational skills a place in Rossi's four-stage process (2002), align them with stage one: Assessment, recognizing and describing the problem. But with their evocation of expectancy of change, and expression of curiosity and hope, relational skills impel trance toward the commotion of stage two, Incubation.

Disruptive Skills

Once more: Hypnosis is about cultivating and influencing trance. Trance is the process of plasticity: changing our minds. As we have explained, novelty often creates trance openings and so, in health care, novelty starts with the clinical encounter. Enacting the basic skills and rapport-building strategies discussed so far are unusual: Intensely person-centered interactions feel different, like something is happening. Relational skills, used effectively, not only secure rapport but also compel plasticity. Beyond these abilities, and contained by rapport, disruptive skills encourage disassembly of conditioned learning, memory, and behavior by (1) actuating embodied "ideomotor" processes, (2) utilizing dissociation and differentiation, and (3) promoting uncertainty.

Actuating the Embodied Mind

However we might agree to define "sub-," "un-," or "non-conscious," and assuming that its existence is worth defining, we might agree that it includes our implicitly learned conditioning: what we know how to do without knowing how we know how to do it. Our minds' most-travelled routes. What we have practiced the most. Where and how we get stuck. Our ruts. As we have repeated: because the mind is embodied all conditioned learnings are, too. So cultivating trance for beneficial change always involves body-based stuff: movement, gestures, yoga, and the "dance" of nonverbal communication.

Many writers on clinical hypnosis consider recognizing a conscious-nonconscious split as requisite (see O'Hanlon, 2009; Yapko, 2012; Zeig, 1994). One can evoke it verbally: "While you are aware of hearing what I am saying with your conscious mind, your non-conscious mind is also listening and interpreting what these words mean at deeper level." Clinicians using hypnosis allude to it as a sense of involuntariness in arm levitation when they say, "It will float up all by itself," or that a given finger on one hand representing "Yes," "No," or "Maybe" can move in nonconscious response to questions (Hill & Rossi, 2017; Rossi & Cheek, 1988). These are contrived and externally imposed attempts to cultivate plasticity in our conditioned learning by actuating the embodied mind. They are classically referred to as ideomotor signaling.

While we consider this type of cultivation basic and essential to "being hypnotic," we tend to practice it in a more naturalistic, less directive, and more evocative way. One enactment is in the Basic Skill we have called kneading, since it continually draws attention to, and thereby integrates, nonconsciously derived behaviors: "That was a big breath," and, "Right. You closed those eyes for a moment." Ernest Rossi has taught us that this skill can be practiced even more implicitly and with a sense of fascination and wonder. He will acknowledge a furrowing of the brow, a sigh, a subtle shift of position with "Yes!" "Right!" "Just like that!" "Wow. Something is happening!" He will even use unfinished sentences like, "Isn't it good to know …" This increasingly-refined focus on subtle and minimal movements, as manifestations of deeper and significant processes, can be experienced as extremely powerful by the person in care.

To foster this embodied plasticity, we can add more specific meaning and novelty to these gestures. Statements such as, "Your eyes closed for a moment. Perhaps they can do that again so you can find out if it helps you see better in your mind's imagination," can promote change. Less directively, so can queries like "Your eyes closed for a moment. What will you discover when you do that again? Will they stay closed until you have learned something new?" Notice these are an extension and combination of the basic skills we labelled kneading and wandering.

When the person in care is expressively gesturing with their arms and hands, those motions can be made conscious, mirrored by the clinician, and even directed. Combining Cheek's use of ideomotor signaling with the spontaneity of arm and hand gestures, Hill and Rossi (2017) developed an entire protocol of therapeutic interaction based on acknowledging and facilitating symbolically embodied change through the client's opposing or "mirroring" hands. A version of this is illustrated in Robinson's interaction with George and his clenched fist in the second episode of Robinson's Story ("George and Robinson"). At a more holistic level, whole body movements such as yoga positions, stretching, serial muscle tightening and relaxation, and walking can be used to meaningfully activate embodied change toward something new (Rossi 2018a & 2018b; Rossi, Mortimer, & Rossi, 2015). I (LIS) routinely give young people who come to my office for therapy a choice of where to sit. After our initial visit, many have benefitted by choosing my desk chair because, as one boy explained, "That's where you find the answers." I (JHL) add that my clients often ask, "What do you learn about me from where I sit?" to which I respond, "What do *you* learn about you?")

There is a place for prescribed and contrived ideomotor signaling, both in training and practice. But for the most part, these are directive, clinician-originated exercises. We often introduce breathing awareness, progressive muscle relaxation, arm levitation with imaginary kites or balloons, or imagining that opposing hands are magnets so the client can "feel" an imagined attracting-and-repulsing magnetic field. We present these experiences not as hypnotic inductions, but as examples, purposefully unrelated (at least explicitly) to the person's problem, of how the mind is embodied. In doing so we cultivate that understanding. They serve to show what is possible. They are exhibits. Not therapy. When we are doing hypnosis to drive therapeutic change, we utilize what the client *already* does and knows how to do, just as Robinson makes use of George's clenched fist and Lulu chooses gymnastics.

Finally, when actuating the embodied mind toward therapeutic change, we rarely promote physical relaxation. We are aligning disruptive skills with the activation energy of stage two (Incubation) toward stage three (Illumination) of Rossi's Four-Stage model. As Rossi (Rossi & Rossi, 2019) noted about Milton H. Erickson's practice:

> Erickson (Erickson & Rossi, 2014) frequently commented that successful hand levitation requires activating muscle tonus (the slight continuous contraction characteristic of a muscle at rest) on a deep physiological level. Erickson's patients would often tremble, vibrate, shake, sweat, and feel hot with the strain they were experiencing—the opposite of the traditional passive hypnotic induction via quiet suggestions for relaxation and sleep. Erickson's hand levitation technique activated the patient's

> mind and body while they were receiving positive inspiring suggestions for therapeutically reconstructing themselves. Erickson, of course, did use the traditional passive eye fixation techniques with relaxation suggestions when they were appropriate, but there was always a special twinkle in his eyes when he used the active hand levitation approach that he seemed proudest of—he got his patients to work and sweat just as farmers and laborers did! What was the work and sweat all about? There seemed to be some secret and unexpected therapeutic efficacy associated with activating the patient's mind-body while administering positive therapeutic suggestions.
>
> (p. 22)

Dissociation and Differentiation

While engaging and disrupting embodied learning, we also disrupt cognitive conditioning. Again, this starts with the basic skills that we have termed wondering and wandering. The client says that they were anxious, or had a headache, or experienced some other problem before the appointment but now they feel a lot better. The clinician does not ask, "What you *think* happened?" or "Why did those symptoms *go away*?" These questions request a theory, and imply a lack of agency and self-efficacy. "Those symptoms" are "other"—an object, a thing separate from the client. Moreover, the symptoms are made to seem somehow sentient; they can autonomously "happen" and "go away." Instead, hypnotically, we can imply, integrate, and reframe this allopathic construct. The clinician wonders aloud, "How did you *do* that?" We are asking questions for which the conscious answer is almost always, "I don't know." Of course, we don't know how we know what we know ... until we learn about it.

We can further drive cognitive disruption with the use of dissociative language, multisensory imagery, the skill of congression, interspersal of ideas in the content of our speech, variations in its prosody, and stretching problems out on imagined scales (scaling). We will touch on these. But first we need to get at their functional essence. These approaches are best posed as questions, even when they are statements, as in, "Part of you knows the answer to that, does it not?" As clinicians, our focus is not on what the answer is. We are focused on what the question *does.*

All of these cognitively disrupting strategies serve a common purpose: they initiate an internal "transderivational" search. Simply put, transderivational searches occur across a broad field for "fuzzy" (as compared to precise) matches of meaning or context. Transderivational search-promoting queries such as, "How do you do that?" and, "Part of you knows the answer to that, does it not?" and even, "What is the sound of one hand clapping?" reflexively (nonconsciously) prompt an internal lack of certainty, and motivation to resolve this with an answer. But if the questions are sufficiently vague, then a broader and deeper—hence transderivational—quest is required. Rossi and

Rossi (2007) have suggested a different term, to more accurately detail the components of the searching *experience* rather than the origins (derivations) of the answers. They consider these "implicit" (since there is no explicit directive to search) "processing" (an evaluative act) "heuristics" (autonomous self-discovery). So, these cognitively disruptive skills are designed to intensify trance by questioning what we thought we knew. Once the question is posed, the clinician observes the effect: what the question does.

Dissociative language starts disrupting by replacing possessive adjectives, such as "your" with the definite article "the" or the demonstratives "that" or "those." One might ask, "How does [*the* or *that*] hand feel?," "It's all right to let *those* eyes close," and "Can you look at *those* hands as if you have never noticed them?"—in contrast with "your hand(s)" or "your eyes." In addition to the trance-opening novelty of this syntax, the semantics imply dissociation, a disruption of habituated body relations that changes experience. There is also something regressive—evocative of a beginner's mind, hence congressive—about this usage, since there must have been a time in our infancy when we became fascinated by the body we inhabited and how we connected to it. Related to this dissociative language is the use of homophone, rhyme, alliteration, and other lyrical syntax. These act as implicit processing heuristics because of the associations of form—poetic, musical, and the related meanings of homophones—in addition to content. Recall what came to your mind previously when we associated "rapt presence" with "wrapped presents."

Dissociative language also has a nonverbal component. In a sense, this is the emotional embodiment of language as music and dance. The range of inflection, pitch, pace, volume, facial expression, gestures, and postures of the clinician are all intentionally brought into play. They cannot be exemplified well in a book, but the theme of their disruptive use has to do with braking normal patterns of speech. I (LIS) often ask a young person who has successfully used self-regulatory skills to diminish procedural pain and anxiety, for example, "Who did that?" They respond with a meek "Me?" as their voice inflects, in question, toward a higher pitch. I repeat their prosody so they can hear it, then ask them to notice how it feels to reverse the change and start the speech at a high pitch, lowering it dramatically, while repeating the word, "Me." We practice, repeatedly, turning up the volume to make it emphatic. Reflexively, their posture and facial expression grow in determination as well. They announce, "Me!"—and change their minds.

It is impossible to catalog all of this music and dance and how to integrate it disruptively, since these skills are not scored but improvised, like jazz, with each new encounter. But these moves have certainly been studied. For example, there is a delightful book by Sandor Feldman (1959) entitled *Mannerisms of Speech and Gestures in Everyday Life*. And Conversational Analysis has begun to be applied to investigate these aspects of hypnosis in particular, enabling more insight into prosodic rhapsody of therapeutic language (Sugarman et al., 2018).

Of all the nonverbal messages, perhaps the pauses speak loudest: the silence following a question; during and then after internal reflection; after eyes reopen; when an emotional change is signaled in the facial expression; and as the tears begin. These silences, accompanied by eye-contact and that rapt presence, convey concern and curiosity in what the other is doing, a space for the person in care to fill. They are evocative of faith and trust as in, "You know just what to do." Sometimes silences seem the most respectful form of communication. We find we use silence more and more as a means of appreciating the client's autonomy, as the internal ferment of Rossi's stage two (Incubation) peaks toward stage three (Illumination).

Dissociative language scales up to dissociated experience, including imagining oneself enacting behavior elsewhere in space and time, with alternative auditory, olfactory, kinesthetic, tactile, and visual imagery. Guided imagery is so often used in therapeutic experiences that it is often synonymous with hypnosis. But we are not referring to a clinician who prescribes and describes an imagined experience based on *their* ideas of what would be beneficial for a given client or a given problem. We are not promoting casting of spells; we consider the practice of prescribed imagery limited at best, and potentially harmful. Contrast that practice with one in which the client has begun to recount an important, perhaps even traumatic experience, at which they would like to be a peaceful observer and, when appropriate, the clinician inquires about,

> What the ears hear there [Note the disruptive imposition of the homophone "here" next to "there."] while you can still hear my voice in the background here ["hear" and "here" again]… and with that next breath in, notice the scents [homophone with "sense"] of the air there [rhyme] that the nose knows [homophone] … and whether you're moving or still, there [also means, "you're still there"] … and what is moving you or around you [implication of the emotional meaning of a "moving experience"] up close and farther away, in the distance … and whether the weather [homophones] there is wonderfully warm or comfortably cool [alliteration] and how that feels on the skin and the face … and of course, the colors and edges of things [regressive and elemental introduction of visual imagery] also close in and far away, what the eyes see there.

These are evocations (not prescriptions) of multiple representational modes, expressed lyrically in order to drive trance. Incidentally, I (LIS) tend to evoke sensory modes in this order—auditory, olfactory, kinesthetic, tactile, then visual. Because we tend to over-rely on visual imagery, but many tend to use auditory and olfactory imagery more habitually (as in musical "earworms" and people's lingering scents). So there can be disruptive novelty even in ways one prioritizes sensory experiences.

This dissociative imagery can be extended to stories and discussions that metaphorically evoke change. Milton Erickson famously talked for hours about gardening with a man dying of disseminated cancer. He emphasized, with interspersal of certain words and his prosody, the natural order of growth and death in the garden and in our lives, thereby evoking comfort (see Haley, 1993). This is also exemplified near the end of Lulu's narrative as she processes the symbology of Vergil's storytelling. Arguably, this enactment of our principle of *Narrative Listening*, using stories to heal, is the oldest form of the healer's art.

Role-played interactions are another form of dissociated trance cultivation. We previously mentioned the boy who chose to gain new perspective by sitting in the clinician's chair. In this way, he was representing the authoritative, remedial part of himself. More broadly conceived, facilitating dialogue between different aspects of the self, Watkins and Watkins (1997) defined the theory and practice of "Ego-State Therapy." We often carry out an imaginal version of this as we have people in care carefully externalize, describe, and even hallucinate a part of themselves, sitting in a formerly empty office chair, then have a compassionate conversation with that part of themselves. We also actuate an embodied experience in this exercise. We have the person in care scan their body, once the problematic part has separated. We inquire, using basic skills of kneading and wondering, about what has changed and how they will maintain that change once the separated self reintegrates.

Representational modes can be utilized for disruption and change. Recall that we can listen for the implied sensory or conceptual metaphor—the representational mode—in the client's speech ("I see what you mean," "I can't get over it," etc.). Then use those same modes to enhance rapport. Shifting them promotes change. Here is an example.

> I (LIS) worked with a very bright early adolescent who suffered "writer's block." Despite superb academic ability, his grades were suffering because, when it came to expressive writing (an essay, report, critique), his mind and hands "froze." He could not bring himself to write on a keyboard, with a pencil and paper, or even dictate to a person or voice-to-text device. A variety of reasonable approaches to resolve this problem failed to help him. Expressive writing terrified him. Here is what worked. We explored the history of that frozen, terrified feeling by peeling back layers of memory to an early experience of youth baseball, the summer that he was seven years old. He recalled standing at the plate, holding the metal bat upright while the coach threw the ball from the pitcher's mound for him to hit. He was terrified of being struck and hurt by the ball, so he stood there, "frozen stiff." He would not swing the bat. He readied for the pain of the ball's impact on his chest or arms or leg. He recalled seeing the coach's mouth yelling at him to "Swing the bat! Hit the ball!" but he did not hear the sound. That was his earliest experience of the feeling that would become writer's block.
>
> He gave me permission to recite this experience once more. I described the warm, early summer day, the breeze carrying the scent of new-mown

> grass, the sounds of children and their parents playing, the easy loose swing of the bat and the resounding "Ping!" as he simply swung through the ball then watched it bound across the field as everyone cheered … then yelled, "Run! Run! Run!" So he did.

He started writing again the next day.

This adolescent's representational modes for the limiting experience were kinesthetic (stiff), tactile (cold, anticipating pain), and visual (the coach and the ball). The account was retold with olfactory (new mown grass) and auditory (children playing, "Ping!") imagery. Ease of movement and warmth were added for good measure. Maybe it was simply circumstance that he started writing again. But we certainly played with this memory. We add this brief reminder that these reorganizations of perspective happen spontaneously, outside of therapy. We all have experienced this. They happen in our stories. Here, we are highlighting the strategies that facilitate shifts that lead to new learning, and of course, changing our minds.

It is critical to understand that the skills for driving a disruptive trance are deployed in response to the trance manifestations of the person in care. In turn, clinicians facilitate, or "knead," these subtle behaviors. We tune our mix of skills to the curiosity, confusion, uncertainty, facial expression, eye-closure, breathing, and postural changes of the client within the processing of our clinician's trance. During the week that I (LIS) wrote the first draft of this chapter, I met with a bright young college student who has been in my care for a decade.

> He met criteria for high-functioning autism spectrum disorder, had a few good friends, and had successfully transitioned to college life as an engineering and graphics major. But now, during the summer, working at a restaurant, he was having increasing anxiety about the impending move to career and living more independently. He found himself increasingly "stuck" and "spinning my wheels" when he did not have the daily structure imposed by coursework. It was increasingly hard to leave the house, call a friend, or even make simple improvements, "like, I don't know, brushing my teeth more often." He said, "I am really looking forward to what's next. I want to live on my own and stuff. But, for some reason, I am getting complacent. Even though I really want to figure this out on my own, part of me wishes that someone would just tell me what to do!"
>
> Knowing his strong oppositional and autonomous traits, his aversion to anything "hypnotic" or "meditative," and his proclivity—as a budding engineer—to understand how things work, I replied that I wished I could "just tell him what to do," and left that statement suspended. After a long silence, I told him that I was going to explain what happened with another young man who was stuck, "But, of course, he was younger than you, and I don't know if any of this will be relevant." Then I proceeded to carefully

> and slowly detail the story of the boy with writer's block, complete with explanations of the underlying strategies of shifting representational modes. At first the telling was interactive, interspersed with my questions such as, "You know?" "So what do you think I did?" and, "Do you understand?" as we discussed engrams and sensory memory. But, as the story progressed, he became more and more still, and his eyes closed. Then his eyes moved, searching beneath the lids. So, my recital became one-sided, lilting, with the prosody appropriate for a younger and younger person. When I concluded with, "He started writing again the next day." The young man, remained still, brow furrowed, apparently in deep concentration. After a few long minutes—silences are hard—he sighed deeply. So I said, "Right. Take all the time you need." Then, after another two minutes or so he shifted in the chair. I added, "Yes. And will your eyes open after another sigh, when you know that part of you will continue to figure this out even when you are not thinking about it?" After another pause, he slowly nodded, stretched, opened his eyes and said, rising to leave, "All I want to say is that it makes some sense."

By the time I have written the last draft of this chapter, I can report that this interaction had the hoped-for effect. He is changing his routines and engaging in social activities out of the house. More importantly, he feels capable of doing this.

Disruptive skills bring the person in care to stage three (Illumination): A moment of confusion, disorientation, a threshold, a liminal experience. While we and others have referred to it as an "AHA!" moment, it is perhaps more often a "Huh?" moment, when we experience uncertainty and "not-knowing." Rossi and Rossi (2019) liken this to quantum experiencing because, as we have mentioned in Chapter 4, it is when we are most open and anything is possible. Often, this peak of evocation in trance passes with amnesia, but there is a subsequent change nonetheless. We have a confusing therapeutic experience that we put to the back of our mind, and then we notice hours, days, or weeks later that we have started getting up earlier, that we have returned to exercise, that we brush our teeth more regularly. The boy with the writer's block later claimed amnesia for content of that office encounter.

Skills for Renewal

We choose "renewal" here because it is broader than "resolving," "healing," or "repairing." We imagine renewal subsumes these. These skills are about facilitating the slow, nonconscious reassembly into new patterns of engrams that have been scattered and twisted by the trance of disruption. These strategies are exemplified at the end of the previous clinical vignette. They are aimed, first, at returning trance direction back to the person in care. It is as if we are saying, "I helped you take this apart, now it's yours to put it together!" But more, we intend that our disruptive influence, founded on rapport, will prevent the client from allowing those pieces to fall back together as before. They probably can't, if Heraclitus is correct about the river. Our goal is to have the person in care leave the encounter in the process of changing their mind. The title of one of the most well-known books about the work of Milton H. Erickson, *My Voice Will Go With You* (Erickson, 1991), speaks to this end.

The skills for renewal are simple, when compared to the previous sets: rapport and disruption. We can divide them into two types: "continuing questions," and "souvenirs" (commonly called "post-hypnotic suggestions").

The first skill in renewal strategies is silence. Recognizing that the person in care needs to begin their reintegrative process, we leave them to their own internal devices. After all that creative and disruptive effort, why would we say, "Here, let me put that back together for you"? These are the silences that we find the most satisfying. We figure that the longer they continue, the deeper the impact, the more the client is owning the process, and the more work is getting done.

But at some point we have run out of time: the next patient is waiting, the procedure needs to start, or has finished. And we want to assure that the process of change both continues and is rekindled. So we start talking again when we observe some clue from the client. Rossi (1993) has proposed a formula for what we are calling continuing questions. "Will you/your"—some behavior change that signals to the clinician and the patient that they are ready to resume usual awareness, such as eyes opening—"when you know that/your"—trance process—"can continue to a satisfying understanding/conclusion/decision, etc." Hence, in our previous example, "Yes. And will your eyes open after another sigh, when you know that part of you will continue to figure this out, even when you are not thinking about it?" We can also sow other seeds for kindling the process.

> I don't know when what we did here today will next come to mind. Maybe it will be when you open the door to your home, or after dinner, or as you dream tonight. Maybe you will let it surprise you … . I wonder how much of this you will remember at our next visit, when you are sitting in that chair there again, and how much it will be helpful to not remember?

These continuing questions are part of how we let our voices follow our patients.

Classically, post-hypnotic suggestions involve the hypnotist planting a nonconscious link between their embedded cue and the subject's future behavior. Famously depicted in fictions such as the *Manchurian Candidate* (Demme, 2004), post-hypnotic suggestions imply external control. This can be used in beneficial ways; for example, a pre-operative post-hypnotic suggestion that, "Every time you feel the blood pressure cuff tighten around your arm, you can remind yourself that you are well-cared for, and you will find yourself expanding your lungs with a deep, refreshing breath." More autonomously, a person in care can be asked to,

> let come to mind [not 'think of'] some part of this experience—an image, an idea, my voice, that chair—that your mind's imagination will use to remind you of what you began to learn today, like a souvenir that brings with it a fond memory ...

Renewal strategies presume that stage four (Verification) of Rossi's four-stage process will unfold for the most part after the encounter, as the client lives into their answers. The purpose of integrating hypnosis into encounters is to propel that transformation.

A central theme in the application of therapeutic hypnosis, as we are describing it, is evocation. We are not providing answers or solutions to fix a person's problems, even though at times, the ideas discussed become adopted as solutions. Our intention is to join in and add impetus to the internal discovery of new possibilities for healing, health, and hope. The machinery beneath the mindset is unique to each person seeking care. They are the experts on how they run it. Clinicians are the wide-eyed and curious sorcerer's apprentices. This approach was first reported by Milton H. Erickson as "Techniques of Utilization" (1959). About them he wrote:

> These techniques are, in essence, no more than a simple reversal of the usual procedure of inducing hypnosis. Ordinarily, trance induction is based upon securing from the patient some form of initial acceptance and cooperation with the operator. In *Techniques of Utilization* the usual procedure is reversed to an initial acceptance of the patient's presenting behavior by the operator and a ready cooperation with it by the operator, however seemingly adverse that presenting behavior may appear to be in the clinical situation.
>
> (pp. 3–4)

The essence of this utilization approach is to recognize that each person comes to care with all of the resources for healing and change that they need. The roles of the clinician are to aid them in that realization, and to encourage them to get started. We are making this observation about utilization because we want to contrast, once more, this expansive and overlapping range of skills for rapport, disruption, and renewal with the narrow, linear, and limiting formal hypnotic practice. That legacy approach brings to mind a narrow path through a wondrous wood. We prefer to bound off the path, or ignore it altogether. Reconsider how a prescriptive induction, suggestion, re-alerting path to treat a person's problem compares to the creative, heuristic cultivation of possibilities.

Principled Therapeutic Hypnosis: Finding the Art

As we near the close of this critical chapter in our treatise, we want to revisit those four principles—or, perhaps better, clinician perspectives—that we called *Systems Thinking, Temporal Touring, Relational Being,* and *Narrative Listening.* How do we take these into account? What is their place in this mix of basic skills, rapport, disruption, and renewal? Because we are writers, we think of them as four managing editors who are looking over our shoulders and asking us questions and guiding us as we interact therapeutically with our patients.

The *Systems Thinking* editor asks us to appreciate that the patient's flood of emotion and tears, to which we are a party, are also a change in inflammatory and immune response and underlying gene expression. That reminder may cause us to say something about that possibility.

The *Temporal Touring* editor keeps us moving back and forward in the client's history, using our congression skills, taking the long view.

The *Relational Being* editor keeps us cognizant of the clinician's trance, so we don't stray away down our diagnostic and hypothetical paths, away from the person in care. This editor keeps us mindful of empathy, attachment, and how to love the space between us and the client. The editor mostly asks, "Is that for you or the client?"

The *Narrative Listening* editor points out thematic elements—certain words, metaphors, jokes, etc.—that can be used to bring coherence and a narrative arc to the interaction.

Because these perspectives and attitudes transcend individual skills and strategies, guiding their use in the overall current of the encounter, we consider them the discipline and the art of hypnosis.

What Isn't Hypnosis

We hope it is becoming clear that therapeutic hypnosis as a skill set—as compared to a procedure or a ritual—is fungible. By that, we mean it can be integrated into all interpersonal interactions. Perhaps it is more accurate to write that it is *already* part of all encounters, just neither necessarily intentional, beneficial, or artful. Sociologist James Maddock (1994) once claimed, "All hypnosis is not therapy. But all therapy is hypnotic." Assan Alladin (2008) has compared the outcomes of cognitive behavioral therapy within and without a hypnotic frame. Meditative practices access trance and disrupt our connections to pain, our thought-traffic, our self-ishness. Guided imagery, neurolinguistic programming, yoga, and eye-movement desensitization and reprocessing are subsets of our conceptualization of hypnosis[3]: a limited and specific use of skills that cultivate plasticity and (hopefully beneficial) influence.

When teaching about "mind-body" therapy, our colleague Mark Weisberg (2016, personal communication) asks the audience to call out some mind-body techniques and he writes them down in large letters on the board. They shout,

"Yoga! Hypnosis! Meditation! Biofeedback! EMDR!" and so forth. When they are done he asks, "Why did no one mention surgery, physical therapy, or taking medication?" The obvious answer is that when we engage in these interventions, we narrow our frame of reference to the allopathic treatment of a targeted problem, as if it can exist outside of our minds and the therapeutic milieu—as if the problem is more real than we are. This leads us to our point, and criticism, that, while therapeutic, hypnosis is not therapy *per se*, any therapeutic intervention, from a surgical procedure to cognitive behavioral therapy to guided imagery to progressive muscle relaxation, can be performed—and usually is—without an intentional hypnotic frame. Our criticism is that many authors and experts in the field blur this distinction between therapeutic intervention and hypnosis, as "hypnotherapy." As we have stated, Milton Erickson claimed not to use hypnosis to cure but in order to cultivate change. Obviously, we agree. Why does it matter? It matters because, when we confuse hypnosis-as-skill-set with therapy-as-procedure, we limit the integration of hypnosis, its fungibility, and its potential.

Hypnosis as the Heart of an Emerging Health Care Paradigm

To close this long pivotal, chapter and the opening section of this book, we position hypnosis as the center, the base, the heart, or the mother ship—however you best imagine it—of an emerging paradigm of heath and care. We have referenced this claim repeatedly, but now that we have better explained what we mean by hypnosis, we can articulate it with more specificity. In our introduction, we introduced Thomas Kuhn's scientific paradigms as they pertain to health care, and George Engel's biopsychosocial model, as emergent from the reductionist, categorical, allopathic model of medical care. That biomedical model, and the paradigm around it, is neither person-centered, nor does it include the complexity of the embodied mind, experiences, and relationships. That paradigm has served our species well for the last century or so, during a dramatic improvement in our well-being, increased longevity, and a stunning increase in cost. Since therapeutic hypnosis cultivates plasticity throughout the embodied mind by utilizing a person's unique and individual resources, we contend that it not only broadens and empowers the effectiveness of allopathic interventions, but it provides unexplored territory for recruiting our innate resources to greater effect. As James Braid wrote,

> … it appears to me quite certain that the imagination has never been so much under our control, or capable of being made to act in the same beneficial and uniform manner, by any other mode of management hitherto known.
>
> (Braid, 1843, p. 5)

Questions and Assignments for Further Discussion

1. Often the prescriptive and problem-based use of hypnosis is the practice of lay hypnotists and licensed clinicians works. Clients and patients stop smoking or have less pain or stress. Why is the more person-centered and creative approach advocated in this chapter any better?
2. What is meant by the clinician's trance and what does this have to do with the therapeutic relationship? Can't a relationship be therapeutic without it?
3. What are some of the systemic messages in health care that limit the effectiveness of the person-centered approach? (he's a no-show; he's non-compliant; she's asthmatic)
4. If trance is defined as how we "go plastic," but we are always changing our minds to some extent, what isn't a trance?

Notes

1 There are reports of harm associated with being a volunteer for stage hypnotists (see Heap, 2000).

2 We have received resistance to using this term from a variety of clinician-bakers. There are many different ways to knead dough. Some have argued that their violent method for kneading dough (pounding, throwing, and fisting) is not an apt metaphor for how they would work with people in their care. The value of the metaphor is that folding the outside manifestations back in (both in dough and in people's awareness) contributes to a change in elasticity and resilience. With dough it is tactile. With people it is psychobiological. In our defense, one can effectively knead dough very gently by simply folding the outside in, over and over again, with rests in between. This seems to work as well as beating the dough up.

3 Though we are certain that their originators would disagree with our subsuming.

References

Alladin, A. (2008). *Cognitive hypnotherapy: An integrated approach to the treatment of emotional disorders.* Chichester, UK: John Wiley.

Alter, D. S., & Sugarman, L. I. (2017). Reorienting hypnosis education. *American Journal of Clinical Hypnosis, 59*(3), 235–259. doi:10.1080/00029157.2016.1231657

Bourdieu, P. (1977). *Outline of a theory of practice.* London, UK: Cambridge University Press. doi:10.1017/CBO9780511812507

Braid, J. (1843). Neurypnology; or, the rationale of nervous sleep, considered in relation to animal magnetism [pdf]. London, UK: John Churchill. Retrieved from https://books.google.com/books?id=rLMnuwEACAAJ&dq=neurypnology&hl=en&sa=X&ved=2ahUKEwjApZTEz7zkAhVFUt8KHbTgAtYQ6AEwBHoECAUQAQ.

Demme, J. (2004). *The Manchurian candidate* [Motion picture]. Hollywood, California: Paramount Pictures.

Erickson, M., & Rossi, E. (2014). Experiencing hypnosis. In E. Rossi, R. Erickson-Klein & K. Rossi (Eds.), *The collected works of Milton H. Erickson, Vol. 12: Therapeutic approaches to altered states* (pp. 63–64). Phoenix, AZ: The Milton H. Erickson Foundation Press (Original work published 1981).

Erickson, M. H. (1959). Further clinical techniques of hypnosis: Utilization techniques. *American Journal of Clinical Hypnosis*, *2*(1), 3–21. doi:10.1080/00029157.1959.10401792

Erickson, M. H. (1991). *My voice will go with you* (S. Rosen, Ed.). New York, NY: W. W. Norton.

Feldman, S. S. (1959). *Mannerisms of speech and gestures in everyday life*. New York, NY: International Universities Press.

Gordon, D. (2017). *Therapeutic metaphors: Helping others through the looking glass*. Tucson, AZ: David Gordon.

Haley, J. (1993). *Uncommon therapy: The psychiatric techniques of Milton H. Erickson, M.D.* paperback reissue. New York, NY: W. W. Norton.

Heap, M. P. (2000). The alleged dangers of stage hypnosis. *Contemporary Hypnosis*, *17*(3), 117–126. doi:10.1002/ch.200

Hill, R., & Rossi, E. L. (2017). *The practitioner's guide to mirroring hands: A client-responsive therapy that facilitates natural problem-solving and mind-body healing*. Carmarthen, UK: Crown House.

Hope, A. E., & Sugarman, L. I. (2015). Orienting hypnosis. *American Journal of Clinical Hypnosis*, *57*(3), 212–229. doi:10.1080/00029157.2014.976787

Lakoff, G., & Johnson, M. (1980). *Metaphors we live by*. Chicago, IL: University of Chicago Press.

Lang, E., & Laser, E. (2011) *Patient sedation without medication: Rapid rapport and quick hypnotic techniques a resource guide for doctors, nurses, and technologists*. Albany, California: Center Stage Books.

Linden, J. H. (1999). Discussion of symposium: Enhancing healing: The contributions of hypnosis to women's health care. *American Journal of Clinical Hypnosis*, *42*(2), 140–145. doi:10.1080/00029157.1999.10701731

Linden, J. H. (2003). Playful metaphors. *American Journal of Clinical Hypnosis*, *45*(3), 245–250. doi:10.1080/00029157.2003.10403530

Maddock, J. (1994). Trance: A generic model for clinical interaction. *Presented to the Minnesota Society for Clinical Hypnosis*. April 14, 1994. Unpublished.

O'Hanlon, W. H. (2009). *A guide to trance land: A practical handbook of Ericksonian and solution-oriented hypnosis*. New York, NY: W. W. Norton.

Olness, K. N. (2006). *Hypnosis in pediatric practice: Imaginative medicine in action* [DVD]. Sugarman, L. I. (Director/Producer). Carmarthen, Wales: Crown House.

Rosenberg, C. E. (2002). The tyranny of diagnosis: Specific entities and individual experience. *Milbank Quarterly*, *80*(2), 237–260. doi:10.1111/1468-0009.t01-1-00003

Rossi, E. L. (1993). *The psychobiology of mind-body healing: New concepts of therapeutic hypnosis* (2nd ed.). New York, NY: W.W. Norton.

Rossi, E. L. (2002). *The psychobiology of gene expression: Neuroscience and neurogenesis in hypnosis and the healing arts*. New York, NY: W. W. Norton.

Rossi, E. L., & Cheek, D. B. (1988). *Mind-body therapy: Ideodynamic healing in hypnosis*. New York, NY: W. W. Norton.

Rossi, E. L., & Rossi, K. L. (2007). What is a suggestion? The neuroscience of implicit processing heuristics in therapeutic hypnosis and psychotherapy. *American Journal of Clinical Hypnosis, 49*(4), 267–281. doi:10.1080/00029157.2007.10524504

Rossi, E. L., & Rossi, K. L. (2019). Milton H. Erickson's paths of effective psychotherapy. *Science of Psychotherapy*. Retrieved from www.thescienceofpsychotherapy.com/milton-h-ericksons-paths-of-effective-psychotherapy/

Rossi, K. (2018a). The yoga of creative consciousness and cognition in neuropsychotherapy, Part 1. *The Neuropsychotherapist, 6*(10), 20–40.

Rossi, K. (2018b). The yoga of creative consciousness and cognition in neuropsychotherapy, Part 2. *The Neuropsychotherapist, 6*(11), 21–40. Retrieved from: www.thescienceofpsychotherapy.com/wp-content/uploads/2018/11/TNPTV6I11Yoga2PrintVersion.pdf

Rossi, K., Mortimer, J., & Rossi, E. (2015). Integration of classical yoga and the 4-stage creative process of modern science. *International Journal of Public Mental Health and Neurosciences*. Retrieved from www.evolutionofpsychotherapy.com/download/handouts/Ernest-Rossi-Integration-of-Classical-Yoga-and-the-4-Stage-Creative-Process-of-Modern-Science.pdf.

Siegel, D. J. (2012). *The developing mind: How relationships and the brain interact to shape who we are*. New York, NY: Guilford.

Sugarman, L. I., Schafer, P. M., Alter, D. S., & Reid, D. B. (2018). Learning hypnosis wide awake: Can we teach hypnosis hypnotically? *American Journal of Clinical Hypnosis, 61*(2), 140–148. doi:10.1080/00029157.2018.1437710

Teleska, J., & Sugarman, L. I. (1997). Hypnotic abilities. In L. I. Sugarman & W. C. Wester (Eds.), *Therapeutic hypnosis with children and adolescents* (2nd ed., pp. 64–88). Carmarthen, U.K.: Crown House.

Wark, D. M. (2006). Alert hypnosis: A review and case report. *American Journal of Clinical Hypnosis, 48*, 291–300. doi:10.1080/00029157.2006.10401536

Watkins, H. H., & Watkins, J. G. (1997). *Ego states: Theory and therapy*. New York, NY: W. W. Norton.

Williams, W. C. (1984). *The Doctor Stories*. New York, NY: New Directions. (Original work published 1932).

Yapko, M. (2012). *Trancework: An introduction to the practice of clinical hypnosis*. New York, NY: Routledge.

Zeig, J. K. (1994). *Ericksonian methods: The essence of the story*. Levittown, PA: Brunner/Mazel.

Part II

Developmental Imperatives

Lulu's Story

Blood

So anyway a couple weeks ago I looked on the internet and read about "cutting"—"self-harm" they call it. At first I thought—*Crazy Mazy! Why would anyone do that?* But then a while later I realized I was wondering how I could find something very sharp. I was very curious—would it hurt much? Or bleed much? Could I find a razor, something sharper than a kitchen knife? It was a little project I was doing all on my own. It took a couple days to find my cutting tool. I used the upstairs bathroom because it has a door lock, and I did it in the afternoon, at about 4 p.m, when I knew no one else in the family would be home.

I tried it again a few times that week. It was a really strange thing to do. I just needed to try it. And I did it one time this week, too. But then I stopped. Because I'm curious—not crazy.

Lulu Goes to the Doctor

A little while ago, Mom took me to a new doctor. I'll call him Doctor M. I don't like him. I don't want to say his name or think about him. Supposedly, I needed to go to Doctor M so he could evaluate my progress, to see if the ankle was healing properly. But I don't like how I feel when I mention Doctor M. Doctor M is crazy. After that one time, I told Mom no more Doctor M, period! Mom could tell I was serious. We won't go to Doctor M again.

I'm not happy. But no crazy stuff either.

Sheila Talks

Then the next week Mom says we should go to see someone named Sheila, "just to talk". I ask who's Sheila? A doctor? Mom says No, not a doctor. Sheila is a person to talk to. A safe person. I say Not a doctor? No, Mom says. I told you. A safe person.

So we go to Sheila and "just talk." Sheila seems nice. After a while, Sheila asks if Mom can wait outside. I say OK, so Mom leaves the room. Sheila asks if there is anything I want to talk about. I say like what? What's important to you, Sheila says. Something you'd like me to know?

I thought why would I want to tell something to Sheila? I don't even know her. But I don't want to seem like one of the "special needs" kids. My needs aren't special. Just ordinary. So to pass the time I talk about gymnastics, and how doing vaults is like flying, and how a perfect landing is electricity, like a bolt of lightning. You're flying, and all of the kinetic energy of your body suddenly hits the mat SMACK! like a nail struck by a hammer. But now I've got this injury. Now I can't do gymnastics and it's like I'm holding my breath until I can do it again.

So then, when we're finally talking about something I actually do care about, Sheila says time is up, and we'll talk again next week. I'm thinking, *What a colossal waste of time that was.*

Why would I come back next week? After I leave I realize I have been feeling like I was really holding my breath about touching that fear of falling. Of being caught in the headlights.

But the next week, we do come back. And we do meet again. And talk. I tell Sheila about how there are people who cut themselves to deal with their feelings. I ask do people actually do that? She says Yes. She acts cool about it. She changes the subject. She says it must be very difficult to not be able to do gymnastics while you're healing. Well, right. But thinking about that makes me not want to talk anymore. About anything.

Another thing Sheila said, was my bones could be fragile because I was malnourished as a child. That really annoyed me. That's like making excuses. One thing I've learned in gymnastics is nobody wants to hear excuses. Everyone always says I'm so light, so my bones are under less stress. Like that makes it easy? Gymnastics is not easy.

But I don't want to talk about these things. Next Sheila's going to ask when the injury will be healed again. And she's going to say that I'm not so light as I used to be because I can't work out as much and because of puberty. But that happens to all of us. We're getting nowhere. What's the point? It seems like next Sheila's going to say I can't do gymnastics anymore.

So today we had a meeting – Mom, Sheila, and me. I think they knew about the cutting already, but I tell them as if they didn't. It doesn't need to be a secret. It was just something I did. Mom admits that she found a razor blade at the back of my bottom dresser drawer. So she knew I was cutting. Otherwise, why would she be looking through my dresser? Sheila said it would feel better once I told, but I don't feel better. I pretend to Mom that I feel better. But my stomach hurts. I pretend I'm just tired; I decide to go to bed early.

Except that then I realize that now I feel the need to cut more than ever. But I can't do it now because Mom is constantly watching and listening.

I don't want to talk to Sheila anymore. I wish I hadn't talked to her at all.

Lulu and Aliyah

I had almost forgotten how my Dad had a plan to help find answers about where I came from. But one day he announced at dinner time that there is a person who lives in America and is related to me. We aren't sure, but we may be cousins. She's ten years older than me, and she is named Aliyah. She came from a tiny village in Africa, nearby where I came from.

Dad figured out where Aliyah lives and has tracked her down. She now also lives in America. She's a poet, a storyteller.

I'm so excited! Aliyah is going to come to live with my family for a few weeks during her summer break from college!!!

Here's what I already know about Aliyah. She is a genius! It's funny because no one seems to notice how super-smart Aliyah is. It doesn't bother her, but it doesn't seem fair to me.

Now Aliyah has been here for ten days. One thing I have learned is that she has very strict rules. When she tells a story, kids have to keep their TV and cell phones off, so other kids in the neighborhood can listen to her stories without being distracted. And she is serious about it. One kid tried to check his phone when Aliyah was about to tell a story. Aliyah just said *"Out! You know the rules!"* and pointed to the door.

One story Aliyah told was about a newborn baby. It was a real-life story Aliyah heard from a woman in her village. When she told the story, it was like a song. I wished I could sing the way she did. I've noticed how some people have a rhythm when they tell a story, or just when they talk, so it sounds like a poem or a song. I don't have that gift, but I remember how Aliyah would close her eyes as she sang, and sometimes take on the voices of the people in the story.

"Quiet down now you kids," Aliyah would say again, sitting on our front porch steps, "sit here and listen to the song I'm going to sing." It happened in the ancient land where sometimes it seems the land has been lived on so long that it's been all used up. But the story goes like this: In that time, the earth went dry, the crops stopped growing, and the elders decided that the whole village had to move. Travelers spoke of well water, well beyond the horizon. The villagers meant to walk an unbending line across the waste lands to the west. All they could carry were the few hard hopes they held in their hands and pockets. They feared the hunger would take them all, though sometimes people on the way gave them food—gave it so the villagers would move on, keep walking, some thought, and it wasn't all they needed, but they were glad to have it. What they found was so much more walking, all to find the far side of more and more walking.

In that troop of walkers, that walking village, was one young woman who carried a baby in her womb. It was a little girl, a baby who was almost ready to be born, a baby—who may have been *you*, cousin Lulu! Ah, now I have your attention! Yes, the baby in this story might have been our own little Lulu!

Usually the walkers would walk in the dark because it was so hot in the day, and at night the elders found their way by the moon and the stars.

Men and boys were not welcome while the baby girl was being born, but when it was time for the mother to push the baby out, the village had to stop walking for a day, and some went on, without the rest. Then the mother had this little one in her arms. Do you think that little one was *you, Lulu*? Maybe it was! But the mother was worried, so worried, because this little baby was not getting fed. How could the young mother feed her little baby girl if the little one wouldn't suckle, wouldn't take the teat?

God help me, the mother sang, *Need someone to help me*, she sang. But there was no one there to help. Auntie used to help with babies, but she was gone. *And Lord, Lord, make this baby stop crying*! The long night went on and on, and stars crowded the sky, and the baby—she doesn't know what time it is. She goes on crying so hard. *I need somebody who knows newborn babies. Everyone says just leave her be; just let her cry herself to sleep*, they say. But that can't be the answer. She's my sweet baby. I can't let her cry. I can't let anyone hurt my baby—*Oh, my sweet one. Why do you cry like this? I pick you up and still you cry. How it cuts me when you cry!*

Oh my sweet—Oh my sweaty baby. Look at you now—Feel that sweat in that cold desert night. All that crying is hard work! Oh baby, what do you want? You don't even know, do you, you sweet baby thing. But now we remember what Auntie used to do, back when we were all together, when we were still a village—a village full of family. Auntie used to hold a baby and walk through the village and sway from side to side and sing silly songs like, "Tiny baby, tell me why! Tiny baby want to cry!" She could quiet any baby, but she's not here.

And how long! *How long will this tiny baby keep crying? Come on now, I know you want your Mama's milk. I know you want it. And—ah! There you go! There you go! That's good now, baby, you my littlest baby, you my only baby, hush-sh-shush, that's alright now. You're my good baby girl now!*

Here you are, little baby, nursing right over your mother's heart. You're suckling right where you can feel your mother's breathing. You'll be with your mother now, and we'll see your Daddy again someday, somehow, and he'll take your mother in his arms like he used to do and hold your mother so hard—so hard it made her breathing stop, so hard she thought her ribs would break, but it didn't hurt her, it made her strong as steel. It made her fly, far, far away.

Lulu in the Desert

Aliyah said it seems she left most of our words far away in the North of Africa. The mercy is that there is so much I cannot remember. Mom showed me a picture of what she says is me, still in the refugee camp. Five years old. No one else in the picture. Just little girl Me, with arms like matchsticks. Eyes too big for my face. But no sadness.

Aliyah wanted me to tell stories about my life. She wanted me to give her stories that she could put away in her wonderful mind. I said no, I wish I could, but I remember nothing, only the blue sky and the white clouds and the tents, row by row by row. And Aliyah said—See? Look! You're telling the story already! Every detail is a story! So tell us now! What else do you remember about the camp, with the tents, and the blue sky and the white clouds? It took me a little while, but this is what I told to Aliyah:

In the camp, I took our water jug every morning and every evening and waited in the queue. But I only filled the jug halfway, because if I took more, it would be too heavy for me to carry. I laughed with the other girls waiting for water. When I took the water to my mother, my birth mother, she would tell me all about my father. He went far off to be a soldier. She said he would be making a home ready for us where we will grow squashes and yams and melons and all kinds of good food. He will return one day and give us all the love he's saving for my mother and me, and we will be so happy together.

In the camp, people smiled when I went by. I could make people happy when I smiled, so I always smiled. In the camp, all the tents were white, and pitched in straight rows. At the end of each row, it was nothing but white sand. Sky always blue with white tents far off. My birth Mama told me that people sometimes go to their white tents at the edge of the land and float up into the blue sky, all the way back to where they began. She said that at the edge of the land there is deep blue water, water as blue as sky as far as you can see, and sometimes people get into boats and float away across the blue water.

And this I remember: I remember how one day I came back with water in my jug and my birth Mama was not there in the tent. The rice was neat and ready to cook, but she was not there. I said, "Mama?" She didn't answer.

But I knew where she was. She went home to plant our garden and get our house ready for us to live there. She must be ready to grow food for my Dad and me when we return home.

But I could not live alone in the meantime. I was only five. This is when they took my picture to help find a new Mama and Dad to look after me.

So then it was just as my birth mother taught me. We went inside a white cloud and went high, high above the other clouds. We flew away, and I worried, a little, that we were traveling too far, too fast. I thought, how could I find my way back to my home? And how would I find my birth mother again?

But then I fell asleep in my soft chair and all was a wondrous confusion for a long time after that. Everything was strange. I didn't know I was in America, and at first I couldn't understand a word of what my American family was saying to me.

6 Developmental Currents

Main Ideas

1. All developmental frames of reference (e.g., Piaget, Erikson, Freud) reflect various aspects of biological imperatives that influence the direction of plasticity (trance), like currents in a river.
2. How one learns to negotiate critical imperatives (e.g., walking, communication, sexual expression) is the basis for experiential resources.
3. The struggle to master these developmental imperatives can also be viewed through the psychobiological lens of Rossi's Four-Stage Model.

> Caterpillar, caterpillar what did you do?
> I made a cocoon and I grew and grew.
> Then I turned into a butterfly when I made wings
> And I flew in the sky and I saw new things.
> Cause that's what happens when you're alive.
> We learn to change as we struggle to survive.
> And that's the gift that we all share,
> With our feet on the ground and our heads in the air.
> ~ First verse and chorus of "The Caterpillar Song"
> by Laurence I. Sugarman

As I (LIS) write, outside on a fresh summer morning, there is next to me, hanging in a mesh container, a monarch chrysalis. My wife, concerned about the decline in the population of North American Monarchs, rescued a caterpillar from the milkweeds that abound in our yard in order to ensure its successful development. Two days ago, the caterpillar was munching on the milkweed leaf in its new home. Yesterday morning it climbed to the top of the mesh and hung there by its tail, like a comma. So I sat next to it and wrote, looking up frequently, anticipating its next act. I was absorbed in writing for about 90 minutes before I checked again … to see a chameleon-green chrysalis, hanging like a smooth little pinecone, where once was a caterpillar. I said out loud, "You've grown up so fast! How did you know to do that?"

So far our book has presented conceptual frameworks, definitions, and science's contributions to the evolution of minds and how we can change them. We have introduced hypnosis in terms of the embodied mind and the plasticity of trance. Moving forward, we consider development, developmental struggles, trauma, attachment, and resilience separately, even though they are inevitably interwoven. We acknowledge that this separation is artificial. We do so to give each concept the attention it deserves. All of these factors are at play in the embodied mind. They recombine in our therapeutic interactions.

In the next three chapters, we turn to the effects of our development on therapeutic interactions, as well as the reverse: how those interactions may influence development. This next part of our book builds on these ideas and delves deeper into understanding how we become who we are, what evokes plasticity, and how incorporating the skills and principles of hypnosis leads to changing minds. This segment begins by explaining what we mean by human development. It explores the history of developmental psychology and revisits, from a developmental perspective, Rossi's four-stage Novelty-Numinosum-Neurogenesis Effect (2002). It frames developmental tasks as governing currents in trance/plasticity. Recognizing and utilizing these are essential to our work with hypnosis, and exemplify the use of these salient forces through the life-cycle, from infant to elder.

Development is the evolutionary playing-out of countless, contingent, and progressive algorithms, like a forking cascade of falling dominoes. This dynamism, like our explanation of mind, radiates out from one dividing egg to the spreading of our wings (if we are to become a butterfly), taking our first steps, or even writing a book. Development is both relentless and infinitely malleable. Its trajectory is shaped by how we move through our challenges and, especially, our relationships. The force of development—our self-expression—is limited only by our emerging sense of our own potential, our self-efficacy, and self-determination. It becomes a governing influence in trance. It determines how and why we "go plastic." If we are determined to make a chrysalis; take those first courageous baby steps; test our adolescent autonomy, like Stevie; or confront our developmental decline, like George; then other motivations and tasks fade in relevance. Thus, we can imagine developmental tasks as governing currents in the flow of our trances.

A chapter on human development is history in reverse. Development looks forward, while history looks backwards. Yet it is difficult—if not impossible—to separate these two experiences. Our development depends on our history. Our history is biased by our changing memories, causing us to reshape our experience of our past development from our future perspectives.

Development includes everything that allows one cell to proliferate into each of us. We assign categories and labels to aspects of these experiences, to place some order on the creative chaos of becoming. The most well-known labels for various of these aspects are: Motor, Cognitive, Language, Emotional, Social Skills, Sexual, Moral, Identity. Each of these categories projects onto a lifelong functional trajectory. Our sense of time plays a role in the narratives we create to explain ourselves. This is one reason that *Temporal Touring* is a key principle in changing minds. Let's look at Lulu's story to understand what this means.

Lulu lost her birth name. She grew to the age of five in a refugee camp. She dimly remembers rows of white tents, blue sky with white clouds, relentless sun, water to be carried, a father far away, fighting, and danger. She remembers being alone with her mother, a woman in fear all of the time. This time included her mother's pregnancy, and thus, Lulu's prenatal environment. Lulu grew up in this climate of apprehension, uncertainty, and threat. Each of these variables sculpted her narrative and her sense of self. Each of these components impacted her developmental work: learning to support herself on her own two legs, to explore, to imagine with toys and, ultimately, to assert herself. This climate affected her perceptions, emotional agility, sense of safety, and visceral responses: gastrointestinal, metabolic, hormonal, autonomic.

Did she experience—and thereby encode in her young mind—her first wobbly steps as the freedom to run toward something new, or away to safety? Was her agility in climbing rocks in camp with the other children valued as a way to hide from those who might hurt her and take her away, as she had witnessed with others? Was a first doll a baby to be rescued from starvation? Her skinny arms and legs, the results of her own malnourishment, were signs of a starving body. But how did her mind experience and value the nutrients and the water and the security of the people she trusted to foster the fullness of her development? And how does her contemporary memory know what parts of her history to select and suppress as she forms relationships, including the relationship with herself?

In the camp and upon her adoption, clinicians may have duly written down diagnoses, listed the traumas Lulu must have endured, and tracked the ages at which each was encountered. They likely considered her deficits and risk factors. They began to form a picture of how Lulu's developmental stages were affected by her ordeals. They labeled her with developmental delays: how she tracked compared to their norms. They assessed what could be repaired with nutrition and education. They considered how to supply what was missing. They looked forward to her next stages of development, predicting future growth on the basis of the past. They judged Lulu as moving through a series of developmental hoops to land on—or miss—milestones. But, of course, Lulu was neither performing, nor a laboratory animal. She was forming embodied memories and experiences as her developmental drives pushed her on to make sense of her world and thrive in it. Later, she pursued gymnastics. How, we might ask, did this choice grow from her early developmental experiences, her learning to run, and her climbing of rocks? How might a clinician have helped her access this experiential information to be utilized as a body of resources?

Development arises from our history, but propels us forward. Its goal is progressive. The two perspectives, looking backward and forward, are essential to the building of relationships in the present. The snapshots of our brief clinical encounters are moments in our clients' lives, frozen in time. They are best held with the past and future in mind as we *wonder* (and *wander*) about the risks and resources developed along the way. This is the basis for the principal of *Temporal Touring*, enacted in the clinical skill of congression, and explains why a developmental perspective is a crucial ingredient in the use of hypnosis for healing and health. Maintaining an awareness of development forcefully contributes to a caregiver's ability to create a climate for changing minds. That is the therapeutic message of this chapter.

Developmental Science

Developmental psychology is a young science. Its child-focused roots include John Locke's (1690) imagining the mind of the infant and child as a blank slate or "*tabula rasa,*" and Jean-Jacques Rousseau, (1979) idea of innate, unfolding blueprints of developmental stages. Darwin first formed his methodological innovation of recording observations over time by systematically studying his own son's development (Hellal & Lorch, 2010). Developmental psychology paralleled child psychiatry, which itself is less than 100 years old, and built more on the abnormal than normal (Silberman, 2015). Like most sciences, psychology and its subdomains are constantly changing, being modified and deepened. Today, developmental psychology includes the entire range of human growth, birth to death.

Traditionally, conceptualizations of development included Erik Erikson's broad measure of the psychosocial conflicts present in eight stages of life (1950); Freud's emphasis on biological contributions to the psyche, in his theory of psychosexual development (Freud, 1962); Piaget's measures of intellect and cognitive development (1954); and numerous tables of developmental milestones that cover the four domains of motor, social/emotional, language, and cognitive development. Other major contributions include Mahler's Separation-Individuation theory (1968), Watson (1913) and Skinner's (1938) behaviorism, Bowlby's (1958, 1969) attachment theory, Bandura's (1977) social learning theory, Vygotsky's (1978) sociocultural theory, Dewey's educational theories (1938), Kübler-Ross (1969) stages of dying, and Kohlberg's (Kohlberg, Levine, & Hewer, 1983) and Gilligan's (1982) moral theories. No single theory unifies these various perspectives. All of these theories look from the outside, at the infant's, child's, adolescent's, and adult's manifested behavior, to make inferences about the workings on the inside: mind and consciousness. Further detailing each of these contributions is beyond the scope of this book, but we will unpack several of them as they relate to development and how we change minds.

Since the "Decade of the Brain" research of the 1990s (Jones, 1999), an explosion of information on neuroscience and genomics has enhanced our understanding of development. This has allowed researchers to offer new hypotheses, and confirm some old ones, by looking from the inside of the brain and body, to the workings of the developing brain and embodied mind. A foundational shift was the realization that development, at its deepest biological level, is an enduring, lifetime process. The central nervous system continues to forge new and prune old internal connections, as well as build bridges between brain and body that consolidate the embodied mind in a dynamic manner. Further, we have discovered that we keep pluripotent nerve stem cells in our hippocampi—the seat of memory management—ready to recruit to strengthen our learning, for all of our lives (Kandel, Schwartz, Jessell, Siegelbaum, & Hudspeth, 2013). The recognition of this ongoing growth and change led to the adoption of the term "neuroplasticity" to refer to the brain's ability to reorganize itself and, more popularly, to the newfound awareness that we can endlessly learn to change our minds. It means that the tendency to rigidity described by Doidge's "Plastic Paradox" (2015; see Chapter 4) is not inevitable. We are always capable of creating new experiential resources. The more we practice changing, the better we get.

Beyond neurocentric studies, others have considered a more systemic perspective on development. Porges's (2011) polyvagal theory (see also Chapters 3 and 4) helped clarify the embodied body-brain connections that inform attention to our environment both for survival and protection through social engagement. LeDoux (1996) explored how emotions—themselves embodied—are inextricably tied to the maturation of the brain, giving credence to their critical role in dealing with trauma and developing resilience. Damasio (2018) has contributed to our understanding of the creation of consciousness within the meld of the biopsychosocial that ultimately separates humans from other creatures. Looking backwards through these conceptual frames provides a more integrated view of development from a microscopic to the macroscopic systems level. That is what we mean by *Systems Thinking*, as we interact hypnotically.

Stanley Greenspan's (1997) three decades of research on child development attempted to integrate domains of sensory perception, emotion, attention/cortical arousal, relatedness, intention, and development of consciousness (via symbology) into a whole. Essentially, Greenspan introduced the notion of a developing mind, as we have conceived it. Greenspan proposes six emotional stages of mind development, which have been further detailed by Perry (2009) into a "neurosequential model" (see also Chapter 8). Similarly, Daniel Siegel (2015) has studied and conceptualized the neurodevelopmental aspects of attachment and subsequent social relatedness that we will discuss in more detail in the next section (Chapters 9 through 11) of this book.

Greenspan linked genetics with intra-uterine, family, and cultural environments as compounding factors in development, such that nature and nurture became another false dichotomy. In this way, his efforts contribute to understanding the countless variables that make us who we are, and defy the capacity of any researcher or any single theoretical approach to account for them. Our development is more than the sum of its statistical measures. This is especially true since we tend to rely on the statistical parameters of the normal distribution curve, while learning more about development from the exceptional, i.e., those outside that range. To help our clients, we have to temper the norms with our wisdom that each person is unique, an "N" of one, formed more from chance than from calculation. We are all outliers in some way … and it is in the arena of what makes us exceptional that the resources for change and healing lie.

When we were newborns, being hungry, feeling alone, wanting touch, or needing sleep arose from developmental imperatives. Developmental imperatives drive need. Multiple factors impacted both how those needs were met and what we learned as babies in the fulfillment of those needs. These factors include the genes we possess, their priority for expression in the moment, the neurohumoral climate of the womb we resided in previously, the nutrients available, our caregivers' ability to recognize and respond to us in ways that promote resilience, the safety of the neighborhood, the rules of the culture, and so on.

In order for neurons to make new connections via the neurotropic factors and the drive of the dopaminergic "want system," an activation must occur from an experience. Since we start as sensing and emoting beings that are fully dependent on others for survival, perception is more primitive and determinant than cognition. Next, we begin to "catalogue affective reactions to sensory experiences" (Greenspan, 1997, p. 19.) That experience is felt. It is embodied. These emotional experiences are believed to organize the mind, to provide a structure that sorts events into emotionally felt categories, and later leads to thinking, and then to language. Emotional embodiment can be thought of as one of the experiential resources clinicians must tap into to if they intend to assist growth and change. Activating perception via emotion enables retrieval of memories, often only at an unconscious level. These may emerge as felt sensory shifts—interoceptions—that are enacted and exposed as behavioral changes including, but not limited to, eye-movement, facial expression, breathing rate, and posture. These can be detected as "trance openings" and utilized by the astute clinician. Words for these experiences are last to emerge, if they ever do.

Updating Developmental Theories in a Hypnotic Framework

Piaget (1954) strove to describe the structure of cognitive development by theorizing four stages that he gleaned from careful observation and testing of his hypotheses. The sensorimotor stage, in which the child experiences the world through movement and senses and learns object permanence is now further supported by our understanding of mirror neurons, the infant's emotional readiness, and relational wiring. During these first two years of life, trance openings involve movement, senses, and emotions. This is when language is developing. We sing lullabies and rock babies to sooth and calm, nourish them with mother's milk, smile, frown, cry, and adjust our faces, voices, and movements, utilizing hypnotic techniques instinctively. Think of baby Lulu crying with her mother on their desert trek or the many mother-baby scenes you have experienced or imagined. The polyvagal theory posits that social orientation and the perception of threat/danger interact in ways that can be fundamental to our developing minds. We learn to understand who is safe. When this developmental synchrony is dis-coordinated or missing, we increase our risk for psychiatric disorders.

Motor skills are further acquired in the preoperational stage, during which Piaget watched how children learned the concepts of size, volume, quantity, and relationships, and how they tested what they saw in the world. From two to seven, healthy children are in motion: they learn by doing, they invent, experiment, build, shape, imagine, and test the world. So much is new. Adventures open them to attending, to curiosity, to learning. In this receptive state, new ideas (i.e., suggestions), are incorporated in the integration of ideas and development of self. The child who wakes from a bad dream and seeks a grownup for comfort can be asked, in this "plastic" state, how they would give the bad dream a new ending—to change it and to remove the bad parts. The very notion of a self begins to move beyond the me and I of the "terrible twos" to an increasingly nuanced sense that more fully emerges in adolescence. Lulu, at five, lost her home, her family, her country, and even aspects of her sense of self, and had to begin anew. What did this do to her sense of self? She was left with different selves to know and merge.

In the concrete operational stage, roughly ages seven to 11, children begin to have rules and some logic, that influence how they think and tell their stories. They play games to see how rules are made and broken and refashioned, and are ever inventive in ways to win and achieve. Yet they are literal in their reasoning. "Can you tell me your name?" is answered with, "Yes." Their imagination is full of what they have experienced in the world, and sprinkled with novelty as they step into their imaginary worlds. These are the trance moments, when care-givers join in those worlds with them, and offer "suggestions" that shift or reframe emotions and perceptions. In a sense, the care-givers help recolor experiences in a different shade. Until the child reaches the formal operational stage, during which abstract reasoning emerges, suggestions are best received when they are more literal than metaphorical. Abstract reasoning is made possible by the rapid growth of the frontal lobes during adolescence. The trance openings are met with more resistance, in part due to autonomy needs, requiring different skills from the caregiver.

The formation of identity, during which the narrative of the self becomes a steady focus, was a central theme in Erikson's Psychosocial Stages (1950). During adolescence, the openings to trance are even more directly personal and emotional. By the final stage, "Maturity," the self is reflective. We revisit and reexamine our lives, looking for integrity, hoping to accept ourselves as we prepare for our own departure. This stage is a somewhat older version of adolescence, but with more experience and wisdom. The Pennsylvania Dutch expression, "Too soon old, too late smart," no longer rings true. Aging, due in part to our increasing longevity, brings benefits. We are smarter because of more experience and relieved, thanks to brain research, to know we could not have done certain things earlier because our minds were not yet fully developed. So our trance openings become more reflective and our past experiences become resources.

Freud (1962), too, provided a step-wise theory, drawing from his medical perspective that each disease has antecedents to be uncovered. From his patients' narratives and symptoms, he looked backwards to early development for explanations. The idea that the past influences the present continues as a legacy in most psychotherapy. And yet, as we have learned from newer studies of memory, our recall is fallible, flexible, and the act of remembering is not essential to our growth and learning. Freud's theory of psycho-sexual development was the first to openly address a topic that had been silenced and is still evolving with our awareness: gender fluidity. While some of his hypotheses have not been confirmed, his practice of combining empirical research with clinical observation created a more detailed portrait of our developing minds.

All of these researchers, clinicians, and theorists would likely heartily agree that human development is multifaceted, complex and, to various extents, idiosyncratic. They would probably concur that they are all proverbial blind men describing the elephant, or, less proverbially but perhaps more accurately, describing a caterpillar becoming a butterfly. What we are now asking is: How do the elephant, caterpillar, and butterfly feel about and learn from their experiences? That is what we will explore next.

Developmental Achievements Are Hypnotic Resources

The unique internal experience and encoding of our developmental struggles form our risks and resources. The risks arise from our genetics and expand to the maladaptive ruts into which we keep falling. For example, "Why does that person keep choosing partners who are so needy?" In our story, why does Stevie consider Micky a friend? Our resources, also genomic in origin, arise from our lessons in courage: the battle scars of falling on our diapers repeatedly as we learned to walk. Our hearts only feel like they break. We actually become more courageous, by going through the process of healing.

To access these risks and resources as clinicians, we mine those developmental episodes that we consider inflection points. We wonder about the elements of those critical developmental task experiences that made us who we are, and ask how we can use them for the rest of our lives. We do this by posing hypnotic questions. We ask—both to better understand those in our care and to disruptively launch an implicit processing heuristic—the same question asked of the caterpillar: "How did you know to do that?"

To better explain how developmental achievements can be resources that are utilized hypnotically in clinical settings, let's consider a collection of vignettes.

Early Childhood: Separation Anxiety and Psychosomatic Symptoms

Danny, age five, came to treatment because of severe cyclic vomiting not due to any detectable metabolic disease. He had been hospitalized several times in the past year. As a result, his physicians had recommended psychotherapy. There was no clear etiology, so his diagnosis was tentative, and available information from the parents was conflicting and vague. Danny's parents were divorced, and the custodial arrangement complex, as they lived hours apart. I (JHL) knew that meeting Danny would reveal much more than these sparse details. At our first meeting, Danny came with mother and sat close to her while eyeing the toys in the playroom.

"Do you know why your mother has brought you here today?," I asked.

"No," he replied with a shake of his head.

"What might be a reason?," I inquired.

"Because I was bad?," he asked.

"Hmmm." I paused to observe mother and child's interaction. "What might be another reason?"

"To play with the cars over there?"

"Yes, that is exactly right!" I responded. "Shall we do that, while mom waits out there?"

Mom left, saying in a low tone, "I can't believe he is separating so easily."

Danny was already busy with the cars. He engaged the miniature cars into "good guy, bad guy" scenarios, alternating roles, then added a police car which quickly became the bad guy. Next, he became a super hero and solved all of the bad guy issues. This little fellow was working hard to figure out the rules of life—what is good, what is bad, an age appropriate task—while conveying themes of unpredictability and helplessness. As I observed him, I wondered to myself what his home life was like. Only super heroes could really solve complex problems. During our play together, there were many moments of disruption: a question, a comment, doing something unexpected. All occurred in a safe, fun, and respectful manner.

What were the hypnotic moments that shifted perspective? As he careened a truck out of control on the pretend road, headed for my car, I asked, "Who can be safe around that kind of driver?"

"Better get out of the way," he yelled. "Good idea! Thanks for the warning," I said, "It helps to be prepared."

With each comment, I responded to his movements, his facial expressions, his sounds, and his rhythms: manifestations of his embodied mind. He was earnest, focused, tense, tricky, and anxious as the bad guy. He was smart, commanding, and self-assured as the good guy. All these emotions were enacted, as resources, through his play. Each of my comments intended to build on the developmental achievements—the resources expressed in the good and bad guy behaviors—while resonating and mirroring the embodied emotions. The cars "gassed up." They went to the garage for repairs. They parked when they were done with their travels. These were predictable and necessary events. There was no discussion of his stomach, of vomiting, or of anxiety. Instead, we were focused on how to be in charge, how to get out of the way, how to stay safe in a world where good and bad were confusing.

As treatment continued, Danny had no further stomach or vomiting issues. Anxiety reduced, and he adopted more and more of the super-hero's qualities, including listening more to his body's needs, to drink when he was thirsty, to eat when he was hungry, and to bathroom when his bladder or bowels required that.

You might ask how this therapeutic example contrasts with such evidenced-based interventions as cognitive behavioral therapy. How does this organic, person-centered, and responsive interaction fit with those formalized constructs? The answer is that these formulaic interventions tend to omit relational, temporal, developmental, or systems principles. They do not include room for the clinician to respond idiosyncratically to the spontaneous and unique abilities of the person in care, who may be at multiple simultaneous developmental ages. We will discuss this further in our closing chapter.

A basic hypnotic principle—thinking and responding developmentally—invites the clinician to use gestures, evoke sensory experiences, arouse the cortex, be relational, and foster the interactions that can lead to new neuronal connections. Clinicians can provide opportunities for reparative experiences to augment the missing, fledgling, or ruptured developmental stage. Danny needed safer attachment figures.

Late Childhood: Social Communication

We can imagine our character Lyle, at age 11, in fifth grade, friendless after his friend Kenneth moved away. Developing social skills is a many-stepped ordeal during childhood. Lyle could engage with his stuffed animals; he could line up his army men, providing a defense against the world. He loved the warmth and closeness of his favorite soft toys, and felt strong when his army men defended his world. How do we use these strengths to assist Lyle in navigating among his peers? Lyle likes school and he loves to write. His teacher, fortunately, noticed Lyle's sadness when his friend moved away and sent him to the school counselor (C).

C: "You must be missing Kenneth since he moved away. I know I am missing him."

L: "Yeah. Wish he were still here."

C: "Me, too. I bet he is missing all of us. It would be fun to write him and tell him some stories about what is happening in his old school."

L: (His face lighting up) "Yeah, like when dufus Bob dropped the teacher's papers and they blew out the window!"

C: (Laughing) "Or last week, when your class went to the aquarium?"

L: "Oh, yeah, he would love to hear about how Sammy stuck his hand in the shark tank. I thought the teacher was going to blow a gasket!"

Empathic, hopeful, accepting, resonating with Lyle's memories, the counselor evokes the emotional, embodied memories that remind Lyle he is part of a community, even with the loss of his best friend. The counselor opens the door that allows Lyle to make stories—his innate talent—of his memories that at once continue his attachment to his only friend and help him identify himself as someone who would *not* drop the teacher's papers or stick his hand in the shark tank. Even though he may not yet grasp who he is, it is developmentally appropriate and necessary for him to first understand and articulate who he is not. The counselor's relating to these developmental imperatives by evoking his narrative abilities is an example of a developmentally aware response. Imagine that she wonders out loud about how the act of writing will bring him new insight and confidence, even new friends (an implicit processing heuristic). If she encourages the writing and telling of these stories in this way, then she is being even more hypnotic.

Adolescence: Identity and Individuation

According to her mom, 15-year-old Alex had begged to start therapy. At her first session, after I (JHL) asked her what brought her to this place, she replied, "I just wanted to see what it would feel like." She was quiet, alternating between avoiding eye contact and long, unblinking stares with her eyes locked on mine. Her dress revealed more than her words. She wore loosely draped male clothes, sneakers several sizes too big, partly-shaved hair with a mullet mane, and baseball cap. Where was she developmentally? Likely in the throes of sorting out identity. Alex is an accomplished student, writer, poet, and musician, so we spent our time learning about each other through those avenues. She was searching for a place to reveal her-/himself that would be safe and different from home. I approached him/her with humor and appealed to his/her love of words.

"I understand you love to write. You love poetry. Do you have a poem you could share?"

S/he responded by reciting a poem that she loved.

"Amazing," I said, adding, "I never got beyond, "Roses are red, and so are noses—"

S/he laughed. Her/his facial expression softened, "That's not how it goes," s/he replied.

"Says who?" I asked, and so we approached, implicitly, challenging the world's rules on gender.

We purposely write with the s/he to remind us that the exploring, the transition, was not to be confined by words, but needed to be inclusive while inconclusive. Gender dysphoria, the label Alex knew inside out, failed to capture the struggles that accompany defining oneself. Alex struggled, told his parents he was trans, and found a new name for himself. His story is still evolving.

Young Adult: Change Can also Occur Without Conscious Awareness.

Sarah, age 25, was in psychotherapy for about a year. One day, after a session with her doctor, Sarah noticed that she was walking confidently for the first time, without showing any of her previous pervasive anxiety. Sarah marveled at the absence of those familiar uneasy feelings, but had no idea how they had left her. She knew how anxiety felt: the tightness in her chest and stomach, the worry and constant dread. Its absence was not the feeling of something missing, like forgetting her phone or keys. This was a calm, a quiet; something new and inviting. She needed to test whether this new feeling was durable. She wanted it to be. Sarah recalled an image that had plagued her since she was a little girl when she had been cautioned about it one Halloween before trick-or-treating. It was the sensory image of biting into an apple … with a razor blade hidden inside. The image stopped short of the physical pain. The dread was in the potential. That experience, which had haunted her persistently in spite of all reason for decades, had simply lost its potency. She could no longer feel the image, nor the shock that went with it. It was gone. So was all the feeling of anxiety that had resided so enduringly in her body. No amount of reasoning, logic, or careful analysis revealed what caused the shift, but she knew something about the way she related to her doctor was the catalyst. Hadn't she experienced this new feeling after leaving the office? In some intuitive way, she understood that the change came from a shift in a very early, preverbal experience, something that occurred even before the iconic apple.

At its core, changing our minds involves encouraging growth and maturation. It requires accessing the felt experience, activating arousal in the cortex, and providing safety in the relationship. Was the safety of the doctor-patient relationship novel? Did this novelty activate attention and begin to link to early formative life experiences? The doctor had heard Sarah's stories of family life: turbulent, chaotic, and full of dread. She had resonated with the ups and downs of Sarah's experiences, without judgment and full of welcoming silences. While Sarah was unable to identify what had happened, what caused the profound shift, we can hypothesize that the plasticity of trance during treatment evoked an opening for feeling safe, providing a missing experience.

The Traumatized Adult: Early Impact

As the infant moves from sensing to relating to interacting with intention and becoming an "I," s/he is developing an awareness of boundaries and of agency. The "terrible twos" occur when the doing for oneself is more important than meeting a need. Holding the juice cup presides over satisfying thirst. When nurtured, this will grow over time into communicating for the sake of communicating and not just to meet a need. Any trauma along that developmental road will affect how the emotions not only shape cognitive abilities, but also shape the personality, including defenses and the individual coping strategies.

For example, 30 year-old Tanya lost her eye in an accident at age four. While playing with her friends, she had leaned forward to see a toy screwdriver at the very moment her friend moved it toward her face so she could see it better. It pierced her in the eye, and she lost the cornea at a time predating corneal transplantation. Realizing she was alone, friendless, and unhappy, she gathered the courage to come to therapy. Tanya presented in therapy as a flattened, two-dimensional version of a person. While academically very capable, she moved in the world like a shadow on the periphery. Quiet, her face often without emotion, her unmoving prosthetic eye noticeably different from her seeing eye, she did not even mention her trauma until the therapist (JHL) inquired directly. Most of the tragic event was repressed. There was little conscious memory for what had happened, and no awareness of how the accident affected her current functioning. As Tanya slowly recovered memories of this traumatic incident, she talked about losing herself, her "I," when she lost the eye. She guessed that she had heard "I" when the doctors had said "eye." She could not see the world properly with just one eye. She was separated from her parents for long periods while in the hospital, since this happened before parents were permitted to stay with their hospitalized children. The pain that developed while the physicians tried to save the eye had been excruciating. Her trauma had returned her to the state of being a dependent infant, but in a state of fear and pain. She had to re-grow her sense of self, of the "I." She had to relearn agency and boundaries. Clinically, in our work, we both needed to see (sic) her as an infant, but with adult resources.

"Your little self was curious. You had an experience that seemed to say, 'Curiosity hurts the cat.'"

"Kills the cat," she interrupted.

"That's curious," I continued, "Your curiosity hurt your eye; did it kill the cat?"

"Maybe that's what I thought: that I died."

"Curious," I repeated, "Very curious. I'm curious that you are now curious about what happened."

This vein of inquiry, of comment, done with genuine curiosity and authentic wonder, is an example of the many clinical strategies based on our four hypnotic principles: *Systems Thinking, Temporal Touring, Relational Being,* and *Narrative Listening.* It disrupts patterns, creating novelty and thus, the potential for change. Slowly, she became a three-dimensional person of substance, less afraid and more assertive. This is a vivid example of how the consequences from traumatic events can throw developmental imperatives off track. Healthy growth and development depend on curiosity and exploration. These had been obstructed by her early trauma and were now enacted in her therapy.

Developmental Thinking with Adults

We can apply developmental thinking to working with any adult. It is helpful to think of adults as children in grown up bodies and to find the experiential resources from their past development. How one learns to negotiate critical imperatives (e.g., walking, communication, sexual expression) is the basis for experiential resources. Few adults recall when they first walked, talked, or were toilet trained, but they can recall events of heightened emotion. We might ask: What was your best birthday celebration? Did you ever go to the emergency room? Was there a family vacation you loved? Who was your favorite teacher? These are questions that invite curiosity, promote temporal touring, heuristic processing, and stir emotions. All of these together—evoking the feelings, gaining attention, being interested and present—begin a cascade of internal, embodied responses. This stimulates the non-conscious and pushes to the surface the items needed for change. The responses will also exhibit preferred modes of coping, defensives, and other clues to the style of navigating earlier developmental imperatives. Each becomes useful for determining what the clinician can suggest or say. Are there corrective lessons, corrective lenses, corrective orienting, new perceptions, or new movements that can unlock old patterns, loosen old associations, and make space for reorganizing the mind?

Sometimes the most confusing and challenging clients respond to relating developmentally. The key to understanding many difficult presentations is placing the psychological response in a developmental framework (Silva, 2004, p. 158). Mysterious disease processes that yield no significant diagnostic findings from routine tests often have their basis in early childhood experiences or traumas. These are implicitly remembered, outside of conscious awareness, but still exerting an effect on the person (Silva, 2004, p. 248). Polly's story exemplifies this.

Polly was a 40-year-old woman who had experienced many losses in the few years prior to starting therapy. She began therapy because she was chronically tired and unable to get out of bed on many days, following an episode of an influenza-like illness. No test results confirmed any "biological" explanation for her fatigue. Like many people in her position, she scoured the internet looking for ways to explain her symptoms. If Robinson were treating her, he would have known to search for the traumas in her past (there were many), to help activate her experiential resources for survival (also many), and to reorganize the lessons learned through the new, attuned relationship with her. These rich results, produced by applying hypnotic skills, can never be achieved with medication alone, even when medications help to reduce symptoms. Polly's memories of all the times she had struggled through to a new solution were activated, and this time, she found new solutions by asserting herself, empowered to go forward while looking back at what no longer worked, and openly grieving her many losses.

Aging

Development, as we have emphasized, is lifelong. We move through a series of milestones of firsts: graduations, marriages, new jobs, starting a family; then losses of parents, friends, and health, and oftentimes mind and self as we have known them. Aging is replete with ironies. What we have claimed as our strengths can become our losses. Our deficits may become new strengths. Our hard-won autonomy may revert to dependency—why are those adult diapers branded "Depends"? Our goals and aspirations are reexamined, the looking back often consuming more time than the looking forward. There is so much more history than energy. We have an accumulation of aches and pains, each one a reminder of what we have endured, struggled through and learned. We call this wisdom. We engage in broader commitments, embrace and care for others, and transform ourselves as we reflect on our lifetimes, as does Robinson's patient George. Or we don't.

This is illustrated in one more developmental vignette. An accomplished researcher of the mind and author began, for the first time in his adult life, to have recurrent nightmares at age 86. He awoke from them with dread and had been wondering if he was dying. He described the dreams in great detail. All started out as experiences from his more vital and generative past: gaining his first academic position, driving to lecture at a large gathering, on his way to receive an achievement award. Each started with familiar confidence and exhilaration. Each turned dark and ominous: the elevator was stuck, he could not remember where he parked his car, he lost his way to the ceremony and they revoked the award. In each case he felt he was edging toward dementia, losing his mind, and most profoundly "my sense of self." He feared "What my mind is telling me." In a series of reflections and respectfully silent processing over about 90 minutes, I (LIS) wondered with him whether the chosen emotion may be misapplied. Could he have forgotten how he brazenly used to explore? Wander to unknown experiences? Challenge long held assumptions? Struggle through confusion to enlightenment? Savor the "AHA!" moments? The next day he shared that he was feeling much better and, with a smile, said that processing these dreams "Must be how I'm keeping my wits about me these days," and that he was, "Preparing my mind for the next great adventure, whatever it might bring."

Action to Language to Ideas: Importance of Movement

Returning to Greenspan's stages of development, the toddler's foray into willful reciprocity is an interactive stage that sets in motion a movement from the fulfillment of desires attained through actions (e.g., the comfort of suckling at mother's breast), to the use of verbal symbols—language development—that leads to ideas. An action defines a desire in the same way that a verbal symbol will later define an idea (Greenspan, 1997, p. 59). Hypnotic skills include acute attention to nonverbal behavior. The smallest movements of our clients can reveal the early actions related to desires and needs. These movements, often unconscious, are glimpses into their past, doorways to explore, as are Rossi's hand mirroring technique and Levine's somatic experiencing approach. The clinician need not and cannot know what they truly signal, just that they are enactments of underlying shifts and growing plasticity to acknowledge and engage with. Until recently, emotional embodiment as an experiential resource has been sorely missing in most treatment modalities other than the hypnosis skill set. Ideodynamic techniques have always been taught in the hypnotic skill set. A nod or shake of the head, a "yes finger" or "no finger," can bypass the language center and hook into emotions. Unlike other psychological treatment approaches, hypnotic techniques integrate the mind and body in a developmental context.

Once language is acquired, the ability to use verbal symbols for expression makes it attractive. On the surface, it seems to make treatment easier, until one begins to think developmentally. Much of what requires "relearning" has its roots in the first year of life and predates language. Our work must keep this in mind. At the same time, using language in novel and creative ways can unleash patterns, too.

Asking a client to talk with their body, to "ask the tummy what it needs to feel better," or the head what it needs to be rid of migraines, captures attention and activates an internal awareness of the body's resources. In this heuristic process a person regresses to those years where imaginary play—included talking with dolls or imaginary friends—and emotional expression found safe outlets. Most adults usually "hear" clinicians' questions, answers, and advice through the filter of their preferred coping strategies, needs, and wishes. Repeating their words, perhaps in a shifting context or with different emphasis—another mirroring technique—can also unlock patterns and stimulate neuroplastic changes.

Research suggests that the words we use can target different parts of the mind, adding a laser-like possibility to hypnotic suggestions. Amir Raz and his colleagues found that carefully crafted suggestions could change focal brain activity (Raz, Fan, & Posner, 2005). David Spiegel (2007) reported that functional magnetic resonance imagery signaled increased activity in the somatosensory cortex when pain was experienced. However, when patients were told, "The pain will not bother you," brain activity increased in the anterior cingulate gyrus. Jensen (2011a), Jensen (2011b) described how therapeutic communication can alleviate pain with language directed at different functional sites. The symbols—the words we use for thinking and communicating—have an emotional and relational connection that are developmentally and, to varying degrees, idiosyncratically rooted. There is promise that this research will transfer to our daily interactions with clients.

The struggles to master the developmental imperatives, to move through the stages of human growth, have parallels to Rossi's four-stage model of the creative process (2002). There is some overlap, which reminds us that patterns at the cellular level are replayed throughout the body in other systems, at higher and higher levels. During data collection (stage one), the sensations that produce information are gathered. Incubation (stage two) is the cauldron of feelings, where there is review, conflict, and negative experiences. Arousal of the cortical functions extends through both these stages. This is followed by a period of inner work, in which perceptions can morph and repattern as the brain reorganizes experience. Illumination (stage three) is a time of intuition, even insight, and positive change—like the experience of Sarah, described above, who was suddenly free of anxiety. The body begins to relax and there is less arousal, as new synapses form. In Verification (stage four), the experience is translated into words, thinking occurs, and a new experience is encoded, both in the brain and in the person's life.

Each of the experiences that propel our development from dependence to autonomy travels through a similar, four-stage process. Sensations flood the infant during the initial data collection stage, who expresses them with crying and smiling through a prolonged incubation. How these feelings are matched, nurtured, responded to, or ignored during illumination helps organize the mind through the verification stage. A need gets met and is associated with a feeling, leaving a trail to follow the next time that particular need presents itself. Bit by bit, cycle by cycle, in fits and bursts, the infant moves toward symbols that will become the words that further organize her mind. Learning to live through this disruptive unfolding, and using that learning resourcefully, is at the heart of experiencing our development and growth. Relating to these embodied cycles, then responding to them authentically, is the key to developmental awareness in therapeutic hypnosis.

Our Four Principles, which we have likened to managing editors, also play roles in thinking, relating, and responding developmentally.

Temporal Touring is most evident. As clinicians, we are accessing prior and future developmental achievements as lessons and resources. We are also mindful of the current developmental imperatives that are churning within the person in our care.

Systems Thinking plays a role, because we need to include in our responses both the internal mind systems and the sociocultural systems that impact the person in our care. Internally, we account for cognitive development versus decline, the surging of hormonal tides versus their retreat, and the client's quest for identity versus their impending loss of self. From a sociocultural systems perspective, we consider how this person's developmental expression—gender, developmental diversity, race, aging, recovery from loss or addiction—can best play out within the larger system.

Relational Being, in the developmental context, involves determining the developmental age of the person in care with whom we are relating. Are we reconstructing a three-dimensional self with an infant, as in the vignette of the woman who lost her eye as a young child? Are we projecting toward the unknown of aging and dying by supporting the client in the use of their life's best resources?

Within a developmental frame, *Narrative Listening* involves the playful stories we co-create while playing with miniature cars; the storylines—as in George's haunting from Orwell's rats, and those of the elderly man's nightmares—that we borrow; and of course, the narrative arcs that we give our developmental accomplishments, as Lyle, Lulu, George, and Robinson are destined to do.

Growth is hard. It happens in struggles and leaps. Like learning, we feel the energy expended to develop, to mature, to age. It is like a series of temper tantrums, ebbing and flowing; like emerging from a chrysalis. Growth finds a way.

Having set this developmental frame in place and exposed its governing power, in the next chapter we will examine notions of resistance and acceptance in change, both therapeutic and not, that are inevitable facets of growing up.

Questions and Assignments for Further Discussion

1. Given your understanding of the hypnosis skills from Chapter 5, discuss possible answers to the question raised in this chapter with regard to Lulu's past history: "How might a clinician have helped her access this experiential information to be utilized as a body of resources?" (p.)
2. List iconic developmental processes, such as egg-to-caterpillar-to-chrysalis-to-butterfly, that can be used as therapeutic metaphors.
3. How might the personal meditative or contemplative practice that focuses only on the present, the "now," be used beneficially within a developmental framework? In other words, how would you teach these skills differently to six-year-olds versus, 12, 18, and 30-year-olds?
4. What behavioral findings characterize a developmental "inflection point"?

References

Bandura, A. (1977). *Social learning theory.* Englewood Cliffs, NJ: Prentice Hall.

Bowlby, J. (1958). The nature of the child's tie to his mother. *International Journal of Psychoanalysis, 39*, 350–371. Retrieved from www.psychology.sunysb.edu/attachment/online/nature%20of%20the%20childs%20tie%20bowlby.pdf.

Bowlby, J. (1969). *Attachment. Attachment and loss: Vol. 1. Loss.* New York, NY: Basic Books.

Damasio, A. (2018). *The strange order of things: Life, feeling, and the making of cultures.* New York, NY: Pantheon.

Dewey, J. (1938). *Experience and education.* New York, NY: Touchstone.

Doidge, N. (2015). Hypnosis, neuroplasticity, and the plastic parodox. *American Journal of Clinical Hypnosis, 57*(3), 349–354. doi:10.1080/00029157.2015.985572

Erikson, E. (1950). *Childhood and society.* New York, NY: W. W. Norton.

Freud, S. (1962). *Three essays on the theory of sexuality.* (J. Strachey, Trans.). New York, NY: Basic Books (Original work published 1905).

Gilligan, C. (1982). *In a different voice: Psychological theory and women's development.* Cambridge, MA: Harvard University Press.

Greenspan, S. (1997). *The growth of the mind.* Reading, MA: Perseus Books.

Hellal, P., & Lorch, M. (2010). Darwin's contribution to the study of child development and language acquisition. *Language & History, 53*(1), 1–14. doi:10.1179/175975310X12640878626147

Jensen, M. (2011b). *Hypnosis for chronic pain management.* New York, NY: Oxford.

Jensen, M. P. (2011a). The neurophysiology of pain perception and hypnotic analgesia: Implications for clinical practice. *American Journal of Clinical Hypnosis, 51*(2), 123–148. doi:10.1080/00029157.2008.10401654

Jones, E. G., & Mendell, L. M. (1999). Assessing the decade of the brain. *Science, 284* (5415), 739. doi:10.1126/science.284.5415.739

Kandel, E. R., Schwartz, J. H., Jessell, T. M., Siegelbaum, S. A., & Hudspeth, A. J. (Eds.). (2013). *Principles of neural science* (5th ed.). New York, NY: McGraw-Hill.

Kohlberg, L., Levine, C., & Hewer, A. (1983). *Moral stages: A current formulation and a response to critics.* Basel, NY: Karger.

Kübler-Ross, E. (1969). *On death and dying.* New York, NY: Routledge.

LeDoux, J. (1996). *The emotional brain.* New York, NY: Touchstone.

Locke, J. (1690). *An essay concerning humane understanding.* London, UK: Thomas Basset.

Mahler, M. S. (1968). *On human symbiosis and the vicissitudes of individuation.* Madison Connecticutt and New York: International Universities Press.

Perry, B. (2009). Examining child maltreatment through a neurodevelopmental lens: Clinical applications of the neurosequential model of therapeutics. *Journal of Loss and Trauma, 14,* 240–255. doi:10.1080/15325020903004350

Piaget, J. (1954). *The construction of reality in the child.* New York, NY: Basic Books.

Porges, S. (2011). *The polyvagal theory.* New York, NY: W. W. Norton.

Raz, A., Fan, J., & Posner, M. I. (2005). Hypnotic suggestion reduces conflict in the human brain. *Proceedings of the National Academy of Sciences, 102*(28), 9978–9983. doi:10.1073/pnas.0503064102

Rossi, E. L. (2002). *The psychobiology of gene expression: Neuroscience and neurogenesis in hypnosis and the healing arts.* New York, NY: W. W. Norton.

Rousseau, J. J. (1979). *Émile* (A. Bloom, Trans.). New York, NY: Basic Books.

Siegel, D. (2015). *The developing mind.* New York, NY: Guilford.

Silberman, S. (2015). *Neurotribes: The legacy of autism and the future of neurodiversity.* New York, NY: Penguin Random House.

Silva, R. (Ed.). (2004). *Posttraumatic stress disorders in children and adolescents handbook.* New York, NY: W.W. Norton & Co.

Skinner, B. F. (1938). *The behavior of organisms.* New York: Appleton-Century-Crofts.

Spiegel, D. (2007). The mind prepared: Hypnosis in surgery. *Journal of the National Cancer Institute, 99*(17), 1280–1281. doi:10.1093/jnci/djm131

Vygotsky, L. S. (1978). *Mind in society.* Cambridge, MA: Harvard University Press.

Watson, J. B. (1913). Psychology as the behaviorist views it. *Psychological Review, 20*(2), 158–177. doi:10.1037/h0074428

Lyle's Story

Lyle in High School

We could call her Olivia. Because to me she looked just almost exactly like the teenaged Juliet in the 1968 Franco Zeffirelli movie version of *Romeo and Juliet*, as played by 16-year-old Olivia Hussey—long straight black hair, dark eyes, and that curvy femaleness that is like nothing else on earth. I have watched that DVD of *Romeo and Juliet* I don't know how many times. And I always have come away with a weirdly comforted feeling about how Romeo and Juliet both committed suicide *accidentally*. It was all just a misunderstanding. In a way, no one can be blamed for the disaster at the end because everything was logical and well-intentioned. But then I always go back and watch it again, because the outcome is so ridiculous—it wasn't logical at all; it's agonizing. It shouldn't have happened. When I think of it, my mind goes dark.

The girl I'm calling Olivia sits just two rows away from me in calculus class, usually wearing one in a series of totally distracting short skirts.

What can be done when we encounter such stunning beauty so closely? Is there some kind of instruction manual that can get me through this?

Romeo sure seemed to have studied the book: Leap up and climb over the high walls guarding the Capulet residence, lock on at the sight of your Juliet, recite a few lines of passionately, seemingly spontaneous, iambic pentameter—which give rise to responsive lines from Juliet—and then—climb up the vines that rise to Juliet's balcony, exchange a few more breathless words and kisses, make a date for the following day. And then? Here is the critical part. Somehow Romeo secretly finds his way to Juliet's bedroom and spends the night there, his body doing the thing men's bodies so sorely want to do. After that, in the movie, there is a glimpse of a naked Juliet as she fearfully rolls out of bed and urges Romeo to dress quickly and flee, by the same way he came, lest he be found out by Juliet's hot-tempered family.

Lyle can't compare Romeo's almost instantaneous amorous success to his own painful predicament. But the class has just recently begun studying geometry, and it's plain that it is an ideal means of transferring beautiful forms—points, lines, triangles, cubes, trapezoids, octahedrons—from textbook pages to the suggestible and freshly plowed brains of a classroom full of unsuspecting high-school sophomores.

Can Lyle speak to her? No. Lyle does not know how to converse. He only makes people laugh by accident. Does Olivia want to make Lyle talk by mistake, like when he was—and maybe still is—known in school as "Bonehead"? Or does Olivia want to tell him something? After never having spoken to him or heard him speak in her entire life? No. Why would she do that?

And does her body want what Lyle's body wants—that is, the feminine inverse of whatever Lyle's body is currently crying for? Well—why would she want that? And if she doesn't, will Lyle experience this agony of need every day for months? Years? Forever? How could he possibly traverse that oceanic row-boat of a gap from Lyle to Girl, or Girl to Lyle?

But look. There's Sam Crow. Although—could that even be his real name? Doesn't matter. Look. Wait—*look!* There he goes, he's walking right up to her! He's talking to her, as if she knew him, as if she had sent him an invitation in the mail to drop by her desk after math class. So easy. For him. And she's *smiling*—at Crow! And Crow isn't even halfway smart. Is she going to talk to him? Really? Does it happen like that? How did Crow do that?

For just an instant, Lyle remembers the stuffed animals he had back when he was a kid. Whatever happened to those animals? Lyle could make use of that tiger, that lion, that leopard just about now. Yeah, he wishes he had a tiger companion, or a daemon familiar, like in Philip Pullman's *The Golden Compass*, that could change shape and kill in an instant—a saber-toothed tiger, with unstoppable strength and quickness, with bloody fangs and claws. Imagine my saber-toothed tiger leaping, cracking Crow's spine at the neck, killing him instantly.

Yes, and "When the stars threw down their spears/and water'd heaven with their tears," we must ask, "Did he smile his work to see?/Did he who made the lamb make thee?"

Yes, this is a conundrum, a question we can only shake our heads at, for who could make the murderous tiger and then—perhaps upon the very next day—give life to the little lamb, and bestow upon it "clothing of delight/Softest clothing, wooly bright."

And in the same way, the fierce tiger daemon could turn into a butterfly, with many eyes on its delicate black and blue wings, to observe secret events, silently and undetected. And in the same way, William Blake bestowed upon the world his fiery poems and the products of his tortured, twisted intellect in the form, not of violence, but of the kindest kind of art, poetry.

Olivia Meets Lyle

A few things about Lyle. How we met. It was basically a mistake. I was standing in the high school parking lot. It was September, early in our senior year of high school. There was a little group of the black students who were talking and smoking after school. This one tall boy offered me a cigarette. I said no thanks; I don't smoke. At which—I don't know why—the boy took a cigarette out of the pack, lit it, and held it up by my face. He said something like, "Just try it. Come on. Everybody here's smoking." I didn't like this kind of pressure. So I said, "Oh, hey, there's somebody I know. Thanks, I have to go and say hi." And I slipped away and started walking without looking back.

Actually it was a ruse—I hadn't recognized anyone. But, in case the tall boy was still watching, I looked up the sidewalk to the first boy I saw coming and went up to him, acting like we were friends. Then I noticed a couple things: One, I actually had seen this boy before—he was in my math class. Two, he was a weird kind of geeky-looking person. But I'd made my move, so I had to stick to it.

Was it all a coincidence? He says, actually, no. He'd been secretly admiring her ever since tenth grade, he says, and had slowed his walk that day in the hope of seeing her close up.

I said, "I need a little help. Just walk with me out to the curb. You get it?" But I'd picked the wrong guy for this duty. He was just confused. When we got to the curb, I thanked him and told him I needed to wait here for my ride. That was his hint to go away.

But he couldn't take a hint. What did Captain Moonrocket say? He said, "You're very beautiful."

I gave him a skeptical look, and a laugh.

"You're in my math class," he said. "So you must be smart." Now—that rated a kooky look. Was he making fun of me? Or am I making fun of him?

"I will show you my music if you want," he said. OK, this was weird, but I happen to be a big music fan. So I said, "What instrument do you play?"

And here was the hook; he says: "I play all the instruments. I play the world."

Olivia and the Bullies

Another thing about this weird kid, Lyle, is that he's kind of out of touch. A few days after we met, we were walking down the hall toward class together, just briefly—kind of awkwardly, because it wasn't like we were dating or anything, just talking for a minute, and I heard some boy's voice saying, "Oh, hey, look! It's Chunky-girl and Punky-boy!" And then, "Yeah, I'm talking about you, Bonehead!"

"Just ignore them," I said.

"Ignore who?" Lyle said.

"Those bullies."

"Bullies?"

We kept walking and left the bullies behind. "Lyle. Are you trying to tell me you didn't hear those people teasing us?"

"What people?"

"You're a strange kid, Lyle."

"Well. I do hear differently. Or—it's more like, if it's not music, I don't hear it."

"Really? That is totally out-there, Lyle. I never heard of that. Do you have some kind of selective hearing?"

"Maybe. That would explain why I didn't hear what they said. So I guess I do have 'selective hearing'"

Well, I sure could hear it. So apparently when I speak, Lyle hears music. Kind of spooky to think of it that way.

But I knew what it was about—it was that Lyle is white, and some people think I need to stay on my side of the color line. But Lyle had no clue about that. How you can live in America your whole life and not get that—well, I guess that's Lyle.

7 The Dynamics of "Resistance" and "Acceptance"

Main Ideas

1. The notion of "resistance" in therapeutic change can be conceptualized as the avoidance of a struggle with developmental imperatives, consciously or not, by the clinician or the person seeking care.
2. The notion of "acceptance," and a basis for therapeutic alliance, can be conceptualized as the clinician discerning, encouraging inclusion of, and then utilizing those developmental imperatives, metaphorically "going with the current."
3. Developmental imperatives often are at odds (e.g., autonomy and support), both within and between individuals in the system.

In Chapter 6, we explored human development from a hypnotic perspective. We presented the framework of developmental tasks as governing currents in trance/plasticity: directions our development compels itself to go. Those currents never flow smoothly. We even encountered **resistance** while collaborating on this chapter about resistance. Our different experiences of resistance, and historical associations with the term, were obstacles to our consensus. In this chapter, we explore how hypnosis skills can facilitate the interplay of our developmental currents, around and through obstacles. We illustrate hypnosis principles applied to the developmental trials of person-centered care. Changing minds is a dynamic and uncertain process that is tested with surprising undercurrents.

This struggle with opposing forces is essential to therapeutic change. Both resistance and acceptance are at play in our response to stressors. Alert/relaxed, vigilant/at-ease, active/at rest, aroused/inhibited, are part of the rhythm of the Basic Resting and Activity Cycle (BRAC), our embodied ultradian rhythms. That's just how it goes.

Progressive Muscle Relaxation was once the preferred soothing balm of modern psychotherapy. First developed in 1908 by Harvard Medical School

Physician Edmund Jacobson as a non-hypnotic technique to relieve stress, it became an essential practice in hypnosis and many other so-called "mind-body" practices (Jacobson, 1929). Eyes closed, prone, and silent, clients were encouraged to attentively scan from head to toe, or feet to forehead, often as directed by the clinician, first tensing muscles and then letting go of the tension. For some, awareness of muscle tension led to relief of accumulated stress. Contract, release, contract, release, and focus on the calm of letting go. In its hypnotic incarnation, the experience of tightening and relaxation could be utilized to encourage one to move beyond the thinking part of the mind and into the body: sensing its outline in space, and feeling the embodied mind's give and take. The sequential tightening and loosening, from chest and abdomen, to fists and toes, also provided an implicit reference to negotiating our life's currents—going with or against the flow, navigating around obstacles, or not. This meaning further extended to the relationship between care-receiver and care-giver. As persons in care, did we accept the clinician's directing of our progressive muscle relaxation exercise and follow clinician's lead, starting with the feet or head? Or did we resist, and in so doing, express our need for self-determination? As care-givers, did we promote and follow the client's emergent self-direction and encourage self-discovery—"Wonder where the tension and release will spread next …"—or did we follow a directive script?

Resistance and acceptance feel like opposites, especially when contracting or releasing muscles. Psychologically, resistance and acceptance can be a false dichotomy. Both are necessary for development. These concepts are cemented in a relational framework: we resist or accept something (imagined or real) in the encounter with another. Sapolsky (2017) refers to the default state of mind as trusting. But the amygdala fuels vigilance, and we learn distrust. It deactivates, and we learn trust. We can only know one by experiencing the other. These opposing forces of distrust and trust underlie all of our developmental processes, and are in relationship to other.

Resistance can be holding back, avoiding difficult moments, both current and past. It can be both self-protective and self-comforting. It can be expressed as projection ("That's your problem, not mine"), as defensiveness, and as silence. It can be fighting all the way to defeat. Resistance feels like swimming against the current. Resisting can be a good thing. Resisting the urge to express violent emotions, for instance, is a worthwhile struggle.

Acceptance can be welcoming, or resigning to what is and what has been. It feels like floating with the current, sometimes—but not always—toward a good end. It can be the readiness to do something different, change direction, accept help, or take time to stop and reflect. Acceptance does not necessarily mean liking or affirming. It can also mean a degree of assent or compromise.

Resistance and acceptance have similarities. They both take energy. Floating with the current also involves resisting a natural tendency to drag, to get stuck, or to sink. The sigh and shrug of agreement is such an expenditure. Acceptance is always letting go of something. The acts of resisting and accepting require that we construct the skills for tolerating discomfort, strong emotions, and failure. "You spend more effort and time telling me why you can't wash the dishes than it would take to wash them," says the beleaguered parent to the harried child.

The apparent dichotomy between resistance and acceptance resolves when we consider them from a different level: from outside of the raging battle or, to continue our stream metaphor, from the shore. When we understand that resistance is the buildup of energy that allows for and reaches a threshold of change—renewal, reintegration, repair, and healing—then resistance becomes the necessary prerequisite for acceptance. Together, they create the rush and roar of the rapids. To use another metaphor, they are integral to the dance. The dance is the larger system; the next level up. Whether we are considering the buildup of ligands influencing cell receptors, the threshold that triggers genomic transcription, the tidal surge of hormones, the courage to take first steps, waking up in the morning, deciding to stand up and speak, or a community's fight against injustice, the dance progresses through its build and release. Resistance flows into acceptance flows into resistance and so on.

Therapeutic hypnosis is a skill set that allows clinicians to both join in and change the dance. The clinician's trance is one of unconditional acceptance, valuing the person in care with concern. We wonder in our behavior and questions: how did you learn to dance like that? We probe to discover strengths, especially in behaviors or ideas that on the surface seem challenging because they are "maladaptive" or "resistant." Sometimes we realize, with the authority of our training and experience, that if the other person continues to dance like that, they will get hurt. We respond in turn, with our concentration and curiosity, even gently challenging to explore with them better and healthier ways to dance through resistance and acceptance. In this way we develop a therapeutic alliance: i.e., the rapport and the motivation for change. We become models of tolerance for the struggles and messiness of living. In short, our acceptance of the person in our care promotes their acceptance of help. This is a bidirectional, mutually reciprocal process.

In moving with resistance, we can use it disruptively. Clinicians can even introduce resistance, challenging the mindset of the person in care toward the acceptance of a new frame. We often learn that from our patients. There was a little girl who came to my (LIS) office for a cast check. Her father reported the nature of her fracture. She spoke up defiantly, "I don't have a broken leg! I have a healing leg!"

In this chapter we will explore resistance and acceptance as two sides of the same coin and provide examples of hypnotic skills that utilize this false dichotomy as a resource.

Resistant Clients and Clinicians

In the legacy model of hypnosis, resistance was used to signify oppositional behavior on the part of the person in care. It was presented to clinicians as an obstacle to surmount that resided in the client, not in the relationship. For example, the Standards of Training of the American Society of Clinical Hypnosis (Dickens, Jacobs, Thomas, Thomson, & Wagaman, 2019) provide the following guidance for treating resistance in clinical settings:

> Strategies for managing resistance include: patient/client education/re-education; separating hypnosis from the presenting problem; enhancing rapport; aligning patient/client and clinician goals; use of metaphor or teaching tales; accept and utilize patient/client responses; and more permissive and indirect strategies.
>
> (p. 17)

Implicit in these instructions for "managing resistance" is the notion of hypnosis as a discrete procedure, something that the clinician does primarily to, not with, the client; something, therefore, that the client can resist.

The term resistance was borrowed from psychoanalytic theory, where it had a related but different meaning. In psychoanalytic theory, resistance was understood to have unconscious roots, to be part of a defensive system against external threats such as remembering or confronting trauma. It was self-protective. When viewed in the light of hypnosis as a set of relational skills, however, resistance can be productively explored, not as an obstruction to be removed but as a resource for change.

Clinicians also use the terms "resistant" and "accepting" for those in their care, indicating the degree of ease with which a person complies with prescribed therapy. The terms can equally apply to the clinician's willingness to understand those in their care. It is noteworthy that, in conventional treatment, clinicians attend to resistance more than acceptance. Clinicians anticipate "No" before "Yes." They often objectify or, worse, complain about the persons who come to them for care. In their exasperations and inadequacies, clinicians are prone to tell those in their care what to do, ignore their clients' ideas or wishes, project blame onto them and, in so doing, inadvertently prompt the resistance they attribute to their clients.

Being directive—dictating the direction of progressive relaxation—is often an expression of clinician-generated resistance. That, in turn, can be reflected by the "resistant" client who desires or needs a person-centered approach. Scripted, procedural approaches—however reproducible—tend to be inattentive to clients' individual needs. Of course, the opposite extreme is also problematic. The clinician who insists on being fully and only responsive to their client, while providing no structure, is likely to have a person in their care who asks, in exasperation, "Would you just tell me what to do?!"

What can the clinician do to work with the struggles of accepting and resisting growth within a person-centered frame? What do we do hypnotically to promote a climate for change within the ebb and flow?

A few years into my (LIS) initial career as a primary care pediatrician, I had a lesson in resistance and acceptance. A large, loud, and argumentative father demanded that his 18-month-old needed a speech evaluation. The little girl only had a five or six clear words—"no!" chief among them, but also "please." She was not speaking in phrases, let alone formed sentences. In fact, she was advanced. She was meeting expressive language criteria for a two-year-old. I showed her father with great authority where she placed on the Denver Developmental Screening Test. "I don't care what you think! I want a specialist!" he insisted. I was seething. I may not have known much, that early in my pediatric practice, but I knew that girl had no speech delay. I was the gate-keeper to healthcare, the person in charge of a judicious use of resources. He was being unreasonable and uncooperative. I told him that I would consider it.

At that time, we rented office space to a group of child and family psychologists. I presented my problem with this father to the elder of that group. I remember vividly that I stood in the doorway to his office as he listened, smiled, and then simply said, "Give him what he wants." It may be obvious advice to you, dear reader, but it broke like a dam over me. I made the referral. He was reassured. He and I got along wonderfully thereafter. His daughter is a 30-year-old school teacher as I write. Resistance. Acceptance.

Ideally, each interaction with a client starts with unconditional acceptance and valuing the person by the clinician. We have all experienced meeting a client we did not like initially. Put differently, we resist finding something about them to like and value. Our relational posture from the start works better when we adopt an accepting, nonjudgmental, and inviting posture. Together we discover their strengths, especially in behaviors or ideas that on the surface seem maladaptive. We are also models of tolerance for the struggles and messiness of living, and this allows for the same in our clients. We tell stories of our failures and what we learned. In other words, our acceptance of ourselves, and of the person in our care, promotes their acceptance of help. This is a reciprocal process. Resistance and acceptance are in flux between the care-giver and care-receiver.

Creating Safety

What are the elements that create safety in clinical encounters? On one side, both clinicians and clients tend to be vigilant in their environment, attracted to novelty but wary of the unexpected, of danger. Each is in their own trance of readiness and opening. The amygdala, with its alarm bell, is centered in the brain's limbic system, waiting to be activated by the unpredictable encounter. By creating an emotionally open environment, we activate a default process of trust (Sapolsky, 2017). The alarm is not triggered. We welcome the client's self-protection, and join with it. We acknowledge and agree with them, when they tell us that they really did not want to come to the office today. Notice how Robinson accepts, then waits through George's hesitancy, as their encounter begins.

We spend our lifetimes learning how to identify what it is that we feel, how to accept these feelings within ourselves, and how to express them to others.

Some of what we learn (e.g., violent rage, shame) may be less useful, and needs refining or nuanced relearning. In large part, our development is about what we learn in that struggle of emotional realization. Creating safety in therapeutic relationships requires emotional acceptance by, and demonstration of, this type of emotional competence This is how we care. That care was tragically lacking at Stevie's therapy visits. Creating safety means making room for resistance.

Resistance and Acceptance as Resources

So how can this ongoing struggle of resistance and acceptance within each of us and within the dynamic healing relationship be utilized as a resource? Here is an all-too-common example, to illustrate these forces at work in a young mind, and a hypnotic reframing of resistance as a resource:

Eight-year-old Lyle does not want to do his homework. It is too hard. He feels stupid when he cannot add the numbers or read the words. At home, he hides his homework, knowing the consequences he will face the next day from his teacher. He seeks comfort in talking with his stuffed animals. This is preferable to the loneliness, self-loathing, and shame he experiences when Dad yells at him for "being so stupid." It is part of why he never talks when Dad is around. In school, Lyle will wrestle with addition and reading when a tutor is sitting privately with him, praising his efforts, joining in his complaints about the "stupidness" of school, then encouraging him to take on the next math problem or the next sentence. "Lyle, you sure know how to complain. You are a much better complainer than me. I like how you can argue. As you grow up, you could choose to become great lawyer who can argue in court and win. I would want you to be my lawyer," says the tutor. Lyle smiles to himself and digs into the next math problem or sounds out the words in the next sentence.

Lyle finds motivation to change in the attuned, appreciative, developmentally progressive, and person-centered manner of the tutor who transforms his complaints into a strength. Lyle's experiences in school and with his father have left him feeling that his learning abilities aren't good enough. The tutor disrupts this mindset by considering him to be worthy of adult support and demonstrating ways to accept himself in his inevitable developmental struggle. The tutor doesn't have to know about Lyle's father. The tutor unsettles Lyle's complaints by engaging in acceptance and possibility. This is hypnotic. In his processing of its novelty, Lyle shifts in his oscillation between the need to master the numbers and words, and the fear of failure and shaming if he is inadequate. He wants to be as good as or better than others, and wants to reject what is difficult or uncomfortable, like his father's disapproval. To trust or distrust? To accept or resist? The emotional relationships in the river of development are part of what moves us along or gets us stuck. Lyle learns tolerance for school work through his relationship with the disruptive tutor.

Acceptance and resistance can also be used as a measure of progress. Clients may say they are finished with treatment, when the clinician believes otherwise. The client may need time to integrate new learning, rest from a struggle, live with their new frame of reference. They may want a second opinion. Making decisions, choosing, and differing with others are steps in becoming autonomous. The relationship stretches and the tension increases. There is tension and release over what can and cannot be controlled, en route to independence and autonomy. Joining with our clients as they decide how to take a break from or leave our care can foster their growth. Within the hypnotic relationship, we hold all of these dichotomies. A young man in my care who did not like that I (LIS) consistently held him to account for his choices, stormed out of my office in anger, shouting, "We're done!" He showed up on time for his next visit two weeks later, saying, "I didn't say we were done *forever*. I knew I could always come back."

Because all of us have unique developmental histories, we also have singular types of limitations and blind spots that constitute a form of hidden resistance. These can create obstacles in care-giving that unwittingly create resistance. The story character Lulu demonstrates how each of us is a unique composition of experiential resources. Her story may have begun with her exposure *in utero* to her mother's abundant stress hormones. These would have shaped Lulu's developing mind, from gene expression to early brain development. Lulu has been a starving refugee in Sudan, losing both of her parents and experiencing even more stresses, which we can only imagine. These experiences distinctively formed not only her developing mind, but her perspectives and abilities.

Most of us would never have experienced Lulu's developmental course, so we see a baby learning to walk, a child holding a doll, men in jeeps driving by, or even a water pump and hose quite differently than does Lulu. This would be likely and especially true of most of her care-givers, after she arrived in her adoptive country. They likely approached her with their scientific training and clinical methodologies that were designed to limit bias and assumptions, to generate hypotheses and collect data to support or rule-out potential diagnoses. They were likely kind and empathic, but they could not possibly know or fully appreciate how Lulu was building her uniquely derived experiential resources into her sense of self. Nor was Lulu capable of explaining to them what they did not know how to explore.

This type of hidden resistance can be resolved in hypnotic relationships through the clinician's self-awareness and ability to accept uncertainty and not knowing. The self-observation that is part of the clinician's trance keeps us from falling in love with our own hypotheses about the person in our care and our methods to treat them. We cannot help wondering in our clinical minds about how Lulu coped and is coping. What happened to her? What has she experienced? What forces of nature have shaped her development and growth? What was disrupted, and what was repaired? What risks and resources did she retain from that learning? But we have to remind ourselves that this is all about our projection and training, not Lulu's lived experience.

What actually matters is not how Lulu developed—even though it makes a compelling and edifying story—but what she knows how to do to help herself. Lulu at this moment, here in an imagined clinical encounter, is the most current product of her amazing development. Instead of attempting to collect all of that history as if it is actually, objectively, and factually accessible, we need to pay more attention to what our questions *do* than to what the answers *are*. If we had the opportunity to engage with Lulu about her feelings of alienation, we might ask "Lulu, what happens in your body when you are enjoying gymnastics?" "How did you come to be curious about your birth mother and father?" "How do you experience calm?" Each question is worded to evoke emotion, to access resources, to relay **attunement** and acceptance. With each question, we watch how her posture, facial expression, facial blood-flow, and eye-movements change. Each of these responses is acknowledged by expressing wonder and interest. In so doing, we bypass our need to know all about who Lulu was, and help her develop her sense of who she is becoming. We define and evaluate the quality of human interactions by these abilities to be sensitive and responsive (Richter, 2004).

Development is uneven, so resistance and acceptance play roles in developmental progress. We can conceptualize them as the ebb and flow of readiness for change. There are children who talk precociously at age one, but who will not use the toilet proficiently until age four—and those who do the opposite. Some adults start great and enduring marriages in their twenties; others do not. It is our nature to compare and contrast ourselves developmentally. I am too short or too tall; have no beard or too much; am happy in my job or not. These internal assessments are manifestations of resistance and acceptance, and of readiness for change, or not.

When we evoke these developmental inflections during our clinical encounters, they look like trance openings: pauses in speech, changes in breathing and facial blood flow, looking away, a bit of catalepsy. We use hypnosis therapeutically to encourage progress during those opportunities. We address the child or adult through the trance openings. We share the emotional experience of it. We find a name for it: "Yes. That is [hard, confusing, frustrating, sad, uncertain, etc.]." We encourage our clients to experience the struggles, to own that accomplishment, to adjust, adapt, and change what they can. "How can you stay with that feeling a bit more, while you learn something from it?" This is both disruptive, and supportive advancement toward something new: Rossi's stage two, Incubation. It is most explicitly enacted in Robinson's encounter with George, but it takes place more subtly in others of our stories.

Resistance Is When Something Is Missing

We have previously framed drives toward developmental accomplishments (e.g., learning to walk, finding identity or intimate partnership) as governing currents in the flow of growth and learning. More functionally, we can consider those drives as ways in which we are particularly motivated toward where we want to go, and thus, how we are most plastic. Developmental drives are where the action is, so in hypnotic interactions, we go with the flow of development. Sometimes, every other direction is met with resistance, so the current developmental drive is where acceptance lies.

I (LIS) recall, when I was a little boy, coming along in the car with my mother and my brother—ten years my senior, so about 16 years old—to the doctor. My brother had acute infections in both eyes, but refused to use the eye drops the doctor had prescribed. My mother had failed to convince him otherwise, despite her exaggerated threats of blindness and institutionalization. There were a lot of histrionics as I sat in the back seat of the car on the trip to the office. In the exam room, I remember watching as the calm doctor meticulously examined my brother's eyes, then simply and quietly stated, "No girl would ever look at guy with eyes like this." My brother put the drops in his own eyes right then, and they went on to heal quickly. Thereafter, he became meticulous about his appearance. I also remember that it was a very quiet ride home.

Aspects of teenage development highlight the value of resistance and acceptance struggles. Disagreeing with adults and surging toward independence are both expected behaviors in a developing teen. Rejecting adults at school, and preferring peers, is a swing between resisting grownup advice and accepting peer wisdom, however faulty the latter may be. The rejection—the resistance—is necessary as one starts to take steps toward independence. As the teen gets angry, or pushes back, or rejects the clinician, it is a good sign that the teen is struggling with the developmental task of becoming independent. For the adult who has not yet individuated, rejecting the clinician's advice may be a sign of healthy growth. The developmental lens helps to distinguish what struggles keep us caught, and which are moving obstacles.

As it occurs in our process for change, resistance comes from many sources. There may be fear from not knowing, or from imagining what to expect from the caregiver. Will they place a label on our struggle, as in Stevie's story, or a dreaded diagnosis? Developmentally, the client will still need structure and security while hoping to preserve autonomy and identity in the face of health challenges. There may be a lack of rapport. The relationship, for whatever reason, may not be a good fit without opportunity to repair attachment. There may be a lack of readiness for change, typically because resources for change are not identified or in place. This may also include a dearth of motivation or energy to learn because the client is depleted of energy, hope, and motivation. There may be a reluctance to give up their sense of control, and a misperception that one has to do so. There may be past negative experience with therapy or medical treatment. There may even be issues of secondary gain (the perceived benefit of having the problem), or religious or cultural beliefs that interfere with the process. The list of reasons for client resistance is endless. In each reason for resistance lies symptoms and direction for treatment. Of course, one has to remember that anyone who has made the effort to consult a clinician is already challenging themselves to change and grow. The list of motivators for acceptance is also endless. Hope is essential.

A person must have intrinsic motivation in order to want to undertake change. Sometimes the person in care cannot and will not ride on the clinician's motivation for them to change. Assuming the patient is intrinsically motivated, resistance to change can be understood as a sign that something is missing.

How does the clinician interact to help the patient find out what must be included, in order for them to undertake action? Does this individual have the internal and external resources necessary to make the change? Does the clinician have the resources to assist them to do so? Either way, the motivating resources are missing.

Assuming intrinsic motivation in a therapeutic setting, what we call resistance can be understood as an effort by the client, the clinician, or both to either (1) to move away from what is felt to be overwhelming, (2) to provide self-comfort, and/or (3) to slow down the process of change, so that the individual can keep up, not be or feel overwhelmed, and thereby learn the most from the experience.

Solid, responsible, reliable George, on the precipice of retirement and staring at the abyss of "old-age," meets with Robinson about a sleep problem. Part of him hopes that the diagnosis he's been given might bring simple treatment: nice and neat. Part of him fears that it won't. He brings so much other loss and concern to the encounter that he reveals his growing fear that this is actually an inflection point in his life; something "I can't fix myself." Regrets, losses, and shame slip out as he talks. Here is a fear of acceptance because it would mean resignation. Must he accept what he sees as the loss, with aging, of his identity as the guy who can fix things? Robinson knows, in his clinician's trance, that George would resist anything that does not align with the developmental imperative—the hidden agenda—that he has brought to the office. So Robinson reflects back George's strengths, that indeed he is actively engaging with this important part of his life. "I think you are here, right now, to start making some sense of all of this. I think that you've felt pulled apart in a lot of directions. I think you deserve to feel a lot better about yourself …" Even more, in his non-directive and fascinated approach, Robinson turns the tables on George, implicitly insisting that *only* he can "fix" this, and that he already has all the tools to do it. George moves from a fear of resignation to a "righteous" anger and determination.

But resistance, as they say, is a two-person sport. It cannot derive only from the client's side. Clinicians are developing, too. We know that Robinson is struggling with impending fatherhood, and the tasks required to succeed as a partner, with new demands on his time and resources. He is preoccupied, non-consciously viewing his clinical work from this new place, such that he sees new details and misses others in his assessment and attunement with clients. He knows, at a deeper level, that he must find new meaning in all of his roles. We would submit that most clinicians become resistant when they feel their competence challenged by those in their care. This can be direct, as in "Doctor, do you know what you are doing?" or implicit, as the clinician encounters a person whom they find challenging to help. That challenge, in turn, can be that the problem is hard to understand or treat. And it may be that the person with the problem is difficult for the clinician to relate to. Of the many ways that clinicians can overcome their resistance, the first is to recognize it. Once we understand its source, using the clinician's trance of attunement, we join with the client in discovering the strengths in both parties, to create a solution.

Negative Effects

Related to this idea of resistance is another term in the hypnosis literature: "negative effects." It has been defined as "Unexpected, unwanted thoughts, feelings or behaviors during or after hypnosis which are inconsistent with agreed (sic) goals and interfere with the hypnotic process." (Machovec, 1988, p. 46). According to Machovec, 20% of people experiencing "hypnosis" had these effects. They could include dizziness, headaches, nausea, confusion or disorientation, anxiety or panic, difficulties coming out of trance, distortion of perceptions, depression, psychotic symptoms, even suicide (Frauman, Lynn, & Brentar, 1993, p. 100). Most common were physical complaints or cognitive distortions.

This notion of negative effects is probably a mislabeling at least, and an effect of directive hypnosis at worst. Note that these reports almost always involve hypnosis-as-procedure in a problem-based (not person-centered) treatment. Hypnosis, defined and used as we have discussed in Chapter 5—as an evocative skill set that is integrated into conversation and across the range of clinical encounters—may elicit somatosensory cues to felt senses, to traumatic memories, to the unpredictable or unknown, that can be explored with the person in care. In doing so, the skilled hypnosis clinician utilizes these evoked trance phenomena to help the person in care gain insight and change conditioned behaviors and symptoms.

In whatever form resistance may masquerade, most often ill effects of treatment are related to the struggle of feeling safe with the clinician, recalling painful memory, expressing and tolerating difficult emotions. Transference, the unconscious redirection of emotions onto another, is at play between the care-giver and client. Our family and relational dynamics can affect our caregiving work, as we unconsciously replay patterns. Sometimes the physical manifestations of a client's underlying issues may lead us to understand the origins of a developmental disruption. The headaches, nausea, or panic with which they present may be embodied memories that we can explore and change. Their cognitive manifestations, distorted perceptions, remaining in trance, or disorganized thoughts can also lead us to information about what needs to change.

Repair and healing of disruptions in development require the presence of a loving, nonjudgmental, soothing figure. When we experience resources for safe attachment, we shift our brain chemistry to be more supported by oxytocin. Oxytocin helps the brain to rewire, to change perceptions, to unlearn old patterns (Lanius, 2019). The clinician provides hope, identifies the developmental challenge, and provides recognition of the resources of the person in our care. In this manner, the climate for change is readied. The person can strive for mastery and learning and still wish to avoid and suppress conflictual material, underlying traumas, and old wounds. This tension produces the oscillating rhythm of growth, the dance of falling down and getting up.

The Secret about Secrets

Often, what is being left out is also being hidden, like underlying rocks in the river; the obstacles that are impeding growth. Resistance can be exposed when clients hide issues or keep secrets. This can occur consciously; for example, when a client does not want to share their alcohol abuse or sexual dysfunction. Or it may be unconscious hiding, where clinical material is repressed or dissociated. In either case, the act of hiding tells us something about the person's developmental disruption.

At age eight, Casey's mother brought her for treatment because she was anxious that her daughter was gaining weight at an alarming rate. Her mother was distressed that Casey was eating candy that she ferreted from the cupboards. She lied about doing so, and hid the wrappers between the cushions of the sofa. It was tempting to conceptualize this problem as one related to healthy eating, or a power struggle between parent and child. But those explanations missed a key element: the secretive behavior of rummaging when mother was not looking, of hiding the evidence, of denying, lying, or wrongdoing. What else was she keeping secret? As I (JHL) observed her dollhouse play, with a repetitive scene of her doll going into the bathroom to wash its hands, I suspected the secret was related to this traumatic play (Gil, 1998). During the play scenes, I introduced doll friends who asked questions to evoke emotion about this reoccurring action. "Are the hands clean after all that washing? Isn't it hard to keep washing? Did you get something terrible on your hands?" Casey's doll did not answer, but would abruptly leave the bathroom. "Is she mad that I asked why she washes so much? I wonder if she is embarrassed?" I persisted, offering a range of emotions to which Casey might relate. I also offered a range of possible behaviors, introducing adult dolls who went into the bathroom while Casey's doll was there, invading privacy and voicing different scenarios. "Sorry, I didn't know you were in here," or "can I be in here with you?" or, "here, let me help you." After several weeks of this evocative play therapy, Casey revealed to her mother that she had been sexually abused by a family friend. Once the secret was out, there were no more candy wrappers in the sofa.

Stevie's struggle with her gender is another example of keeping a secret. As Stevie began to notice discomfort with bodily changes, she grew confused and distressed. Ignoring the feelings, or focusing on other thoughts, only worked briefly. Distraction was inadequate. The pressing need to address the out-of-sync, ego-dystonic, internal feeling persisted. Resisting these feelings took too much energy. Stevie chose the dissociated escape of opiates, and the relatively accepting relationship, however harmful, with Micky, over the implicit judgments of the therapist, her parents and, as Stevie felt it, the rest of the world.

The secret about secrets is that they are profoundly important, and revealing of a developmental disruption. As with all symptoms, some manifestation of the secret (e.g., handwashing, stealing, social withdrawal) point to the solution. Developmental progression is supported and nurtured when we create an accepting climate for resistance. All responses from a client are therapeutically useful. When we normalize, educate, and demystify in a nonjudgmental manner, providing clients choice, collaboration, safety, and our curious presence, then there is space to change. We can do this from the posture of the curious and wondering clinician's trance, asking gently disruptive questions about how the person in care has learned and practiced those manifestations of their secrets. For example, what might have happened if Stevie had encountered a counselor, a therapist, or a doctor who expressed interest in Stevie's writing, shared the wonder and confusion about the requirement to choose a defined gender, marveled at Stevie's metaphorical juxtaposition of "The Lady or the Tyger." The only limitations are our willingness to join in, using our skills.

Thinking in Family Systems

A mother's stress impacts her children outside of the uterus, as well. It often looks like resistant and avoidant behavior. Seven-year-old Tina had stomach aches on most days. Medical evaluation found no evidence of illness or abnormality, and the doctor recommended a psychological assessment and treatment. The psychologist found that Tina's mother, recently divorced, wanted her child to feel better immediately. She could not attune to her daughter's worries, talking over and at her whenever Tina expressed her feelings. "I miss my daddy," was met by mother saying, "We can't do anything about that. I told you that. Just get over it." Contrast that response with: "Yes, honey, it hurts when Daddy does not visit or call. It must feel terrible. It will not always feel this way. It will change for the better." Mother could not tolerate her daughter's pain about the divorce. Thus, Tina had no model for learning to tolerate her own disappointments. Parents often feel responsible for their child's pain. Their child's pain tells parents they have failed to protect their child from hurt. Teaching parents to tolerate their children's pain in the process of developing is sometimes as simple as helping parents become aware of their own pain: Breathing with a parent, helping them tune into the pain of feeling parental failure, accepting that marriages do end, and that there is pain with that ending. Accepting instead of avoiding creates novelty and openings. In the clinician's trance of attunement, we can talk about painful endings and model calm understanding. In this way, we create the safe and healing space of a relationship with the parent, who may in turn face their child's discomfort. From that starting place, the child, too, will benefit.

Suggestions, Solutions, Success

Hypnotic skills add ease and improved effectiveness to our clinical encounters. The more skills added to the clinician's repertoire, the more resources we have at hand in order to respond therapeutically to others.

Hypnosis can bring forth unconscious material quickly, like a depth-finder that discovers the rocks beneath the surface. This is vital to cultivate change. Trance is the biological process that reveals the readiness for what needs to change. Access to a range of unconscious processes—emotional, imaginative, or visceral—can be more readily evoked when hypnosis is integrated into our practice. This requires the skills to manage timing, pacing, and intensity, especially when we encounter fragile ego structures. When we accept the unconscious offering as a resource for change, we will be most effective in assisting the people in our care.

Acceptance of change, of our suggestions, of our disrupting influence, starts with the acceptance of the relationship. It continues with the client's awareness that the clinician understands what the client wants and will accompany him/her on that journey of repair, growth, and renewal.

At the beginning of this chapter, we described progressive relaxation as the alternation of holding and dispersing tension. Hypnosis, as we conceive it, is almost never about being relaxed. It is about the oscillations of opening and closing to novelty; determining what can be trusted and what is dangerous, right now. Our trances happen as we and our clients struggle to grow. Acceptance of and resistance to change are both struggles. These struggles propel us through developmental shifts. When we label a client "resistant," we miss the importance and the meaning of the client's struggle, and the opportunity they provide for our own learning.

Questions and Assignments for Further Discussion

1. Consider your own definitions of resistance and acceptance and discuss them in terms of the struggle and outcome. How do your definitions relate to a developmental imperative?
2. Secrets are often very important holders of keys to changing the mind. Find a secret of one of the characters in the stories and discuss ways to therapeutically evoke emotions around that secret.
3. What is the relationship between family, community, and societal systems and the experience of developmental inflection points (e.g., starting school, becoming sexually active, starting to drive a car, voting)? Choose an example of developmental disruption, then describe how it resonates through family, community and larger social systems.

References

Dickens, M., Jacobs, D., Thomas, J., Thomson, L., & Wagaman, L. (2019) Standards of training – Level I: Fundamentals of clinical hypnosis workshop [PDF]. Retrieved October 2, 2019 from www.asch.net/Portals/0/Emma_Folder/Level1SoT-Final.pdf?ver=2019-08-08-125933-130.

Frauman, D., Lynn, S., & Brentar, J. (1993). Prevention and therapeutic management of "negative effects" in hypnotherapy. In J. W. Rhue, S. Lynn, & I. Kirsch (Eds.), *Handbook of clinical hypnosis* (pp. 95–120). Washington, DC: American Psychological Association. doi:10.1037/10274-005

Gil, E. (1998). *Play therapy for severe psychological trauma.* New York, NY: Guilford Press.

Jacobson, E. (1929). *Progressive relaxation.* Chicago, IL: University of Chicago Press.

Lanius, U. F., Paulsen, S. L., & Corrigan, F. M. (2014). *Neurobiology and treatment of traumatic dissociation: Toward an embodied self.* New York, NY: Springer.

Machovec, F. J. (1988). Hypnosis complications, risk factors, and prevention. *American Journal of Clinical Hypnosis, 31*(1), 40–49. doi:10.1080/00029157.1988.10402766

Richter, L. (2004). The importance of caregiver-child interactions for the survival and healthy development of young children. Geneva, Switzerland: World Health Organization. Retrieved October 2, 2019 from https://apps.who.int/iris/bitstream/handle/10665/42878/924159134X.pdf;jsessionid=BD7D3DC1CDF327B87C7F40FE0AD157D5?sequence=1

Sapolsky, R. (2017). *Behave: The biology of humans at our best and worst.* New York, NY: Penguin.

Robinson's Story

Missed Exits

(This takes place four years before the previous episode)

Ah. It was a sound of nearly silent dismay. Then a slightly more audible trace of annoyance. *Ah!* A pause. A sigh. Exasperation. *Missed my exit on the 690,* Robinson thought. *Why did that happen?*

Well, presumably, it happened because he was distracted, thinking about something else. But he's always thinking of something else. There is always something else, and something else beyond that else. Always a voice, beneath many more voices.

Everyone wants to know why things are the way they are. The patients assume Robinson knows all, and that it's just a question of whether he'll let on. He's the doctor. Which is to say, the teacher. The teachers are the ones who can, ostensibly, teach because, after all, they know all, and see all.

But it seems all Robinson can offer is a process. And the reason for that can be a long way to seek. Ha. Why did he miss his exit? Why did he disrupt the process?

No great harm done, though. Later on, after dinner, he settles into his home office. Only the sandwich crumbs on the empty plate remain. He is in his desk chair, alert, caffeinated, prepared to think clearly and move forward. He'll surely make some sense of the papers and books piled before him.

So. Here he sits. A long moment has occurred, broken only when Robinson realizes that he has been staring at the waste basket across the room. It is a blue waste basket. Though its blueness has no significance. Perhaps he is simply tired. He has a lot on his plate.

Or perhaps it is the tiny dose of antidepressant he has just begun taking, a dose that is almost certainly too small to have any perceptible effect. And yet—here he is, his gaze locked for no reason on a blue waste basket for—how long? Just long enough to notice. Long enough that, upon reflection, Robinson can detect a very minor, insignificant, unmeasurable shift in his consciousness, possibly traceable to the medication. Or not. These are, apparently, the only known, or suspected, effects of the pills—the only ones

Robinson, at least, can observe and report: one, a tendency to stare at waste baskets and two, a recent history of missing one or more exits on the freeway.

And yet, insignificant as these effects almost certainly are, Robinson realizes, there is a congruence between the vocabulary he has used in thinking about these issues and the vocabulary employed to discuss therapeutic hypnosis that he has just been reading about in the texts and papers on his desk. He is thinking that he will need to reread the passages about the "trance." At this point, however, Robinson realizes that he has been harboring a certain resistance to this whole subject. After all, if staring at a waste basket and inconveniently missing a freeway exit are all the trance has to offer, skepticism is probably warranted.

Why was it that he ever hazarded down that strange road called "hypnosis"? Wasn't he strange enough already in medical school? Training at the Mecca in Baltimore? In this suburban internal medicine practice? Living in this neighborhood? In this house? … a black man? How many missed exits is that? Why even consider stranger things?

Hypnosis. Another sigh. Not exasperation this time. This time confusion. Why does he need this? Need this. He does. And a blue waste basket.

A couple of dozen patients a day, every day, after day. Treating their risk factors as they drift down, inerrantly down, inadvertently accumulating the ills of American living: diabetes, obesity, high blood pressure, tired joints, sleeplessness, anxiety, aging, anxiety, loss, anxiety, depression. Advice, pamphlets, prescriptions, and referrals. Treating their risk factors. Treating with magic pills and pamphlets. Tricks and treats.

Yes. The usual annual succession of children came to the door last week. Trick-or-treating in their customary costumes. Ghouls and goblins. Dark Vodou magic. And that night, Robinson dreamt the dream that still haunts him, year after year. Starting with the cool humid night air, so late in the moonlight, behind their little blue house in the hills beyond Port-au-Prince. Hiding with Mama in the ditch in the dark. That booming voice exploding inside. That big scary man! He was wailing in *kreyòl*, breaking up furniture. Percussion to his bass. Mama held Robinson's skinny body close, while she whispered, "Shhhhhh, *ti bebe*, Shhhh, *ti bebe*. He drinking is all." And little Robinson holding back hot tears, eyes wide, afraid to breathe. And then as always the dream becomes a terrifying recollection, and Robinson's chest constricts as he remembers that big man's *Vodou* funeral, in their house with the *Manbo* and *Houngan* and all the people dancing and singing and the drums and flutes and the smell of hot coffee—coffee, so the big man's soul could make his exit in good company—so it could let go, and travel safe. Robinson's, big and little, fears of what he cannot see. Tricks and treatments and trances. He awoke from that dream sequence both hot and cold, like always.

Now, Robinson is staring at the blue waste basket. Papers on hypnosis for irritable bowel syndrome and PTSD and pain, all stacked, waiting, on his desk. Yellow highlighter. One book open to trance inductions. A shudder and sigh … this time of starting again.

And Shani has been leaning in the doorway. Looking at him with that beautiful smile. Slowly shaking her head, at him. "What you doin', baby?" The melody of her voice. "You need some sleep." His wondrous wife with those almond eyes and that high forehead. No islanders in her. Her people had to have been West African royalty before their slavery time. She carries herself that way. Though now different with that round belly, caressed so casually under her hand. She ambles over to drape him in a hug. "I've got a hearing, early, with Judge T tomorrow," say her warm lips against his head. "So I am heading up. Your son wants a good night hug." Robinson embraces her and the boy in her belly from his desk chair, saying, "You, let your Mama sleep, little one." Then, "I just want to read a bit. Not long." He watches her leave. She turns to smile at him watching her leave.

He finds himself fixing on the empty plate, now. So much on it. Shani must know. His awkward distance. He is so scared to say. So ashamed at his hidden relief when those first two pregnancies did not take. Or is he ashamed of the hiding? His dishonest comfort and consolation of her.

What kind of man *is* he? Well yes. That is the question. A man whose idea of a father is a big black monster. A man who, knowing that, still helped create an innocent son, stretching and kicking in his kind wife's belly. How can this man father, be a father to, foster the young life a black son, now, in this America? Him? Really? This is a man whose non-conscious trance-mind would have him miss his exit … and go where? He leans back in his chair to shut his eyes. Just a moment.

The charge nurse, Brenda, pokes her head into the on-call room where he is just barely sleeping, in his blue hospital scrubs. "Robinson, get up. It's time."

Is little Esther dying? Now? Little Esther has been *not* dying. He shakes his mind awake as he follows Brenda onto the ward to Esther's room, now full of hushed family with lights dimmed. There is the table-top fake Christmas tree: the little lights glowing and the candy canes drooping on its wire branches.

Esther has been in the back corner single-bed room on the pediatric ward —where fourth year medical student Robinson is assigned this December— for two long weeks. And not dying. The youngest of eight children, each adopted over a period of two decades by this amazing man and woman. These supernatural parents. Esther is six years old, though she looks older and smaller. She has been losing her battle with germs that the HIV virus have let invade her body since birth in Port-au-Prince. She has been in this bed, in this room not dying from AIDS, patiently waiting for all her family to come home from everywhere. Her sister from college in California. Her oldest brother and his wife, have just arrived from Ramstein, Germany, stationed with the Air Force. Snowflakes watering on his dress blue uniform coat and hat on the chair by the door.

Esther's white-haired Mama, lying next to her child on the bed amidst the tubing, sees Robinson in the doorway and whispers, "Robinson's come, my sweet girl." Esther's big red-rimmed eyelids quiver and chapped lips curve up ever so slightly as Robinson is drawn by some power into the room by the bedside, to kneeling at the bedside, to sing gently to her in soft *kreyòl* …

Somehow, he knows. We all know somehow, that she has been waiting and not dying until we, her family, are all there, with all of our varied racial blends and families of origin. Now, in the early hours of Christmas morning on the quiet hospital pediatric school-age unit all are there together … So she can let her soul fly free, protected in good company. Make her exit.

And he knows he is dreaming. He has dreamt this dream before. Or is he dreaming that he has dreamt this dream before? An endless dream hall of dream mirrors? Dizzy. He remembers that Christmastime in the hospital and that family and Esther. That was real. Some vague nausea building. And, now at the edge of waking, Esther is here, smiling, somehow a young woman, calling Robinson, "*Tonton*" (uncle) and nodding at him, kneeling as if she knows. Knows what? "You can sing for your little boy," her mind tells Robinson without saying the words.

And Robinson jolts upright in his desk chair, still covered by the emotional mist. What? How? As the rumble rises in his belly. He inhales deeply, fully awake. The gorge rises. He bolts across the office to grab the blue wastebasket, and kneeling over it, vomits up everything that had been on his plate.

8 Effects of Trauma and Chronic Disease

> **Main Ideas**
>
> 1. Everyone experiences traumatizing events, but not every becomes traumatized.
> 2. By disrupting developmental imperatives, both trauma and chronic disease threaten the development of competent experiential resources.
> 3. Trauma evokes as a trance of survival. Hypnosis can help change that trance.
> 4. Chronic disease need not be traumatizing, but still disrupts and interrupts developmental imperatives.
> 5. Poverty and oppression increase the likelihood of detrimental effects of trauma and chronic disease.

The preceding chapter defined the way in which we frame the struggles of growth and development, using the plasticity of trance and our hypnosis skill set. Many of those struggles come from traumatic events in our lives. In this chapter we detail the nature of trauma, its universality, its disruption of development, its embodiment, and its effects. We will define trauma, explain its relationship to hypnosis, and conceptualize trauma systemically. In this way, trauma-informed clinicians may better appreciate the background of those in their care. Finally, we explain and illustrate strategies to treat the trance of trauma by utilizing hypnosis with the four principles that we have promoted.

Subjective Experience as a Vital Sign

In 2001, the US Joint Commission on the Accreditation of Healthcare Organizations (JCAHO, 2001) added pain assessment to their requirements for evaluation of patients' well-being. As a result, many health care organizations came to refer to pain as a fifth vital sign, along with blood pressure, heart and respiratory rates, and temperature. This mandate[1] was significant from the vantage point of the biomedical paradigm. It conferred a hospitalized patient's verbal report of a subjective experience equal status with physiologically and mechanically derived data as part of a "vital" assessment of well-being. The forces behind this pronouncement were many, but of particular importance were the recognitions that there was no other objective measure of pain that had been standardized and validated. It established that not asking a patient about their experience of pain could omit data that was critical to their care. While pain histories are standard, raising ongoing subjective pain experience to the status of a mandated "vital sign" was new.

Adding pain—a subjective manifestation of a multidimensional experience—to a traditionally objective and medical standard created change in health and care. Some predicted that a measure of trauma would be the next vital sign (Linden, 2005). Trauma, after all, was arguably an even more "vital" and formative measure of how we make up our minds, live our lives, relate to others, and face challenges to our health. Interestingly, increased awareness of the impact of the pain experience on one's mind and molecules helped us to understand that trauma, too, is embodied and systemic.

Defining Trauma

There is much debate and research about what constitutes a traumatic experience. We all agree that some events in our life shape us unalterably, but trauma researchers and clinicians do not yet agree on what elements form the tipping point, the threshold over which we pass that makes those events so potent and injurious. One widely used definition is that trauma overwhelms a person's ability to cope. We may simply lack the resources to withstand an event without being wounded in some way, from which we need to heal. The flow of information and energy across the brain may be too much for the embodied mind to manage by itself (Siegel & Doidge, 2010). So we can look at trauma from two perspectives: the characteristics of the event(s) and the person's capacity to manage them. We can do little about the former: events over which we have no control. So our discussion about helping people who live with trauma in this chapter, and our parsing of resilience in Chapter 11, will focus on growing our capacities to cope and grow through traumatizing events.

Here are our definitions. "Trauma" is commonly used to refer to a single event or act: a motor vehicle accident or an act of violence. We do not use it that way. We use trauma to mean a *way of living* with the wounds and scars of the embodied mind. This kind of living is usually dysfunctional, painful, and brings one to care. These injuries are often traced back to traumatic or traumatizing events. But there are always antecedents (genetic, genomic, experiential, relational, etc.) that increased the likelihood of an event being traumatizing in a given individual's life. This is most clearly portrayed in the lives of Robinson, George, Lulu, and Lyle. Put simply, an event or act can only be traumatic or traumatizing if, in retrospect, it produced trauma. As we have described development, trauma can best be understood retrospectively but must be healed progressively.

Trauma is a Universal and Multidimensional Phenomenon

Everyone experiences trauma. Each vignette that we have included in this treatise, and each of our story characters, involves somebody struggling with the impact of a traumatic event. Lulu is an adopted refugee. Robinson grew up poor and frightened. George is traumatized by impending loss with age. Stevie struggles with gender definition. Lyle is insecure, alone, and looking for connection. In each story, there are developmental imperatives that move these characters toward learning from these experiences and healing. Trauma includes the dimensions of embodied systems, relationships, and development. Each character moves through these domains toward a hoped-for future.

Trauma is a somatic experience. At its worst it leaves us helpless to act, immobilized, with the brain in a hyperalert state (Van der Kolk, 2019). Research points to the many protective systems in the body—e.g., neurological, endocrinologic, and immunological—that activate under stress, which are termed embodied trauma. Consider George's recounting of his dream about rats. He described Orwell's book and the torturer making use of a person's worst fear; i.e., Winston with a cage of rats on his head. George feels disgust at the very thought of rats. When he awakens from his dream, he feels rats under the covers, at the foot of his bed. He has visceral, auditory, and visual responses. He has stored the image from the book as embodied sensations associated with the emotions of disgust and fear. The dream and its traumatic associations are a somatic experience.

Trauma is also a relational experience. Since our minds are biologically social, in affecting our embodied minds, trauma must affect our relationships, and vice versa. This includes our clinical relationships. Social relationships are also a resource for managing our body's responses (Siegel, 2019). One essential contribution from the clinical relationship is hope: providing hope of feeling better, providing hope that one will become well again. When we speak of relational being, it includes this capacity to be the container of hope, in recognition of how trauma can render us not only helpless but hopeless. Of course, relationships can also be injurious and traumatic. Undue influence—limiting freedom of choice and substituting another's choice or desire for the person's own—can be understood as a relational abuse of hypnotic skills that is contrary to ethical clinical and research canons of doing no harm, acting beneficially, and respecting autonomy (CIOMS, 2016). From child and intimate partner abuse to cult indoctrination and human enslavement, instances of relational trauma involving undue influence likely far outnumber the use of therapeutic hypnosis for healing and repair. This is also part of Lulu's story.

Trauma unequivocally affects and is affected by our development. Employing a developmental framework helps to make sense of the broad variation in responses to potentially traumatizing events. Children have fewer resources for coping, by virtue of their age and limited experiences. The term "trauma-by-proxy" was introduced because the developmentally young are vulnerable to feeling another's trauma as if it is their own. They may see news images of an earthquake on television, replete with alarmed, anxious faces and voices of reporters, and feel as if they have just been in an earthquake. The three-year-old's unfolding understanding of reality, geography and time renders them vulnerable to being confused about what is occurring where and to whom. Even in the absence of their own traumatic event, it is as if they respond to another's in a personal, identified manner. As another example, watching scary video games or horror movies can produce trauma-by-proxy in the young. The four-year-old will tell you that a zombie ran after them, as though it was real. Developmentally older children may know that the zombies are not real, but watching zombies in games or movies can still activate fears formed earlier, and cause them to emerge in nightmares. Our susceptibility to being traumatized continues to develop as early traumatic experiences interact with our growing capacities to cope, as with George and Lulu.

Trauma fundamentally affects identity formation. The fields of philosophy and existentialism gave us the term "existential crisis" (Sartre, 1948). This expression was once commonly used to describe responses to traumatic events because, in disrupting our development, they often drove us to question the meaning, value, and purpose of our lives.

Early trauma discussions distinguished between trauma with a small "t" (e.g., falling down and scraping your knee) or Trauma with a capital "T" (e.g., losing your family in an airplane accident), in an effort to recognize the influence of events from a child's perspective. Early developmental experiences influence self-regulation and self-determination (Ryan & Deci, 2017), as well as social connectedness and emotional well-being, a point we will amplify in following chapters.

Trauma is one of the more powerful of those early experiences, especially because it disempowers us. When we assess its impact, developmental thinking reminds us that a child's experience and an adult's experience of the same event are not equivalent. Hence, on the one hand, a clinician looking through an adult lens may miss many youthful experiences that have traumatic consequences for a child, such as a move from one's original neighborhood, or being lost in the store and unable to find one's parent. On the other, the clinician may expect an event such as the kitchen catching fire to be traumatic, while a two-year-old may have experienced this as a fun adventure in which the nice firemen came and no one was hurt. The phenomena of trauma are universal. Their effects are specific.

The multidimensionality of trauma's effects challenges our system of care. Because trauma is embodied, relational, and developmental, its potency and effects impact and must be addressed through these domains. In disrupting the direction of our embodied mind's development, trauma is, by our definition, hypnotic. How clinicians keep these dimensions in mind as they express curiosity about a person's history of trauma opens doors to a hypnotic evocation of experiential resources.

Trauma's Entry into Health Care

While pain was being recognized as a vital dimension of physical health, research in and awareness of psychological trauma were growing exponentially. Assessing the physical dimensions of traumatic injury—wound depth, projectile trajectory—was as old as health care itself. People with broken bones, ruptured appendices, bullet wounds, and heart attacks have always filled emergency rooms, where medical training has been geared to respond swiftly and knowledgeably to their bodies' visible wounds. But the magnitude of the impact of the psychological components of trauma is best exemplified in the US by two national events in the second half of the 20th century.

First was the growing awareness of child maltreatment, originating with the publication of Kempe, Silverman, Steele, Droegemueller, and Silver's (1962) article on the "Battered Child Syndrome." Physicians began to recognize and record injuries in children that did not fit with parents' or care-givers' descriptions of their causes. With that recognition, clinicians had to take on roles and develop skills beyond diagnosing and setting fractures. Physicians raised awareness nationally, advocating for more sensitive and responsive clinical care for these traumatized children within the health system, and better education and support for their care-givers.

The second event was the Vietnam war. The minds of soldiers returning from combat, with limbs lost and memories of dying comrades, continued to experience the flashbacks of warfare (Benedek & Ursano, 2009; Herman, 1992). The name "Post-Traumatic Stress Disorder" (PTSD) was applied to this phenomenon and entered the psychiatric lexicon with the third edition of the American Psychiatry Association's *Diagnostic and Statistical Manual* (*DSM-III*; APA, 1980). It was distinguished from conditions that were deemed inherent to the individual (e.g., a traumatic neurosis) by having an externally derived etiology, an inciting traumatic event that impacted the individual (Friedman, 2014). The initial diagnostic entry lacked criteria for a developmental assessment and was void of the relational component that is now considered significant. This new term was used retroactively to describe survivors of the Holocaust, the bombing of Hiroshima and Nagasaki, and other societal (man against man[2]) atrocities. The framers of the *DSM-III* reasoned that events antecedent to trauma were extraordinary, exceeding the emotional coping resources of normal individuals. Thus, trauma was a kind of emotional scarring in response to perceived existential threat. This formulation, the sheer volume of affected returning military, and the many clients who self-diagnosed their PTSD, motivated medical practice to broaden its treatment responsiveness. As the world experienced humanitarian crises with increasing frequency, a melding phenomenon began in American medicine. Treating trauma became a whole-body endeavor, or as some colleagues reflectively wrote, it required a "mindbody" approach, the two words were inseparable (M. Weisberg, personal communication, March, 1998).

The diagnosis of trauma, both physical and mental, and the recognition of its prevalence, was a societal crisis that tentatively bridged the siloes of medicine and psychology. It compelled us to reckon with the artificial body-mind dichotomy that had come to characterize much of western allopathic medicine. The 1970's consciousness-raising about sexual, physical, and verbal abuse of children demarcated the psychological components of trauma. Psychology heartily responded with the development of the field of family therapy.

The mental health crisis that put PTSD in the diagnostic nomenclature also compelled medicine and psychology to integrate their work. Many people who suffered from trauma did not seek help beyond their local physician. Anecdotally, psychologists working in Veterans' Administration health centers in the US have told me (LIS) that the veterans most affected by PTSD exhibit the most denial and minimalizing of symptoms, typically claiming that, "Other guys went through much more than me" (C. Crane, personal communication, May, 2018). As a result, that local physician became the portal for help, often beyond his or her training or skill. An unintended and important outcome of caring for traumatized children and veterans was that clinicians needed to become aware of their own emotional vulnerability when treating trauma. They also needed skills to cope with their own traumatization.

Complementary and alternative approaches (e.g., eye-movement dissociation and reprocessing, acupuncture, neurofeedback) proliferated partly as a result of the failures of limited medical interventions, and the public need for faster and better results (Lake, 2014). Between 1970 and 2000, the number of books on the topic of identifying trauma, treating trauma, understanding humanity's propensity for and revulsion of violence, pointed to the explosion of theories, research, and treatments. Guidelines for treatment slowly emerged (Weine et al., 2002). An important outcome of this trauma research was learning how early traumatic experiences can affect brain development (Perry, 2009).

At the same time clinicians were learning about trauma, they were experiencing the risks of treating those who were traumatized. Helping people adapt to their experiences is immensely rewarding, when their suffering eases. Treating the effects of trauma means being present as a patient tells their story and experiences the emotions and the bodily sensations that go with it. Trauma, it turns out, is embodied and relational for all parties in the therapeutic system. Its effects are contagious. "Vicarious traumatization" (McCann & Pearlman, 1990b)—how we change as a result of our empathic responses to another's trauma—was recognized as a risk factor for developing PTSD. Complementary terms for vicarious traumatization are "secondary traumatization" or "compassion fatigue" (Figley, 1995). Like burnout (Freudenberger, 1974), without awareness, recognition, and self-care, these exposures can leave clinicians and other care-givers physically and emotionally exhausted, in our own existential crises.

We portray some of this contagion in Robinson's story. Robinson exhibits vicarious traumatization as he encounters Little Esther as a medical student. He feels deeply for her, and in addition this evokes his own unresolved childhood fears of his father. This experience stays with him in dreams as he approaches his own fatherhood, which then leads him and his wife to therapy.

Without appropriate self-care, compassion fatigue can lead to poor sleep, poor eating, substance abuse, depression, and the very symptoms we are helping our clients to reduce. Promoting well-being in the people we care for requires the practice and modeling of self-care. From a social systems perspective, the recognition and treatment of the clinician's susceptibility to the contagion of vicarious traumatization is a departure from the legacy of the reductionist biomedical model. Within that paradigm, the trend had been toward increasing diagnostic categorization and treatment protocols—which has served, however unintentionally, to promote avoidance of vicarious traumatization through disengagement and objectification.

Trauma-Informed: Do You Ever Feel Unsafe at Home?

Trauma did not become a vital sign like pain. It did, however, earn a vital place in health care. It yielded a new approach, referred to as "trauma-informed" care (Salasin, 2011). Trauma-informed care focuses on understanding, recognizing, and responding to the effects of all types of trauma and the ways that an individual lives in trauma.[3] It is a direct application of many psychological principles in trauma treatment. It is being researched and applied in a variety of settings (Stringer, 2019) and, we posit, can be enhanced with the integration of hypnosis skills.

To be a trauma-informed clinician is to recognize the formative and client-specific influences of trauma. A trauma-informed clinician sites along the lifetime of each individual, looking for signs of trauma and how it may have affected development, relationships, aspirations, and health. *Temporal Touring, Narrative Listening,* and *Relational Being* are practiced from this stance. Trauma-informed practices often start in the examining room with the routine question, "Do you ever feel unsafe at home?"—an inquiry about domestic violence or its echoes. This direct question may not yield a direct answer. But trauma-informed clinicians learn to observe the non-verbal, body language response to that question: what the question elicits. They learn that asking it gently and impartially can open doors to awareness, and then to therapy. The aim of the query is to expose any impact of trauma without retraumatizing the individual. Evoking emotions in the context of a strong therapeutic alliance, a safe and accepting relational being, may produce abreactions. These intense moments of emotional expression can appear as retraumatizing. They can be uncomfortable for the clinicians, who therefore may avoid them with the intention of protecting the client. In fact, this avoidance is not protective. No change occurs when emotions are not evoked. How we evoke repressed emotion facilitates change.

Whatever the client's response, hypnosis skills apply to the struggle of changing the effects of trauma. The clinician's trance serves to accept and normalize the strength of the emotion, thereby depotentiating it. Disruptive elements such as the use of dissociative language, dissociative imagery (e.g., reconstructing traumatic experiences from a different point of view), and time distortion can assist the person to regain empowerment and regulation, reminding them that this struggle is how we learn and change. Finally, the use of continuing questions, post-hypnotic souvenirs, and—perhaps most powerfully—silence that gives room for illumination and "AHA!" moments, allow that person to progress toward reintegration.

A Developmental Definition of Trauma

We can refine the definition of trauma from a developmental perspective. Supporting our thesis to envision the individual as layered from micro (cellular) to macro (social) systems, trauma may be seen as a disruption of developmental imperatives: from gene, to cell receptors, to synapses, to body, to mind, to family and society. What does this mean?

We experience trauma, then manage and learn from it, in stepwise and expansive fashion. A simple example: A one-year-old is learning to walk. Sitting on the floor, he grabs the edge of the sofa, pulls himself up, and traverses its edge, his little fingers steadying his balance. He lets go and takes a few steps. Then he falls. Then he wails. The fall disrupts his emerging drive to master the complexity of walking. This is a small potential of trauma. He quiets, reaches up, grabs the sofa, and starts all over. With practice, he lets go. He accumulates experience. Falling down is usual when we are in the process of learning to walk. Walking, in fact, is the act of controlled falling, repairing trauma potentials. Soon he's potentially traumatizing his parents by disrupting their drive to protect and keep him safe. Then they, too, have to overcome these slightly larger potentials of trauma to allow him more exploration … and more potential traumas.

Human growth and development, in all of the complexity with which we examined it in Chapter 6, is the skeletal framework upon which we layer the flesh of temperament, personality, attachment, family dynamics, intellect, physical and mental well-being, and more. Collectively, this construction adds up to a euphemistic kind of "normal." If normal is average, what lies standard deviations away from the average is a disruption of development. The infant who is abandoned or beaten. The toddler who is diagnosed with Cystic Fibrosis. The elementary school student who is struck by lightning. The teen who is hospitalized with alcohol poisoning. The college student who is raped. The young adult diagnosed with Multiple Sclerosis. The middle-aged woman, told she has breast cancer. The man in mid-life crisis who undergoes open-heart surgery. The elderly person, facing loss of self with dementia. Each experiences a disrupting event in their development. These experiences—outside the boundaries of normal—populate our common list of traumata that, in some form, disorder each of our lives. In disturbing our developmental trajectories, trauma evokes plasticity for eventual recovery, learning, and sometimes, scarring. In that way it is hypnotic—and so, hypnosis is useful in treating trauma.

Earlier definitions of trauma included criteria of sudden events that were overwhelming and disruptive to one's frame of reference or to the meaning we make of events (McCann & Pearlman, 1990a). These definitions did not fully consider the spectrum of vulnerability—from in-utero to adult experiences—with regard to effects on mind and brain development. Later definitions addressed the effects on physiology, arousal or avoidance symptoms, and the stress-response system's ways of coping with or adapting to something experienced as threatening.

A "trauma" and what is "traumatic" are not necessarily interchangeable. In theory, the noun refers to some shared, common understanding of what is beyond the normal experience. The adjective refers to an individual's response to the threat to his or her survival. Viewed from a neurobiological stance, anything that alerts us to a threat to our survival can be a trauma. We might think of the trance for survival as the starting place for all trauma.

Surviving is arguably the most basic developmental imperative. The dark night that limits vision, the snake rustling in the grass, or the tiger lurking in the jungle may be phylogenetic fears meant to alert us to action. Which comes first, the fear of snakes, or the snake bite that teaches us to be afraid? Developmental imperatives, such as menses and menopause, may be disruptors to development and evoke the trance of survival. Every girl recalls the start of her menses; for some, it is traumatic. When a man experiences erectile dysfunction, it is usually traumatic. When a parent learns their female child is becoming a trans-male, it is traumatic for the relational dynamics. Trauma not only leads to dysregulation, it also is dysregulating of the emotional distance with other human beings (Schore, 2019). An aspect of development is disrupted, so we go plastic, and the meaning we give to the event—our response to the event—creates the traumatization (Gil, 1998). Hypnosis has a powerful role in revising the wounded response.

Our responses are determined by genetics, epigenetics, and experience (Perry, 2009). As with most efforts to normalize the human experience, it turns out that context, personality, early formative life experiences, intellect, culture, and belief hinder any consensual definition of either trauma or what is experienced as traumatic. Still, some parameters are useful to remind us of the ubiquity of trauma, and to guide us in what to look for and ask about as we design interventions to lessen their negative impact on an individual's development.

Identifying Trauma

While recognizing that individual coping and developmental age are significant in the genesis of trauma, so are the type of events. There is no comprehensive list of trauma events, but for the purposes of assessment and treatment, we can place them into basic categories (Pynoos, 1994). We have culled our own list of traumata from the experiences of our clients. Each reminds us of what to listen for in the client's narrative, what may emerge in their care, and what to ask about. The list includes:

(1) Verbal, physical, and sexual abuse (this includes victimizations, homicide, rape, and suicide).
(2) Accidents.
(3) Chronic illness and medical procedures.
(4) Death (loss of parent, sibling, relative, friend, pet) or "hidden" losses (changed schools, lost an election, a job, a place on the team).
(5) Divorce or separation; family pathology.
(6) Natural disasters; terrorism is a subcategory because it requires large-scale responses.
(7) War.

When considering kinds of potentially traumatizing events, those perpetrated by other humans are more difficult to heal from and more likely to be perpetuated intergenerationally. In contrast, the response to a natural disaster often creates a communal response, which enables more positive coping (De Zulueta, 1993).

Chronic illness is listed as a separate trauma because of its distinguishing characteristics. Chronic illness is enduring and often progressive. This means it taxes a person's coping resources on a daily basis. This amounts to a persistent assault on hope, an ongoing series of demands and crises. The effect on the family system is intensified when there is a genetic contribution to the chronic disease. Parents grieve their ignorance of genes unknowingly passed on to their child. Children, including as adults, see their parents as a source of their lifelong challenge. Illness causes us to look back and determine what else we could have been done preventively. This search of our past for a sense of control is usually fruitless. Healing requires forgiveness. The poet Buddy Wakefield says that forgiveness starts with "the release of all hope for a better past" (Wakefield, 2012). Of course, this reflective revisioning can occur with any bad event we wish we could have avoided. With chronic illness, this is complicated by the experience of being at odds with one's body. "How did I miss that sign of illness? Why did I not do something sooner? Why did my body not give me better signals?" Furthermore, many chronic illnesses are not overtly visible. This may mean they are under-considered in social relationships, which can undermine empathy.

Chronic Illness and Hypnosis

In my (JHL) clinical practice with children, I am often afforded the opportunity of knowing a child well into their adult years. The magnitude of history that accompanies these long relationships is something physicians once regularly enjoyed. Barbara was one such client. At eight years of age, she began treatment for anxiety and panic, which accompanied every illness. Barbara had cystic fibrosis (CF). A mild upper-respiratory infection, cold, or any irritant that made her breathing difficult, would set off her worries of not being able to catch her breath. She was smart and sensitive. She already understood that CF meant an early death. This was a lot for a youngster to manage. Anxiety creates a trance opening. When fear is activated, we orient toward danger and novelty, becoming plastic. In our first session, I asked Barbara to teach me what she thought I needed to know about her illness so that I could help her. [Clinical comments in italics.] *Being person-centered and letting her choose what was important.*

B: "My lungs get filled with gunk. My parents have to do physical therapy [chest percussion] with me every day to loosen the stuff so I can get it out."

J: I handed B a stuffed animal and asked, "Can you show me what that looks like when they do that therapy?"

B: Tense and focused, B thumped on the back of the stuffed gorilla. "Like this."

J: "Wow, that takes a lot of energy. How do you know when you're finished?"

B: "Well, you are never finished. You do it every day."
B was watching me as she said this. A clear lesson in chronicity: it is "never finished."

J: "The gorilla wants to go play. How long will this thumping take, today?"
Can time distortion make this today and not everyday?

B: "You never know. I think he's done for now."
Health is unpredictable and I have some control over decisions.

B learned to use her imagination to calm herself, to go on fantasy travel in which she was courageous and adventuresome. She met a guide on her journey.

J: "Can you tell me about the guide?"

B: "It is a small chameleon, green, and has suction cups for feet."
Her imagination was giving her a very useful companion.

Barbara wanted help with self-care. She did not like the dependence on others that her condition necessitated. This tension between the developmental imperative toward autonomy and the need to rely on others is a distinctive feature of most chronic illness. Medical procedures seemed unending, and young Barbara struggled to accept the routine. Her family relationships were supportive, but as Barbara entered adolescence, her need for individuation caused more stress, since she still relied on her parents for percussive treatments. She was sure she would not live past 20, and she avoided dating. I hoped for Barbara to learn to advocate for herself, to be aware of the ongoing medical research that promised more hopeful outcomes. At various times, she would come in to address a reoccurrence of anxiety. This came after a serious illness, some loss of function, and facing her mortality.

B: "My best CF friend had a very sudden and serious decline. She got a lung transplant. Even the doctors were scared she wouldn't make it."

J: *What does it feel like when your doctors are afraid, I wondered.* "How is she doing?," I asked.

B: "Really well, but she posts everything about her progress online. It's so weird." She said this looking away, a distressed and thoughtful expression on her face.

J: "Not your style. You prefer privacy, to be discreet, and to manage on your own." *I was reinforcing one of her many resources for coping.* "It sounds like you do not enjoy reading the details."

B: "I am coming to realize that exposing myself to too much online stuff about CF isn't good. I identify with everyone and think it's going to happen to me."

J: "Hmmm—you identify with everyone? Like when you were sure you would not live past 20?" (B was now 35.) "What about the folks who are doing really well?"

B: Smiling. "Right, I am only looking at the ones doing poorly. I am going to stop for a while, give myself a break." *Barbara knew what she needed to do to restore her homeostasis. Her condition was only traumatic at times, no longer all the time.*

The younger and more frequently we experience trauma, the more it is likely to become what Van der Kolk (2005) refers to as complex or developmental trauma. This category includes both prenatal and relational trauma (Schore, 1994). From the field of interpersonal neurobiology we have learned that a pregnant mother's stress and emotional regulation affects the development of the fetus's brain and its potential for regulating emotion and responses to novelty. The terms "complex" or "early" trauma highlight the awareness of the developmental continuum. Once we view trauma as a disruptor of development, all trauma is developmental.

Relational Trauma and Undue Influence

There is no clearer manifestation of the hypnotic elements in trauma than in the harmful indoctrination of others. Examples of harmful undue influence include but are not limited to: destructive cults, mind control, brainwashing, parental alienation, estrangement, unethical hypnosis, abusive relationships, human trafficking, multi-level marketing, and violent extremism. As Steven Hassan (2018) teaches, the spectrum of undue influence employs, for nefarious purposes, all of the hypnotic skills we have presented to produce identity-damaging effects (Hassan & Shah, 2019). Hassan's "BITE Model" categorizes the types of control inflicted by perpetrators of this type of trauma (Hassan, 2018). BITE is an acronym for **B**ehavioral control, **I**nformational control, **T**hought control, and **E**motional control. These also label the domains of treatment in which the therapist engages, in the challenging task of evoking innate and individual potentials of identity and self for rebuilding. Intriguingly, Hassan relates that even young adults who were born into cults seem to have a core and inviolable sense of self, awaiting free expression (S. Hassan, personal communication, August, 2015).

Trauma is Embodied and Systemic

Everyone has experienced traumatic events, and all of us carry some somatic and relational fallout, as embodied memories from these traumatic experiences. Anxiety, depression, rage, and violence are felt experiences that are both evoked and calmed in our social interactions. Siegel (2019) considers three brain networks that are required and must collaborate for healthy development, and thus, coping with trauma. The default, or primary, is the survival network that interacts with the autonomic (fight, flight, freeze, and vagal) systems. Next, the salience network helps prioritize what is important to consider. Third, and most recently evolved, the executive network plans and organizes. We can become traumatized when these networks cannot fully cooperate with each other. That is what we mean by a traumatic event overwhelming our ability to cope.

In this way trauma creates fear, causes internal chaos, and impairs planning or meaning-making. The goal of therapy is to evoke these sensations, change their temporal (time of day) and symbolic (the meaning of getting back into the car after one has been in a car accident) relationships, and provide a re-integrating experience, so the embodied mind can begin to restore balance. This must occur in a relational context of unconditional acceptance. Being present with the person in our care, to provide a safe and secure environment while they process their physical sensations, talk about what is welling up inside of them, and engage the executive functions, helps to coordinate each of these three networks, so there may be renewal and re-integration. We add that this process aligns, once again, both with Rossi's four stages of the Novelty-Numinosum-Neurogenesis Effect (2002) and the rapport-disrupt-renewal skills of hypnosis.

Trauma is both personal and communal. To address it requires systems thinking. The impact of neglect, poverty, substance abuse, and maltreatment on neurodevelopment may cause more trauma in the world than shocking events that get news coverage. Until our healing disciplines reach out beyond emergency departments and therapy rooms to inform the public about the interplay between development, society, and trauma, these early negative influences on growing minds will continue without satisfactory prevention and treatment.

Reducing the Effects of Trauma

Given our discussion so far, we can simply define being traumatized as experiencing a threat to survival that impairs the creation of competent experiential resources. In turn, failure to create these experiential resources disrupts our development. The defensively oriented sympathetic nervous system behaviorally produces what is commonly referred to as the "fight, flight, or freeze" response. It is reflexive to perceived external threat, triggering prior to conscious mitigation. If this system remains in high arousal, called increased sympathetic tone, it can produce long-term damage to our entire central nervous system, especially when we are young, developing, and so, most malleable. What changes the brain, changes the mind. The successful healing of traumatic experiences goes beyond just surviving sympathetic arousal. Flexibility, functioning in the face of the unexpected, and a world-view that adapts to change and accepts human limitations are vital components of resilience (Linley, 2003). A positive outcome from a traumatic event includes repair of developmental "wounds" and the building of resources for resilience. Moreover, it involves the rebuilding of agency and self-determination. These goals are as requisite for the battered child as they are for the soldier with flashbacks.

Psychiatrist and researcher Bruce Perry created the Neurosequential Model of Therapeutics (NMT, 2009) to ground treatment of traumatized children in a neurodevelopmental perspective. The therapeutic model includes taking a developmental history, and an assessment of current functioning. It matches symptoms to developmental age and identifies what is missing or in need of developmental progress or repair. It then recommends interventions based on the map of the brain's need for development. If early deficits have affected the more primitive regions of the brain, then cognitive or behavioral treatments (which characterize many psychotherapy treatments) will be inadequate. Instead, providing patterned, repetitive neural input, such as rhythmic breathing, music, repetitive movement, yoga, balancing exercises, and other somatosensory interventions are needed to provide use-dependent alternations in brain function. This is effective in restorative neurology with stroke patients, and can provide organizing and regulating input to the brainstem and neural networks, which reduces trauma symptoms of anxiety and impulsivity (Perry, 2009.). These embodied and relational approaches align with the hypnosis skills set.

Remember the discussion about progressive muscle relaxation (PMR) in Chapter 7? We made the point that hypnosis is not about relaxing, and in fact requires some tension. However, the breathing, muscle movement, repetition, soothing imagery, calm voice, and slow pacing of PMR incorporates pro-social parts of the nervous system through building awareness of the body's responses. We calm first in the face of others' calm (Linden, 2014). The presence of the clinician provides containment for our unregulated emotions. PMR is an embodied, person-centered, and disruptive experience that fosters better self-regulation and agency, thereby changing the brain and embodied mind.

Adding the Hypnosis Skill Set

Perry (2009) considered a continuum of adaptive responses to threat. This spectrum emphasized the universal hardwiring of our stress-response system in the face of fear, to promote survival. He points out that we respond adaptively and there is no one correct way to do so. He combined five key elements, common to the experience of both trauma and trance (i.e., how we go plastic): (1) Sense of time, (2) Arousal, (3) Dissociation, (4) Regulating brain region, (5) Cognitive style, and (6) Internal state.

Perry's work seems to reflect his hypnosis training (personal communication, 2006). His inclusion of a sense of time and dissociation are two phenomena routinely evoked and used in disruptive hypnotic techniques. Dissociation is the break in the continuity of consciousness, memory, identity, or perception. In *My Brilliant Friend,* author Elena Ferrante (2012, p. 89) describes this as "dissolving margins," capturing the unsayable, the dissolution and disappearance of previous experiential contexts and boundaries: what we thought we knew for certain, even our sense of self. When we go plastic, continuity is disrupted. This creates an opening for modulating perceptions. Dissociation's temporal relative is a distortion in the tracking of time. We use the now-flexible sense of time to move forward and backward; hence, *Temporal Touring.* In trauma treatment, by the process of being present, marking past, present and future, we evoke dissociated affect, co-create narratives, label sensory experiences, and imagine non-traumatic scenarios, in order to help restore continuity. The hypnosis skill set incorporates awareness of and responses to behavioral changes of the embodied mind: gestures, facial changes, words. This interaction allows people to change their minds.

Viewed through Perry's (2009) spectrum, when we are adapting to extreme, potent trauma, we are in an internal state of terror. There is no sense of time; arousal may be aggressive ("fighting"), or dissociative (fainting, "freezing"); the brainstem is responding while other parts of the brain are overridden or shut down; and the cognitive style is reflexive (without thought), not reflective. Somnambulistic trance seems to share these features. The patient who undergoes surgery without chemical anesthesia, instead choosing to utilize these dissociative, adaptive capacities, illustrates the plasticity of both trance and trauma responses.

When little Lulu was separated from her mother and moved into a new environment, she likely experienced terror. She may have had a temper tantrum or grown mute. She likely had no memory of the length of time that she travelled from the refugee camp to the new adoptive home. Memory formation and thinking at the age of five are not fully developed. Misunderstanding and misperceptions make the young child vulnerable to memory errors and condensation of experiences (Terr, 1994). Lulu's mind was undoubtedly flooded with messenger molecules signaling alarm and discord, initiating a cascade of dysfunction for her developing mind.

Each of these variables—time, associative networks, autonomic functions—are explained in the trance phenomena, principles, and skills of hypnosis previously described in Part I. What "goes in" during the trance of survival can "come out" during a therapeutically evoked trance. Stress response symptoms can be changed and modified, using the hypnotic skill set to direct a trance experience.

If surviving trauma involves trance (i.e., is formative), then further addressing the parallels between the experiences of trance and trauma will clarify the usefulness of the hypnosis skill set. Do you remember in childhood when someone would jump from a hidden place and yell, "Boo!" and scare the "living daylights" out of you? Danger captures our attention. It also narrows and focuses our attention on the immediate. It activates our survival mode and increases sensing, while lessening thinking. Time becomes distorted. Our other sensory perceptions are altered: some intensified, some diminished. In that moment of shocked surprise, maybe you even felt the energy flow of adrenaline (the neurohormone that increases our ability to remember) course through your body. In this survival mode, we are highly responsive to the influence of others. As one emergency room physician often stated, "People in the ER are in trance, waiting for someone to take charge of their trance" (D. Ewin, personal communication, March, 1990).

In using the hypnotic skill set, we engage with the trance-activated mind in order to change it. We either identify the existing trance receptivity (people in distress or suffering), or evoke it with the use of novelty to capture attention, always in a container of safety and protection. We breathe together, create rhythms that are soothing and repetitive, and pace words of comfort and strength, such as "yes," "that's right," or the phrase, "so difficult to do." In the treatment of trauma, most of what we say is geared to those lower (evolutionarily more primitive) brain regions, so the sound, rhythm, flow, and cadence of our speech matter. It is how the lower brain region "listens" and activates, which will allow the more complex parts of the brain to reorganize and, later, absorb suggestive corrective messages. This is also supported by the aforementioned work of Porges (2011), that links regulating the rhythmicity of language, breathing, and thus, heart rate variability, with increasing vagal tone and social engagement. In all these ways, using the hypnotic relationship to tap into the neural and humoral pathways involving bonding, attachment, affiliation, and social communication (Perry, 2009; Porges, 2011), while being cognizant of the stress-response pathways, creates the potentiation for change. Hypnotic principles and skills incorporate the potential of the relational and the survival trance to change the mind.

Skills for Reducing Trauma Symptoms

We can apply each of our principles to reduce symptoms from trauma. Earlier, we discussed the distortion of time that often accompanies a traumatic event. Our clients often feel as if they are still experiencing what was traumatic, even though the actual event has ended. Distortions in our sense of time accompany fear and threats to our survival. Helping a patient identify when that fear began, and then the first point at which they knew they were safe, thus "bookending" an event, begins to provide a containing and comforting timeframe from which to heal. Inquiring about these "time stamps" evokes memories and emotions. Implicitly, it conveys that the traumatizing event is over. What is being recalled and felt are memories. Note that the endpoint, the first experience of post-traumatic safety, may be in the moment of answering the question in the clinician's office.

Here is an example of the "bookend approach." Erin entered my (JHL) care after a winter car accident because she was experiencing panic attacks, any time she had to drive.

J: "That sounds like a very scary experience." I said, after she described the accident.

E: "Yeah," her eyes focused on the floor with a dazed expression.

J: "This may seem like an odd question, but when did you know you were safe after this accident?"

E: Looking very surprised, she said, "When my husband arrived to get my daughter and me from the side of the road." *The event had an ending.*

J: "And when did you first feel danger in your car?"

E: "When I couldn't turn the steering wheel. I felt the car swerving, and tried to keep it on the road, but the steering wheel was frozen. I just felt, oh no!" *Now the event has a beginning.*

These bookends in time permit a story to be created of the event, giving language to what had so far been an experienced set of embodied responses to her survival being threatened. Erin's panic attacks, with sweaty palms, thumping in the chest, kinesthetic and visual flashbacks of the car rolling over, etc., are an unprocessed story.

This is where the principle of *Narrative Listening* is applied. Our memory is reactivated and facilitated by organizing facts along different kinds of narrative arc. To create a sense of coherence and meaning, we organize along a time line, building emotions to a peak and then to resolution, or along somatosensory experiences, or—perhaps most profoundly—in some combination. The clinician listens for the missing pieces and the exaggerated moments. We listen for the "I don't knows." These often point the way to what is stored somatically. They are often the beginning of those implicit processing heuristics. We observe the responses to the person in our care: eye-movements, shifts in posture and breathing, furrowed brows. We ask questions with attention to our tone, volume, speed. We match or model the elements of each emotion. In this way we elicit details, evoke emotions, and discover the sequence of events. The embodied mind stores all of our experiences. These are often wordless. They are engrams, recorded as gestures, sounds, smells, and a whole range of motor and sensory elements, arranged in specific contexts, often without thought. Consider the interplay of these elements, and how one might respond to their enactment in Erin's words, facial expressions, and gestures, as involving *Systems Thinking*. The experiences can be accessed safely through activating visual, muscle, and sensory memories. Together with the trusted caregiver using their clinician's trance, we co-create the narrative in words.

As Erin described her car accident, I interrupted

J: "Where were you when the car stopped moving?" *My voice expressed calm, curiosity and concern.*

E: "I was in my seat, the seat belt kept me from flying all over. I was reaching back for my daughter." *E's voice grew louder, faster and more urgent.*

J: *In a quiet, slow voice I inquired,* "Can you show me how you were reaching? How far was your daughter from you? If I am your daughter, show me where I would be." *Our place in space is one of the most durable memories of our experiences. Where we were when such-and-such happened is an avenue to pursue to tell the story, and helps the patient access embodied memories.*

E: *She moves her body to stage the accident.* "I was in the driver's seat, here." *She points to where she is seated, letting me know she is in the story now. Her eyes are dazed, her speech slow.* "The car was upright, after it had rolled over. We were on the snow bank at the side of the road"

J: "Which side *were* you on?" *I interrupt, noting with emphasis she is telling the story in the past tense.*

E: "The same side I was driving on!" *she says with irritation; her eyes now look into mine.*

J: "That's right—it happened then, and it's over." *I speak softly, slowly, our eyes still locked together.* "You are all right. And your daughter? You reached back?" *I use the past tense to implicitly convey it is over.*

E: "She was ok. Crying, we were both crying. But we were both ok." *She has likely taken in the message of being alive.* "Just some bruising from the seat belt."

Erin began to embody the story of the accident. Other open-ended questions then evoked what her perceptions had stored. What time of day was it? What did the sky look like? What was the temperature of the air? The weather? What could she see outside the car? Did she feel the movement of her body? What was she wearing?

I put each of these pieces together and repeated the story back to her, reminding her that her body's automatic reflexes did what the brain does best: they enabled her survival.

J: "Erin, that was quite a scary moment in time. The car feeling out of control, then you feeling out of control, and terrified you and your daughter would get hurt. Your brain was working to enable your survival and your daughter's, just as your brain knows how to drive, and has done so carefully for 30 some years. You called your husband. He came, and getting in his car, you knew you were ok. You're safely telling me the story now."

I remained positive, listing her strengths, co-creating the story, processing the sensations, using a soothing, comforting tone. Observing her responses, I saw her calm. Her breathing was more regular. She smiled.

J: "I wonder if you can imagine right now, getting into your car before the accident, as you have done so many times—to run errands, to drive your daughter to school? All those times, was it easy to get behind the wheel and go where you needed to go?"

Now Erin has an opportunity to draw on her history and practice what she already knows: driving without panic.

E: Smiling. "Yes, it was easy before the accident. I can do this."

There is agency and empowerment in Erin's words. Trauma renders us helpless and overwhelmed. A valuable outcome of resolving trauma's sequelae is the installation and restoration of able coping resources.

In order to elicit Erin's coping mechanisms, to help her resolve her traumatic responses (panic attack symptoms) to driving, we apply each of our four principles. We are attuned, sensitive, and responsive to her. We are aware of her relations with others. We listen and then comment. Each suggestion is calculated to assist in putting the experience into words, to help it become an emotional story. We use time, *Temporal Touring*, to start and end the traumatic experience, and then suggest she can look forward to driving free of anxiety, as she has done in the past.

To begin by telling her she is fine, and the accident is over, would have been both ineffective and superficial. Her mind could not have taken that message in because it does not fit with the experience of its own underlying sympathetic nervous system arousal, nor the resulting effects throughout the embodied mind. We have to start where the system is and mirror it, matching its capabilities, and help lead it to a new conclusion, one that enhances coping. Erin wanted to drive in winter without fear of another accident. Evoking memories of her many years of safely driving her daughter without incident restored her sense of efficacy.

I asked what she had learned from the car accident. The question surprised her. "Anyone is vulnerable in a car, and I need to keep driving," she replied. This question invited making meaning of her experience, transforming the traumatic event into a resource. It is similar to Beverly James's (1989, p. 203) game for children. She encourages them to make friends with their scar. Coping with adversity and resilient thinking now were experiential resources for Erin.

Therapeutic interventions are supposed to be safe, but that is not always the case. They can inadvertently create a sense of danger. A well-meaning therapist can be ignorant and diagnosis-based, rather than person-centered. Or perhaps they are more enthralled with their technique and process than with the person in their care.

Contrast the preceding interactions with an encounter in which the suggestions and advice are about conformity, rigid morality, or an unconscious bias that leaks through the language choice. For example, during a psychotherapy session with a gender dysphoric girl (not yet transitioning), I (JHL) learned her/his father was going to be away for several weeks. This would leave my client with her/his sister and mother at home. I started to comment on the opportunity for girl time but, seeing the tensed look on my client's face, I caught myself in my unconscious bias. I still saw my client as one of the girls. Fortunately, I was able to quickly correct and add that while mom and sister hung out, my client would have some time for her/himself. Her/his face relaxed.

When we are not attuned, and not matching our clients' emotions, we risk shaming them. In their already frightened survival trance process, this may cause them to hide their worries and to suffer in an alienated silence. If the caregiver is authoritarian or self-righteous, or their hubris limits empathy, the person in care can be traumatized. Stevie seems to have encountered some of this type of interaction with the therapist.

Of course, people who have experienced developmental trauma are particularly vulnerable to being retraumatized. To restate, trauma is not just an event. The response to trauma may become a way of living as if one's life depended on it. It can become a way of surviving, not living. An entire field of dissociative identity disorder (DID) and its sub-discipline of ego-state therapy (Phillips & Frederick, 1995; Watkins & Watkins, 1997) have emerged alongside the study of the mind and how it is impacted by trauma. One way the mind manages overwhelming events is to dis-associate from what is happening. For example, children who were sexually abused sometimes report floating out of their bodies. As adults, the same floating may occur whenever something scary or dangerous occurs. When we experience life as dangerous and unpredictable, we remain in the survival trance.

You may "leave your body" in order to cope, to feel some control, to feel less helpless. In the short term that is useful, such as when we suggest to the mother in labor that she imagine floating to the ceiling of the birthing room, so she may watch her baby being born. In the long term, to live on the ceiling is to be a victim, without the agency to feel embodied and whole. As our many examples have shown, traumatization is an experience in which one struggles to maintain one's ability for self-determination amidst ghosts of past threats, while living perilously into the unknown (see Ryan & Deci, 2017). Inherent in person-centered hypnotic approaches is the evocation of a sense of agency and self-determination. This agency, empowerment, and becoming active move us from victim to victor, from helpless to independent, to becoming capable of changing our minds.

Remember there is a disproportional and formative valence in early childhood experiences (Perry, 2009). The child raised in life-threatening circumstances of poverty, neglect, maltreatment, family pathology, or war is likely to be in survival mode. If the stress-response system has been tuned to zoning out, to dissociating, it has learned to avoid so as not to be hurt. If the stress-response system has been tuned to aggression and to fighting, it has learned to hurt the other first, so as not to be hurt by the other (Perry, 2009). Current understanding of dissociative identity mechanisms is that part of surviving is an arrangement of coping responses among different parts of the developing entity. DID theory is beyond the scope of this book, but using hypnotic skills and principles to address the dissociative aspects of trauma responses is quite valuable. As noted earlier, what "goes in" during the trance of survival, can "come out" during a therapeutically evoked trance.

As we align and attune with our clients, we may mistake trauma-bonding for "secure attachment" (James, 1989). Naively, in the beginning of my (JHL) career, while working in elementary schools, I would enjoy walking into the building where, within a few feet of the door, I felt like the Pied Piper. I would be surrounded by children competing to hold my hands, hugging my arms, and happily accompanying me to my destination. I thought it was sweet, and was curious about its dynamics. This instantaneous connection is a feature of traumatic bonding. Like attachment, the bond is experienced as essential for survival, but it is motivated by terror in the face of those we are dependent upon. It is a PTSD response. The goal of a trauma bond is to look after our care-giver in the interest of our own safety. These children were likely conditioned to have traumatic bonds with abusive caregivers, and in seeking connection with me, used their automated responses. They may also have been seeking healthy connection. As we will learn in the next chapter, healthy attachment is loving, it takes time to grow, and it fosters autonomy, individuation, and self-mastery.

People are social animals, relational beings. Trauma responses not only occur at an individual level, but also at the community level. Families, tribes, cities, countries, and entire cultures can experience a traumatic event and be unable to offer one another the protection and support for coping. An important characteristic of the approach we are describing is its applicability to any level of system organization. Whether thinking of the cellular activation in an individual or an epidemic of infectious disease, the same skills and principles apply to promote changing minds. In the next section, we will examine the roles of attachment in our development, and thus in the hypnotic relationship. Studies of resilience consistently and emphatically demonstrate that healthy relationships heal (Linden, 2020).

Questions and Assignments for Further Discussion

1. Each of the characters in the stories has had trauma in their lives. What are some of the antecedents that shaped their later responses to traumatic events?
2. In this chapter we explore the narratives of a person's life written by our development and responses to trauma. How might you expect your health care provider to learn about your traumas?
3. Given that being susceptible to trauma, especially interpersonal trauma, is part of being human, speculate on care-giving and health care practices that can foster preventive resilience, sort of a trauma-immunization, as well as practices that increase susceptibility.

Notes

1 Since 2016 the JCAHO has denied both the mandate and pain as a vital sign. This may be related to the opioid crisis, but is also evidence of the entrenchment of the health care system, and its difficulty systemically with managing public policy and politics. www.jointcommission.org/joint_commission_statement_on_pain_management/

2 We are aware of the gendered comment here, describing the existential nature of traumas endured at the hands of another human being. An astonishing 75% of violent crime is perpetrated by men (USDOJ, 2010, Table 38), and about 77% of the time, men are the victims of murder (Kellerman & Mercy, 1992). So, while admittedly not fully inclusive, this gendered language is apt for most of human violence.

3 As per our definition of trauma being a way of living, "living with trauma" is more accurate usage than "coping" with trauma. The latter externalizes the trauma from the person, as if it can be dissected. The former recognizes that trauma is something a person manages on an ongoing basis, which can be changed.

References

American Psychiatric Association (APA). (1980). *Diagnostic and statistical manual of mental health disorders* (3rd ed.). Washington, DC: APA Press.

Benedek, D. M., & Ursano, R. J. (2009). Posttraumatic stress disorder: From phenomenology to clinical practice. *FOCUS: The Journal of Lifelong Learning in Psychiatry, 7*, 160–175. doi:10.1176/foc.7.2.foc160

Council for International Organizations of Medical Sciences (CIOMS). (2016). *International ethical guidelines for health-related research involving humans* (4th ed.). Geneva, Switzerland: CIOMS.

De Zulueta, F. (1993). *From pain to violence.* Northvale, NJ: Jason Aronson.

Ferrante, E. (2012). *My brilliant friend* (A. Goldstein, Trans.). New York, NY: Europa Editions.

Figley, C. R. (1995). Compassion fatigue as secondary traumatic stress disorder: An overview. In C. R. Figley (Ed.), *Compassion fatigue: Coping with secondary traumatic stress disorder in those who treat the traumatized* (pp. 1–20). Philadelphia, PA: Brunner/Mazel.

Freudenberger, H. J. (1974). Staff burn-out. *Journal of Social Issues, 30*(1), 159–165. doi:10.1111/j.1540-4560.1974.tb00706.x

Friedman, M. J. (2014). PTSD history and overview. In *PTSD: National Center for PTSD. U.S. Department of Veterans Affairs.* Retrieved from www.ptsd.va.gov/professional/treat/essentials/history_ptsd.asp

Gil, E. (1998). *Play therapy for severe psychological trauma.* Videotape and manual. New York, NY: Guilford.

Hassan, S. (2018). *Combating cult mind control* (4th ed.). Newton, MA: Freedom of Mind Press.

Hassan, S., & Shah, M. J. (2019). The anatomy of undue influence used by terrorist cults and traffickers to induce helplessness and trauma, so creating false identities. *Ethics, Medicine and Public Health, 8*, 97–107. doi:10.1016/j.jemep.2019.03.002

Herman, J. L. (1992). *Trauma and recovery.* New York, NY: Basic Books.

James, B. (1989). *Treating traumatized children.* Lexington, MA: Heath.

Joint Commission on the Accreditation of Healthcare Organizations (JCAHO). (2001). Pain standards for 2001. Retrieved from www.jointcommission.org/assets/1/6/2001_Pain_Standards.pdf

Kellerman, A. L., & Mercy, J. A. (1992). Men, women, and murder: Gender-specific differences in rates of fatal violence and victimization. *Journal of Trauma, 33*(1), 1–5. doi:10.1097/00005373-199207000-00001

Kempe, C. H., Silverman, F. N., Steele, B. F., Droegemueller, W., & Silver, H. K. (1962). The battered child syndrome. *Journal of the American Medical Association, 181*, 17–24. Retrieved from doi:https://citeseerx.ist.psu.edu/viewdoc/download?doi=10.1.1.589.5168&rep=rep1&type=pdf

Lake, J. H. (2014). A review of select CAM modalities for the prevention and treatment of PTSD. *Psychiatric Times, 31*(7), 29. Retrieved from: www.psychiatrictimes.com/integrative-psychiatry/review-select-cam-modalities-prevention-and-treatment-ptsd

Linden, J. H. (2005). In the face of trauma: Building resilience in children. Regional Postgraduate Teaching Morning and Grand Rounds, University of Rochester Medical Center, Rochester, NY (April 19-20, 2005).

Linden, J. H. (2014). Hypnosis in childhood trauma. In L. I. Sugarman & W. C. Wester (Eds.), *Therapeutic hypnosis with children and adolescents* (2nd ed., pp. 143–166). Williston, VT: Crown House.

Linden, J. H. (2020). Relationship factors in the theater of the imagination: Hypnosis with children and adolescents. *American Journal of Clinical Hypnosis, 62*(1–2), 60–73. doi:10.1080/00029157.2019.1568961

Linley, P. A. (2003). Positive adaptation to trauma: Wisdom as both process and outcome. *Journal of Traumatic Stress, 16*(6), 601–610. https://doi.org/10.1023/B:JOTS.0000004086.64509.09

McCann, I. L., & Pearlman, L. A. (1990a). *Psychological trauma and the adult survivor: Theory, therapy, and transformation*. New York, NY: Brunner/Mazel.

McCann, I. L., & Pearlman, L. A. (1990b). Vicarious traumatization: A framework for understanding the psychological effects of working with victims. *Journal of Traumatic Stress, 3*, 131–149. doi:10.1002/jts.2490030110

Perry, B. (2009). Examining child maltreatment through a neurodevelopmental lens: Clinical applications of the neurosequential model of therapeutics. *Journal of Loss and Trauma, 14*, 240–255. doi:10.1080/15325020903004350

Phillips, M., & Frederick, C. (1995). *Healing the divided self: Clinical and Ericksonian hypnotherapy for dissociative and post-traumatic conditions*. New York, NY: W. W. Norton.

Porges, S. W. (2011). *The polyvagal theory: Neurophysiological foundations of emotions, attachment, communication, and self-regulation*. New York: W. W. Norton.

Pynoos, R. (Ed.). (1994). *Posttraumatic stress disorder: A clinical review*. Litherville, MD: Sidran.

Rossi, E. L. (2002). *The psychobiology of gene expression: Neuroscience and neurogenesis in hypnosis and the healing arts*. New York, NY: W. W. Norton.

Ryan, R. M., & Deci, E. L. (2017). *Self-determination theory: Basic psychological needs in motivation, development, and wellness*. New York, NY: Guilford.

Salasin, S. (2011). Sine qua non for public health. *National Council Magazine, 18*(2), 18. Retrieved from: www.thenationalcouncil.org/wp-content/uploads/2012/11/NC-Mag-Trauma-Web-Email.pdf

Sartre, J. P. (1948). *Existentialism is a humanism* (P. Mairet, Trans.). Paris, France: Methuen.

Schore, A. (1994). *Affect regulation and the origin of the self: The neurobiology of emotional development*. Hillsdale, NJ: Lawrence Erlbaum.

Schore, A. (2019). The neurobiology of attachment. In *National Institute for the Clinical Application of Behavior Medicine*, Treating Trauma Master Series. www.nicabm.com/program/treating-trauma-master/

Siegel, D. (2019) The neurobiology of trauma. In *National Institute for the Clinical Application of Behavior Medicine*, Treating Trauma Master Series. www.nicabm.com/program/treating-trauma-master/

Siegel, D., & Doidge, N. (2010). The mind that changes the brain. In *R. Cassidy Seminar*, Feb. 26–27, 2010, Philadelphia, PA.

Stringer, H. (2019). Improving mental health for inmates. *Monitor on Psychology*, *50*(3), 47–52. Retrieved from: www.apa.org/monitor/2019/03/mental-heath-inmates

Terr, L. (1994). *Unchained memories*. New York, NY: Basic Books.

United States Department of Justice (USDOJ). Office of Justice Programs. Bureau of Justice Statistics. (2010). National Crime Victimization Survey, 2007. Ann Arbor, MI: Inter-university Consortium for Political and Social Research [distributor]. Retrieved from https://bjs.gov/content/pub/pdf/cvus0702.pdf

Van der Kolk, B. A. (2005). Developmental trauma disorder: Towards a rational diagnosis for children with complex trauma histories. *Psychiatric Annals*, *35*(5), 401–408. Retrieved from: https://is.muni.cz/el/1423/jaro2013/PSY403/um/Developmental_Trauma_Disorder_Kolk.pdf

Van der Kolk, B. A. (2019). The neurobiology of trauma. In *National Institute for the Clinical Application of Behavior Medicine*, Treating Trauma Master Series. doi:10.13109/prkk.2009.58.8.572. Retrieved from www.nicabm.com/program/treating-trauma-master/

Wakefield, B. (2012). Free air! TEDxUSU, Nov. 29, 2012. Office of Research & Graduate Studies, Utah State University. Retrieved from www.youtube.com/watch?v=5n6413nx6b0 and https://genius.com/Buddy-wakefield-free-air-annotated

Watkins, J. G., & Watkins, H. H. (1997). *Ego states: Theory and therapy*. New York, NY: W.W. Norton.

Weine, S., Danieli, Y., Silove, D., van Ommeren, M., Fairbank, J. A., & Saul, J. (2002). Guidelines for international training in mental health and psychosocial interventions for trauma exposed populations in clinical and community settings. *Psychiatry: Interpersonal and Biological Processes*, *65*(2), 156–164. doi:10.1521/psyc.65.2.156.19936

Lulu's Story

Bad News

After school today, my America Mom sat me down in the kitchen and gave me a fresh-baked gingerbread man and a glass of milk. When I'd eaten, she said she had something very sad to tell me: My Africa Mama died years ago, in the refugee camp. I was so shocked, I was already sobbing by the time Mom's sentence was ended. Immediately I thought of the story Aliyah told about the mother, and the baby who might have been me. But my America Mom hugged me and held me tight, and she explained how hard it had been to decide when to tell me. There was no good time. And your father, she said, we held out hope for a long time, believing he would be found, but it seems likely he was forced into the army and killed long ago in the fighting. I did not cry louder when I heard this—I never even met my father, never even saw a photograph of him. But hearing this news, that both of my parents were gone, that I'd been orphaned for many years, without realizing it, gave me such a feeling of devastation. I had no home to go to except the one I was sitting in. I quieted down; I felt a sense of awe at the emptiness that was now in the center of my life. And I sat staring at the crumbs left from the pieces of gingerbread man.

And then I picked up the biggest crumb and popped it into my mouth.

Why Lulu Was Unhappy

For a long time, Lulu was not happy, but she didn't know why. She knew that her America Mom and Dad had contacted Aliyah in the hope that finding someone who came from the same place in Africa she was from would cheer her up.

But when it was time for Aliyah to go back to college, Lulu was still sad. Aliyah leaving was just one more thing Lulu had to be sad about.

But then, suddenly, Lulu was crying, and suddenly Lulu knew what she was crying about. Lulu and her America family were all gathered on the front porch waiting for the taxi to pick up Aliyah to go to the airport. But when Lulu began to cry, it was not ordinary crying. She was crying so hard she could not stop, even though her Mom was right there to comfort her.

She was crying so hard because years ago Lulu needed protection and there was no protection, and Lulu needed understanding and there was no understanding. And Lulu was very sad, but she was even more angry—angry because it suddenly came to her that if Dr. M had done this to her, then he surely had done it to other girls. He had acted as if her body was his to play with. He had acted as if it didn't matter that he was dishonest about why he was there and what he intended to do to her there. He had invaded her space without asking for permission and without even a vague gesture seeking consent. But Dr. M did not know that he was playing with fire. He did not know something Lulu had learned about fear.

At first, when Lulu tried to remember what happened in Dr. M's office, she remembered nothing. Nothing at all. Or when she tried to remember it was all confusion and anxiety. Everyone said you have to go see Dr. M if you have a gymnastics injury. Lulu didn't know why they say that—an ankle is an ankle. But Mom took Lulu in to see him anyway. And while Lulu's Mom was busy in the outer office filling out paper work, Dr. M asked Lulu to get on the examination table. He started talking in a soft, gentle voice, and then, after a while, he started massaging her calf muscles, which made her very uneasy. Lulu noticed that Dr. M did not seem to be attending to her ankle. What does massaging the calf have to with treating a broken ankle? He didn't even look at the ankle. But everyone said Dr. M has unusual and effective techniques, and the calf and the ankle aren't far apart, so—maybe? Maybe this actually makes sense? It would be so embarrassing to need to leap off the table and run away, broken ankle and all. But Lulu desperately wanted to do just that.

Dr. M kept talking, though Lulu couldn't say what he was talking about, and then he very gently asked Lulu to lean back until she was lying on her back. And then he was massaging one thigh and then the other. And Lulu was feeling that terror. She remembered running in the camp. It was dark. Running away from something with Mama and other women and girls between the tents. There were men in cars and uniforms. She remembers a scream as an older girl tripped and fell. The men grabbing her and laughing, hitting her. Holding her. Blood. Fear in the headlights.

And Lulu knew; she knew what was going on. She had fallen on her ankle but was not going to be held down. She was going to make Dr. M stop. As he helped her reach over and sit up she twisted away from him, and yelled, "Hentue!" Dr. M stopped, surprised, eyes wide. A deer in the headlights. Lulu marched out, refusing to limp, right through the waiting room and past her America mother and out the office door. She felt like she was … fire. She mouthed that word "Hentue" to herself, over and over, like it was a wonderful treasure she had found deep inside.

Her Mom followed, bewildered, as the receptionist said something about making an appointment to see Dr. M again the following week. Lulu had no intention of ever going back. Lulu began to summon the courage to explain to her Mom what had happened.

Part III

Attachments, Relationships, and Modeling

9 Trance and Attachment

Main Ideas

1. Primary attachment sets engrams for coping with developmental imperatives.
2. How we learn to respond intentionally, with unconditional acceptance, drives self-regulatory capacity in the other.
3. Resilient and congruent primary attachment is the both the immunization and the antidote to what traumatizes.

As discussed in parts I and II, independence, autonomy, and self-determination are core, evolutionarily mechanisms, around which we grow our minds. This may be uniquely true for humans. We spend most of our lives building and then maintaining our independence and autonomy. Ironically, we do not and cannot do this alone. To strive toward independence, we begin with dependence on others. For healthy development, we need those we depend upon to respond to us. This chapter focuses on that interaction: the trance of infant-caregiver, the primacy of bonding and attachment, and what that has to do with plasticity and hypnosis skills, especially the clinician's trance.

The Role of Relationship in Development

Relationships are a powerful driver of how we go plastic, grow, and change our minds. We tend to determine "developmental success" retrospectively, attributing it to some intersections of nature and nurture in the formative years. This especially holds for the first year of life and its impact on all the rest.

The human infant, if all goes well, arrives in the world with its unfiltered and unfocused senses intact, crying for help, and fully dependent on others for its survival. So much happens after that arrival, much of which is unexpected and unanticipated by bewildered parents and caregivers. The newborn's task is to cope with and manage the internal tensions created by emotions. As parents and caregivers, we are launched into a world of mystery and discovery as we watch this creature unfold and transform. It seems all too intricate to comprehend. Perhaps this is the reason we are intrigued by the stories of feral children (Arai, 2000; Perry & Szalavitz, 2017). We wonder, "What is the nature of being raised without nurturance?" One without the other seems frightening.

Primary Attachment

While developmental drives are forces in the flow of trance, development is also relational. Developmental success requires the structure of essential human interactions to foster attachment or bonding. It is important to unpack this idea of attachment, as it is the precursor to rapport or alliance and, so, the power of therapeutic relationships to effect change (Peebles-Kleiger, 2002). Attachment is about the response to our emotions, and whether those responses provide safety. The outcome of these interactions determines to some extent how we later develop our emotional self-regulation. Over time we internalize the responses (conditioning) we receive and thus our expectations of other's responses to us begins. Many events that will occur along the road from infant to adult cannot be predicted but are fervently imagined. As we will detail in the following chapter, the parental trance, like the clinician's trance, begins even before the child is born. Clinicians cultivate parental trance when we ask parents, "What are you most worried will happen? What fears do you have for your infant?" Despite this foreshadowing, the foreseeable future seems never to occur. All we know is that these first interactions and primary relationships are vital. In order for our children to survive and thrive, we need caregivers and parenting, but what kind?

Theories of psychological and physiological growth that emerged to address this question grew in parallel and within the sociological context of the industrial revolution and World War I. A little over a century ago children were seen primarily as small adults. At the beginning of the 20th century leading scientific efforts of notables such as James (1950), Janet (Reed, 1987), Freud (Wollheim, 1981), and Piaget (1997) were concerned with the question of what promotes healthy human development. Each considered the requirements for timely and resilient development. Psychoanalytic theory is noted for placing caregivers and those we care for under the microscope. It proposed steps in development. It introduced concepts of transference and object loss as ideas for explaining and changing the ill effects of the early child and parent interactions. The principle of *Relational Being* in our reconceptualization frames hypnosis as an interpersonal phenomenon (Baker, personal communication, July 29, 2019), which spans both the psychoanalytic and socio-cognitive models. Baker and Spiegel (2019) note the shift in the use of hypnosis from the first half of the 20th century to the second half. It moved from a focus on abreactions and regression to promote insight, to an emphasis on more relationally oriented approaches in which the interactive moments between caregiver and the person in our care were used to repair developmental disruptions and promote growth.

The psychoanalytic perspective of Baker (1981), Brown and Fromm (1986), and Diamond (1984, 1987) reflected the cultural swing from a self and internalized focus to a community and external focus which foreshadowed our principles of people functioning in nested systems and growing (healthy or otherwise) as a result of relating. These theoretical ideas established that parents and parenting were potent influences on the development of children. The process and nature of that influence remained in question.

René Spitz (1887–1974) delved into this question. Starting in the 1930's, he studied institutionalized infants, questioning what happens in the absence of parents' nurturing involvement. He carefully described the withdrawn, depressed infants in overcrowded orphanages, where care was limited to basics of food and toileting and without the playful and loving interactions from caregivers. Spitz (1945) referred to partial emotional deprivation as "anaclitic depression," meaning the emotional effect of losing a loved object. He termed the more extreme and devastating condition resulting from the absence of caregivers "hospitalism." The infants to whom this term was applied lived but did not gain weight or develop optimally. Missing essential relational ingredients impaired their ability to metabolize nutrients. Evidence mounted that relational ingredients provided by caregivers mattered as much, if not more than, providing nutritional ingredients.

However it is that we are engineered—hormonally, genetically, or socially—to find the small version of ourselves curious and cute, the baby version of mammals generally evokes a surge of nurturing (Lorenz, 1973). This may be what invites nurturing behavior from the caregiver. The attuned interplay of infant and caregiver is joyful to watch. Consider the following:

Six-year-old Lisa played kitten in the therapy room. She mewed for food, found the mother cat for warmth, rolled a ball for fun, knocked over her kitten siblings on unsteady paws, and waited to be cuddled, nestling into her soft blanket home. She played kitty, while instructing me (JHL) how to be mother cat. For Lisa, being a baby kitten was a mixture of mirroring what mom was doing with her new born baby sister, wishing this for herself, and maintaining her more developmentally evolved self that knew how to mother. Lisa's play illustrated how layered development is—Lisa can be baby, mother, herself, and another mammal—and how development can be seen as a series of relationships. Bronfenbrenner & Morris (2007) posited just this idea: that human development across the life span is the experience of "complex reciprocal interactions" (p. 797).

Attachment Theory

A succinct review of attachment theory will allow us to map its relationship to hypnosis principles and skills. Brown and Elliott (2016) provide a more comprehensive and detailed history of contributions to attachment theory that are beyond the scope of this book.

Attachment theory has its roots in developmental studies of infants' responses to parental absence and loss. John Bowlby (1969) was a leading theorist in this area and coined the terms "maternal deprivation" and "attachment behaviors." Influenced by Lorenz's (1973) imprinting experiments with ducklings and their mothers, he surmised similar instinctual patterns for human infants. He called these "fixed action patterns" and "care-seeking and protective behaviors," which served to keep the mother nearby (Bowlby, 1969, p. 66). Prior to this notion of physical attachment, feeding of infants was thought to be key in bonding.

Bowlby's ideas were supported by Harlow's (1958) monkey experiments studying the elements of infant/caregiver dependency. Harlow separated baby monkeys from their biological mothers at birth. He gave them a choice of an inanimate surrogate cloth mother or wire one, and found they preferred the cloth. His experiments revealed that soft contact was important. Even when the surrogate cloth mother was not fitted with a feeding nipple, the baby monkeys sought the surrogates for comfort. Bonding, he surmised, was more than just meeting the physiological need of hunger. When frightened, the monkeys that had the soft cloth surrogate exhibited what was considered normal comfort seeking with the surrogate. In contrast the monkeys raised with wire surrogates, threw themselves on the floor. Again, he surmised infant-child bonding was related to some emotional, affectional component. Based on his work with monkeys, Harlow (1958) distinguished care-seeking behavior—as a component of attachment—from dependency. The latter was quickly outgrown and neither directed toward a specific person nor associated with strong emotion. Care-seeking attachment behavior, in contrast, was a reciprocal emotional interaction that was unique to the dyad.

These findings further supported our understanding that relating, as a function of the mind, is embodied. Infants need physical and sensory interaction to feel protected. Caregivers' responses to infant's proximity-seeking yields an attachment bond. The young need **attunement**—validating, affirming, and accepting emotional responses—from the caregiver. Scientific experiments and study were being applied to tease out the details of what literature, art, and music had endlessly portrayed as a sacred loving space between mother and child.

Historically, our minds summoned images of mothers when we thought of the infant's primary caregiver. For this reason, mothers and maternal behavior were ripe for critical review in scientific study. Mothers were seen as the cause for failures in their child's development, a point of view unintentionally reinforced by developing psychoanalytic theory. At one time, infants' deformations were blamed on the mother's character (Solomon, 2012, p. 119). Autism was attributed to the behavior of "refrigerator mothers," a term adopted after Kanner's (1943) description of the criteria for autism, which described cold, uncaring mothers. These theories were later discredited. But they are damaging nonetheless, since these biases reinforced the notion that all parents have to blame themselves for any hardship that befalls their child. As research on attachment advanced, the role of maternal behavior became more specified. Winnicott (1971) proposed the "good enough mother," later popularized by Bettelheim's (1987) "good enough parent." The template for attachment continued to be reconfigured, well beyond wire surrogates.

Bowlby (1969) was also interested in the exploratory behavior of infants which he theorized was opposite to attachment. Ainsworth (1971) furthered Bowlby's attachment studies. Her seminal work investigated one-year-olds and their interactions with their mothers (and later, their fathers). She employed precise variables observing toddlers as they began to move about their environment away from their mother. Her interest, like Harlow's, was in the quality of the attachment. Her research was designed to learn more about the importance of a secure base in infant attachment. She created a laboratory paradigm that she labelled "The Strange Situation." It had eight distinct steps: (1) An infant and its mother are introduced into an unfamiliar room strewn with toys. (2) They are observed together for three minutes. (3) A stranger is introduced into the room in the next three minutes, is silent, then speaks with mother, then with the infant. (4) Mother leaves, and the infant and stranger are together for three minutes. (5) Mother returns to comforts the child and the stranger leaves. (6) The mother leaves, again, and the child is alone for three minutes. (7) The stranger returns and focuses on the infant for three minutes. (8) Finally, the mother returns and comforts the infant while the stranger leaves. Ainsworth coded specific behavioral observations including body posture, smiling, locomotion, crying, vocalization as well as four dimensions of interaction: proximity, initiating contact, avoidance, and resistance. She found that in response to the "Strange Situation" the varied relating patterns of these one-year-old infants were likely formed even earlier in their development and revealed that a prototype for future relating is laid down very early in development.

The children's patterns of attachment were categorized as "secure" or "insecure." The insecure were further subdivided into "anxious" or "avoidant." Main and Solomon (1986) later added another grouping, the "insecure-disorganized/disoriented attached." Over time, this latter group showed more dissociative behaviors throughout their childhoods. Dissociative behaviors in mothers were also predictive of more disorganized attached behaviors in their infants. As studies in trauma increased in the 1970's, spurred by increased awareness of child abuse and the return of US draftees from the war in Vietnam, attachment theory emerged as playing a key role in understanding traumatic reactions. The prototype that was laid down early in caregiver-infant attachment, predicted the coping resources available to us later, under stress. Temperament, socio-economic factors, and cultural influences affected one's psychological make up, too, but the stability of attachment patterns over time and their link to the concept of alliance in psychological treatment made attachment worthy of more study.

The coping styles that were later incorporated into the criteria of post-traumatic stress disorder were built on the anxious or avoidant styles, posited to have been laid down in the infants' early development. Early secure attachment was linked to positive outcomes in complex trauma (Brown & Elliott, 2016). Both self-development and affect regulation appear to grow out of the quality of attachment. Infant studies confirm that the most robust self-regulation skills are acquired within the context of attuned attachment (Schore, 1997). In short: interpersonal relationships are "trance-formational." They shape the "how" of our plasticity: coping, adaptation, and how we do or do not change our minds. So how do we use what we know to help others change their minds?

Since the Ainsworth studies on mother child attachment entered the literature, the discourse has broadened in linking biology to relational development. Amy Banks, an advocate for the new psychology of women (Miller, 1976) and its focus on mutuality, sees our maturation as increasing relational complexity (Banks & Hirschman, 2015). She notes that through a relational lens, one sees the child that leaves the mother to explore the world not as separating but rather widening the connection circle of those with whom it can relate and trust for support. Margaret Mahler's (Mahler, Pine, & Bergman, 2008) concept of separation—individuation while useful to explain aspects of becoming independent, may have inadvertently lost the balanced view of the importance of connection in the process of growing. Similarly, Maier and Seligman's (2016) research on learned helplessness, when revisited, yielded the yin and yang of resilience, grit, and flow.

The relational-cultural theory developed in the 1970s by Jordan and others at the, then, Stone Center (1991), predated the neuroscience of relational communication which Porges polyvagal theory and Schore's (2013) biology of communication of our right brain to another's right brain incorporates. Tronick (2007), who studied mother-infant behavior, describes the developmental concept of implicit relational knowing which refers to the idea that we perceive others mental states unconsciously. Each of these new additions to our understanding of the biology of relating strengthen our argument for the cracking paradigm in health and care and advocacy for hypnosis principles and skills at the heart of changing minds.

Protohypnosis and Imaginative Involvement

We all know nurturing behaviors. We associate cradling and rocking the newborn in one's arms, studying with wonder the infant's eyes and body, humming melodies, kissing the soft skin, and murmuring loving words with nurturing behaviors. The new parent learns how these behaviors bring responses from the infant whose orienting response is seeking safety and satiety. Schore's (1994) research on affect regulation reveals the neuroendocrine and neurohormonal effects that visual communications of both pleasure and interest have on the developing brain of the infant.

Our responses to the infant and to one another systemically affect the entire embodied mind. Swaying, caressing, even *mesmerizing* the infant into calm, and quiet attention, perhaps even drifting into sleep, are behaviors that developmental psychologist and psychiatrist Josephine Hilgard (1970) considered *protohypnosis* an embryonic and safe prototype for trance and influence.

Josephine Hilgard's (1970) study of hypnotic responsivity in adults revealed that their early relationships with their parents were related to a concept of imaginative involvement. Young children (ages two to seven) did not behave as adults did during scripted hypnosis procedure. As compared to older children, adolescents and adults who usually close their eyes when they engage in imaginative and internally-directed reverie, younger children used their imaginations with their eyes open. Hilgard inferred but did not elucidate the developmental differences, while Vandenberg (2002) analyzed the role of development to clarify the variations in hypnotic responses across ages.

Hilgard found, in her search to understand the role of biology in hypnotic responsiveness, that past experiences that allowed the free play of imagination, absorption in an experience, and a separation from reality yielded adults who were more hypnotizable with the Stanford Scales (Weitzenhoffer & Hilgard, 1959, 1962, 1963, 1967). Her exploration of imaginative involvement and transference, the rapport between therapist and subject, highlighted the significance of relational factors. The seemingly innate behaviors of mothers, the suspected hardwiring of empathizing, soothing, and comforting in order to quiet a distressed infant, offered insights into the infant-mother interaction that looked like spontaneous trance. Hilgard's detailed depiction of hypnotic phenomena led to our seeing these phenomena outside of the context of procedural, legacy model hypnosis. This is an example of the ability of nature and nurture to propel and reinforce one another. The mother can learn what works with her infant's nascent biology: emotions, temperament, genetics (expressed or suppressed), intelligence, and more. In turn, the mother's responsive nurturing complements those innate characteristics, and so the interpersonal biology of attachment deepens.

When babies and their caregivers gaze at each other, their patterns of neural activity synchronize in what is hypothesized as preparation for their increased communication (Leong, V., Byrne, E., Clackson, K., Georgieva, S., Lam, S. & Wass, S. 2017). The interaction of caregiver and care receiver, learning to attune to one another while becoming increasingly attentive and absorbed, mutually synchronizing their breathing, heart rates, levels of muscle tension and movements has been posited as the early infant-parent template of joining in systemic, psychobiological plasticity (Banyai, Meszaros, & Csokay, 1982; Varga & Kekecs, 2014). Psychology is returning to its natural focus on the study of human experience. Still it is hard to think of mother's love in purely biological measurements.

Amidst the synchronized neural activity, the infant is learning even more. She experiences how her smiles can elicit a change on mother's face (Tronick, 2009); how her cries bring food to her mouth; how her wails bring her to rest on the warm, familiar body that hums her to sleep. This productive rapture between the child and caregiver is essential to basic development. Otherwise there is "failure to thrive," and Spitz's (1945) century old anaclitic depression and hospitalism.

We have come to know that attachment, the bonding between infant and caregiver, is foundational and therefore certainly *protohypnotic*. As humans grow, the quality of that early attachment shapes us and our later interactions, including especially the therapeutic ones.

From Templates to Change

As we continue to unravel the secrets of bonding between infant and caregiver, we have learned that empathy, that ability to understand and be sensitive to the emotions of others, is not in uniform quantities among parents. Mother feels a cold draft, so she puts the socks on the baby, only to watch as the baby removes them. Father loves baseball. His first present of a baseball glove for his son is discarded in favor of the baby doll. What each parent does next uncovers their capacity to attune to their child's needs. Will she scold or delight in the baby's exploration? Will he express disapproval or celebrate his son's caring for the toy doll?

The parent who accepts the child unconditionally, is kind and loving, attunes to their discoveries in a way that encourages responses, encourages the child's psychobiological agility. We might say that the parents' response-ability encourages the child's trance-ability. To be unconditional is to suspend judgment. To see the child's uniqueness and nurture him or her is the art of parenting, and practicing health care. It is difficult to begin from a place of "radical unknowingness," abandoning assumptions and expectations, as Haas (2018) puts it "As long as I don't assume *anything* about a person in my care, I may learn something that will help." (p. 97). Note the similarities with what we have termed the "clinician's trance."

We humans are critical, tend to harbor biases (e.g., mother-blaming), to form beliefs, and to be tribal, all of which affects our interactions, especially with our children. Implicit bias, which is nonconscious and emotional in nature, challenges all caregiving relationships and is difficult to overcome (Chisolm-Straker & Straker, 2017). Learning to see individuals rather than stereotypes or diagnoses, seeing people in terms of strengths rather than their weaknesses, and caring collaboratively are all strategies that enable caregivers to move beyond implicit biases to provide unconditional caring.

Modeling and Family Systems

If one quality of primary attachment is that it is predictive, as all of the evidence shows, how do we educate parents to synchronize, to be unconditionally loving? As facilitators and modelers, we develop rapport, attune, empathize, connect, be with, and form new attachments, which alter old patterns of interacting. To paraphrase Albert Schweitzer: Modeling isn't a form of education. Modeling is the only form of education. Modeling the behaviors, with parents and infants is the starting place. This requires consideration of the family system.

Families are systems in which the complexity and dynamics of attachment can be viewed and addressed. Each family member is portraying an attachment pattern, and the clinician can be challenged discerning the composite interactions. I (JHL) grew disturbed while observing two young parents with their 18-month-old toddler. The parents, engaged in bickering and hostile interactions, ignored the child who wandered the treatment room holding her stuffed animal. The child drew closer to me with each loud exchange from the parents. I gestured her closer, bent toward her, talked with her soothingly about the toy she held, regarded her face, smiled, and then said aloud, "It is hard to listen to grownups when they fight." Her small arms reached up to me. "Would you like to sit here with me?," I asked. She nodded, and I lifted her to sit next to me. The parents remained oblivious to my interaction with their daughter. We sat together as their fighting continued, neither hearing the other. I engaged her with questions about her toy, each question designed to convey possible comfort: Did her stuffed animal have a name? Was it her friend? Did she sleep with it at night? She nestled closer. I struggled with what to do to get the parents' attention. To the parents I commented, "Have you noticed your daughter's response to your arguing?" They looked at her and said, "Oh, she likes you." I was not sure where to begin with my response. "Maybe," I ventured, "Isn't it curious she came to me while you two were busy fighting? I wonder if she needed to feel safe with all the noise. I wonder how you two feel when you are fighting." My uncertain groping to shift their attention seemed to work for the moment. The room grew silent and the mother commented that she hated the fighting. In my mind, I thought, "Round one, how many more to go? Fighting is their coping style." Attention refocused, danger lessened, I was calculating where I might be able to effect change for this family. How could I model attuning to the toddler's upset, while attuning to the parents? Where do we place the lever to best create systemic change?

This discordant family, while engrossed in their fighting, were inattentive to their child's needs. The child sought me out apparently searching for safety and avoiding danger. Fear is compelling. It tells us our survival is threatened. This active comfort-seeking on the part of the toddler was protective, but her avoidance of the parents revealed the insecurity of the attachment. The parents' inability to attune to their daughter's discomfort exposed something about the quality of their own early attachments.

In some families, attachment is disorganized, and relationships are tenuous. The bonds that develop are dysfunctional and disturbed, even traumatic. A trauma-bond relationship may appear to be a form of attachment but it has different goals. The child's main objective becomes tending to the adult's emotional needs and limiting intense feelings. It is hypothesized that trauma-bonds originate in terror, often instantaneously, through domination and fear, mastery of others rather than self, obedience to the will of others, while still experiencing the other as essential for survival (James, 1994). The parent to whom the child turns for safety can be the object of danger, leaving the child with what Main and Solomon (1986) considers fear without solution. In an adult, a traumatic experience may also create a traumatic bond, such as described in the term "Stockholm syndrome" or "capture-bonding," in which a terrified person develops what looks like empathy for his captor. A similar traumatic bond may also develop in cults (Hassan, 2018). Trauma bonds are a response to unbearable fright and the need to survive but lack the relational building blocks of attunement and responsivity needed for resilience. In contrast, secure attachment is characterized by love, reciprocity, and caring.

What about the effects of disrupted attachment, such as we see in Robinson, Lulu, Lyle, and Stevie? What repairs and heals these ruptures? What sparks the systemic plasticity to promote restoration of progressive development? Whatever creates resilience also heals the traumas encountered in dynamic human relationships. Investing in healthy relationships, which are unconditionally loving, trusting, authentic, enduring, and strongly embodied, produces children with self-love, self-esteem, empathy, self-efficacy, and autonomy, ingredients for resilience. The key ingredients of predictability, constancy, calming regulation, and hope of the therapeutic relationship provide missing and needed experiences of healthy attachment. The rapport, relating, attuning, and responding to the body's narrative create the rhythms and climate of attachment to repair and restore emotional regulation (Peebles-Kleiger, 2002, p. 157).

Successful therapeutic relationships contain these elements, composed artfully from the music (prosody), dance (posture and gestures), lyrics (verbal content) of communication. Attachment research has turned attention onto the quality of relationships. Strong, social, emotionally satisfying relationships increase survival rates, according to accumulating evidence (Holt-Lunstad, Smith, & Layton, 2010). Biological survival and interpersonal skills are combined in the practice of clinical care. This generates plasticity. What we experience with our caregivers in early life sets us on a path, and this path is mutable. Hypnosis communication skills are the vehicle for this changing of minds.

Beyond the clinician's trance, what are the items in the hypnotic skill set that foster relating for change? Sensitivity and responsivity are fundamental to the nature of our interactions (Richter, 2004). What are the social-emotional skills and how are these empathic competencies learned or taught?

Accruing research supports the view that mindfulness techniques, observing ourselves without reacting or judging, increases emotional and somatic awareness (Yapko, 2011). With awareness of emotions and their influence in the body, one can then learn stress tolerance. With practice, this can produce emotional regulation. But the practice of mindfulness alone is not relational. It is not designed to repair attachment. It serves as an opportunity to reset reactivity, but does not go further. It does not seek to change perceptions or narratives. Hypnosis skills go further than mindfulness in the pursuit of autonomy and resiliency. When we add the clinician's trance we become models of healthy attachment and strong social relationships.

In sum, secure attachment, attuned relationships, and clinical hypnotic communication are foundational concepts for developing resilience. Resilience is to the socio-emotional individual what immunity is to the cell. Resilience seems less abundant in those we see in our clinical care. That should come as no surprise since secure attachment provides protection from illness. Our new mission as caregivers is to be aware of how prevalent insecurity is. For this we also need to think systemically, to consider the social support, relationships, and communities our clients belong to. The context of people's lives, societal stressors, and loneliness affect the strength or weakness of attachments. We can focus on the individual's uniqueness and strength, helping them to use these resources to find meaning, belonging and safety in their world. If we provide the elements of healthy, secure attachment, we can become the cloth surrogates that provide what is needed for changing minds. Resilient and congruent primary attachment is both the immunization and antidote to what stresses or traumatizes. When the foundation is insecure, caregivers with clinical hypnosis skills recreate an environment for security, thus inoculating against stress, building immunity, and changing minds.

The Complex Ecology of Interpersonal Relationships

As caregivers, we often collaborate with one another in the care of our patients. These relationships can be invaluable, intense, rewarding, and sometimes frustrating but often entrancing. The emotions that are evoked in our caring mean we are likely to experience the same plasticity with our colleagues as with our clients. We can apply the same set of hypnotic principles and skills: a developmental lens, accessing strengths and deficits, building rapport, listening to the narrative, entering their emotional world, and trusting the process of creativity, per Rossi's four-stage model of the Novelty-Numinosum-Neurogenesis affect.

> I (JHL) received a series of distressing voicemails from a primary care physician (PCP) about a client whose care we shared and who was often

> late for appointments. My phone message in response to the PCP started with, Thank you for reaching out and letting me know how distressed you were [*Acceptance and valuing her emotions*]. You sounded both worried for and angry with our mutual client [*Resonance*]. I have experienced these feelings too, and they sometimes leave me wondering how effective I can be [*Our mutual identities are impacted*]. I am glad to learn she made it to see you. I think her showing up, however late, is a statement of her investment in getting well [*Shifting perspective, reframing*]. I smiled when you said in your message that treating infections is easier than treating people with mental health issues. Perhaps we can think of her as a "superbug." That will move both of us toward a cure [*Alliance for change, joining*]. Look forward to our continued collaboration.

This example is a microcosm of the complex ecology of interpersonal relationships in health and care. We all are products of our early attachment experiences, which influence the nature of our relating. In this chapter we have illustrated *how* healthy relationships build on characteristics in the process we refer to as trance: how they help us "go plastic." Relationships are a powerful driver of plasticity. As we will discuss in our closing chapter, the integrity of our interpersonal professional relationships reflects the health care paradigm. How clinicians care for each other within the health care system resonates with how we care for patients and clients.

Questions and Assignments for Further Discussion

1. This chapter explores bonding, attachment, and how those processes utilize our genetic predisposition to connect. What advantages does this predisposition afford humans?
2. Speculate on, compare, and contrast the characteristics of maternal attachment that Robinson, Lulu, Lyle, and Stevie had with their mothers.
3. From the content of this chapter, summarize and speculate on what it is about the unconditionally positive fascination of a care-provider that stimulates psychobiological plasticity.

References

Ainsworth, M. D. S., Bell, S. M., & Stayton, D. J. (1971). Individual differences in strange- situation behavior of one-year-olds. In H. R. Schaffer (Ed.), *The origins of human social relations* (pp. 17–58). New York, NY: Academic Press.

Arai, A. G. (2000). The "wild child" of 1990s Japan. *South Atlantic Quarterly, 99*(4), 841–864. doi:10.1215/00382876-99-4-841

Baker, E. L. (1981). An hypnotherapeutic approach to enhance object relatedness in psychotic patients. *International Journal of Clinical & Experimental Hypnosis, 29*(2), 136–147. doi:10.1080/00207148108409154

Baker, E. L., & Spiegel, E. (2019). Dancing in the in-between: Hypnosis, transitional space, and therapeutic action. *American Journal of Clinical Hypnosis, 62*(1-2), 31–59. doi:10.1080/00029157.2019.1585328

Banks, A., & Hirschman, L. A. (2015). *Wired to connect: The surprising link between brain science and strong, healthy relationships*. New York, NY: Jeremy Tarcher/Penguin.

Banyai, E., Meszaros, I., & Csokay, L. (1982). Interaction between hypnotist and subject: A psychophysiologic approach. *International Journal of Clinical and Experimental Hypnosis, 30*, 193–205. doi:10.1007/978-1-4684-4913-6_7

Bettelheim, B. (1987). *A good enough parent: A book on child-rearing*. New York, NY: Alfred A. Knopf.

Bowlby, J. (1969). *Attachment and loss, Vol. 1*. New York, NY: Basic Books.

Bronfenbrenner, U., & Morris, P. (2007). The bioecological model of human development. In *Handbook of child psychology* (pp. 793–828). doi:10.1002/9780470147658.chpsy0114

Brown, D. P., & Elliott, D. S. (2016). *Attachment disturbances in adults*. NY: W.W. Norton.

Brown, D. P., & Fromm, E. (1986). *Hypnotherapy & hypnoanalysis*. Hillsdale, NJ: Lawrence Erlbaum Associates.

Chisolm-Straker, M., & Straker, H. O. (2017). Implicit bias in US medicine: Complex findings and incomplete conclusions. *International Journal of Human Rights in Healthcare, 10*(43–55). doi:10.1108/IJHRH-11-2015-0038

Diamond, M. J. (1984). It takes two to tango: Some thoughts on the neglected importance of the hypnotist in an interactive hypnotherapeutic relationship. *American Journal of Clinical Hypnosis, 27*(1), 3–13. doi:10.1080/00029157.1984.10402582

Diamond, M. J. (1987). The interactional basis of hypnotic experience: On the relational dimensions of hypnosis. *International Journal of Clinical and Experimental Hypnosis, 35*(2), 95–115. doi:10.1080/00207148708416046

Haas, L. (2018). Memoirs of disease and disbelief. *New Yorker*, June 4 & 11, 2018, pp. 93–97. Retrieved from www.newyorker.com/magazine/2018/06/04/memoirs-of-disease-and-disbelief

Harlow, H. (1958). The nature of love. *American Psychologist, 13*, 673–685. doi:10.1037/h0047884. Retrieved from http://psychclassics.yorku.ca/Harlow/love.htm?session=A19sRVsBY90pGgZLqKsmx52pUJ

Hassan, S. (2018). *Combatting cult mind-control*. Newton, MA: Freedom of Mind Press.

Hilgard, J. (1970). *Personality and hypnosis: A study of imaginative involvement*. Chicago, IL: University of Chicago Press.

Holt-Lunstad, J., Smith, T. B., & Layton, J. B. (2010). Social relationships and mortality risk: A meta-analytic review. *PLoS Medicine, 7*(7), e1000316. doi:10.1371/journal.pmed.1000316

James, B. (1994). *Handbook for the treatment of attachment-trauma problems in children*. New York, NY: Free Press.

James, W. (1950). *The principles of psychology*. New York, NY: Dover. (Original work published 1890).

Jordan, J., Kaplan, A., Miller, J. B., Stiver, I., & Surrey, J. (1991). *Women's growth in connection: Writings from the Stone Center*. New York, NY: Guilford.

Kanner, L. (1943). Autistic disturbances of affective contact [pdf]. *Nervous Child, 2*, 217–250. Retrieved from http://mail.neurodiversity.com/library_kanner_1943.pdf

Leong, V., Byrne, E., Clackson, K., Georgieva, S., Lam, S., & Wass, S. (2017). Speaker gaze increases information coupling between infant and adult brains. *Proceedings of the National Academy of Sciences, 114*. doi:10.1073/pnas.1702493114

Lorenz, K., & Leyhausen, P. (1973). *Motivation of human and animal behavior: An ethological view*. New York, NY: D. Van Nostrand.

Mahler, M. S., Pine, F., & Bergman, A. (2008). *The psychological birth of the human infant: Symbiosis and individuation*. New York, NY: Basic Books.

Maier, S. F., & Seligman, M. E. P. (2016). Learned helplessness at fifty: Insights from neuroscience. *Psychological Review, 123*(4), 349–367. doi:10.1037/rev0000033

Main, M., & Solomon, J. (1986). Discovery of a new, insecure-disorganized/disoriented attachment pattern. In M. Yogman & T. B. Brazelton (Eds.), *Affective development in infancy* (pp. 95–124). Norwood, NJ: Ablex.

Miller, J. B. (1976). *Toward a new psychology of women*. Boston, MA: Beacon Press.

Peebles-Kleiger, M. J. (2002). *Beginnings: The art and science of planning psychotherapy*. Hillsdale, NJ: Analytic Press.

Perry, B., & Szalavitz, M. (2017). *The boy who was raised as a dog*. New York, NY: Basic Books.

Piaget, J. (1997). *The child's conception of the world*. (J. & A. Tomlinson, Trans.). New York, NY: Routledge (Original work published 1925).

Reed, G. F. (1987). Janet, Pierre. In R. Gregory (Ed.), *Oxford Companion to the Mind* (pp. 397–398). Oxford, UK: Oxford University Press.

Richter, L. (2004). *The importance of caregiver-child interactions for the survival of healthy development of young children*. Geneva, Switzerland: World Health Organization. Retrieved from https://apps.who.int/iris/bitstream/handle/10665/42878/924159134X.pdf;jsessionid=BD7D3DC1CDF327B87C7F40FE0AD157D5?sequence=1

Schore, A. N. (1994). *Affect regulation and the origin of the self: Neurobiology of emotional development*. Hillsdale, NJ: Lawrence Erlbaum.

Schore, A. N. (1997). Early organization of the nonlinear right brain and the development of a predisposition to psychiatric disorders. *Development and Psychopathology, 9*, 595–631. doi:10.1017/S0954579497001363

Schore, A. N. (2013). *The science of the art of psychotherapy*. New York, NY: W.W. Norton.

Solomon, A. (2012). *Far from the tree*. New York, NY: Scribner.

Spitz, R. A. (1945). Hospitalism: An inquiry into the genesis of psychiatric conditions in early childhood. *Psychoanalytic Study of the Child, 1*, 53–74. doi:10.1080/00797308.1945.11823126

Tronick, E. Z. (2007). *The neurobehavioral and social emotional development of infants and children*. New York, NY: W.W. Norton.

Tronick, E. Z. (2009). Still face experiments. Retrieved from www.youtube.com/watch?v=apzXGEbZht0

Vandenberg, B. (2002). Hypnotic responsivity from a developmental perspective. *International Journal of Clinical and Experimental Hypnosis., 50*(3), 229–247. doi:10.1080/00207140208410101

Varga, K., & Kekecs, Z. (2014). Oxytocin and cortisol in the hypnotic interaction. *International Journal of Clinical and Experimental Hypnosis, 62*(1), 111–128. doi:10.1080/00207144.2013.841494

Weitzenhoffer, A. M., & Hilgard, E. R. (1959). Stanford hypnotic susceptibility scale: Forms A and B. Palo Alto, CA: Consulting Psychologists Press.
Weitzenhoffer, A. M., & Hilgard, E. R. (1962). Stanford hypnotic susceptibility scale: Forms C. Palo Alto, CA: Consulting Psychologists Press.
Weitzenhoffer, A. M., & Hilgard, E. R. (1963). Stanford profile scales of hypnotic susceptibility scale: Forms I and II. Palo Alto, CA: Consulting Psychologists Press.
Weitzenhoffer, A. M., & Hilgard, E. R. (1967). Revised Stanford profile scales of hypnotic susceptibility scale: Forms I and II. Palo Alto, CA: Consulting Psychologists Press.
Winnicott, D. W. (1971). *Playing and reality*. New York, NY: Basic Books.
Wollheim, R. (1981). *Sigmund Freud*. New York, NY: Cambridge University Press.
Yapko, M. (2011). *Mindfulness and hypnosis*. NY: W.W. Norton.

Stevie's Story

Stevie's Identity

OK. Back home now, writing from within the heavy security of a chosen Stevie identity. And you say "What?," and you say "Stevie, talk Inglish. What is it? The Lady or the Tyger?" But the Stevie brain of today is racing way past logic. Like doing 80 in a 25 mph zone.

And then there is this: how it feels to take a pill and suddenly get steady. The addicts at Hayden High are high. All. Right. They don't make sense, but at least they make English. At least they know when the White Rabbit has gone down the rabbit hole. And can spot a chipmunk on a hollow log. Am I right?

And wow—Is this Bambiland? Rabbits and chipmunks? Is Bambi coming up next?

OK. This is definitely something about a shaman and the sacred space of the forest. That's where Stevie will go to find healing; but listen – is that the front door opening? Is that the shaman from the magical forest? Did Stevie take shrooms this morning? Did Stevie call for some more magic?

Mmm. Can't actually remember … Or—wait—is that Dad calling up the stairs?

But why would Dad be calling to Stevie's room when Stevie is supposed to be at school?

Oh no! It's for a reason! It's because Dad was going to take Stevie to that therapist today. That's why Stevie was thinking about going down the rabbit hole this morning. Stevie can't turn off that craziness that keeps pouring out of that Stevie brain like water out of a garden hose.

But let's stay calm. Just dallying with you, dear reader, and mean you no harm. Just starting a new paragraph, adding some new text; it seemed the paragraph needed a bit of space, a bit more calm and quiet to begin the new day.

And furthermore. This sequence of text began by proposing the topic of "Identity." Hence. Some additional thoughts on that subject:

Stevie is pointing to an identity owed to a very own-ness. No one can root Stevie-ness out of the now. Even if, even when, Stevie slips under for good and all. Even when the only citizens at last stop groping for the right pronoun to mention or omit, Stevie will always be the one who was here, the haggard ghostly prognosticator, the poet, Edgar the Poe, who I think once also resided upon Raven Lane. Stevie will be the one who declined, who resigned, from the Stevie family and all that came with it, through the power of an unchanging wish and a flickering vaporous identity, and who remained Stevie purely out of a choice. And in the cosmic story, the comic larder where the stars are kept, the home of Stevie that started here and stopped in this selfsame place, that stew that triggers wild guffaws when-even or wherever God stumbles upon the evidence of—um—ah—forgot what I was about to write.

So—did I take something psychedelic this morning? No. No, I'm positive. Almost positive. That was yesterday. Yesterday was Sunday, so the therapy session is today. Positive. Why would we go to therapy on a Sunday?

All curiosity needs to consider is Micky and his cache of cash, the cash money paid to Micky so other high school citizens can buy illicit pills. And where is the ultimate source of that cash? Look no further than thy father's house, and no deeper than certain anonymously retained bills, filched from thy mother's purse. To be plain, cash has been stolen from those who are closest by those who are most in need because no pretext existed for taking cash by some other means. Some may maintain that the cashless young should not resort to theft to remedy their circumstances. Of course, everyone agrees; Stevie, for example, should take that deadly dull library job Ms. Abood recommended Stevie for, except that then parents would stop providing walking-around money, assuming it was needless. So it's better just to get stuff by stealing from parents.

And don't the parents really want their offspring safe and steady? So, if they ever could possibly know that the vaporous soup forming into a Stevie becomes so very gelled with the magic of shaman's pills and shrooms, wouldn't they open their caches? Don't they want that for me? Could they ever be people who want who Stevie wants to be? Throw that thought away.

And by shoplifting, as well, of course. Although the shoplifting is more of an adventure than a reliable source of income. It's a thrill to think of Stevie's 100% record of lifting free merchandise from Wagner's, never yet apprehended.

OK, but Stevie can't possibly go to this therapy session; can't possibly invite this Doctor Hip into the Stevie brain. It's true, Stevie did talk to Dad about it, but did not agree to do it. But now it's the day. And—Stevie can't do it. No. Out of the question. Too high. Unless …

I'll call back down the stairs. Obviously—if I'm supposed to go to the shrink's office then I don't need to stress about being at home on a school day.

Mmm. That was a good moment of clarity, was it not?

But my brain is in such a stew. I don't want moments of clarity; I need a whole lifetime of clarity.

"Stevie! Time to go! Now! Are you ready?"

"OK, Dad! I'm coming!"

OK. I can be cool. How much did I consume? Whoa. Don't know. More than I should have, apparently. Dizzy. Majorly.

But it's going to be the same as the last time: I will just sit there not saying anything because what is there to say? Am I going to suddenly start chatting about whether I'm a boy or a girl? And how am I supposed to know the answer? Once upon a time—well, it used to be so righteous and simple. Who gets to decide? Obviously, I get to decide. It's my body, and my brain.

And in the meantime, everybody's been talking about that kid who OD'd in a stall in the boy's room at Glen High School. They had the naloxone on hand but the kid had already turned blue and they didn't give him the shot in time. I wonder if Hayden High is equipped to deal with an emergency like that. Everybody always assumes that it can't happen here.

"*Now*, Stevie. Come on! We're going to be late!"

That is—what will it be? The Lady, or the Tyger?

10 The Trance of Parenting

Parsing the Paradox

Main Ideas

1. Parental developmental tasks relate to, and seem to conflict with, those of their children.
2. A primary parental paradox is that expressions of the need to protect can serve to undermine autonomy and resilience in their children.
3. Children seem to behave in just the ways that provoke their parents to change in beneficial ways. "When parents do what their children *need*, it often serves the parents' personal development."

In preceding chapters, we weighed the importance of attachment and attunement in the developing mind, and considered how both affect and can be affected by hypnosis. We noted how the qualities of primary relationships—mother, father, siblings—resonate through the growing infant and child, along their life-course and then into therapeutic relationships. In this chapter, we shift that focus from the mind and trances of the developing person to the minds and trances of their developing parents. We will explore the wiring and activity of what we will call the trance of parenting. Then we will explain the hazards of that trance, what we label the "Parental Paradox." Finally, with a series of examples, we will demonstrate how the skills of hypnosis can be used to disrupt and redirect the parental trance to be more beneficial and satisfying for parents and their children.

Parenting is, obviously, a special relationship. Exceptional not just for its formative impact on the changing child but also because it is inherently conflicted. With one hand, parents strive to protect their child from peril. With the other, they encourage productive exploration of the unknown. The balance is precarious. How far do we let them fall before they grow their wings? At what point do our rescues imbue failure? Real dangers lurk on both sides. The stakes rise with the child's increasing abilities. Despite their parents' efforts, children's minds are shaped by the scars of injuries and swelling of successes. Parental resources for negotiating this balance derive from their own childhood lessons, in *their* parents' care. Scaling down to epigenetics, parenting patterns, like transgenerational waves, wash over children, who in turn become moms and dads, or choose not to, and on it goes.

Each of us recalls those things that our parents did that we promised ourselves *we* would never do, or never forget to do, if we were ever to become parents ourselves. Then, becoming parents, we struggle to make good on those promises to ourselves. It is that effort—to either transcend or hold on to those formative lessons in order to do better for our own children—that motivates plasticity in parents' minds. But this is a different drive for change and growth than most of the developmental tasks and relational interactions we've discussed. It is different because the focus of change is not the parent but the child. The motivation tends toward selflessness and sacrifice. It hinges on the unsettled bargain that if I, as the parent, do everything right, my kid will be okay. If this were an actual hypnotic conversation, we would follow that last sentence with a long period of silence, allowing its poignancy to sink in deeply.

The trance of parenting is distinctive. It is impactful, conflicted, and directed not on the parent who generates it, but the child who interprets it. So there is a special role for therapeutic hypnosis in helping parents encourage healthy children. That's where we'll start.

Practicing the Parenting Trance, Or, Adventures in Catastrophizing

The default behaviors of parenting, when engaged with the child, seem binary. As parents, it's as though we are either chasing, yelling, anticipating, or reminding, with toddler-raising patience, or we are cuddling, caring, and absorbed in comfort. That amygdala in the center of our brains that we have described as the arbiter of emotion, seems to be either blaring warnings or crooning lullabies. Panic or peace. We don't seem to find much time for the middle. On those occasions that we do—when Robinson plays cars with his son, Lulu's adoptive parents cheer at her gymnastics events, or we run alongside-of-not-holding-onto the child learning to ride the bike—those moments feel more like fortunate happenstance than intentional. It is difficult to extend those moments and to make them purposeful.

This all makes some sense from an evolutionary perspective. First, we need to keep saber-toothed tigers from eating our young. Then we need to envelop our kids in as much secure contact and loving care as we can. These needs are felt strongly, sometimes surprisingly so, by parents. Emotionally intelligent, poised, and competent people, once they become parents, can feel like emotional wrecks. The sleep-deprivation contributes, of course. If we consider these dual parental drives from the standpoint of their effects on the infant and child's developing mind, then we can understand that they are enacted as behaviors that teach the difference between vigilance and safety. Perry (2017), Siegel (2012), and Brown and Elliot (2016), culling from their own research and that of many others, illustrate that inadequate parental attachment—an inadequate balance of these two drives—fundamentally diminishes emotional range, resilience, and agility, such that the attachment-starved infant or child primarily favors a "freeze" response in relation to novelty and social engagement. So from a relational and modeling perspective, it makes sense that parents are so intensely compelled to act this way, at least at the beginning.[1] This balancing act forms a foundation for the trance of parenting.

Time-travel is another contributing feature of the Parenting Trance. Parents simultaneously sample experiences from their own childhood and project themselves into their child's future. Of course, most of this is non-conscious, conditioned, and embodied. The mother holding her baby knows that she was also held. Such common and daily events as the child's starting school, making and losing a first friend, learning to ride and falling off of a bicycle trigger the parent's own conditioned learnings that influence their responses. Without being mindful, parents project those responses onto the child, again, often protectively. At the same time, parents cannot help but plan who their child will come to be. They reflexively cultivate their child's development along that course. This is most evident with gender. Traditionally, as soon as we know their anatomic makeup, we begin to "gender" our children in our minds, our views of them, in more profound ways than how to clothe and name them. In many cultures, race, ethnicity, class, caste, family occupations, and traditions further determine, and so shape, the expectations of who a child is to become. Future paths may be more open in diverse and egalitarian societies, especially among more privileged groups, but parents will still imagine and impose on their children's futures. These future-orientations shape parents' current behaviors that are then projected as expectations on to the growing child.

While parents are becoming engaged with this balancing act, time-traveling and meddling with their child's futures implicitly over their first few months, children start doing something uniquely mammalian and singularly human: they begin to make up their own minds. They begin to express autonomy, preference, a desire for self-determination, even opposition. They begin to test and defy everything. The parent of a particularly rambunctious and athletic toddler, a child who seemed to hold no fear of heights, remarked, "She thinks that gravity is an opinion."

Children become intensely sensitive to infringements on the widening boundaries of their autonomy. The toddler asks for a drink of juice. The parent considers this an opportunity for learning and asks the child which colored cup they want to choose, "The red one, the blue one, the yellow one, or the green one?" The toddler replies to each choice with an emphatic "No!" The parent sighs and patiently presents the choices again, getting the same responses. The parent asks, "Do you still want juice?" The child nods, "Yes." The parent, now exasperated, asks, "Then what?!" The toddler points to the cups and insists, "*I* choose!" then proceeds to point and name the cup colors, mimicking the parent. The child resented being *given* a choice. They wanted to *make their own*.

With their child's inevitable and accelerating drive for self-determination, parents increasingly realize that the window of opportunity to protect, direct, and shape their child's mind is closing. That's assuming that the window was ever open very much in the first place. Parents become both delighted —"Look what he did all by himself!"—and horrified—"Look what he did all by himself!"—by their child's behavior. The conflict intensifies in the parent's mind, fueled by the social environment. Saber-toothed tigers may be extinct, but the newsfeed and social media expose bigger and more insidious threats, from environmental toxins to mass shootings in elementary schools. These promote vicarious traumatization of parents. The default, underlying parental mode becomes one of anticipating harm to their child. In these ways, the child's mandatory and autonomous development, coupled with the parent's sensitized perceptions of danger, align to intensify parental catastrophizing. If you aren't worried, you aren't paying attention.

The foregoing conflicted and catastrophic time-traveling is the basis, the circuitry and engrams, for the parental trance, which is why we've referred to it as the default. We are calling this a trance, rather than an attitude or stance, because it is a practiced form of psychobiological plasticity within the parent's mind: a reinforced rut from genomics to behavior. It is not in the parent's hourly consciousness. The trance activates as parents project their child's current behavior into the future, almost always toward a bad end. When the infant falls on her diaper, the child runs from parents at the park, erupts into a tantrum, is late for school, the adolescent starts swearing, won't clean their room, doesn't say where they have been, etc.,—all of these natural forays into autonomy trigger parental projections, time-travelling from past and future.

As parents, we reflexively predict the catastrophic outcome of these behaviors. Parents have been saying, likely forever, "If you keep doing that, you will end up …" then conjuring some horrific outcome. Of course, saying it to the child is a strategic warning, but parents feel it more. It builds inside, mostly unexpressed. The reflexive, protective trance of parenting, rooted in our evolution, is set up to predict future calamity from present performance, to continually wonder about what can go wrong. After all, we did not get to this point as a species by mistaking the saber-toothed tiger in the bush for a gentle breeze. We also call it a trance because we are going to present how therapeutic hypnosis—a skill set to influence plasticity in helpful ways—can help change it.

Posing the Parental Paradox

However protective it might be, the parental trance is not benign. It is enacted in behaviors that can be interpreted, and often are, as indicative of both the fear of the unknown and the lack of faith in the child's abilities to handle that uncertainty.

The parent's conscious intention when reminding, warning, checking over, and (unwelcomed) accompanying, is preventive and protective. It is also to model anticipatory behavior, to put readiness into the child's mind. We expect that children will internalize this, learn how to be prepared, especially the more we repeat ourselves. So far, so good. We must do these things. But there's a catch.

Children have never been parents, let alone adults. They are not very good at taking the long view. They do not occupy their minds with past and future projections as their parents do. They certainly don't do "patience." Their developmental priorities are more immediate and autonomous. They don't say in their minds, "I think I will learn to walk sometime next week, perhaps on Thursday." Their drives for autonomy ("It is *my* idea"), heuristics ("Let *me* figure it out"), and self-determination ("*I* choose how") are both relentless and desirable. As a result, they tend to offer one of two responses to parents who are in the throes of expressing the protective parental trance: opposition and acceptance.

Opposition is easy to understand. We have all done it. It is not surprising that "No!" is consistently among the first five words children learn to say in their first two years, considering how often they hear it. As parents continue to remind, opposition tends to increase. We can define "nagging" as when parents tell the child something that: (1) the child already knows and (2) they don't want to hear at that moment. Through adolescence and into adulthood, this type of response can meld with autonomy to produce parental rejection, withholding information, and distancing from parents. We find ourselves saying of our parents, "They really don't know me." Even as these feelings dissipate with our own maturity, they leave residue. When in my sixties (JHL) my 92-year-old mother reminded me to take my umbrella on a cloudy day, I quietly muttered angry expletives. She remained in her parental trance, so I was in my rejection trance.

The second response, acceptance, is more insidious, and therefore, perhaps more potent. The more parents repeat their preventive and protective reminders, the more their children begin to wonder, "Maybe they're right. Maybe I ought to be concerned. Maybe I can't do stuff on my own." Especially when a child has struggled with their own sense of competency and self-efficacy, when they have been traumatized, their self-image can internalize parental caution. In short, if the child is susceptible, they catch the contagion of anxiety inherent in the parental trance.

I (LIS) have the opportunity to demonstrate this profoundly in my clinical practice on a regular basis. To help children experience the embodiment of their anxiety, I use skin conductance biofeedback. Sweat gland activity in the palms and fingers conducts small amounts of current and correlates sensitively with sympathetic nervous system activity. So, with electrodes strapped to the child's fingers and a video display showing a bar graph of their "Stress Level" (which is actually electrical conductance), I ask them to lower the bar (increasing electrical resistance by drying up sweat glands) on the screen beneath a given threshold, represented by a line across the graph. I situate the parent and child such that the both can see the display and me, but not each other. As the child figures out how to lower their stress toward the line on the graph—by breathing slowly and being really still, for example—I intentionally nod toward the parent to say, nonverbally, "Watch this," then say out loud to the child, "This is hard. Here, let me help you." Then I raise the threshold closer to their stress level, making it easier for them to reach. Reliably and within seconds, the child's stress level *rises*, moving *away* from the threshold line. I let them struggle at that new level. Then I repeat the process, each time first capturing the parent's attention. After another repetition or two, with the child's stress level substantially higher, we stop and process. Parents are often stunned by the real-time and objective evidence that unsolicited offers for help raise their child's anxiety.

The parental paradox comes down to this: the more we help, the more we hinder. The more we protect our children from life's challenges, the more they are unable to face them. It is a paradox, because the fundamental drives of both parties—parents' drive to protect, and children's drive toward autonomy—are in conflict and required. As a result, most children grow up with a mixture of both responses: some opposition and some acceptance of anxiety. It is also a false dichotomy, of course. There are a lot of creative and helpful encounters in between meeting saber-toothed tigers and never letting our children go. The question becomes, how do parents make more of those creative and helpful encounters happen on purpose?

Hypnotically Parsing the Parental Paradox and Resetting the Parental Trance

The hypnosis skill set—building rapport, disrupting entrenched plasticity in the embodied mind, promoting renewal from that disruption—can powerfully help parents transcend their conditioning and the trap of the parental paradox. For the rest of the chapter, we will explore, using vignettes, how the parenting trance can change with hypnotic interventions that parse the parental paradox. In the next chapter, we will take this theme further into helping parents lead the way toward fostering resilience and coping in families.

The Prenatal Visit

Just as their fetus is maturing toward birth and babyhood in a mother's womb, nascent parental trances are forming in parallel. Ostensibly, prenatal pediatric visits are for collecting a family history of risk factors, providing counseling about newborn care, and establishing a collaborative relationship with the clinical practice. But meeting with prospective parents provides the clinician a rich opportunity to creatively evoke antecedents of their attitudes and then set loose implicit processing heuristics into their developing parental minds. Besides, in applying our principles of *Thinking Systemically* and *Narrative Listening*, there is really no such thing as "taking a history." Memory retrieval doesn't work that way. So, in this novel setting (i.e., plasticity-enhancing), full of anticipation toward the impending birth or adoption, we have the opportunity to co-construct a narrative with these pending mothers and fathers.

Within this relational context, we recognize that family histories are family lore that function to form parental mindsets in the present and anticipation for the future. For example, the expectant father and his uncle both had their appendixes removed as children. His uncle had complications because it was "taken out too late." While it is highly unlikely that these episodes of appendicitis were genetically predetermined or related, it is inevitable and normal that this man's baby will, in the natural course of its infancy, have some gastrointestinal distress, complete with spitting up and vomiting. Knowing this, the clinician may be tempted to anticipatorily reassure the father with the statistical improbability that these episodes predict appendicitis problems for his child. The father may even volunteer that he knows this family history "probably has nothing to do" with *his* baby. But we are not dealing with facts or cognition. Both of these parents live with their approaching leap into the uncertainties of parenthood. We are interacting with elements of a coalescing trance of parenthood.

So instead of simply reassuring, the clinician can make a note that this inevitability will warrant more and sensitive care because of the symptoms' innate associations. More, the clinician can wonder out loud—modeling their comfort with not-knowing—"Well! That's interesting. Good to know. We can look forward to learning what your baby makes of that bit of family history as they grow up." Even more determinative family data that may carry higher risk can be framed with possibilities of positive outcomes, including and especially mental illness and substance abuse, countering tendency toward catastrophizing. The clinician can be the person in the relationship who keeps recognizing that this family story is yet to be told.

In addition to anticipating and reframing medical and genetic risk factors that infiltrate the parental trance, there are the parents' parenting stories. I (LIS) enjoyed surprising parents by asking about this with novelty. I would raise it near the end of the visit, after completing and reviewing the history form and orienting them to the practice. "Just one more set of questions," I would say. Then I would make the following inquiries. How did your parents raise you? What parts of that do you want to keep? What have you promised yourself you will never do? How are you different from them? How are you alike? All of these questions, and the conversations that followed, were implicit processing heuristics, designed to start disrupting the conditioning that these people were heirs to. So I was interested in the "how" of each parent's responses—to both the questions and to each other—as much as the "what." Equally importantly, in this developing therapeutic relationship, it delivered the message: We talk about this stuff here.

The Newborn Exam

The first examination of the infant in the hospital in front of the parents affords a dramatic opportunity to instill positivity, resilience, and hope. I (LIS) would enjoy taking part in this first doctor-patient relationship with an infant, and celebrating its unique qualities. It is a set up for hypnosis because it is a truly novel moment for all involved. Here are the elements of what I used to perform. First, I would enter the room and ignore the parents completely, focusing only on the infant. I would introduce myself to the infant and ask, "What name are they giving you?" Then, as I proceeded through the physical examination, I would comment positively on his or her blood flow, muscle strength, heart, breathing, abdominal organs, etc., as if the infant has consciously and intentionally made them all this way. "You have grown yourself a good, strong heart." One way to get an infant to open their eyes is to change their orientation in space. I would raise the infant into an upright prone position at eye level. They would open their eyes and reflexively arch their neck, holding their head up. Then I could be impressed with their demonstration of postural control and beautiful eyes. This speaks powerfully to the infant's nascent autonomy in the face of utter dependency. The authoritative clinician is establishing a positive relationship in acknowledging the infant's resilience over their fragility. Finally, I would give the *infant* guidance and instructions (including scheduling a first appointment) on feeding, hygiene, sleep position, developing a schedule, while their fascinated parents listened and processed this information, even more so because they were overhearing it. Sometimes I would say, "You'll get all the sleep you need, but your parents won't." I would end with something like, "Please be patient with your parents, you have a lot to teach them. Make sure they understand what you need. But they won't always do what you want." Then, finally, with the baby bundled, I would turn to the parents and ask if they had any questions.

In addition to its obvious novelty, the intention of this performance was to disrupt conditioned perceptions of the infant as helpless, unaware, asocial, unintelligent. Equally importantly, it casts the parents as the novices that they are (even with subsequent babies) while imbuing the baby with hidden wisdom. It emphasizes the fundamental value and work of responding to our kid's needs, but carefully considering their wants. It closes with an implicit processing heuristic, readying the parents to observe and learn from their baby's cues. How do I know this was hypnotic in its effect? Because, for decades of pediatric practice, as their children grew, parents would reminisce, "I will never forget that first newborn exam."

We must add that not all newborn exams reveal a healthy, strong, mature, perfectly formed infant. This revelation can feel devastating to parents, activating their catastrophizing reflex. In those conditions, it is even more important to be infant-centered and strength-based. "So, you seem to have been assigned some challenges. We wonder what will you make of them and what barriers can we help get out of your way." When an infant arrives with a recognizable syndrome—meaning a studied constellation of findings linked to an identified prognosis and treatment—we can pronounce audaciously, "It's good to know that you meet criteria for [——] syndrome. But of course, you also have [baby's full name] syndrome, so we can wonder what kind of person with [———-] syndrome you are going to become."

The Phantom Test

Harmful experiences that take place during the intensity of the newborn period can also have enduring effects. I (LIS) asked the parents of a two-year-old girl to meet with me for counseling. We were all concerned about their little girl's angry, defiant, and testing behavior. Mother, who had taken leave from her professional career to stay home with her daughter, was feeling exhausted and inadequate. Father was bewildered. Both expressed concern that their daughter had a neurodevelopmental condition. The child, the first-born after an uncomplicated pregnancy, labor, and delivery, was developing normally, aside from the ferocity of her temper. The only apparently relevant family history was that mother's sister had delivered a baby two years prior who was six weeks premature and so had been hospitalized for a month with breathing, feeding, apnea, and jaundice problems. Now four-years-old, the niece had various developmental delays.

I had worked repeatedly over the last year with the mother to help her practice consistent scheduling, limit-setting, time-out, and engagement for desired behavior. But the mother found it very difficult to follow through. She said, "I am just so worried that something's wrong with her." It finally dawned on me to ask her the basis of her concern, even though there was nothing I knew of in the child's history to warrant it. She replied, "You know. It's because of that jaundice problem she had after she was born." I was confused and concerned that I had missed something. I had no record nor did I recall her having a jaundice problem. After I got over my embarrassment, I told them so. I promised to look into it.

My investigation revealed that late on the second postnatal night, a newborn nursery nurse had told the mother that the baby looked jaundiced, so she was going to bring the baby back to the nursery to have a blood test. Then the shift changed, the on-call physician examined the baby, was unconcerned, and did not order the test. But the mother never knew, never asked (perhaps due to her fear and sleep deprivation), and so, never received the results. Instead, the worry took root and grew so that the parents saw the child as fragile and vulnerable, despite the fact that she was a tyrant. It would be great if the story ended with the parents finding out the truth and changing their behavior. But that is not what happened. It took years of work and family therapy for these parents to feel confident enough to stand up to their child. Such is the power of events occurring early in the impressionable trance of parenthood.

The Blue Backpack and Other Evocative Cartoons

When, during a session with a parent, or parents, and their child, we encounter evidence of the parental paradox—the struggle between trying to help and trying to get out of the child's way—I (LIS) will launch into a story or an imagined cartoon designed to disrupt and redirect the parental trance. Because it seems a non-sequitur, there is novelty. The stories and images appeal to various representational sensory modes with multisensory imagery, meaningful icons that can act as post-hypnotic "souvenirs," as discussed in Chapter 5. The stories are varied in order to tune them to the language, experiences, and sensory modes of the parents and child. The value of the stories is that, as in our principle of *Narrative Listening,* they provide a compelling and coherent container for the implicit information. Sometimes stories and imagery are like a well-insulated coffee mug: they hold difficult-to-handle information, so that you can drink it in slowly and carefully.

The Blue Backpack

You know, that reminds me of a story. It's the little boy's first day of kindergarten. A month ago the mother helped him pick out a blue backpack to hold all his new kindergarten stuff: crayons, scissors, lined papers … and a change of underwear and pants. Now she is getting ready to go with him to the bus stop for that big step up. She really has quite a mix of strong feelings that she is struggling to hold back as she reminds him, "Don't forget your blue backpack." She helps him put it on, and off they go to join the other kids and parents gathered at the curb. The backpack looks huge on him. He looks so determined as he climbs those steps … and does not look back.

Then suddenly he's in second grade and tells his mom that she doesn't need her to wait for the bus with him anymore. She sighs as she says, "Okay." But she insists on a hug and kiss, reminding him, "Don't forget your blue backpack." He yells "Got it, Mom!" over his shoulder just before the screen door slams behind him and he runs off to his friends at the street corner.

Then in fifth grade he is getting tall and gives her a hurried kiss and half-hug after rushing breakfast. She yells after him, "Don't forget your blue backpack," and he replies, annoyed, "Okay!" as the door slams.

Then he's 13 … 14 … 16, oversleeping, grabbing some toast, and rushing out the house as if she, at her morning coffee, doesn't exist. There is no response as she offers, "Love you. Have a good day … Don't forget your blue backpack," in his wake.

They have lugged the last container of his packed belongings up the stairs and into his dorm room at college and he is distracted, ready to explore, unsure of how to say goodbye, how to feel. He allows a hug and has endured a list of her reminders, including that he will call her tomorrow. At the doorway, she cannot help but turn back and ask, "You got your new backpack, right?" It is blue.

What's with this blue backpack? You know what it is, don't you? It's an icon, a good luck charm, a special coin, a rabbit's foot. It is easier to hold in our hearts than what it represents. It's a prayer. It means, "Please don't die today."

Parents all over the world, some with better reason than others, do something like this. They may not even be aware of it. But they feel the need to do it, to keep their kid safe.

And it is not benign. You see, the kid has been hearing this all his life. "*Don't forget your blue backpack.*" Over and over and over again. It's this annoying thing his mother or father keeps saying. Like he's an idiot. Like he would *ever* forget his stuff. He has *never* forgotten his backpack! She doesn't even know what's in it. She doesn't even know me, that's why I don't tell her stuff. She treats me like I can't do anything right. But, he wonders quietly, what if she is kind of right? What if I am an idiot about things, some things. What if I really can't do stuff without her reminding me? What if I can't make it on my own? So the blue backpack means different things to different people. Parent's prayers are often overheard and misunderstood.

Catastrophizing attachment

So, imagine this cartoon. You and your wife, your son, your daughter, and the dog are all standing in the smoking, charred ruins of what used to be your home. Your faces are streaked with soot, and the cartoonist has drawn little wisps of smoke rising from your singed hair. You are all stunned, and staring at your son who is holding a lighter, saying, "Whoops. My mistake." Got it? Okay, here is the question. Do you love him any less?

Imagining estrangement

Having asked about and sketched the young person's dreams and hopes for their future, we can use and improve upon specific elements from the young person's future projection and characteristics—including those that challenge the parents—while occasionally checking with them for accuracy. We turn to the parents and say, "Let me ask you a question. Imagine that your child is 20 years older. They are living in Chicago, in a beautiful condominium. Not married … yet, but lots of great and supportive friends. They are an architect who really loves what they do and the people they work with. The people in the architectural firm really value their creativity and ability to collaborate. They play in the local mixed-gender soccer league, and coach in the youth league. They still play the saxophone in a jazz group, with gigs at some clubs. Works out. No longer eats meat. Is happy, healthy, successful and loved" After a pause, "There is just one catch … They want nothing to do with you and you have not communicated for a decade. How is that for you?"

Changing Trajectories

The course of our children's development rarely follows that of parental dreams. As in *Romeo and Juliet*, literature and theater are replete with stories of children finding their own way, despite and in opposition to their parents. Of course, these autonomous expressions don't occur in single dramatic productions, but as diverging paths laid in the walking. Metaphorically, our children negotiate a maze in which the walls are constructed of family values and circumstances. Then they begin to test the walls and break them down, increasingly asking, with their behaviors, "Why is that wall there? Why do we do it this way?" The force of these questions is somewhat determined by the permissiveness of the larger culture: race, ethnicity, class, caste, family occupations, and traditions.

From a (family) systems perspective, we might say that our children test our relative values. They ask with their behavior, at least, "Which is more important to you, my chosen self-actualization or your measures of success?" In this way, and uncannily, our children often challenge us as parents in just the ways we have struggled to grow. For example, consider the father, perhaps Lyle's father, who was raised in a large, noisy family of people who yelled. Lyle is a boy with sensory sensitivity, especially to loud voices. When Lyle's father yells, he only evokes his son's fight-or-flight response, and so is ineffective at communicating any content. The boy requires his father to develop the self-regulation to speak softly. More, he requires that his father make this change a priority over expressing his authority. It is as if our children, who are in the business of deploying their embodied minds, are asking their parents, "Show me how you change your minds. Then I will change mine." In their book, *Everyday Blessings,* Myla and Jon Kabat-Zinn (2014) frame this as each child being the director of their parent's development, sort of like little Zen masters. While they may be quite annoying, we ought to respect these powerful teachers.

This way of relating becomes a powerful enactment of *Relational Being, Narrative Listening,* and *Systems Thinking* when using hypnosis with parents. The shift is disruptive, exemplified in the previous example of the newborn exam. Stevie's adolescence and gender confusion typify an adolescent struggle that challenges parents. A father in my (LIS) practice could be like Stevie's. He was wrestling with his male-born adolescent's gender dysphoria. As a little boy, this patient was diagnosed with high-functioning autism spectrum disorder. The child was socially reticent, primarily focused on learning music and reading books, and while avoidant of popular competitive team sports, was intensely focused on the martial arts. His father found this challenging since none of these were his interests, and this father didn't know how to join in. Quite naturally, he faulted himself for his son's developmental differences. "I didn't spend enough time with him … uh, her, I don't know." Now 16 years old, with no evidence of autism and taller than both of her parents, his child identifies as female, dresses accordingly, has chosen a different name and is socially active, a martial arts instructor, and an accomplished young musician and composer. Father feels paralyzed in his relationship. "I don't know how to talk with … her … anymore."

In our hypnotic conversation, we evoked images and icons—achieving her first yellow-belt as a young boy, a first music recital, stories read together at bed time—during which father was not only present and supportive, but more nurturing and emotionally demonstrative then his own father had been, and also excited about his child's accomplishments. Then we shifted to a decade into his trans daughter's future—simply accepting, without question, that profound shift. We collaborated in constructing her imagined course—the orchestral debut of her first symphony, the adoration of her friends, a loving partner, and even a new level of cultural acceptance—then imagining his ongoing pride and continuing caring support. We added themes of coherence: how he kept and read all of the programs from recitals and concerts, looking for her name, which was different from her birth name, and how the future orchestral concert contained her biography, and his name, too. This was rapport-building, disruptive imagery, and seeding elements of renewal: a hypnotic process, complete with father's tears.

About a month later, I read a letter to the editor in the local paper imploring parents of all children to fight for equal rights for people across the range of gender expression. The author noted that this may not have been the world of our childhood, but that parents "must prepare their children for the changing future with love and respect." It was written by this father. I wrote to him, asking him to come in to share what he was learning. In our encounter, he explained that after he came home from our visit, his daughter, "Just looked different. It was hard to explain." He started asking her about her plans for her future, and he was surprised that she responded thoughtfully. They had started having conversations. "I guess she knows that I am not trying to control her … if I ever could." He added, "But I am still worried, maybe even more than I used to be." This confused me, so I asked him to explain. He replied, "I'm not concerned about her gender choice. I am concerned someone's gonna kill her. We have to work on that."

Teaching Parents Self-Hypnosis

In these types of encounters, parents can learn the pitfalls of the parenting paradox, and how to alter the trance of parenting. They can catch themselves nagging protectively and begin to ask their child questions instead. They can balance reflexive catastrophizing with intentional and courageous imagining of their children's success. Most fundamentally, they can catch their own fear of saber-toothed tigers that underlies the contagion of anxiety and replace it with self-calming, breathing, and progressive muscle relaxation. So, when they are ready to learn and practice, it is a real pleasure to collaborate with parents in developing a self-hypnotic meditative exercise—based on the unique components of their relationship with their child—that roughly follows this format:

> In anticipation of your day and the unexpected events that will trigger worry about your child, catch the next breath in and hold it briefly, before letting it out, and noticing the decrease in muscle tension that goes with that breathing out, with a pause at the bottom. Stay with those ten-second breaths until you have noticed a change toward feeling more calm, comfortable, and in control. [*This is an evocation of increased vagal tone and embodiment.*] Keep doing that, as you shift your thinking and your mind's imagination from concern about the known and unknown worries that you will encounter, to modeling competence and confidence for your child … knowing just the right thing to say … knowing that it's okay to say and do nothing at all when they are safely finding their own way. Even recall those times when they surprised you by knowing just what to do. [*Competent acceptance of uncertainty. The opposite of anxiety. Pause to allow those reframed memories to activate*]. Then challenge your mind's imagination to look forward to future surprise accomplishments in your child's life … that you had no idea how they would turn your love and support into that kind of healthy living. Doing this thing or that thing … [*Another pause*]. Then with that perspective in mind, let it change your breathing and posture to one of excitement and anticipation for who your child is becoming. You can notice the back and shoulders and abdominal muscles shift toward a confident, dignified posture. You need not concern yourself with any internal thoughts of doubt; you will not fail to caution them or protect them when it is really needed. You know they will never again [some past experience that scared the child in the past, like chasing a ball into the street, getting lost in the store]. They keep learning and growing from these lessons because you have helped them learn how to change their minds. Before you finish this exercise for now, return your attention to your breathing and remember that, over the next day, whenever you need to bring these feelings and images to mind, all you will need to do is to give yourself one or two of these deep breaths, allow your posture to shift, and thank yourself for taking good care. You can wonder when you will do that next. [*Post-hypnotic souvenir with a "continuing question" and processing heuristic.*]

In this chapter, we purposefully focused on the parent's trances and perspective, in order to address the quandary of the Parental Paradox. Parents cannot really control their children's outcomes. How they become aware of, and act on, that inefficacy with poise and compassion is the key to their parenting, and their own development. In our careful attention to helping our children become the people we hope they can be, they teach us to become the people we have always needed to be. That difficult shift, that change of mind, is powerfully facilitated with hypnosis. I (LIS) recently found myself saying to a father in clinic "You know, it is pretty unclear how or whether anything we do as parents has much of an effect on who our kids become. So the bottom line is that we need to stop measuring our effectiveness as parents by how our kids act and what they do" He was disturbed by this and, as an engineer, I think he was bothered by the fuzziness of this logic, and my apparent disregard for what seemed to him (and most of us) an obvious cause-and-effect relationship. That is precisely the disruption I was aiming for. So he replied, "Are you telling me to give up on my kid?!" I smiled and said, "No. I am saying that we need to judge our behavior as parents not by how our *kids* act, but by the way *we* act."

Questions and Assignments for Further Discussion

1. Cite and compare examples of parental catastrophizing in this book's stories.
2. Using lessons from this chapter, how might you counsel a parent on their interactions and limit-setting (their parenting) who has just learned their child has been the victim of abuse or other trauma? Consider Lulu's adoptive mother as an example.
3. Speculate on how heath care delivery methods can both exacerbate and ameliorate the tendency toward parental catastrophizing.

Note

1 We are aware that, as we write this and long after this book is out of print, there will be parents and children on the planet living in desperation, with few resources, stuck in this bimodal existence. That is represented by little Lulu's early years. Parenting in the context of actual existential and traumatizing threat is real and dire, but not the primary focus of this chapter.

References

Brown, D. P., & Elliot, D. S. (2016). *Attachment disturbances in adults: Treatment for comprehensive repair.* New York: W.W. Norton.

Kabat-Zinn, M., & Kabat-Zinn, J. (2014). *Everyday blessings: The inner work of mindful parenting.* New York, NY: Hachette.

Perry, B. D. (2017). *The boy who was raised as a dog, and other stories from a child psychiatrist's notebook.* New York, NY: Basic Books.

Siegel, D. J. (2012). *The developing mind.* New York, NY: Guilford.

Lyle's Story

Olivia Hears Lyle's Music

OK. So I did feel strange—some weird kind of geek, for one, and a white boy to boot. But something made me trust that Lyle was not up to something. He really wanted to show me his music—whatever he meant by "show," and whatever he meant by "music"—and I had my sister drop me off at his house so someone would know where I went. He was sitting on the front steps of the house when we pulled up. We came inside, and I thought he'd offer me a pop or some chips or something, but—no, not even a glass of water. OK. I didn't come for the refreshments, but it was again a sort of alarm bell that he just didn't even know the most basic social conventions.

I looked around, expecting to see some kind of musical gear—microphones, instruments, something—but there was nothing. "We have to go to my bedroom," he said. OK. Sure. I should have known.

"It's all upstairs," he said. "My Mom won't let me set things up in any room but my bedroom." Right. Of course.

At this point, I decided I might as well poke my head in. So we go upstairs, and, well—I'm trying to describe things, OK? But this room was indescribable—so much gear—computers, monitors, speakers—some of them set up, some of them spread out unassembled across the floor, all sorts of cables and wires, some plugged in, some just left in a tangle on the floor—it was a colossal mess.

But the takeaway was the music, which began, softly, as we went up the stairs, and then gradually increased in volume and by quarter tones as I stood and listened. The music pulled me up the stairs. "I wrote this for you," Lyle said, gesturing, "so you should sit here, in this chair. That's the best listening spot. Obviously we have no authentic acoustics, here, but I've been able to create artificial acoustics, so long as you sit in the right place." So, evidently, I got to sit in the magic chair.

Lyle listened, not moving, clearly assuming that I, like him, would not think of moving till the music ended. The music seemed like a sort of fanfare, with a welcoming blast of brass instruments—or that's what it sounded like—but once the music ended, Lyle quickly explained what we had heard. It was music governed by robotics and artificial intelligence, so that the music continually rediscovers itself. According to Lyle, this music also relies upon sound machines that can reproduce virtually any possible musical sound. He pointed to each piece of gear and explained what it could do. I just listened, amazed, understanding a tiny fraction of what he was saying. When he wanted to illustrate a point, he would click a few times and play me a quick succession of musical examples. I realized a lot of those examples were not in any known musical genre.

Lyle explained that since his machines can make any possible sound, he isn't limited by the repetitious sounds of the easily recognizable genres. They are recognizable precisely because they borrow and repeat—in effect, because they are all the same. Lyle says that the musical human voice is the hardest instrument to capture in a synthetic environment, but with dedicated artificial intelligence he is confident that he can capture the human voice and "sing" in ways instrument-bound composers cannot. Meaning, for example, that we will no longer have defined ranges for particular voices in a choir or instrumental orchestra because a single voice can sing any note, however high or low, and however pitch-perfect or in-between it may be.

I suddenly realized how long it had been since I'd checked my phone. I checked it, and then checked it again. All I could say was—"Omigod! I can't believe how long we listened to this music! I have to get home to make dinner! Thanks for the music, Lyle!"

Lyle, Olivia, and Some Heavy Stuff

Lyle and Olivia had started wandering toward her house after school. OK, not exactly *after* school. Time happens. School goes on. And they were not there. But they weren't missing much. Their absences were a technicality.

But then Olivia asks Lyle what college he's going to and he mumbles in reply, so Olivia tries other words. She asks what college he's *applying* to. Lyle again mumbles.

Olivia starts to get annoyed. "Lyle, you're going to college, right? Everybody at this school goes to college. Are your plans top secret information?"

"I don't think I'm going to college. We don't have much money."

"Lyle. Take out a loan. Apply for scholarships. You're smart. Of course you're going to college."

Lyle tries to divert her, asking, "What college are *you* going to?"

"Henh!" Olivia makes an impatient sound. But then she can't help but add: "I'm going to Yale." It's plain that she's proud of this fact.

Lyle also concedes: "I'm sort of not getting along with my parents. My father, really."

"Lyle," she says. "How does not getting along with your father keep you from going to college?"

"Well, he won't fill out any of the forms," Lyle says, "You know. Financial aid, all that."

"What, so you're going to waste your life tossing pizza dough just because your father's being uncooperative?"

At this point, they have walked to the intersection that leads to Olivia's house.

"Let's go around the block again," Lyle says, "I have to explain something."

They turn around and start walking again.

"My father," Lyle says, "believes I can't speak."

"What? How is that possible?" Olivia says. "He lives in the same house you do, right?"

"Right, but here's what happened. I was about five years old. We were at the dinner table. I did something that made my father very angry. I don't know what it was. My father was always yelling and hitting, but this was worse than usual. He got up from the table, grabbed me, and yelled—I'll never forget this—he said—'I'm gonna *shake you up good!*' And that's when he threw me across the room. I was so scared. But I was more angry than scared. I was like a ball of fire in that moment. But I wasn't talking. I was screaming. I was roaring."

"Lyle. You've carried this anger around for twelve years?"

The two of them have stopped walking.

"Lyle." Olivia says, "I don't understand. How does that story explain why your father thinks you can't speak? And even if it does, that still doesn't explain why having a kid who doesn't speak keeps that kid from going to college."

"On question 1: I stopped talking because I was so angry with my father. And on question 2: It's habit now. He never offers to help. My mother talks to me, but, if my father's home, I don't talk back."

"Wow," Olivia says. "You have what is possibly the most dysfunctional family I've ever heard of. But it definitely does not justify your family's behavior. In fact, I think that if we opened up a psychology textbook to the definition for the term 'dysfunctional family,' it would fall open to a big picture of your family."

Unless—wait a minute. Lyle—you write stories, don't you? You write fiction. You—you made this up, didn't you! Or—maybe it's true that you're still very angry; maybe you truly remember and despise that assault on a five-year-old by a grown man. But the part about not speaking to your father for 12 years—that's got to be exaggeration, at best.

"Well," Lyle said, "maybe. But I am still that little boy whose hair caught fire at what his father had done that time, and on many other occasions. And that's what I want you to know about me."

"OK, well, Lyle—you're still trying to punish your father for that one incident, long ago?"

"He never apologized!"

"OK, well, Lyle, listen, you definitely need to fix your part of this problem before it wrecks the rest of your life. Got it?"

11 Evoking Resilience with Autonomy and Uncertainty

Main Ideas

1. Parents can learn to optimize their intentional use of a "parental trance" to both cope with the emotional struggles of parenting and model resilient autonomy for their children.
2. Parents ideally … but not always, "lead the change" in family systems.
3. For the system, the opposite of anxiety is welcoming uncertainty. Parents can learn to model this.
4. Parental disengagement from their children can both evoke and empower in their children's autonomy and resources.
5. Person-centered and evocative hypnotic skills are aimed at encouraging resilience.

Health care is about fostering and hope, helping our clients to live full, meaningful lives, and to restore their best functioning, by being empathically responsive in a climate of possibility. We evoke or utilize potential for naturally occurring plasticity and apply our hypnosis skills to these ends. Why is this focus on potential important? Resiliency—our ability to bounce back, to be elastic and supple, and to be flexible and bending in life's journey—is the essence of health. That is the subject of this chapter.

Through the 80s and 90s of both the last two centuries—from Janet to van der Kolk—clinician-researchers built a foundation for understanding the psychobiology of trauma. The pendulum has more recently swung away from trauma and adversity—painfully disruptive trances—to the study of resilience: trances of agile expectancy. In this chapter we explore resilience in the context of trance, mind, and hypnosis, and how parent-child interactions and family systems can facilitate its development.

A story first. Martin Seligman, the psychologist who initiated learned helplessness research (Maier & Seligman, 2016) was my (JHL) college professor. I remember him as brilliant, insightful, and one of the saddest-looking lecturers of my undergraduate days. My classmates and I were intimidated by him, and often remarked on how unapproachable he seemed. Years after I graduated, I heard the story—perhaps apocryphal—that his five-year-old daughter asked him one day why he looked so sad. His child's question initiated his own reassessment of earlier research. He wanted to know more about the animals that had *not* been deterred by the electric shocks delivered in his lab. Instead of being risk-averse, they were risk takers that pursue their food in spite of the deterrent. This led to his research on learned optimism, and the birth of the field of positive psychology (Seligman, 2006). Some 20 years after my graduation, I happened to walk by Dr. Seligman on the streets of my home town. I recognized him and found myself staring at this now-famous professor. I was surprised when he smiled at me; I was still expecting his stern face.

A five-year-old's curiosity about her father's expression swung the pendulum toward a new path. These changing trajectories can occur at personal, communal, and societal levels. From helplessness to optimism: this shift was neither "right" nor "wrong," but generative. Such insights are essential to how we learn and grow. We are not static in our development, nor in our biology. Changing frames of reference, is a disruptive construct in hypnosis, introduced in Chapter 5, and the key to what we refer to as resilience.

Starting in the 1950s with Werner and Smith (2001), longitudinal research has found that about one third of children who grew up with many adverse experiences became thriving, resilient adults. As Seligman's animal research had shown, some subjects are not deterred by potentially traumatic events. This raised the question: How does resilience emerge?

Bonanno (2004), a trauma and grief researcher who studied adults' ways of coping, distinguished resilience from recovery. He wrote that resilience "reflects the ability to maintain a stable equilibrium … in psychological and physical functioning" (p. 20). Recovery, by contrast, requires a period of decompensation, from which a person has to recuperate but not necessarily learn. In short, resilience is the ability to maintain homeostasis during change. Bonanno suggests resilience is more common in the general population than would be expected from the study of trauma. His research also indicates resilience is reached through multiple pathways. He lists four traits, each an area for research, in those that exhibit resilience. The first, "Hardiness," is the trait of being committed to finding meaningful purpose in life. It includes the belief that one can influence one's surroundings and the outcomes of events, and that one can learn and grow from both positive and negative life experiences. Next, "Self-Enhancement," is the trait of feeling empowered to do what is needed for self-protection. Good self-esteem enables agency, and being able to act on our own behalf prepares us for dealing with life's challenges. The third trait is "Repressive Coping," the ability to dissociate from what is stressful in order to see the glass as half full, which minimizes the feeling of being helpless. Finally, he lists the trait of "Positive Emotion and Laughter," the capacity to be hopeful, find humor in the adverse, and distance oneself from it. This knack allows for "macro" perspectives, "the

10,000 foot view," and less personalization of events. We might summarize these four components simply as being helpful and hopeful.

Research from the Center on the Developing Child at Harvard (2015) reveals that resilience can be developed at any time, and the earlier the better. Their findings show that resilience factors include: trusting relationships; emotional support outside of the family; self-esteem; encouragement of autonomy; hope; responsible risk-taking; a sense of being loveable; scholastic achievement; belief in morality; and unconditional love for someone. Masten (2001) views resilience from a developmental perspective, reporting that children who have healthy development in spite of adversity are resilient. In an article entitled, "*Ordinary Magic: Resilience Processes in Development,*" she looks at the protective factors the young develop, and concludes that "resilience is made up of ordinary processes, rather than extraordinary ones" (p. 227). Adaptation is our evolutionary force. Resiliency is our default mode. We have to learn to get stuck.

Metaphors for resilience have included rubber bands, Jello, branches blowing on a tree, Raggedy Ann dolls, springtime, and all manner of animals—especially cats, who are reputed to have bounced back from close calls with death by virtue of having nine lives. A more fitting metaphor may be the engineering that goes into a skyscraper of reinforced steel that can withstand hurricanes, earthquakes, even bombs. It sways, shakes, and then centers itself, remaining intact. Ginger Rogers—who did everything Fred Astaire did, except in high heels and backwards—certainly exemplifies adaptation and resilience. Robinson, Lulu, and Lyle also exemplify these capabilities, in their own ways.

Note that resilience can only be demonstrated in the face of adversity. It even requires friction to develop and strengthen. Here we remind you about Rossi's Novelty-Numinosum-Neurogenesis Effect and the four stages that underlie it (2002). How well we engage with and encourage others to move through that second incubation stage, then on to insight and integration that builds resilience. *Systems Thinking* can guide our approach to assisting those in our care, to help develop their resilience.

Aligning with the conception of mind, trance, and hypnosis from the beginning of this book, and in keeping with our *Systems Thinking* principle, we can also consider resilience as the development of agility within our embodied minds. For example, what does it take to enter an uncertain social situation (the first day of school, a first date, or new employment) with the proper balance of wariness and acceptance? At the level of the embodied mind, this requires that sympathetic (defensive, fight-or-flight) arousal be juxtaposed with increased vagal tone (social engagement). One needs to have the experiential resources to balance the innate reflex of fight-or-flight with slowed, deep breathing and the evocation of positive emotional experiences. Like all of our learned abilities, this is encoded in psychobiological engrams, our personal stories. Lulu seems to have learned that, in the face of perceived threat, as soon as her heart rate goes up, and her amygdala sounds an alarm, she should pause and activate the opposite reflexes. The more she does this, the more she reinforces that Hebbian network of cellular elements and their underlying genomic proclivities. The more she does it, the better she gets at it. Even if the social system doesn't respond warmly, she will find those whose responses she can cultivate as you can read about at the close of Lulu's story. Just as trauma can lead to ongoing traumatization and traumatic contagion, resilience can be regenerative and infectious. We can teach our embodied minds to embrace uncertainty, from cell to society. Resilience is the ability to change our minds.

Sunny, a six-year-old bright, energetic, youngster, came to treatment when her parents became overwhelmed by her school meltdowns. Though she was only in kindergarten, she already hated school. Asked to do something in the classroom that she did not want to do, or could not yet do, she would argue, cry, throw things, and generally behave in ways that got her removed from the classroom, and often sent home. Sunny had learned what she needed to do to achieve her goal of getting away from the offending structure of school. A side effect of this behavior was that other children found her difficult and "mean." But Sunny was not adapting. She knew how to avoid what she did not like—an important skill—but she did not know how to tolerate discomfort.

To help Sunny, we needed to address her underdeveloped self-regulating skills and her environment. In therapy, Sunny expressed that she did not feel heard. "Nobody listens to me!" When a classmate or teacher failed to hear her concerns, she became incensed. How might she notice her anger, take a deep breath, and use a quieter, calmer voice to speak? She practiced doing this, noticing that as soon as she breathed out, and then in, her feelings slowed down and her voice quieted. It was easier for others to hear her earnest remarks when she spoke that way. She used her imagination to experience herself in the classroom feeling very proud when others listened to her speaking calmly. This is progression into the future, using *Temporal Touring*. She felt her upset feelings as water rolling off of her skin. These shifts in sensory perception produced changes in her emotions, then her behavior.

Next, we addressed the family and classroom systems. Instead of sending Sunny home with each tantrum, could the school provide a safe space, with an adult, where she could remember how to regain her control with self-calming tools, and then return to the classroom? Had the school asked Sunny what resources would help her to do this? Could the teacher welcome her back into the classroom and calmly acknowledge her growing ability to self-regulate? What class activities could be designed for Sunny to practice kindness toward her peers? Sunny made a list of tasks that would give her the opportunity to practice kindness. The teacher instituted a program of "Citizenship Points," awarded when students voluntarily helped others. Sunny appointed herself the politeness observer, complimenting others when they showed the behavior she considered polite. The school was happy to implement these changes, and Sunny's challenging behaviors subsided.

How could her parents respond in ways that would model adaptation and resilience? Instead of Dad asking, "What did you do bad today?" he proposed a treat that she could earn, each day she achieved her classroom goals or citizenship points. He learned to congratulate her efforts and focus on her positive behaviors. With this behavioral focus, he learned to show interest and wonder out loud how she recovered when she lost control. "How did you calm yourself? What does it feel like, to know you can do this?" Over time, Sunny came to expect that her dad would ask her at dinnertime, "What didn't go the way you wanted it to go today? How did you handle it?" She could collect experiences over her school day to share.

It was no surprise that sassy and outspoken Sunny, usually quite honest and accurate in her comments and observations, had witty parents with a sarcastic attitude—the very behavior they did not accept in their daughter.

"It is not okay for her to correct me," said the mother. "That is disrespectful."

"Really?" I said. "What did she correct?"

"She said I should not yell, and that I should look at her when I am talking to her."

"Oh." I responded, "She is telling you what you have taught her, but you don't like how she says it?"

Mom rolled her eyes, put her hands on her hips, and said sarcastically, "Yes, but it's not her place to correct me!"

I smiled and then rolled my eyes, put my hands on my hips—as I had seen Sunny do many times—and repeated mom's words in her tone, adding "I wonder where she learned that?"

Mom looked at me in surprise, and then burst into laughter.

"Yes," she said, "I know that I can be really sarcastic."

"Yes, and she copies you well. I wonder how you can also model politeness, patience, and a kinder tone. Then you can watch how she copies you, without correction."

To model resilience, parents must show their own ability to bend, not break, with the emotional wind. As discussed in the previous chapter, the parental trance is composed of learning to breathe, to take a moment out of the flow, and to feel good about one's own parenting. It consists of seeing the effect of yourself on others, of modeling for yourself, pausing, and imagining the young person being successful, and your comfort in your kids' success, even when your children are furious with you. Positive use of imagination and suggestion are fundamental hypnotic skills.

In the parental trance, unthinking, automatic expression of behavior conditioned from the parent's interactions with their own parents may also emerge. Observing this in ourselves, with mirroring from the clinician, allows us to revisit family rules, words, tone, and styles of discipline to foster more adaptive parenting; i.e., what works best for this child and this situation.

In this same family, the older daughter was sent to school detention for swearing in the playground. Where was she learning those words? She heard them at home when her parents fought. The swear words had become associated with worry about her parents and then, she discovered, with any worry. The clinician explained to the parents how their daughter connected worrying and swearing. In turn, they learned to tell her, if they were arguing, that sometimes adults argue in order to solve problems. They would invite her to suggest solutions, shifting the focus from worry to agency.

Most parents are well-meaning in their parenting efforts. Most children want to please their parents. We think of children as the most vulnerable members of a family, but of course, everyone is vulnerable in the family system. The parent and child can become a behavioral-feedback loop for one another. This loop can be constructive or destructive. When the movement and resonance between parents and children is viewed as a necessary rhythm of the parental dance, the clinicians can use family interactions to encourage processes in which each family member learns something that evokes calm, competence, and confidence.

Hypnosis can mindfully and intentionally change patterns of family interactions to evoke resilience and independence. Sassy Sunny, in the preceding example, avoided eye contact when she was determined not to listen to adults. The parents were taught to request eye contact, and to practice it at quiet times. They learned to do a progressive muscle relaxation technique to teach body awareness, first leading the child, and then having the child lead them through the exercise.

The parent's behavior says, "I change. So can you." This creates positive chain reactions by being intentional, not reactive.

When I (JHL) was a young mother, the phone rang just as my 15-month-old spilled his glass of purple grape juice all over the floor. I answered in a stressed tone (motherhood trance) and blurted out to the unsuspecting caller what had just happened. She said, "You can handle this. It is just spilled juice." Her simple words, calmly spoken, immediately calmed me and restored my perspective. It became a mantra for the many challenges of parenting yet to arise. "I can handle this": Hardiness and Self-Enhancement. "It's just spilled juice": Repressive Coping and Humor. Resilience.

It all begins at home. Developing resilience is a part of growth and development at its best. It is what we do with the social interactions of communication. Another mother said, when she called for an appointment, "I don't know if this is for me, to help me manage my daughter better—or for her, to help reduce her fears." It was, from our perspective, for both. What is hard for most parents is knowing when to engage (resonate) and when to disengage (trust the process).

Resilience Amidst Challenges

Thus far, we have presented rather typical examples that parents and children face. Of course, there may be extraordinary experiences that children and families endure. The child who grows up with a chronic illness or disability may flourish or wilt, due to influences even more significant than a parent's promotion of resilience and independence. For example, they may never be able to be fully independent. This changes not only the child, but the entire family system. The parents experience grief over the loss of the fulfillment of their dreams for their child. How effectively parents deal with this hardship becomes crucial to the health of the child.

A stress-resistant person is a resilient person. Flannery (1987) noted characteristics of stress-resistance which parallel those noted in resilience. There is a sense of personal control from an internal locus of control, developing specific skills for specific situations such as in Robinson performing his medical duties. There is task involvement, doing what a task requires with commitment. It is in the active stance in the face of adversity when Lulu is doing gymnastics. Robinson renews himself by participating in his son's bedtime routine: being the father he did not have. Lyle is challenged by the process of finding a friend and affirmation in his music.

How do we move a person in care toward independence and autonomy? In every parent-child dyad, every experience can have an "Oh, no!" side and the "Oh, yes!" side, i.e., reactive vs. adventurous. Those who tend toward anxiety, turn sympathetic arousal into "Oh, no!"

We can teach parents to express trust in the child's ability to learn, while quieting their innate protective tendencies (see Chapter 10). We can celebrate the parent who lets a toddler feed him- or herself and delights in the few times the spoon reaches the mouth. Competency and resilience are encouraged when the parent allows the child to choose his or her clothes, matching or not, so they learn for themselves what keeps them warm or cool, what earns them stares of disapproval or acceptance by their peers, and whether they care. It is in the behavior of the parent who does not wake the ten-year-old for school, but provides an alarm clock and helps the child figure out how to use it. In each of these and many other examples of parenting, it is possible to teach anticipation and faith rather than anxiety. A father in my (LIS) practice was in the habit of asking his school-aged children at dinner, and with delightful anticipation, "What didn't go as expected today? How did you fail?!" He wanted them to embrace the unexpected and the learning from it. His children must have gone into each day anticipating that they would need to have *something* to report to their father.

Our clinical hypnotic interactions across the age spectrum are aimed at encouraging resilience. The clinician's trance, as we have defined it, involves not only open and non-judgmental acceptance, but authentic beginner's-mind curiosity, as if to say, "I am really interested in how you work!" Such a stance instills faith and hope in the person in care. The use of disruptive skills, too, can provide challenges that test and strengthen the resilience of the client. In George's clinical encounter, Robinson's unexpected and strident response to George's problems prompts an emotional and angry response, for instance. Finally, open-ended integration skills with continuing questions and post-hypnotic wondering leaves it to the person in care to determine, both consciously and non-consciously, what they will do with what they have learned. Person-centered and evocative interactions evoke resilience.

Resilience beyond the Family

Thus far, we have defined resilience and placed its development in the actions of family systems. Parents most often lead this system and model behaviors that are resilient and promote independence. To become autonomous, with confidence to face and manage uncertainty, is the hoped-for outcome of effective parenting. Children develop coping mechanisms in part by virtue of who parents them, and how.

Pathology results when the parenting process fails, and so other participants in our nested system must assume the role of teaching and developing coping skills in children. The neighborhood, the city and its various institutions, the culture, the medical establishment, the nation, and so on: each may take a role in developing healthy adaptations in the young. Just as with the family system, they may do so more or less effectively. We may also note cultural experiences that cause children arousal and therefore reinforce fear: drills and practice lock downs for mass shootings at school; going through airport security; visiting the doctor for vaccinations. These are among the anticipated challenges of life's messy course, so we must ask, "At what level do we intervene?"

In schools. After Hurricane Katrina destroyed the homes of many children in New Orleans, a creative teacher helped her young students create a book about their experiences and their survival (Visser, 2006). Third graders illustrated their fears and losses in the form of three statements (Grotberg, 1995): their strengths ("I am …"), their abilities ("I …"), and their connections ("I have …"), illustrating how we build resilience from resources. A safe adult accepts and supports the children, evokes their emotional experiences, guides them to express these in pictures, and to find meaning in facing life's challenges.

In society. According to Elizabeth Rosenthal (2018), "The central mantra of 'innovation' in the past decade has been 'patient-centered, evidence-based care.' But," she asks, "isn't that the very essence of medicine? What other kind of medical care could there be?" (p. 5). Can medicine truly be client-centered, in this era of for-profit business, in which care receivers are consumers and doctors are commodities? There is a need for every clinician to be aware of failures in these systems, including the biomedical model, which we address more fully in Chapter 12. It is health care's duty to deal with the ills of society. At the very least, none of us should tolerate conditions that do not nourish healthy growth, says Stanley Greenspan (1997). This requires us to address social conditions that do not foster healthy growth, including, increasingly and appropriately, issues of hate as a health risk (ACP, 2017; Krieger, 2017; Shultz, Zakrison, & Galea, 2018).

In the newest guidelines on psychological practice with girls and women, there is an emphasis on resilience (Pappas, 2019). It is teaching that empowerment is more than an internal process like self-confidence or self-improvement. Empowerment includes resisting oppression; it is developed by taking action. This includes taking direct action to help others. Doing something meaningful helps a person with psychopathology. In other words, when we do something to help our clients, we model for them that positive action fosters hardiness and stress-resistance in us and in them. As such, psychology is recognizing its role in repairing an essential relational imperative, furthering adaptation. Resilient clinicians foster resilient clients.

Medicine and psychology are moving beyond symptom relief and recovery to prevention. Developing resilience is essentially preventive and starts from the earliest, prenatal, moments of the child-parent relationship. In the struggles inherent to growing up, in the push and pull of each developmental signpost, applying the hypnosis skills defined and described so far, encourages resilience in each of us.

Questions and Assignments for Further Discussion

1. Bonanno suggest four traits as factors in building resilience. Compare and contrast the significance of those factors in the resilience, or lack of it, of Robinson, Lulu, Lyle and Stevie.
2. Consider the story of Seligman's daughter in the opening of this chapter. Who has been a similar resilience-evoking role model in your life?
3. Discuss ways to influence the parental trance, and move caregivers from "Oh, no" to "Oh, yes" responses.

References

American College of Physicians (ACP). (2017). American College of Physicians says hate crimes are public health issue. Retrieved from www.acponline.org/acp-newsroom/american-college-of-physicians-says-hate-crimes-are-public-health-issue

Bonanno, G. (2004). Loss, trauma, and human resilience. *American Psychologist, 59*(1), 20–28. doi:10.1037/0003-066X.59.1.20

Flannery, R. B., Jr. (1987). From victim to survivor: A stress management approach in the treatment of learned helplessness. In B. A. van der Kolk (Ed.), *Psychological trauma* (pp. 217–232). Washington, DC: American Psychiatric Press.

Greenspan, S. (1997). *The growth of the mind.* Reading, MA: Perseus.

Grotberg, E. H. (1995). A guide to promoting resilience in children: Strengthening the human spirit. In *Early childhood development: Practice and reflections series, v. 8.* The Hague,

Netherlands: Bernard Van Leer Foundation. Retrieved from https://bibalex.org/baifa/Attachment/Documents/115519.pdf

Harvard University Center on the Developing Child (HUCDC). (2015). InBrief: The science of resilience [pdf]. https://46y5eh11fhgw3ve3ytpwxt9r-wpengine.netdna-ssl.com/wp-content/uploads/2015/05/InBrief-The-Science-of-Resilience.pdf

Krieger, N. (2017). Are hate crimes a public health issue? *BMJ Opinion.* Retrieved from https://blogs.bmj.com/bmj/2017/08/24/nancy-krieger-are-hate-crimes-a-public-health-issue/

Maier, S. F., & Seligman, M. E. (2016). Learned helplessness at fifty: Insights from neuroscience. *Psychological Review, 123*(4), 349–367. doi:10.1037/rev0000033

Masten, A. (2001). Ordinary magic. Resilience processes in development. *American Psychologist, 56*(3), 227–238. doi:10.1037//0003-066x.56.3.227

Pappas, S. (2019). Treating women and girls in context. *Monitor on Psychology, 50*(6), 26.

Rosenthal, E. (2018). *An American sickness.* New York, NY: Penguin Press.

Seligman, M. E. P. (2006). *Learned optimism: How to change your mind and your life.* New York, NY: Random House.

Rossi, E. L. (2002). *The psychobiology of gene expression: Neuroscience and neurogenesis in hypnosis and the healing arts.* New York, NY: W. W. Norton.

Shultz, J. M., Zakrison, T. L., & Galea, S. (2018). Hate and the health of populations. *The Milbank Quarterly, 97*(1), 11–15. doi:10.1111/1468-0009.12362 Retrieved from: www.milbank.org/quarterly/articles/hate-and-the-health-of-populations/

Visser, R. (2006). *The story of a storm: A story about Hurricane Katrina.* Brandon, MS: Quail Ridge Press.

Werner, E. E., & Smith, R. S. (2001). *Journeys from childhood to midlife: Risk, resilience, and recovery.* New York, NY: Cornell University Press.

Robinson's Story

Sweet Dreams

(Four years after the previous episode)

Robinson is driving home on the 690 this early darkening autumn evening. He is later than he intended to be. Driving a bit above the limit. He is feeling full. His mind is playing too rich and loud to listen to the radio. Driving home from conducting the first session in this season's "Mind-Body Health" seminar at the teaching hospital. Thirty or so young, interested psychology interns, internal medicine, pediatrics, and family medicine residents and fellows. A general surgery resident! All in scrubs or street clothes. All eager. More women and more varied skin tones on their intelligent faces than when he trained. Gives him hope.

He did what he had done before, but he keeps changing it because it keeps changing him. He asked them where they came from, where they imagined they were going—stressing that word "imagine"—what were their interests outside of health and care—not "medicine." He shared his origin story and his early childhood experiences in Haiti and Vodou. The patients he had known who had healed or not, died or not died, despite his allopathic efforts had naturally kindled his interest in our own innate abilities for healing in concert with our allopathic practices.

Yes. He left out the big scary man and the funeral and how little Esther lived until she died. He could no longer distinguish the memories from the changing dreams anyway.

He also left out the crisis in his marriage. How he became paralyzed with fear and shame at the prospect of becoming a father. How he got sick with worry. How he considered the impact of bridge abutments on 690. How he and Shani went to the couples therapist, Robyn Jackson. The hard trance work they did together there. The volume of tears shed. How that learning had transformed into their hypnotic preparation for a miraculous birth of their son, and his love for them, and how he believes they all saved him. Saved his life. How they still used those skills in their marriage, during waves of trouble. No. He decided to leave all that out. That inflection point. That bend in the river. These young people will find their way.

He went on to define hypnosis and trance, explaining that hypnosis was not the ritual of mind-control still portrayed in the media and by stage hypnotists, nor was it meditation, but a neurobiologically grounded set of interpersonal skills aimed at driving plasticity and so helping people help themselves to change their minds. He touched on some research from neuroimaging, electroencephalography, chronobiology, and psychophysiology to satisfy their needs for scientific rigor. He presented video of Milton Erickson and Ernest Rossi. He showed examples of the Comfort Talk® training from Elvira Lang, scenes of young people using hypnosis during and after their treatment for childhood cancers in Kuttner's *No Fears, No Tears Thirteen Years Later,* then everyday scenes of hypnosis in primary care from Sugarman's *Hypnosis in Pediatric Practice.* He listed his training from conferences, from workshops to supervision.

He closed by demonstrating a ten-minute trance interaction, explicitly using only the basic skills of kneading, wondering, wandering, and "congression" with a Family Medicine resident volunteer. She said she was interested because she'd been having trouble sleeping. While Robinson seemed simply to have an intensely interesting, kind of weird, and somewhat humorous conversation with her. She ended up losing track of time—after: "That was ten minutes! I thought it was, I don't know, like two!"—closing her eyes, and becoming unaware that all eyes in the room were focused on her. While he only asked her questions and gave no advice, she told Robinson that he had given her a lot to think about and that she was … really looking forward to getting some sleep tonight."

Robinson was never confident about these demonstrations so he was almost always surprised at how powerful they were. He felt much more in his element in his office. But he also supposed he set these young folks up for expectation with his preceding presentation and that was partly why it went so well. That and his gentle voice and accent.

Then the questions. The discussion went too long. They all wanted to learn more. The surgical resident, a woman from Puerto Rico, walked with him to his car asking about using hypnosis to improve postoperative outcomes.

So, he was feeling rich and grateful, speeding home in the Autumn evening when he saw the blue-red-blue-red-blue flashing lights in the rearview then heard the siren coming up behind him. Heart stopped. Chest tight. Blinker on. Slowing. Pulling over. A black man, in this car, in this neighborhood. As the police cruiser flew by, wailing, on its way. Elsewhere.

A deep breath. *Ahhh.* Release. Pulling back into traffic. Green bumper sticker on the van ahead reads: "Be the change you want to see in the world—M. Ghandi." Seen it so often before. Sad that it's trite. But wait. This time it reads differently. He always thought that it meant—that *Ghandi* meant—to be the outcome, act the way you want people to act. This time though, the third word stands out, highlighted, though it isn't, at least not on the bumper sticker. It reads, "Be the *change* ... " Then Robinson laughs out loud. He missed his exit.

Three hours later, Robinson quietly closes the door to four-year-old Elijah's room as he steps into the hall. Robinson does Elijah's evenings. Not a chore. A gift. Cleaning up from dinner together. Playing. Tonight with cars. Bath time, with toys in the tub until his little fingers pruned. Brushing teeth. Pajamas. Hug to Mama. Stories read from the *World Folktales* book. Papa does voices. Lights off. Imagining together what kind of dreams he wants to have tonight and report to Papa in the morning. Then a kiss. Then Robinson's heart nearly bursts, every night, when Elijah says, "I love you, Papa," before Robinson can tell Elijah so. "I love you, too. Sweet dreams."

Elijah takes after Robinson. Gentle features on his face, gentle demeanor. Robinson peeks into the little one's room. One-year-old Rose is asleep in her crib. Named for Robinson's mother, Roseline, she already looks like Shani, a princess, and not quiet about it. A force.

Shani is in bed reading, penciling notes on a yellow legal pad. Glasses perched. He smiles at her from the doorway.

"Anything you need from downstairs?"

She looks up. "No, baby. When are you coming to bed?"

"Soon, just want to check on tomorrow."

Robinson sits on his desk chair in his home office. He has taught himself to look at the list of who he is scheduled to see the next day at the office. It is not so much to find out how busy he will be or how the day will go. It is that he has learned that collecting them the night before sets them in motion in his mind. He finds that he can respond to them more carefully the next day. Sometimes he says, "You know, I was thinking about you," when he sees them.

His practice has changed. He has added two comfortable chairs across from each other in his private office at work. Like his partners still do, he used that room to do charting, correspondence, and get away. It is still that, but now he has made it his therapy room. Some drawings on the wall, one by Elijah. Potted plants. He meets with patients there to talk about how to change: pain, sleep, diet, anxiety. He meets monthly with Dr. Robyn Jackson for supervision. His partners refer some of their more difficult patients to him. He is challenged by this work. One of those referred is on tomorrow's list for a second visit. Robinson smiles to himself when he reads the first name: George.

Part IV

Looking Beyond

12 Changing Minds, Shifting Paradigms

Beyond the Biopsychosocial Model

Main Points

1. For good reason, Engel's biopsychosocial model has not been successfully integrated with the categorical/reductionist paradigm.
2. The critical shift is to move beyond diagnosis and treatment to evaluation of risks (e.g., genetic, environmental, cultural) and resources (e.g., intrinsic experiential, family system) to modulate those risks.
3. The skills of person-centered, developmentally-contextualized, and systems-based therapeutic hypnosis form the heart of clinical care in this paradigm.

> We use medicines about which we know little to treat diseases about which we know less in people about whom we know nothing.
>
> Source unknown

Welcome to our final chapter. Here we shift our view beyond the individual minds that we described in our book's first section; the second section's study of governing developmental forces; and the systemic relational effects covered in the third section. Our focus has so far been narrowed to the integration of these elements into the practice of therapeutic hypnosis with individuals and families, and the fictional lives in our stories. Now we move beyond those nested levels, to the health care paradigm. We take a bird's-eye view of the place of hypnosis within a more holistic future model.

We have been assembling disparate concepts and principles about our minds and how we change them, all under the inclusive banner of clinical hypnosis. We have also been explaining and exemplifying how we (LIS and JHL) have been learning to apply these ideas in clinical practice with hypnosis at its core. Through our stories, we have shown how hypnotic elements function outside of clinical settings, albeit in fictional lives. We reasoned at our book's beginning, in defense of our narratives, that literature, and art in general, serves to concentrate reality into more lucid portions. Consistent with our emphasis on the role of story-telling and *Narrative Listening* in healing, we intended our stories to provide impetus for healing our heath care model. Now we gather all of this conceptualized content and application into a vision of a new clinical construct.

We have discussed scientific paradigms. Here, we start with what we mean by the *health care* or *clinical* paradigm. For variety, we will use "model" and "construct" interchangeably with the word paradigm, though they are not quite the same things. You may recall that Kuhn showed that paradigms begin to break as they become more inconsistent with an emerging reality. So we will touch on how the current and dominant health care model is cracking —with increasing morbidity and mortality—under the pressure of its inadequacies. Then we will explore what we imagine as the next construct. Like all paradigm shifts, the subsequent one subsumes the phenomena of previous models. Of course, it also embraces the principles and practices that we have been promoting. The emerging paradigm holds promise for reducing and preventing the suffering accompanying the former construct, and opens possibilities for new knowledge, tools, and practices, and so brings hope.

We are aware that any paradigm, like any system, is really a defined portion of something larger, as we illustrated with our electric kettle in Chapter 3. Our understanding of health and the practice of care cannot be easily separated from the healthcare industry. Healthcare is an operation, or enactment, of the paradigm. It is reasonable to ask—like the chicken or the egg—which came first, the paradigm or the business model? The roots of the current paradigm, as outlined in our first two chapters, seem to have arisen from a pursuit of understanding health and disease, and more deeply, attempts to improve the human condition. But it is also apparent that the current dominant paradigm is good for business, to a point. The primacy of reliance on external therapies over innate abilities to heal both sells and self-perpetuates, until it doesn't. We contend that healthcare and its economic, political, and social ties serve primarily to interact with and entrench the current paradigm, keeping it in place until it stalls. So we must discuss some of that entrenchment.

However, we cannot detail the economic, political, nor cultural change—perhaps "revolution" is more apt—that will be required to accommodate the paradigm shift. Those aspects are beyond our expertise and, frankly, anyone's foresight. Evolution does not occur by vote, consensus, or mandate. One could argue, perhaps cynically, that those human practices too often serve only to begrudgingly yield to or delay progress. As evidence, we point to our current global interactions with the phenomenon of climate change. Here we attempt to conceive of what our evolving scientific understanding of who we are and how we work—our changing minds—means about how we can help each other increase our health. In so doing, we envision the enactment of theories, practices, and tools that are emerging into the next paradigm.

Before deepening our discussion of paradigmatic change, health, and care, let's use our *Narrative Thinking* and *Temporal Touring* principles to time-travel into the new paradigm. Imagine that it is early morning in a teaching hospital, and the medical students, residents, psychology interns, and other professional trainees are rushing around to collect the information that their supervising professionals will be asking them about, as they meet with and discuss the patients under their care. Vital signs, laboratory results, and candidate diagnostic conditions are collated and analyzed on devices linked to quantum computers. The process of differential diagnosis has become automated, along with the latest recommended, evidence-based, allopathic treatments for the patients' unique biogenetic nature. Even the patients can access this information. It is not the subject of clinical discussion or a challenge for the trainees. The supervising clinicians are going to ask questions like:

"How did you evaluate his risks?"

"What are her creative resources?"

"What are her most relevant trance experiences?"

"What are the types and relative impacts of his past traumas?"

"How well does she regulate emotion and upregulate T-Cell immune function?"

"What type of contemplative exercises correlate with his immediate early gene expression?" Imagine that the question the trainees most dread is, "How exactly did you ask the patient that question, and why?" Imagine what the training of these young clinicians is like.

What is a Health Care Paradigm?

We introduced Thomas Kuhn's classical thesis about the structure of scientific revolutions in Chapter 1. Kuhn purposed the term, "paradigm," to name the thing that a given scientific revolution changed. He defined paradigm as a set of beliefs, practices, and tools used in a scientific pursuit. A paradigm works because it creates a coherent way of describing and operating within the world. Paradigms shape relationships between elements of perceived reality, along with ways of using them in our lives. When, for example, we believe that health and illness are determined by a balance of specific types of spiritual forces, then we engage in practices (song, dance, prayer, and sacrifice) to enhance, appease, or dissuade those forces, by using appropriate tools (musical instruments, costumes, incense, sacrificial blades).

When the paradigm involves something as familiar as our health and its care —as compared to the more obscure subjects Kuhn discussed, such as X-rays and chemistry—it affects our daily life. We might pray or engage in other rituals on a daily basis to keep the spirits from making us sick. The paradigm also becomes a major factor in our economics, politics, and society at large.

Like a persuasive argument, when a paradigm is relevant and coherent, it becomes our unquestioned version of reality. Anything that occurs outside of the prevailing paradigm is unrealistic—or, as Kuhn put it, anomalous—meaning, literally, "unnamed." For example, all of the health care discussion in this book has concerned therapy using medications, procedures, surgery, or direct interpersonal communication. Even if we were to provide indisputable proof of non-local, energy-based, and spiritual healing processes, they would be regarded as unrealistic, because this idea is far beyond the current paradigm. The concepts of Pert's (1997) *Molecules of Emotion* and the mechanisms of both placebo effects and psychosocial genomics are more proximate, but just as paradigm-shaking. They require change in the tools, beliefs, and practices of health and care.

The Characteristics of the Dominant Paradigm

As we noted previously, Kuhn did not discuss health care, medicine, or psychology in his book. But there are clearly established beliefs, practices, and tools within health care that compose a paradigm and so, a mindset for providing and receiving treatment. The current foundations evolved primarily from physician and surgical practices. These have strongly influenced the practice of clinical psychology that came later and, as we have also noted in Chapter 2, the modern evolution of clinical hypnosis. We think that the attempt to pack these practices into a biomedical frame is part of the reason that the frame is breaking.

Much of the building of the current paradigm comes from systemic observation—of human behavior, and operative and autopsy findings—and scales down to activity detected under the electron microscope. In other words, the paradigm is based empirically, not philosophically. Since paradigms are, in part, determined by the tools used within them, the tools limit the paradigm. The current paradigm is also oriented pathologically. It was founded primarily on the study and treatment of disease rather than the study and support of health. So, rather than a "health care" or "medical" paradigm (since it has shaped clinical psychology), it is probably accurate to refer to a clinical paradigm as the basis for how we interact with people who come for care.

First, the current clinical paradigm is necessarily and proficiently reductionistic. It is founded on the belief that health and illness can best be explained and affected at the smallest, usually molecular, level. This orientation, along with the tools and techniques that operationalize it, have driven marvelous progress in the last century, from the discoveries of insulin and antibiotics, to customized immunotherapy and transplantation. In part due to this reductionist orientation, the model tends to be categorical. We tend to think in terms of and employ discrete embodied subsystems—immune, neurologic, musculoskeletal, gastrointestinal—as if they operated independently. The power and accomplishments of this categorical reductionism tend to blind us to the systemic interactions, and complexity within the embodied mind, that we described in our opening chapters.

The dominant paradigm is materialistic. That is, in medical settings, its transactions involve substances, procedures, and products that are designed to correct (e.g., surgical repair), replace (e.g., implanted cardiac valves, joints; hormone replacement), activate (e.g., psychostimulants, immunizations), and suppress (e.g., cancer chemotherapy, immunosuppression). To varying extents, this materialism has been extended to psychotherapy. The products are protocols, sometimes manualized, designed to create behavioral, cognitive, or emotional change. Chief among these are cognitive behavioral therapy, protocols for exposure and response prevention and, for people with developmental and behavioral problems, applied behavioral analysis.

Research techniques have contributed to this materialism, because research requires consistent variables. Additionally, the shorter, faster, and easier the protocols—so that anyone can administer them—the more they are valued. While these are necessarily interactive with, and ideally responsive to, the proclivities of the patient, our experience is that they tend to be used in a prescriptive and formulaic fashion. Like the medical examples (e.g., knee replacement, pharmacologic management of high blood pressure), they tend to be algorithm-driven and problem- or diagnosis-based more than person-centered.

The materialism of the dominant paradigm extends to a factory model of care delivery, whether intentionally or accidentally. It reflects the same production-line processes that originated in modern business and now can be found in education: i.e., faster, more productive, and more cost-effective, in order to maximize profits and outcomes. Unfortunately, the latter two do not usually correlate directly, especially in the long term. This model works better with robots than humans. Patients and clients often feel that they are moving through an automated process when they receive assessment and treatment. This depersonalized process diminishes care.

Finally, and most importantly for our thesis, the dominant clinical paradigm is allopathic: "allo-" referring to non-self, as compared to "auto-" for self. Generally, this means it relies on externally-applied treatments: medicines, surgical procedures, and formalized/manualized techniques and protocols for psychological therapies. Externally-derived treatment is a rational extension of an empirical, pathological, reductionist, and categorical perspective of heath and disease. It asks: Since we can observe a specific destructive process giving rise to disease in specific tissue types or organ systems, what do we do to fix it? As a curious consequence, for example, we tend to treat drug effects with drugs.

Cracks in the Paradigm.

From vaccination to synthetic organs, the 150-year hegemony of our empirical, pathological, reductionist, categorical, materialistic, and allopathic clinical paradigm has driven progress in reducing disease, preserving and prolonging life, and expanding our knowledge of how we work, perhaps more expansively than any other period of human existence. It has probably transformed us more profoundly than the last century of advances in transportation or the last 50 years of growth in technological communication and computing. Certainly, it has changed our health and disease narratives and their practices. Despite abundant evidence to the contrary (see Kirsch, 2009), many still refer to emotional and cognitive struggles as a "chemical imbalance," for example.

Over this same time, there have been increasing calls for what others have called "paradigm change" to expand the dominant construct. There have been appeals to broaden the range of therapeutic interventions to emphasize various complementary practices such as dietary change, meditation, inclusion of naturopathic, herbal, homeopathic, traditional Chinese medicine and Ayurvedic practices, philosophies, and therapies. This movement gave rise to the establishment of the National Center for Complementary and Alternative Medicine at the US National Institutes of Health in 1998. The name was changed to the National Institute for Integrative Health in 2014, to recognize inclusion and prevention (NIH, n.d.). Other appeals for paradigm change have aimed to deepen the basis for or application of recognized interventions. Evidence-based medicine has been deemed "paradigm-changing" (EBMWG, 1992). The shift was based on the emergence of increasingly sophisticated methods for performing well-controlled clinical trials that yielded results different from older and more subjective bases—"clinical experience" and anecdote—for clinical decision-making. The current drive toward gene-based "personalized medicine," in which pharmacotherapy is tailored to individual genotype, has also been heralded as paradigmatic. Within clinical psychology, the clarion call of evidenced-based interventions, especially as they compete for the same primacy as medicine, is leaving out uncontrollable variables, such as our individual uniqueness. Is it any surprise that people increasingly voice dissatisfaction with the very caregivers to whom they once turned?

These persistent calls and proposals for paradigm change are symptomatic of ferment throughout the conservative core and at the fringes of the prevailing allopathic model. They speak to phenomena and experiences that the biomedical model does not, or seems unwilling to, consider: spontaneous healing and placebo effects, for example. Often these are examples of exceptions to the rule in individual patients. But each of us is an exception to some rules. Most of us were not participants in any of the research used as a basis for our treatment. This reveals a fundamental gap between health care research and clinical care, a divergence that is intrinsic to the prevailing allopathic paradigm. While the application of well-controlled and population-based outcome research is likely to fulfill the greater good of public health, the same knowledge applied to an individual is problematic. As Tonelli (1998) notes in his critique of evidence-based medicine, "To the extent that relevant differences between individuals cannot be made explicit and quantified, an epistemological gap between research and practice must remain" (p. 1236).

A new health care paradigm and its constituent science must account for the infinite complexity of the individual.

In the half-century years since Kuhn repurposed it, "paradigm" has been an overused term, particularly in health care, where Kuhn never placed it. There does not appear a clear boundary between a profound paradigmatic change and what constitutes merely a new fiefdom or brand. Levin (2017) argues, in his thoughtful paper on a plan for health care paradigm change, that "What is being called a new paradigm may be more an old paradigm in a new wrapper [as compared to] … a thirst to search for and apply genuinely revolutionary knowledge" (p. 52)—for all of these movements are anchored within the dualistic, allopathic model. Returning to Levin (2017),

> All the contingencies of the old paradigm are manifest: the conceptual segregation of healer and healee; the assumption of informational hegemony on the part of the physician; the definition of a healing agent as *thing* given *by* an authority figure *to* a passive recipient.
>
> (p. 51, italics original)

Health care is necessarily relational and collaborative, even when those qualities are being ignored. How the prescription is received is at least as important as what it is for. Prescribing a meditative practice, a plant-based/whole-food diet, an Ayurvedic mixture, or all of these, to normalize high blood pressure in a given patient may well be unorthodox, welcome, and even beneficial, but is it paradigm-busting?

Kuhn posited that persistent anomalies acted as the skirmishes heralding revolutionary paradigm change. Anomalies are those phenomena or behaviors that can neither be ignored nor explained within the prevailing paradigm. They seem supernatural; ghosts in the machine, as mentioned in Chapter 3. They required new knowledge and a frame-shift to accommodate them. Here, we select three such anomalous issues, among many, to illustrate the cracking paradigm: pain treatment, diagnostic non-reality, and placebo research.

Treating Pain

The allopathic treatment of pain is a prime example of the limits and cost of a reductionist and materialist clinical paradigm. Pain—an experience created by the embodied mind—is a signal. It warns of actual or potential injury, though not necessarily mere injury to body tissues. In a real sense, pain is the embodied mind's engram for struggle, and for the process of healing. Pain can characterize Stage 2, Incubation, of Rossi's four-stage model of creative synthesis. A little boy with recurrent pain due to osteogenesis imperfecta (a genetic disease referred to as brittle bone disease), and who was fond of his fleet of toy construction vehicles, referred to pain as, "Guys at work repairing roads. You have to be careful and let them fix it." In short, pain has purpose. How we work through pain is one significant way that we learn to heal.

Pain is also multidimensional, with wide distribution of pain-related sites in our brains, each coordinating different aspects of painful experience: somatosensory, emotional, associative, relational, and cognitive. In identifying this Jensen (2011a, 2011b)) described how therapeutic communication can alleviate pain, by using language directed at different functional sites. While primarily a central nervous system experience, pain is embodied, bidirectionally. Central and autonomic nervous system processes can manifest as somatic pain, and chronic somatic pain can result in changes in the cerebral cortex. Phantom limb pain is associated with trauma, indicating that the psychosocial context of amputation affects the biology of its encoding (Flor, Nikolajsen, & Jensen, 2006). Pain is also relational. We and our primate cousins are "hard-wired," via systems such as Von Economo neurons (Butti, Santos, Uppal, & Hof, 2013), to connect somatosensory information to social-seeking, when in pain. Thus, we have evolved the sensory perception of pain into an intricate whole-organism and sociocultural—or biopsychosocial—experience.

Many clinicians are asked by their patients with complex pain if it is "all in my mind?" The answer must be, "Yes!" All pain, from briefly episodic to chronic, is fully and intricately in our minds. Therefore it is highly amenable to, and requiring of, multidisciplinary strategies (hypnosis, exercise, diet, creative expression, manipulation, and even medication) for change. We must carefully help those little repair guys fix it—whatever "it" is—and grow through the experience.

We merely touch on this rich complexity in order to contrast it with the reductionist take on pain treatment under the prevailing clinical paradigm. For the most part, we have become pain intolerant. We treat pain by chemical dissociation. While the history and detailed pharmacokinetics of medical analgesia is beyond the scope of this book, let it suffice that it has devolved into the use of polypharmacy. We primarily use non-steroidal anti-inflammatory drugs, acetaminophen (paracetamol), and opioids, at a cost of $560–635 billion annually (Tick et al., 2018). Additionally, we use other drugs to treat the side effects these painkillers cause (e.g., gastric erosion, esophagitis), along with pharmacological treatment of opioid addiction. Further, we use drugs to dissociate from the experience, meaning, and lessons of pain. With chronic pain, medication becomes the problem. Regular users of non-opioid medications for pain develop rebound pain phenomena (Lynch & Watson, 2006).

Opioids, in particular, directly co-opt and overpower the dopamine-opiate (want-reward) positive feedback loop (see Chapter 3). They fundamentally impair our tolerance for discomfort (the dopaminergic "want" system) and generate craving for activation of our opiate receptors (the opiate "reward"). A journalist interviewed a man who was addicted to opiates, first prescribed after back surgery. He intricately detailed his daily work of obtaining and processing pills, so that he could inject himself. The reporter asked, "So you do all of this to relieve your pain?" He replied, "Hell, no. I still have pain. I do this just to feel normal." Our experience aligns with this anecdote. When allowed to spiral, eventually the respiratory depressant effect of the opioids overrides everything and, like Stevie, we succumb. This is the ultimate form of dissociation.

The opioid use epidemic that is currently raging in the US is a direct and lethal manifestation of our prevailing health care paradigm. It is thoroughly and regularly documented, including its origins within the healthcare industry. According to the Centers for Disease Control and Prevention (CDC, 2018, p. 14), 11,824,000 people reported abusing opioids nationwide in 2016. Of these, 78,840 received emergency department treatment for overdose (p. 19) and 42,249 died (p. 21). These numbers are likely to be underestimates, because such factors as homelessness and use of illicit synthetic opioids make valid numbers difficult to attain. An estimated 207,584 doses of naloxone were used in 2016, in an attempt to reverse opioid overdoses in the US (Cash et al., 2018). While life-saving, the emphasis on acute drug reversal is like providing fire-extinguishers to people, in order to help those who accidentally burn down their home because they use fireplaces and cook stoves during cold weather. There is emerging evidence that the easy availability of naloxone is correlating with an increase in opioid over-dosage (Doleac & Mukherjee, 2019). As much as pharmaceutical manufacturers, distributors, and governmental entities may be liable, our culture is complicit, to the extent that we rely on medication primarily to "not feel."

Pain is an embodied and inevitable life experience that can be utilized for growth. Clearly, the inability of our empirical, pathological, reductionist, categorical, materialistic, and allopathic clinical model to preventively address the occurrence of pain in our lives is a gaping crack in paradigm. And the race is on, with grant money waiting, for "better" drugs to treat pain.

Diagnostic Non-Reality

The hegemony and reification of diagnoses poses another costly inconsistency in the prevailing paradigm. The dominant clinical paradigm is operationalized through the formalized, differential process of "making the diagnosis." Diagnosis (literally meaning to "know through") is a model for the disease condition affecting a person. The value of diagnoses derived from the notions that (1) measurable and predictable biological factors led to pathological states that could be modeled ("diagnosed") as a culmination of a destructive process or processes; (2) different individuals with common diagnoses therefore manifested common pathophysiology, and thus could and should be treated the same; and (3) to optimize reproducibility and results, prescriptive therapies ought to be delivered in a consistent, formalized, and structured manner. In theory, and certainly within the paradigm, this standard of accurate diagnosis and refined treatment, based upon measurable, evidence-based outcomes, should drive improvement in care. There is no doubt that this paradigm markedly improved modern health and care globally from where it started in the mid-19th century. But diagnoses have also become the "coin of the realm." They are the bases for billing, reimbursement for services, disease classification, and the organization of clinical research. As such, they have become entities with power, hence reified.

But in less than a century, diagnoses and the specificity of disease definition have become social entities that codify and legitimize an increasing variety of behaviors, as well as justifying treatment. These include attention deficit disorder, chronic fatigue syndromes, premenstrual syndrome, road rage, and a variety of behavioral addictions (gambling, sex). Disease-labeling within the prevailing paradigm brings behaviors and characteristics into the paradigm for treatment and study. Diagnostic entities no longer need a clinical-pathologic grounding in the form of laboratory or etiological agent to be realized. "Getting a diagnosis" is sufficient for inclusion into the group, entering social discourse, and deserving treatment. In his compellingly titled essay, "The Tyranny of Diagnosis: Specific Entities and Individual Experience," Rosenberg (2002) notes,

> Philosophers and sociologists of knowledge have voiced an abundance of opinions regarding their epistemological and ontological status, but to the historian, disease entities have become indisputable social actors, real inasmuch as we have believed in them and acted individually and collectively on those beliefs.
>
> (p. 240)

There are two aspects of the power of diagnostic reality that represent cracks in the dominant paradigm. The first is the devaluation and objectification of the individual, and individual differences. The second is that, with increasing definition and specificity, the utility of diagnosis itself begins to break down.

There is an obvious social benefit of having a diagnosis: one is not alone. The affliction under this label is not as alienating. Others share it. On the other hand, once diagnosed, the disease, and so part of the person who has it, becomes subject to bureaucratic management. We must fit ourselves to the disease in order to obtain care. Even more obviously, care is directed toward the disease, not the person. In different ways, this pressure to conform to a diagnostic template is **iatrogenic**, as is illustrated in both George's and Stevie's stories. Indeed, it seems that the pressure of to conform to some type of template or form, in part generated by his/her therapist, is Stevie's central anguish. As Rosenberg (2002) writes, in paradigmatic terms:

> In this sense, a repertoire of disease categories becomes a mediating interface between and among parts of the system. Once articulated, such bureaucratic categories cannot help but exert a variety of substantive effects on individuals and institutional relationships … Thus a poor or homeless person becomes visible to the health care system when diagnosed with an acute ailment but then returns to invisibility once that episode has been managed. It is almost as though the disease, not its victim, justifies treatment. Thus, the employment of seemingly objective disease categories

obscures the conflicted relationships among medicine's moral, technical, and market identities.

(pp. 254–255)

Another aspect of the mediating force of diagnosis within the paradigm is generated from the increasing ability of technology to detect disease antecedents. The detection of elevated blood pressure, blood cholesterol levels, hemoglobin A1c percentages, prostate-specific antigen, lower bone densities, and family histories and genetic markers for depression or bipolar disorder, to name only a few, constitute potential risk factors for pathologically-based diseases but are not themselves symptom-generating or impairing. Some new diagnostic entities link technology to symptoms but offer no solution. George's "REM Sleep Disorder" is one of these. But, once articulated and propagated within the culture as "**proto-diseases**," these conditions take on an emotional reality as entities, as Rosenberg writes, "occupying a position somewhere between warning signal and pathology" (2002, p. 254). Thus, the proliferation of reductionist disease typing and subcategorization, fueled by ever-more-precise technology, creates a **nosological iatrogenesis**. A state of health is impossible if everyone has got something.

This reification of disease and diagnosis, empowering **nosology**, represents anomalous threats to the prevailing paradigm because diagnoses—and even the conceptualization of a disease process as something you can "have"—are models. They are not real. People are real. People are not merely containers for diseases or risk factors. We are enactors and/or preventers. The clinical paradigm is threatened when it is iatrogenic; in other words, when it degrades rather than preserves health. An experienced vocational education teacher told us that, when a student said they could not complete an assignment because of their attentional dysfunction or other diagnostic impairment, she would reply, "Well, what kind of person with [diagnosis] do you intend to be?" The construction of a new clinical paradigm must account for the power of the unique constellation of resources, whatever they may be, that each individual uses to heal.

Placebo Research

This leads us quite naturally to the exploration of those innate resources for healing that are the subject of the field of placebo-effect research. Placebos—purported biologically inert interventions ("sugar pills," sham surgery)—have increasingly been employed as experimental controls in laboratory and clinical research over the last half century. The valid use of such controls is one of the tenets of qualifying research for evidence-based medicine. When standard-of-care therapy, including surgical treatments such as internal mammary artery ligation for angina (Dimond, Kittle, & Crockett, 1960) and osteoarthritis of the knee (Moseley et al., 2002), provided no better outcomes, and worse outcomes when compared to sham surgery, placebo-researchers speculated that the vast majority of medical interventions over the history of care have been placebos: that is, biologically inert at best (Shapiro & Shapiro, 1997).

While the biological ability of say, fox lung, spider webs, mandrake root, or crocodile dung pessaries, may be questionable, their efficacy within the cultural, relational, and narrative context of their use were likely evocative enough of healing resources to activate genomic, physiological and, therefore, systemic effects within the embodied minds of the people to whom they were administered (Moerman, 2002; Shapiro & Shapiro, 1997). Hence, over the last three decades, serious, well-controlled research into the nature of these evoked effects has been undertaken by Fabrizio Benedetti and colleagues at the University of Turin, Ted Kaptchuk and Irving Kirsch at Harvard University, and Alia Crum's laboratory at Stanford University.

Placebo research does not study placebos as a comparator—the basis by which the effectiveness of a so-called "biologically active" substance or procedure is to be measured—in a pragmatic study of drug or procedural effects. Placebo research examines the biopsychosocial effects of the placebo itself, compared to no intervention at all. In other words, placebo research examines those innate biological processes that we enact in response to the expectation and conditioning of an allopathic intervention. As such, placebo research promises to reveal mechanisms of our embodied minds that operate outside of the allopathic paradigm. This research questions what we mean by "biological effect," since the color of pill, the method of administration, the relational context, and the narrative explanation surrounding the delivery of the placebo all have biological effects. The history of health care is a history of placebo effects.

The scope and history of this emerging and disruptive field of inquiry is beyond this book. Interested readers are urged to study the publications of the leaders named above, and in particular Kirsch's (2009) *The Emperor's New Drugs* and Benedetti's (2009) *Placebo Effects* for more information. Benedetti's book is a comprehensive delineation of placebo research methods and findings that is used as a course textbook. In Chapter 3, we discussed an example of one such finding in the mysterious mechanisms of expectation and conditioning with regard to Parkinson's Disease. We call them "ghosts in the machine," because they represent processes outside of our monistic and allopathic biomedical model. Other examples demonstrate the effects of beliefs, expectations, and mindsets on human physiology in clinical populations, including: pain (Tracey, 2010; Wager et al., 2004; Wager, Scott, & Zubieta, 2007), depression (Kirsch, 2009), high blood pressure (Gould, Davies, Mann, Altman, & Raftery, 1981), and irritable bowel syndrome (Kaptchuk et al., 2010) among others. Thus, the assumption that one is receiving a treatment (even when that treatment contains no active pharmacological substance) can elicit a healing response in the body.

This is true in non-clinical populations as well. For instance, it has been shown that mindsets influence biological response to ingestion of food, impact of exercise on health, and physical performance (Crum, Corbin, Brownell, & Salovey, 2011; Crum & Langer, 2007; Turnwald et al., 2018). These psychological variables do not emerge from the ether; rather, they are shaped by the social, narrative, and personal experiential contexts of the individual. The characteristics of physicians, features of a treatment, or the social settings, evoke different physiological changes in different individuals. This likely occurs via psychological intermediates (Buckalew & Coffield, 1982; Colloca & Benedetti, 2009; Crum, Phillips, Goyer, Akinola, & Higgins, 2016; Howe, Goyer, & Crum, 2017). Placebo research has revealed, and continues to reveal, the psychobiological mechanisms that validate the concept of the embodied mind.

The Entrenchment of the Allopathic Paradigm

Before we return to imagining the coming paradigm, we must consider the entrenchment of the current one. We are writing from within the United States, which leads in economically developed countries in per capita health care costs (with a three-trillion-dollar-per-year healthcare industry; Rosenthal, 2018) as a percentage of gross domestic product (GDP), and increasingly trails in life expectancy (OECD, 2019). So we are biased by the current influence of exorbitantly expensive pharmaceuticals, devices, and procedures; the political power of the Pharmaceutical Research and Manufacturers of America (PhRMA); the Medical Device and Manufacturer's Association (MDMA); and their collaboration with the for-profit healthcare insurance and hospital industries (Americas Health Insurance Plans, AHIP; American Hospital Association, AHA) to increase both our reliance upon and the escalating cost of medical and procedural fixes—meaning allopathic treatment—over the potentials of prevention and self-regulation. This machinery is operating during a fundamental national debate about whether access to our health and its security is a right—and a prerequisite to participating in a capitalist, free-market society—or a commodity, controlled from within that economic system. In short, the allopathic healthcare industry churns away profitably while the society considers whether to dismantle it … and suffers, all the while.

Rosenthal (2018), among many others (see Emanuel, 2014; Brill, 2015; Dentzer, 2018), has written a popular, well-researched, and detailed examination of the business of US Healthcare. It concludes with a series of practical recommendations for improving Healthcare and for self-advocacy within the system, including opening the US market to pharmaceuticals manufactured elsewhere, improving patient ownership of their health data, price calculators for procedures, and "Tools to Help You Figure Out Whether a Test or a Procedure is Really Necessary" (Appendix D, p. 352). Notably, the Harvard-trained physician-journalist structured the book in two parts that fit with the medical treatment of a patient—that patient being the business of Healthcare. Accordingly, in the first part, Rosenthal describes the emergence of component problems (the oppressive powers of insurance, hospitals, physician organizations, pharmaceuticals, conglomerates, etc.) as, "History of the Present Illness and Review of

Systems." She titles the second part, "Diagnosis and Treatment: Prescriptions for Taking Back our Healthcare." This example typifies efforts to change health and care from within the paradigm, using its current knowledge, tools, and practices. While valuable and indispensable for self-advocacy, from a systems perspective, this is like attempting to lift one's car off the ground from the driver's seat.

Government-sponsored Healthcare reform measures in the US have focused primarily on increasing access and, more recently, lowering the cost of its various established products. This is akin to attempting to reduce food insecurity and poor nutrition by increasing the availability of fast-food drive-throughs, instead of increasing access to fresh grains, fruits, vegetables, and community gardening. In other words, Healthcare cost and distribution reform has not changed what we mean by health or do about care.

In the end, we expect that the efforts to transform health and care will necessarily transcend Healthcare. A parallel can be found in the Human Genome Project (HGP). In 1988, the tools for unlocking and representing the human genome—the sum of our evolution, so far—were ready for the task. The US Congress agreed to fund the exploration, through the National Institutes of Health and Department of Energy, toward the ambitious goal first articulated by the US National Academy of Sciences:

> … determining the order, or "sequence," of all the bases in our genome's DNA; making maps that show the locations of genes for major sections of all our chromosomes; and producing what are called linkage maps, through which inherited traits (such as those for genetic disease) can be tracked over generations.
>
> (NHGRI, n.d.)

The HGP achieved its goal in 2003. In the process, and increasingly since, we have discovered that "The map is not the territory" (Korzybski, 1931). Specifically, we learned that genomics—the process of gene-expression, the turning on and off of the mapped genetic code—was at least as significant as the code itself. Further, we found that *intra*-generational, daily life experiences, from environmental toxin exposures to the variety of interpersonal interactions and life events that we have written about in this book, mark genes for expression or suppression. And there was another level of social and environmental interaction affecting the enactment of our genetic potential, involving aspects of our lives over which we have control: our diet, our emotional expression, our relationships, and how we repair our traumas. Hence, with the advent of epi-genetics, we have moved from the determinative dogma that "we are our genes," to learning we can, as Ernest Rossi (2004) writes, have "a discourse with our genes."

In a similar way, we consider that we are reaching the limits of the pills and processes of allopathic care, both in medicine and psychology. We begin to recognize that brain care and body care cannot really be functionally separated, any more than can be DNA base-pairs from their expression. Changing the cost-structure for a medication, or shifting patients from the emergency department to the clinic, has little to do with how they use what they receive. So, while acknowledging that paradigms are but parts and products of our societal evolution, we nevertheless will keep to this conceptual level. We believe and expect that our rapidly evolving understanding of how we grow and heal our embodied minds will be a driving force in changing health and care.

Beyond the Biopsychosocial Model: Risks and Resources

In our first chapter, we wrote about how George Engel attempted to expand the inputs into the therapeutic domain beyond history, symptoms, and signs, to include the psychological and social significance of a given person's experience within their culture. The biopsychosocial model also pushed the allopathic paradigm to consider a broader range of treatment outcomes: the effects of the treatment on the person's sense of themselves, and on their relationships within their family and community. (Engel, 1977).

In our first chapter, we juxtaposed Engel's biopsychosocial provocation with Kuhn's examination of paradigm change through scientific revolution. We did this because Engel's model cannot be operationalized within the current clinical paradigm. How would one factor in the complexity of individual experience—innate, distinctive phenomena within one's embodied mind, from gene-expression to behavior—while still grouping people and mediating their treatment through diagnostic entities? How can we promote and evoke health and hope when the dominant materialistic, production-line practice is prescribing medication, products, and lifestyle practices in the face of increasing proto-diseases (Rosenberg, 2002). Everybody has some diagnosis. "Healthy" is not a diagnostic code. We think that a shift must occur.

Let's start by imagining that the diagnosis of specific, pathologically based disease entities (colon cancer, diabetes, dementia) occur outside bracketed regions on a spectrum. The measures within those bracketed regions are labelled as "low risk." When my (LIS) blood pressure is maintained over the day within the low-risk range for my age, that manifestation of my embodied mind is healthy. The same could be said for my weight, the amount of sleep I get, my exercise stamina, the make-up of my gastrointestinal microbiome, my genomic expression of various cancer genes, my immune surveillance of those nefarious gene-products, my mood, the quality of my emotional expression, and my reality-testing. There are—or will be soon—countless, evolving, and likely infinitely-testable aspects of my functioning, available for examination. In fact, Rossi and his colleagues have proposed an "International Psycho-Social and Cultural Bioinformatics" database to house such items (Rossi, Rossi, Yount, Cozzolino, & Iannotti, 2006). To narrow it down, it would probably be best to use my family history and some genetic testing, to determine which of these many parameters pose a risk of moving outside of the "low-risk" bracket. We should also include some basic lifestyle issues; for example, my father died from colon cancer, so diet, alcohol intake, and smoking are also relevant factors. We'll simply call these my risks. As long as I keep them within the brackets (for example, not smoking at all), they are low. My job is to keep them there.

How do I do that? I do that by developing my resources. There are a lot of them, and we don't know their limits. Resources are innate, relational, and material. My innate resources are the most accessible of these. They are my abilities to engage with and control my embodied mind. How do I already know how to lower my blood pressure, sleep well, eat more plant-based foods, express my strongest emotions productively? More importantly, how am I best creative? How do I know how to change my mind? How do I "go plastic"? What are my best trances? What are my hypnotic abilities? These are the resources I can call on, to apply to keeping my risks within the low range. At his second visit with Robinson, George brings those resources out: his love of literature and the power of writing, his love for his family and identifying as a person who responsibly fixes things. Lyle's musical synthesis is how he exercises his plasticity. For Lulu, it is her experience of being a person of the world, and what it takes to create her own story and her own self. For Stevie, it was not having to be formed yet, to be okay feeling indeterminant. For Robinson, it is the practice of hypnosis and the clinician's trance … as well as the gift of being a father and husband.

Ideally, I learned to use these resources when I was little because, in our idealized imagining of this paradigm, my parents and doctors taught me that it was good to use my breathing and imagination whenever I got hurt, or was scared, or found it hard to go to sleep. Relational resources are those people —our family, our teachers, our clinicians, and counselors—who responsibly teach us about, and evoke within us, our abilities to cultivate and apply our trances. A child whose airways are reactive, and meets criteria for asthma, is taught how to change autonomic balance with breathing, changing heart rate variability, and imagining powerful and positive emotional experiences of her own making. She may also use inhaled medication: a material resource. When it was prescribed, the doctor provided a narrative to imagine how it works, so she could "make it work better." I (LIS) once casually asked a child how her medicine was working. She responded, somewhat indignantly, "It doesn't work on its own, you know! You have to make it work."

As an adult, I use all of those resources to minimize my risks of high blood pressure and colon cancer by motivating myself toward a plant-based diet, moderating alcohol, not smoking, engaging in regular, intensive exercise, taking breaks, and having regular colonoscopies, as well as imagining my immune surveillance being extraordinarily vigilant. I can also imagine that my father is grateful that I am doing better than he did. Why not? As that boy said in Chapter 4, "Maybe how I imagine it works is really how it works."

Eventually, inevitably, my risk factors will move beyond some brackets, and part of my embodied mind will meet criteria for a disease-specific diagnosis. But it will not be a "disease entity." How I, or you for that matter, come to meet criteria of a given diagnosis will be unique: the interaction of risks, gene expression, aging, mindset, and so many other yet-to-be-discovered factors. The question will not be, "What disease do you have?" but "How did you come to meet these criteria, and what do you already know to do about it?" With the help of skilled clinicians like Robinson and evocative, person-centered hypnotic techniques, we will struggle a bit more to learn from these challenges how to change pain and immune function, and cope with side effects of useful medication.

We are describing systems of daily living, by which we maximize our innate resources to minimize known and newly discovered risks to home-ostasis. Trance utilization—learning how to change our embodied minds with agility—is at the core of health and care. Meeting criteria for a specific disease is not a failure of innate resources, but a challenge to adapt, and deserving of relational and material support. But other or "allo-" resources, however powerful, are always adjunctive to the innate. We "have to make them work."

In such systems, technology expands to better detect risk factors and our abilities to modulate them. For example, if Jensen's work on the role of increasing low frequency EEG (theta and alpha) power (see Chapter 4) proves an indicator of brain plasticity (i.e. trance), then operant conditioning with EEG neurofeedback can be employed to intensify and deepen self- and **hetero-hypnosis** (Jensen, Adachi, & Hakiman, 2015; Jensen, Adachi, et al., 2015, 2016; Jensen, personal communication, 2019). Prescriptive protocols for how and what to imagine would be irrelevant. What matters will be whatever unique and highly personal way the person in care learns to generate that signal of increased theta activity. It is likely that other markers of plasticity, such as RNA micro-arrays of early gene-expression and changes in autonomic balance, can be combined to develop even more valid and multidimensional proxies.

Similarly, genetic risk surveillance, already and increasingly popular, can expand to examine genomic risk (how we live in such a way to enhance or suppress specific gene expression), which will allow us to monitor how well we are learning to use our genetic endowment healthfully. Again, we envision that this will not be done primarily by protocols in which users are told what to imagine, as much as by encouraging a given individual's embodied mind to "imagine how it really works."

Within this effort, there is huge potential for developing meaningful, wearable biosensors, and combining large amounts of real-time data in ways that tune to the needs of the user. There are still roles for procedures and pharmaceuticals, but even larger roles for determining their specific effects on individuals. Placebo research serves to teach us what is possible for us to do for ourselves.

Imagine the powerful influence of a clinical culture that begins interactions by exploring and valuing your innate resources: asking "What do you already know how to do?" in order to decrease pain, safely express anger and disappointment, and increase immunological resilience. Moreover, imagine that clinicians have been trained to teach you how to explore and expand those abilities. Imagine that they routinely request and update a list of your social resources and their relative value: "Who do you turn to for …?" Imagine that they regularly and sensitively noted and revised your responses to queries about trauma, monitoring not just your words but the qualities of your nonverbal communication. Imagine that such approaches were consistent with data shared across the range of healthcare (the industry), from well-child visit to preoperative evaluation. Imagine that this is what you have come to expect, how you have become conditioned to encounter care. How would that affect your expectations of treatment, beyond, or perhaps instead of, receiving a prescription? Wouldn't those encounters be expressions of the healer's art?

Paradigm change starts with outlandish, even heretical ideas. No one is intelligent or prescient enough to really predict the next paradigm in any science. We know that the current construct costs too much and is achieving diminishing results. We know that we underutilize our capacity for self-regulating our embodied minds at all levels in our current model. We do know that it costs less to use what we already own than to buy stuff. And we know that we are developing an increasing technological facility to measure inputs and outcomes of our innate abilities.

We can imagine that this kind of change is possible. We know that it is necessary. We wrote this book so that you could imagine it, too. As a matter of fact, before you finish reading this chapter, we invite you to do just that. Let your mind wander to a future, idealized health care setting in which your unique innate abilities to regulate inflammation, metabolism, mood, and comfort are valued and sometimes enhanced by medication and procedures. What is the environment like? How do people interact with you? Imagine you are a clinician-collaborator in this setting. How does it feel to be joining in this way with those in your care? Give yourself as long as you like to wander through these scenarios, taking everything in. Then we can wonder together about how we are going to make it happen.

Questions and Assignments for Further Discussion

1. Assuming this more holistic and person-centered paradigm will emerge, speculate on how and in what sector that transformation will begin and why. Will it be among patients and customers? Clinical professionals? Government? The healthcare industry?

2. The emerging model discussed in this chapter and illustrated through the book seems to blur distinctions between the roles of clinical psychologists (and other non-physician mental health care providers) and physicians. Discuss whether and in what ways the clinical roles and competencies of these professions will need change in the new paradigm.
3. Choose a condition requiring biomedical care (e.g., cancer, degenerative arthritis of the knee, insulin-resistant diabetes) and track how it might be evaluated and treated differently in the proposed paradigm than the current one? Does it really require a paradigm change or just integration of new methods?

References

Benedetti, F. (2009). *Placebo effects* (2nd ed.). Oxford, UK: Oxford University Press.

Brill, S. (2015). *America's bitter pill: Money, politics, backroom deals, and the fight to fix our broken healthcare system*. New York, NY: Random House.

Buckalew, L. W., & Coffield, K. E. (1982). An investigation of drug expectancy as a function of capsule color and size and preparation form. *Journal of Clinical Psychopharmacology, 2*(4), 245–248. doi:10.1097/00004714-198208000-00003

Butti, C., Santos, M., Uppal, N., & Hof, P. R. (2013). Von Economo neurons: Clinical and evolutionary perspectives. *Cortex, 49*(1), 312–326. doi:10.1016/j.cortex.2011.10.004

Cash, R. E., Kinsman, J., Crowe, R. P., Rivard, M. K., Faul, M., & Panchal, A. R. (2018). Naloxone administration frequency during emergency medical service events — United States, 2012–2016. *Morbidity and Mortality Weekly Report, 67*, 850–853. doi:10.15585/mmwr.mm6731a2

Colloca, L., & Benedetti, F. (2009). Placebo analgesia induced by social observational learning. *Pain, 144*(1), 28–34. doi:10.1016/j.pain.2009.01.033

Crum, A. J., Corbin, W. R., Brownell, K. D., & Salovey, P. (2011). Mind over milkshakes: Mindsets, not just nutrients, determine ghrelin response. *Health Psychology, 30*(4), 424–429. doi:10.1037/a0023467 Retrieved from: www.dishlab.org/pubs/Crum%202011.pdf

Crum, A. J., & Langer, E. J. (2007). Mind-set matters: Exercise and the placebo effect. *Psychological Science, 18*(2), 165–171. doi:10.1111/j.1467-9280.2007.01867.x

Crum, A. J., Phillips, D. J., Goyer, J. P., Akinola, M., & Higgins, E. T. (2016). Transforming water: Social influence moderates psychological, physiological, and functional response to a placebo product. *PLoSONE, 11*(11), e0167121. doi:10.1371/journal.pone.0167121

Dentzer, S. (2018). *Health care without walls: A road map for reinventing U.S. Health Care*. Independently published. Boston, MA: Network for Excellence in Health Innovation.

Dimond, E. G., Kittle, C. F., & Crockett, J. E. (1960). Comparison of internal mammary artery ligation and sham operation for angina pectoris. *American Journal of Cardiology*, *5*, 483–486. doi:10.1016/0002-9149(60)90105-3

Doleac, J. L., & Mukherjee, A. (2019). The moral hazard of lifesaving innovations: Naloxone access, opioid abuse, and crime. Social Science Research Network. doi:10.2139/ssrn.3135264. Retrieved from https://papers.ssrn.com/sol3/papers.cfm?abstract_id=3135264

Emanuel, E. J. (2014). *Reinventing American health care: How the Affordable Care Act will improve our terribly complex, blatantly unjust, outrageously expensive, grossly inefficient, error prone system.* New York, NY: PublicAffairs.

Engel, G. L. (1977). The need for a new medical model: A challenge for biomedicine. *Science*, *196*(4286), 129–136. doi:10.1126/science.847460

Evidence-Based Medicine Working Group (EBMWG). (1992). Evidence-based medicine: A new approach to teaching the practice of medicine. *Journal of the American Medical Association*, *268*(17), 2420–2425. doi:10.1001/jama.1992.03490170092032

Flor, H., Nikolajsen, L., & Jensen, T. S. (2006). Phantom limb pain: A case of maladaptive CNS plasticity? *Nature Reviews Neuroscience*, *7*, 873–881. doi:10.1038/nrn1991

Gordon, D. (2017). *Therapeutic metaphors: Helping others through the looking glass.* Tucson, AZ: David Gordon. ISBN 9871521227626.

Gould, B. A., Mann, S., Davies, A. B., Altman, D. G., & Raftery, E. B. (1981). Does placebo lower blood-pressure? *Lancet*, *318*(8260-61), 1377–1381. doi:10.1016/s0140-6736(81)92799-9

Howe, L. C., Goyer, J. P., & Crum, A. J. (2017). Harnessing the placebo effect: Exploring the influence of physician characteristics on placebo response. *Health Psychology*, *36*(11), 1074–1082. doi:10.1037/hea0000499

Jensen, M. P. (2011a). The neurophysiology of pain perception and hypnotic analgesia: Implications for clinical practice. *American Journal of Clinical Hypnosis*, *51*(2), 123–148. doi:10.1080/00029157.2008.10401654

Jensen, M. P. (2011b). *Hypnosis for chronic pain management.* New York, NY: Oxford.

Jensen, M. P. (2019, September). Personal communication.

Jensen, M. P., Adachi, T., & Hakiman, S. (2015). Brain oscillations, hypnosis, and hypnotizability. *American Journal of Clinical Hypnosis*, *57*, 230–253. doi:10.1080/00029157.2014.976786

Jensen, M. P., Adachi, T., Tomé-Pires, C., Lee, J., Osman, Z. J., & Miró, J. (2015). Mechanisms of hypnosis: Towards the development of a biopsychosocial model. *International Journal of Clinical and Experimental Hypnosis*, *63*, 34–75. doi:10.1080/00207144.2014.961875

Jensen, M. P., Gianas, A., George, H. R., Sherlin, L. H., Kraft, G. H., & Ehde, D. M. (2016). Use of neurofeedback to enhance response to hypnotic analgesia in individuals with multiple sclerosis. *International Journal of Clinical and Experimental Hypnosis*, *64*, 1–23. doi:10.1080/00207144.2015.1099400

Kaptchuk, T. J., Friedlander, E., Kelley, J. M., Sanchez, M. N., Kokkotou, E., Singer, J. P., … Lembo, A. J. (2010). Placebos without deception: A randomized controlled trial in irritable bowel syndrome. *PLoSONE*, *5*(12), e15591. doi:10.1371/journal.pone.0015591 Retrieved from: https://journals.plos.org/plosone/article/file?id=10.1371/journal.pone.0015591&type=printable

Kirsch, I. (2009). *The emperor's new drugs: Exploding the antidepressant myth.* New York, NY: Random House.

Korzybski, A. (1931). A non-Aristotelian system and its necessity for rigour in mathematics and physics. Proceedings of the American Association for the Advancement of Science in New Orleans, LA, December 28, 1931. Retrieved from https://pdfs.semanticscholar.org/c291/61b8e0971844c0919ea070f6868d28df7adf.pdf?_ga=2.111697860.1131525434.1568904392-734417185.1568904392

Levin, J. (2017). New-paradigm research in medicine: An agenda. *Journal of Scientific Exploration, 31*(1), 49–70. Retrieved from: www.baylorisr.org/wp-content/uploads/2017-JSE-New-Paradigm-Research-in-Medicine.pdf

Lynch, M. E., & Watson, C. P. N. (2006). The pharmacotherapy of chronic pain: A review. *Pain Research and Management, 11*(1), 11–38. doi:10.1155/2006/642568 Retrieved from: http://downloads.hindawi.com/journals/prm/2006/642568.pdf

Moerman, D. E. (2002). *Meaning, medicine, and the placebo effect.* Cambridge, UK: University Press.

Moseley, J. B., O'Malley, K., Petersen, N. J., Menke, T. J., Brody, B. A., Kuykendall, D. H., … Wray, N. P. (2002). A controlled trial of arthroscopic surgery for osteoarthritis of the knee. *New England Journal of Medicine, 347*(2), 81–88. doi:10.1056/NEJMoa013259

National Human Genome Research Institute (NHGRI). (n.d.). What is the human genome project? Retrieved September 25, 2019 from www.genome.gov/human-genome-project/What

National Institutes of Health (NIH). (n.d.). National Center for Complementary and Integrative Health (NCCIH). Retrieved September 19, 2019 from www.nih.gov/about-nih/what-we-do/nih-almanac/national-center-complementary-integrative-health-nccih

Organisation for Economic Co-operation and Development (OECD). (2019). Life expectancy at birth. doi:10.1787/27e0fc9d-en

Pert, C. B. (1997). *Molecules of emotion.* New York, NY: Scribner.

Rosenberg, C. E. (2002). The tyranny of diagnosis: Specific entities and individual experience. *Milbank Quarterly, 80*(2), 237–260. doi:10.1111/1468-0009.t01-1-00003

Rosenthal, E. (2018). *An American sickness.* New York, NY: Penguin.

Rossi, E. L. (2004). *A discourse with our genes: The psychosocial and cultural genomics of therapeutic hypnosis and psychotherapy.* Phoenix, AZ: Zeig, Tucker and Theisen.

Rossi, E. L., Rossi, K., Yount, G., Cozzolino, M., & Iannotti, S. (2006). The bioinformatics of integrative medical insights: Proposals for an international psycho-social and cultural bioinformatics project. *Integrative Medicine Insights.* doi:10.1177/117863370600100002. Retrieved from https://journals.sagepub.com/doi/pdf/10.1177/117863370600100002

Shapiro, A. K., & Shapiro, E. (1997). *The powerful placebo: From ancient priest to modern physician.* Baltimore, MD: Johns Hopkins University Press.

Tick, H., Nielsen, A., Pelletier, K. R., Bonakdar, R., Simmons, S., Glick, R., … The Pain Task Force of the Academic Consortium for Integrative Medicine and Health. (2018). Evidence-based nnpharmaologic strategies for comprehensive pain care: The cosortium pain task force white paper. *Explore, 14*(3), 177–211. https://doi.org/10.1016/j.explore.2018.02.001

Tonelli, M. R. (1998). The philosophical limits of evidence-based medicine. *Academic Medicine, 73*(12), 1234–1240. doi:10.1097/00001888-199812000-00011. Retrieved from www.researchgate.net/publication/13406212_The_Philosophical_Limits_of_Evidence-Based_Medicine/link/5c6741414585156b57fff04b/download

Tracey, I. (2010). Getting the pain you expect: Mechanisms of placebo, nocebo and reappraisal effects in humans. *Nature Medicine, 16*(11), 1277–1283. doi:10.1038/nm.2229

Turnwald, B. P., Goyer, J. P., Boles, D. Z., Silder, A., Delp, S. L., & Crum, A. J. (2018). Learning one's genetic risk changes physiology independent of actual genetic risk. *Nature Human Behaviour, 3*(1), 48–56. doi:10.1038/s41562-018-0483-4

United States Centers doc Disease Control. (2018). CDC National Center for Injury Prevention and Control. Retrieved from https://www.cdc.gov/drugoverdose/pdf/pubs/2018-cdc-drug-surveillance-report.pdf

Wager, T. D., Rilling, J. K., Smith, E. E., Sokolik, A., Casey, K. L., Davidson, R. J., … Cohen, J. D. (2004). Placebo-induced changes in fMRI in the anticipation and experience of pain [pdf]. *Science, 303*(5661), 1162–1167. Retrieved from: https://canlabweb.colorado.edu/files/Wager_2004_Science.pdf

Wager, T. D., Scott, D. J., & Zubieta, J. K. (2007). Placebo effects on human µ-opioid activity during pain. *Proceedings of the National Academy of Sciences, 104*(26), 11056–11061. doi:10.1073/pnas.0702413104 Retrieved from: www.pnas.org/content/pnas/104/26/11056.full.pdf

Epilogue

Lulu

Hello, dear reader. This is Lulu. Wherever you are, I hope you have learned enough about me and my life to care about how things have turned out for me. Here are a couple key points.

I grew up with an avid curiosity about the world and about the country where I was born. I prefer not to identify that country here, but it was certainly North Africa that was the site of some of my most fascinating and terrifying experiences. After college, I went to Africa to be a teacher in a school for girls remarkably dissimilar to our schools in America. The classroom was expected to accommodate at least 65 girls at once.

We were told that the schools were safe. Sadly, this turned out not to be true. Although there was no organized attack, I was the victim of a nighttime assault, wherein I was given the choice of succumbing to rape peacefully or surrendering violently. I rejected both options and instead reminded the attackers about their mothers, their sisters, their girlfriends. Though I did not plan it this way, the conversation I had with the would-be rapists consumed enough time to fend off any prospective attacks.

Did something I learned in my past teach me the poise and fire to resist this assault? Well, the poise and fire are there, wherever they came from. I don't fade from fear. It brings courage. In my mother language "Hentue" means "No."

Lyle

Lyle's Mom, Years Later

I remember the night Lyle was born. Not that I stood by the hospital window and watched the flakes fall, one by one. But I remember how once in a while someone would say "Wow! It's snowing so hard!" And then I woke up the following morning and they brought Lyle in to nurse and I could see how everything out the window was white. And I felt such comfort. I was in a place like I'd never been before. All this snow had fallen, but none of it was my problem. That had never happened before.

For a while, it felt like there was a cushion between me and the real world. And there was a deep, deep exhaustion after the events of last night.

There was a brief moment of stillness, when I expected things to be magical and quiet. And they were! It was quiet, but the moment was over very quickly.

And now Lyle is graduating from college, and he has done very well. I can hardly make sense of that.

I do love Lyle, I do, of course I do, but it's like—well, for example: I never expect a Mother's Day card from Lyle. When he was a boy, he just didn't get it. Even when all the other kids were making cards in school, he'd make something like a card—admittedly, an odd one—and then he'd just leave it in his desk, so I'd never see it.

And it's like that thing he did of pretending he couldn't hear people speak. I went along with it, I admit, because I had to. But not until I had tried for years to get him to admit he could hear. I don't know if it was a delusion, or some kind of strange way of adapting to intolerable thoughts or emotions. But even though we love each other, living with Lyle at times is like living in Candyland. Unreal. Or, it had not been a reality that I knew of or was allowed to enter. Lyle-land.

It's odd how Lyle has turned out to be the star student of the family. His cousins, uncles, and aunts, act as if they've always thought he was "cute" and "gifted", which they haven't. They are revising the history of their confusion and distancing to make a nicer story of it for themselves. We let them have their reality, too.

Let's see how some things have developed:

Olivia, for example. Did Lyle and Olivia seriously hit it off together? I mean, how often does a high school romance develop into a deep permanent relationship? Even if both parties in the relationship find the other very attractive? And even though they have a lot in common—went to the same high school, for example. But then we are not talking about two common people. Even their names fit together. I don't know how often Lyle and Olivia got together with Olivia up at New Haven and Lyle in Boston. But that stopped being mine to know long ago. Lyle would have never gone to college and blossomed there without Olivia's lead. She was the bee that saw he was a rare flower to open.

And Lyle's music. Did Lyle revolutionize music with his robotics and artificial intelligence? Not exactly. Not yet. But only because not enough have heard and felt it yet. He says he has already turned some heads in a "super cool part of the music world." But he never let turning heads be his measure. Lyle is still fully self-contained and now opening. And as a mother, this is all I need to know.

And of course there is Lyle's Dad. Well, intermittently alcohol surely is part of it. Alcohol is what he drank in the same way some people poured alcohol on their wounds. Part of it is anger, pure and simple. Anger at what? I always tried to ask him. But it was never mine to know. Maybe now he will be able to seek some help in that department.

Lyle's position these days is that Dad's a tough nut to crack, but cracking his Dad's nut is no longer Lyle's job. It never was. I used to believe Lyle's Dad was my job, but when a marriage is devoted to protecting son from father, it is not marriage, is it? Loving Lyle and his world helped me know that I could not fix his Dad, or Lyle for that matter, who did not need repair. I fixed me. I moved out when Lyle moved out.

And here is a card—a Mother's Day Card? Is that possible? With a somewhat inscrutable comment from Lyle: "There is always one more note in the music and one more stage where the song never falls silent."

Stevie

Look. Is there a Tyger in there somewhere? Some kind of ferocious unhappiness that was dragging me away from home in the vain hope of finding a colony of Stevie-ish persons where Stevies can live naturally without having to transform into some other kind of creature? OK. That's empty words. Let's move on. Maybe it's supposed to end like this. Lots of pain. There is no Lady. There is no Tyger. Neither one possible answer nor the other. Both equally shitty.

Wasn't there a project underway not to have to make a decision, not to have to take on some form called "gender"? Couldn't we have just let the "I" that is "me" take its time to become something of its own?

Scaldingly cold out here in space. But at the very, very, very least I can let it puff me up and freeze me into a form of its own. Without. Questions. Anymore?

Stevie's Father

Oh, dear reader, please listen to this.

I tried to get her up—and look—oh—jeez. I've reverted to calling him "she"; that is, calling Stevie "she." I'm literally so confused that I don't know—can't talk about my own kid. But it doesn't matter anymore. Doesn't matter what we call Stevie. "Him" or "her," "she" or "he." Does it?

Stevie's Mother

I know that she was taking money from my purse. Part of me knew. Weren't there three twenties, not one? How many times did that happen? How many times did I not ask her? I didn't want to know. I didn't want to know what I wasn't giving her. What she was getting from me without me.

Stevie's Father

I was in the house. She was also in the house. Did I go upstairs and haul her out of bed to go to that therapy session? Didn't I owe it to her and us to get her the hell out of bed? Right in that moment? It wasn't a dentist appointment for god's sake. Like all she needed to do was brush and floss. It's supposed to be therapy.

Weren't we supposed to have done … something … more … by then?

Robinson

My dear reader, I have done my best to tell you this story of who I am becoming, so far. There is an important reason. All of our healing traditions are founded on stories and their telling. There were healing stories in my Voudou childhood. Even our modern, data-driven, technological, and expensive practices are founded on the telling of scientific stories. It is in the sharing and shaping of the stories with others that we begin to change and then to heal.

Through all my medical training—my learning to examine, to test, to evaluate data, to diagnose, to prescribe, to do things *for* people—I knew that I was not becoming a healer. I was not becoming a healer in the way I needed that word to mean. All of the effort to become disciplined, objective, and evidence-based did not add up to who I believed I needed to be. To do that I needed to find my story: from my childhood to my fatherhood. It was in the family lessons from my mother, from Esther, and other patients; even from my father, and certainly from my partner, my wife, and my wondrous children. These tuned my mind so I became able to attend to the stories by those who granted me presence in their care.

I am still learning to listen. I am learning to listen to the words and the melody and dance of their stories. I am learning to improvise and harmonize. I am learning to sway with them in the dance of the averted eyes and the clenched fist, the sentence they begin and then leave unfinished, looking away. I am even learning to respond to their breathing under the stethoscope, their abdominal exam, and their arthritic range of motion. And I have learned to trust, with and beyond all the data, the evidence that joining in this way changes their embodied minds: inflammation and mood all together. I have learned to trust that every prescription I write, every referral I make, and every procedure I perform *for* them is activated by our collaborative story-telling: what they do within themselves. How they know how to heal.

A patient, a chemical engineer, was grateful to me for helping him change his diet, inspiring him to exercise, and facing his metabolic syndrome. He said, "Thank you for being a catalyst." I thought about that. I replied, holding his hand, "Technically, I am not a catalyst. By definition, catalysts are unchanged after the reaction is completed."

So, I am sharing this story because stories change in the telling. I think how we are becoming healers is also changing, and must. All I know is to find my own way. I wrote something in my journal that came to me one evening after looking at tomorrow's schedule. I read it when I need to be reminded. I will share it with you.

"The 'good doctor' is, first of all, just like the rest of us: unsure, questioning, frightened. But this one dares to feel the wounds, and, facing the illness borne of both our poverties and potentials, strives to save the flesh, to save the dreams."

Afterword

In this groundbreaking book, Sugarman, Linden, and Brooks have offered a compelling argument as to how and why the technology driven, disconnected approach of allopathic medicine must be changed. The days when a paternalistically caring practitioner would drive horse and buggy to a patient's home to care for him or her from birth to death have been gone for decades. While the technical aspects of practicing medicine have advanced tremendously since that time, the relational aspects have suffered proportionately. The embodied intimacy and closeness built through years of home visits once allowed doctors to witness a patient at their most vulnerable. Without an abundance of evidence-based treatments, the relationship itself was the physician's greatest tool in healing. The belief that minimizing the power of relationship in medicine is reducing the effectiveness of all treatments is central to Sugarman's, Linden's, and Brooks' transformative approach.

Allopathic medicine, as it has been taught and practiced in the United States over the last half century, has embraced the separate-self model of human development espoused by the dominant culture. In 1928, President Herbert Hoover coined the term "rugged individualism" to describe characteristics of an ideal society member who is totally self-reliant and not dependent on the government for anything. This fierce individualism and the shaming of "normal" neediness have filtered down to all aspects of human life in America, and to a lesser degree throughout Western culture.

The majority of developmental theories that have emerged since the early 20th century promote the belief that human beings are born dependent on their caregivers and that the goal of child-rearing and community-building is to create independent, autonomous individuals capable of competing in a hyper-competitive society. In fact, the "self-made man" is virtually synonymous with the "American Dream," while those mired in dependency are pathologized as immature, weak, and less than. In general, groups with the most social capital are the ones who are seen as being most successful on their own.

Medical doctors are a group with enormous respect and social capital. When I was in medical school in the late 1980's, learning the "art of medicine" required a denial of human needs. Thirty-six hour hospital shifts during clinical rotations and residency left students exhausted and stressed. The cutthroat, survival of the fittest environment, designed to maximize objectivity, left everyone involved with deep empathy deficits, both for themselves and others.

Over the last three decades, changes in the practice of medicine have amplified the disconnect between patients and health care providers. Managed care has limited the time clinicians can spend with patients and building a therapeutic relationship has taken a back seat to a reliance on new technologies for definitive diagnoses. At the same time, there has been a substantial rise in the levels of overall loneliness and isolation.

A 2018 Cigna survey of 20,000 people revealed that almost half of the respondents (47% over the age of 18) reported often feeling alone or left out (Cigna Health Care, 2018). This statistic is not reserved for seniors who are living alone at unprecedented rates. The Generation Z adults (between the age of 18–22) are currently lonelier and unhealthier than previous generations. Relationally, our society is in a death spiral that incidentally cannot be blamed on the Internet. Again, the Cigna (2018) study revealed no difference in loneliness score (20 items, 100=most lonely) between heavy social media users (43.5) and those who have never used social media (41.7). Loneliness is an epidemic in the United States, with lethal consequences.

In his groundbreaking book, *Love and Survival*, cardiologist Dean Ornish (1998), made a compelling case for the power of human connection in health and well-being. His exhaustive review of the literature on the impact of loneliness and isolation (through death, trauma, divorce, and disconnection) on physical and emotional health leads him to conclude that being disconnected is the most important determinant of overall quality of health and death from all causes. Close connections have a bigger impact on health than smoking, exercise, medication use, and all surgical procedures. Yet, allopathic medicine continues to ignore this irrefutable evidence.

Health care providers may contribute to the feelings of alienation by breaking down the body into distinct parts and systems with individual treatments aimed at attacking a specific illness rather than supporting wellness. There is ample evidence that our health care system is not working. Despite spending more than any other developed country on health care per person (Organization for Economic Co-Operation and Development, 2019) a recent Bloomberg (Miller & Lu, 2019) analysis of overall health and well-being ranked the United States behind all other civilized countries (#34 overall). Even with all our technologies and training, we are failing at wellness. It is time for a paradigm shift.

In her book, *This Changes Everything*, Christina Robb (2007) described the relational revolution that emerged from a group of feminist educators and clinicians in the greater Boston area in the 70s and 80s. By listening to women's voices and experiences, researchers and educators (Judy Herman and her colleagues at the Victims of Violence Program, Carol Gilligan and colleagues at Harvard's Graduate School of Education, and Jean Baker Miller and colleagues at The Stone Center at Wellesley College) created an alternative theory of human development where emotional maturity is *not* predicated on separating and individuating from others but rather on developing the capacity for increasingly complex and mutual adult relationships. Indeed, this shift from valuing rugged individualism to valuing healthy human connections has the power to change the trajectory of our current health crisis.

Ironically, the technology that is contributing to a disconnection in medical encounters is also adding valuable information on how and why healthy relationships are essential to emotional and physical well-being. This is the fertile ground for the emerging field of "Relational Neuroscience." In *Wired to Connect: The Surprising Link between Brain Science and Strong Healthy Relationship*, Banks (2015; with Leigh Ann Hirschman) summarized the research that makes it clear why loneliness and disconnection have the power to kill us. The human body functions best in tribes, packs, or communities. For example, the autonomic nervous system evolved in humans (and mammals who need ongoing care-taking for survival of the young) in large part, initially to keep infants close to their care-giver, but also to keep adults close to others who are deemed safe in order to modulate collective stress levels.

As Sugarman, Linden, and Brooks have noted in this text, Stephen Porges' (2011) research identified the "smart vagus nerve"—a branch of the vagus nerve that innervates the muscles of facial expression, the tiny muscles in the inner ear and the muscles in the throat and trachea. As part of a larger social engagement system, the smart vagus is activated when an individual is in contact with close, safe others. A typical interaction usually involves the face opening and the eyebrows raising. Additionally, hearing becomes more attuned and speaking more regular. All of these behaviors and actions are produced by and feedback upon vagal nerve projections such that the vagus system tells the sympathetic nervous system (fight or flight response) to stand down. Essentially, stimulating the vagus nerve through safe relationships helps us feel calmer and less stressed out.

A second piece of seminal research in Relational Neuroscience comes from Eisenberger and Lieberman (2005) who identified the dorsal anterior cingular cortex as a neurological alarm center that activates not only when a person is in physical pain, but also when they are distressed by social rejection and isolation. Being connected to others is so important to our well-being that our nervous system reads social pain and physical pain as equivalent dangers. Pain, physical or emotional, activates the stress response system while being accepted by close others decreases pain and stress levels and improves health and well-being.

A third piece of neuroscience research by Rizzolati and Fabri-Destro (2010) identified the mirror neuron circuitry involved in reading others. This discovery underscored the absurdity of rugged individualism. Discovered entirely by accident, the mirror neuron system was first observed in primates and subsequently explored in humans. In their lab study of the grasp response in macaque monkeys, Rizzolati's group found that the area of the monkey's brain (F5) activated both when the monkey was reaching to pick up a glass or piece of fruit *and* when the monkey was watching another individual grasp something. The activation of the motor area for grasp was stimulated even when the monkey's arm was not moving! This shocking finding stimulated a body of research that tells us that as humans we "know" other people's feelings, actions, and sensations by internally mimicking them in our own nervous system. The mirror neuron system is now understood to be the basis for empathy and intuitive knowing that had previously been a mystery. Resonating with others and building the capacity to resonate or read others accurately is diminished when the mirror neuron system is undermined by our "power-over" culture that encourages a person to "do his own thing" without concern for his impact on others.

A fourth neural pathway important to the healing aspects of relationship is the dopaminergic reward system. Ideally, the dopaminergic reward system stays attached to healthy, supportive relationships so that nurturing and care, hugging, and cuddling cause a release of dopamine, which in turn produces a burst of good, feelings, motivation, and energy. Keeping the connection between dopamine and healthy relationship is essential to overall well-being and is actively undermined when we force people to stand on their own two feet and pathologize interdependency. In fact, the neuroscientist Rachel Wurtzman's (2017) research suggests that the opioid epidemic is directly related to loneliness and isolation. The striatum, which sits at the base of the forebrain and plays a role in decision-making and compulsive, repetitive behaviors, is hypersensitive when a person is disconnected from a social network. This hypersensitivity can lead to a search for a quick reward, and narcotics are just the powerful pain-killers and agents of disembodied dissociation needed to sooth the pain of social isolation.

This brief review of Relational Neuroscience offers insights into why disconnection, loneliness and a culture build on individualism actively undermine health and well-being. There is no doubt that a paradigm shift in medicine needs to incorporate the new science of relationship.

With this book, Sugarman, Linden, and Brooks help us envision that paradigm of change. They remind us of what our bodies already implicitly know: that mutual, supportive relationships heal. More, these authors illustrate—with treatise, vignettes, and stories—how we can harness and leverage the power of healthy relationships at each kind of health care visit. Their relational model of hypnosis is based in part on the Linden's (1999) "5 E's Model of Feminist Hypnotherapy" proposed 20 years ago. According to Linden, hypnosis that is empathic, empowering, egalitarian, ego-strengthening, and embodied is "both a principle and strategy for how to enact hypnosis naturally."

This book is an essential contribution to the growing body of work that has the power to shift the dominant culture in medicine. It encourages clinicians to look up from their microscopic evaluations of disease and see each individual macroscopically. It invites practitioners to add hypnosis to their repertoire of healing techniques not in lieu surgery, antibiotics, and other evidence-based medical practices but in order to increase the effectiveness of these allopathic interventions.

The hypnosis these authors describe is a far cry from that practiced by the stage hypnotist who mysteriously mesmerizes an unwitting attendee to follow an idiosyncratic suggestion. Sugarman, Linden, and Brooks use trance "to mean the *process* of developing plasticity, malleability, flexibility and, further, resilience and agility of mind." Their dyadic trances amplify the healing process by harnessing the autonomic nervous system's natural response to safe connection. Through the process of mutual trance, an individual's ability to heal themselves emerges.

In a culture that often relies on stratification and dichotomies to describe human experience, hypnosis—as Sugarman, Linden, and Brooks have conceived it—just may be the ultimate health care win-win. Combining the macroscopic approach of hypnosis with the microscopic view of technology driven-medicine has the power to amplify the healing process, transform modern medicine, and ultimately improve the health and well-being of our society.

Amy E. Banks, M.D.
Lexington, Massachusetts, USA

References

Banks, A., & Hirschman, L. (2015). *Wired to connect: The surprising link between brain science and strong, healthy relationships*. New York, NY: Jeremy Tarcher/Penguin.

Cigna Health Care. (2018). *Cigna U.S. Loneliness Index.*[Website]. Retrieved from www.multivu.com/players/English/8294451-cigna-us-loneliness-survey/

Eisenberger, N. I., & Lieberman, M. D. (2005). Why it hurts to be left out: The neurocognitive overlap between physical and social pain. In K. D. Williams, J. P. Forgas, & W. von Hippel (Eds.), *Sydney symposium of social psychology series. The social outcast: Ostracism, social exclusion, rejection, and bullying* (pp. 109–127). New York, NY, US: Psychology Press.

Linden, J. H. (1999). Discussion of symposium. Enhancing healing: The contributions of hypnosis to women's health care. *American Journal of Clinical Hypnosis, 42*(2), 140–144. doi:10.1080/00029157.1999.10701731

Miller, L., & Lu, W. (Feb. 24, 2019). *These are the world's healthiest Nations.* [Website] Retrieved from: www.bloomberg.com/news/articles/2019-02-24/spain-tops-italy-as-world-s-healthiest-nation-while-u-s-slips

Organisation for Economic Co-operation and Development (OECD). (2019). *Life Expectancy at Birth.* doi: 10.1787/27e0fc9d-en

Ornish, D. (1998). *Love and survival: 8 Pathways to intimacy and health.* New York, NY: HarperCollins.

Porges, S. W. (2011). *The polyvagal theory: Neurophysiological foundations of emotions, attachment, communication, and self-regulation.* New York, NY: W. W. Norton.

Rizzolatti, G., & Fabbri-Destro, M. (2010). Mirror neurons: From discovery to autism. *Experimental Brain Research, 200*(3–4), 223–237. doi:10.1007/s00221-009-2002-3

Robb, C. (2007). *This changes everything: The relational revolution in psychology.* New York, NY: Farrar, Strauss and Giroux.

Wurtzman, R. (Oct. 2017) *How isolation fuels opioid addiction.* [Video file]. Retrieved from: www.ted.com/talks/rachel_wurzman_how_isolation_fuels_opioid_addiction?language=en

Appendix

American Society of Clinical Hypnosis (ASCH): www.asch.net/. Visit this URL for the nine component sections of ASCH: www.asch.net/Professionals/ComponentSections/ComponentSectionDirectory.aspx.

European Society of Hypnosis (ESH): http://esh-hypnosis.eu/. Visit this website to find the URLs to each of the component societies of ESH, 41 societies in 20 countries.

International Society of Hypnosis (ISH): www.ishhypnosis.org/. Visit this website to find the URLs to each Constituent Society of ISH, 35 societies on five continents.

National Pediatric Hypnosis Training Institute: www.nphti.org/.

Society of Clinical and Experimental Hypnosis (SCEH): www.sceh.us/.

The Milton H. Erickson Foundation: www.erickson-foundation.org/.

Glossary

Afferent Conducting inward or toward the center from the periphery. In the nervous system, afferent nerves conduct toward the brain. Sensory nerves are afferent. In the circulatory system, veins are afferents to the heart. Efferent is the opposite of afferent, meaning conducting outward or away from the center toward the periphery.

Anomalies In the context of paradigm change, this term refers to phenomena that cannot be explained or accounted for from within the paradigm. Increasing anomalies threaten the coherence and authority of the prevailing paradigm.

Attunement In psychology, this is the process of being aware of and in sync with another's emotional state, understanding their moods and adjusting responses to their experience, e.g., an attuned parent knows the baby's cry of hunger, and responds by providing nourishment.

Basic Rest Activity Cycle (BRAC, see also Ultradian Rhythm and Novelty-Neurogenesis-Numinosum Effect) This is a term used for the physiological and behavioral manifestations of the empiric ultradian cycle (80–120 minutes, average 90 minutes). It has been overlaid on this temporal interval as a metabolic, energetic, and behavioral manifestation of the human biological clock that is used to explain periods of more energetic, focused learning or adaptation during the first half of the period, followed by less focus and more repose during the second half. This has been adapted by Rossi and others to support a cyclic "Novelty-Neurogenesis-Numinosum Effect."

Biomedicine The term applied to the model in which medical research and care is reduced to principles of biochemistry, molecular genetics, and cell-biology.

Biopsychosocial Model The term, attributed to George Engel, for the integrative and multidisciplinary model of health care that combines biological, social-environmental, and psychological factors into healing from disease and the promotion of well-being.

Clinical Hypnosis (see also Hypnosis) The use of the interpersonal communication skills and discipline of hypnosis in health care settings, such that context of care is bounded by ethical principles of doing no harm, providing benefit, respecting autonomy, and providing equal access to care for the patient or client. Hypnosis in non-clinical settings is not limited by these ethical canons.

Clinician's Trance (see also Trance) The term used in this book to capture the mindset on the part of the clinician in which they are (1) intensely focused on the communicated content and behaviors of the person in care; (2) deeply curious about the life-experience that informs that content and those behaviors; (3) accepting of the other's values, beliefs, and feelings without judgement; while, (4) hypothesizing about their experiences; and, (5) responding based upon clinical knowledge, experience, and intuition.

Conservative (Plasticity; see also Epithetic) In the context of psychobiological plasticity or trance, this term refers to doing the same thing repeatedly; i.e., strengthening the same psychobiological pattern or engram. Examples include practicing scales on a musical instrument or one's golf swing, memorization of lines in a speech, or engaging in obsessions and compulsions. It is the opposite of epithetic plasticity.

Congression In this book, an invented word that refers to the basic hypnotic skill the clinician uses to project developmental progression and regression. "Con" means "with," and the Latin "gressare" refers to temporal movement, or time-travel.

Construct Validity In clinical research, this term refers to whether the thing being tested actually represents the thing, or construct, that it purports to represent. For example, one may question the construct validity of an investigation of hypnosis if the thing that is measured as a proxy for hypnosis is the ability of a research subject to raise their right arm in response to a suggestion that they imagine that the arm is tied to helium balloons. Hypnosis can be a much broader construct than that.

Demand Characteristics In a psychology experiment, these are subtle cues that may reveal the hypothesis being tested, and thus influence the participants as to what is expected in their responses. Demand characteristics can be understood as a form of implied bias.

Depth (of trance) In the legacy model of hypnosis, depth is a linear, external, and behavioral measure of the intensity of the experience of the hypnotized person. Several scales of hypnosis depth have been developed for research purposes. For example, a person who behaves with catatonia (psychomotor immobility) is considered to be less deeply hypnotized than a person who can experience a visual hallucination, based on some scales. Both the clinical validity of this linear construct and whether intensity correlates with outcome have been questioned.

Development Continuous, sequential changes which occur in both physiological and psychological functions during the lifetime of an individual. Human development is the study of how people develop on physical, intellectual, and social levels.

Developmental Imperatives From the perspective of trance and psychobiological plasticity, developmental urges can be understood as governing currents or drives that steer the direction of that plasticity. For example, the urges to walk, express oneself, establish autonomy, and develop one's sexuality all take priority over other needs during certain periods of our lives. Since hypnosis is defined as a discipline for interpersonal influencing of psychobiological plasticity, such developmental imperatives must be considered.

Ecological Validity In clinical research, this term refers to the whether the conditions under which an experiment is performed are representative of the real-world environment (or ecology) in which the research subjects live.

Embodied Integral to and part of the physical body as compared to something emergent or ephemeral. In this book we refer to feelings, experiences, and the mind as being incorporated into the body, such that they are expressed in behavior symptoms. This contrasts with the notion of the mind being an idea or something insubstantial.

Emergent Properties In system science or cybernetics, and emergent property is a characteristic of a complex system that develops irreducibly, as more than the sum of its parts. The characteristics of water (e.g., expanding upon transition from liquid to solid, the patterns of snowflakes) are properties of neither oxygen nor hydrogen.

Engram In neuroscience, an engram refers to the distinct network of cellular elements and their connectivity, by which memories and experiences are stored. Allport used the term to describe elements of a cellular system that become "auto-associated." In broader, psychobiological terms, an engram can be such a multicellular pattern that extends beyond the central nervous system to include endocrine, metabolic, gastrointestinal, motor, and other somatic responses, since the mind is a complex and embodied system. Ultimately, engrams arise from the genomic proclivities of their component cells.

Epigenetic(s) Processes and mechanisms that determine the likelihood of gene expression, e.g., methylation. The means that underlie genomics.

Epithetic (plasticity, see also Conservative) In the context of psychobiological plasticity or trance, this term refers to doing something completely different and creative. Invented by the authors to be intentionally different than "synthetic." The prefix "syn-" refers to something similar to or like something else, such as synthetic leather. The prefix "epi-" refers to something that is completely different, even tangential or, in the context of trance, inspired or enlightened: an AHA! moment. It is the opposite of conservative plasticity.

Experiential Resources This term refers to the idea that our life experiences—comprised of our memories, lessons, and conditioned learning, both conscious and nonconscious—can be utilized in hypnotic contexts as resources for change in emotion, thinking, and behavior.

Formal Induction (see Induction) In the legacy model of hypnosis, a prescribed procedure (arm levitation, gaze fixation, focus on breathing) to assist someone to experience trance.

Genomics (see Epigenetics) The study of our capacity for gene expression. In contrast to genetics, which concerns gene sequence and endowment, genomics relates to the mechanisms and frequencies of gene transcription or suppression.

Hebb's Axiom The term applied to Donald Hebb's principle that cells that tend to be activated at the same time or in the same sequence tend to become interconnected. It has been simply stated as, "Neurons that fire together wire together." Though originally conceived to apply to the actions of neurons, within the context of the embodied mind, we apply this term broadly to include all body systems.

Hetero-hypnosis The term used to refer to the application of hypnosis between two people in which one is using hypnosis to influence the other. While it is often contrasted with "self-hypnosis" or "auto-hypnosis," it is argued that this is a false distinction and dichotomy, since we are often being influenced by others and often working to preserve our autonomy. In short, all hypnosis is both hetero and auto.

Hypnosis A widely used, variously defined, and frequently misunderstood term. Hypnosis as a procedure (something you can do or perform) is often conflated with hypnosis as an effect (something you can be in or under), presuming a direct relationship between the two. That is why, in this book, we define hypnosis separately from what it may or may not do. We define hypnosis as a collection of skills—a skill set—that can be practiced as a discipline and even an art. The discipline of hypnosis is intended to influence psychobiological plasticity. In other words, hypnosis is a method to change minds. As defined, it is ethically neutral. We argue that most of the hypnosis on the planet is used at least to gain advantage, if not nefariously. Clinical hypnosis, practiced within ethical bounds, is an exception.

Hypnotic Relationship The term to describe the spatial, attuned, and synchronized interaction between the clinician and the person in their care, when the discipline of hypnosis is being used. It is an extension of the Clinician's Trance.

Hypnotizability (see also Construct Validity) A metric, developed from standardized testing, of one's ability to comply with instructions and engage in behaviors that have been deemed hypnotic. The more one complies with instructions toward intended behaviors (e.g., arm levitation, upward gaze, catalepsy, imaginary experiences, responding to post-hypnotic suggestions), the more one is deemed to be susceptible to hypnosis, able to be hypnotized, or "hypnotizable." This construct has been criticized on the basis of construct and ecological validity, and may have little correlation to clinical outcome, but persists in research use to differentiate subjects who are more or less likely to respond to a hypnosis protocol.

Iatrogenesis Derived from the Greek, to mean "that which is brought forth by the healer," this term refers to harm produced in the act of providing health care; e.g., medical and surgical errors, post-operative infections, and opioid addiction.

Induction (see formal induction) In the legacy model of hypnosis, this term refers to a method or ritual for changing the mental state of the client or patient in preparation for hypnosis. It is criticized as being unnecessary, at least.

Implicit Processing Heuristics A term introduced by Rossi and Rossi to describe the purpose of questions and responses to people moving through a hypnotic process, especially to promote change. It more accurately details the components of the searching *experience* rather than the origins of the answers. The instruction is "implicit" (since there is no explicit directive to search); requires "processing" (an evaluative act); and acts as an "heuristic" (autonomous exploration for self-discovery and self-improvement). These cognitively disruptive skills are designed to intensify trance by questioning what we thought we knew. Once the question is posed, the clinician observes the effect: what the question does.

Interoception The term applied to the influx of messenger molecules and afferent (often vagal) nerve impulses that comprise our sense of well-being, safety, and comfort. Commonly referred to as "gut feelings" or "intuition."

Kneading As a basic hypnotic skill, this term refers to the act of commenting and reflecting upon nonverbal, primarily nonconscious, behaviors in another person. In clinical settings this can mean responding to the patient's sigh, postural shift, or facial expression with, "Yes," or "That's right." The use of this skill is both disruptive of normal processes and cultivates awareness of nonconscious processes.

Ligand In biochemistry and pharmacology, a ligand is a substance, usually a macromolecule, that binds to and forms a complex with another substance. In the context of this book, ligands are information molecules (e.g., hormones, immunoglobulins, neurotransmitters) that bind receptors on cell walls, thereby initiating changes in the cell's internal activity.

Liminal An adjective related to thresholds. In this book, the thresholds are in between conscious and nonconscious resources, between struggling with a problem and finding the solution and, more fundamentally, between the sufficiency of a stimulus and the production of change in a system's behavior (e.g., the triggering of gene expression or symptom relief).

Messenger Molecules The collection of substances (peptides and steroid forms) that travel intercellularly within the body and bind cell receptors. Via this binding, they transfer energy into the cell, changing cell function in some way. This term—instead of immunoglobulins, hormones, neurotransmitters, and cytokines, for example—is employed to recognize that these substances function across systems. Immune cells have neurotransmitter receptors. Nerve cells have receptors for cytokines. This usage aligns with the conception of the mind as an integrated, complex system, rather than independent compartments.

Mind (see Emergent Property) Recognizing the varied and indeterminate use of this term, in this book we use the term to mean an emergent property of the complex and embodied systems that are contained within us. Other emergent properties are consciousness and our sense of self.

Mindset In this book, this term refers to a collection of factors that determine an attitude or state of mind in an individual. Mindset can include expectation, conditioning, and the neurohumoral components that underlie it.

Monistic In reference to the biomedical model, this word means a one-to-one, linear, cause-and-effect relationship, such as using penicillin to treat streptococcal pharyngitis. This contrasts with more complex, multifactor, nonlinear, and dynamic relationships, such as those studied in chaos theory.

Narrative Listening One of four orienting principles proposed in this book. This refers to listening for and using the embedded stories in the client's or patient's description, recognizing that the meaning and value of such accounts depends on the coherence of narrative arc.

Neuroplasticity The term used to describe the lifelong adaptability of the central nervous system to change its function and structure in response to life experience: the essence of learning.

Novelty-Neurogenesis-Numinosum Effect (See also Basic Rest Activity Cycle and Ultradian Rhythm): A term coined by Rossi to denote the learning process that aligns with the basic rest activity cycle along ultradian oscillations. Rossi posits that the focus and intensity of the first half of the cycle correlates with inspiration, stimulation of neurogenesis, and enlightenment or discovery that has been appropriated from Jung into the term "numinosum."

Nosology The branch of medical science that deals with the classification of disease.

Paradigm Broadly used to refer to a pattern thoughts and concepts. In this book, and as defined by Kuhn, the term refers to the beliefs, practices, and tools that define an established science. The biomedical paradigm is the prevailing western model for healthcare.

Person-Centered The adjective used to describe a clinical approach in which the determining factors are primarily those characteristics of the person in care. Person-centered care contrasts with diagnosis-, treatment-, and problem-centered care.

Plasticity The ability to change. One's malleability, agility, and adaptability. This can mean susceptibility to being affected by external influence, but it can also be self-determined. Psychobiological plasticity is essential to trance formation and, at its most functional, healing, health, and well-being.

Polyvagal Theory The term coined by Porges to represent the multiple and contradictory roles of the vagus nerve in evolution and development, as an afferent influence from the viscera and projected higher effects on social engagement.

Protodisease A term used by Rosenberg to denote the creation of disease entities out of collections of risk factors or related findings, in order to fulfill requirement for diagnostic reality, as the basis for treatment within the biomedical paradigm.

Protohypnosis A term coined by Josephine Hilgard describing the embryonic, safe, attuned, loving, caressing, attentive behaviors toward an infant, which she considered prototypes for trance and influencing positive change.

Psychobiological Plasticity Agility or and flexibility in the biological systems and psychological manifestations that constitute our minds. How able and willing we are to change our minds, whether or not we are aware of it.

Rapport A term used in clinical encounters to describe the attunement and establishment of the relationship between clinician and person in care.

Receptor Chemical structures, composed of protein and embedded into cell walls, that receive and transduce signals that may be integrated into biological systems.

Relational Being One of four orienting principles proposed in this book. This refers to the clinician's recognition that we are biologically determined to influence each other, so that the nature of the relationship and the effects of rapport, attunement, and modeling are part of trance and healing.

Resistance In the legacy model of hypnosis, a term used to describe a client's rejection of hypnosis, the therapeutic relationship, and/or hypnotic suggestions. In this book, resistance is defined as a necessary dynamic in development and growth.

Self-efficacy A term developed by Bandura to mean how well one can execute courses of action required to deal with prospective situations.

Systems Thinking One of four orienting principles proposed in this book. This refers to the clinical recognition that the clients within our care are parts of open and evolving systems. As such, we must embrace uncertainty in their care, recognize that the effects of our interactions can occur at multiple levels, and understand that such changes are liminal, requiring a degree of resistance and activation energy.

Temporal Touring One of four orienting principles proposed in this book. This involves appreciating the ever-shifting oscillations in the system within which the client is engaged. From short-duration epochs—breathing and heart rate variability changes over minutes—to ultradian rhythms of shifting genomic expression, diurnal rhythms, monthly menstrual cycling, seasonal emotional changes, multi-year developmental periods and, of course, transgenerational life-times, this fourth-dimensional or temporal view recognizes currents of time, at different rates. This means that clinicians need to help those in their care while thinking about interventions and changes progressively. Future and past orientation create plasticity in the fluid present.

Trance Like "mind" and "hypnosis," "trance" is a term with a wide variety of meanings. In this book, it refers to the process (and specifically *not a state*) of increasing psychobiological plasticity that can be induced or evoked with novelty, intensity of relationships, inspiration, and imagination.

Trauma An experience—often but not always linked to an event—that exceeds a person's perceived ability to respond adaptively. Developmental trauma incorporates the concept that the age and resources available to the individual affect the response to the trauma. Trauma becomes a way of living.

Ultradian Rhythm (see also Basic Rest Activity Cycle and Novelty-Neurogenesis-Numinosum Effect) A 80-120 minute (average 90 minutes) chronobiological period that is labelled ultradian because it is less than, and oscillates within, the 24-hour diurnal cycle. During sleep, this rhythm correlates with sleep stages. During wakefulness, we tend to have more rapid electroencephalographic activity, and feel more alert and focused, during the first half of ultradian cycles. We grow more tired and less focused during the latter half. This has been adapted by Rossi and others to support a cyclic "Novelty-Neurogenesis-Numinosum Effect."

Wandering As a basic hypnotic skill, this term refers to the intentional practice of uncertainty. Like wondering, it involves loosening preconceptions of both causation and treatment, as well as prioritizing the client's cues in the encounter's agenda. It is contingent on whatever the person in care has just done or said, and implies progress or movement. Wandering is the progressive exploration of the client's experiential domain.

Wondering As a basic hypnotic skill, this term refers to the intentional practice of uncertainty. Like wandering, it involves loosening preconceptions of both causation and treatment, as well as prioritizing the client's cues in the encounter's agenda. Unlike wandering, it is not contingent on whatever the person in care has just done or said. Wondering is exploration beyond the client's experiential domain.

Subject Index

Author Index

Made in the USA
Monee, IL
13 September 2026

62977356R00193